THE CALIPHATE

WORLD THOUGHT IN TRANSLATION

A joint project of Yale University Press and the MacMillan Center for International and Area Studies at Yale University, World Thought in Translation makes important works of classical and contemporary political, philosophical, legal, and social thought from outside the Western tradition available to English-speaking scholars, students, and general readers. The translations are annotated and accompanied by critical introductions that orient readers to the background in which these texts were written, their initial reception, and their enduring influence within and beyond their own cultures. World Thought in Translation contributes to the study of religious and secular intellectual traditions across cultures and civilizations.

SERIES EDITORS

Stephen Angle
Andrew March
Ian Shapiro

THE CALIPHATE
OR
SUPREME IMAMATE

Al-Khilafah aw al-Imamah al-'Uzma

Muhammad Rashid Rida

Translated and Introduced by Simon A. Wood

Yale
UNIVERSITY
PRESS
New Haven & London

This publication was made possible in part by a grant from the
Carnegie Corporation of New York. The statements made and
views expressed are solely the responsibility of the author.

Also published with assistance from the foundation established in
memory of Calvin Chapin of the Class of 1788, Yale College.

Copyright © 2024 by Simon A. Wood.
All rights reserved.
This book may not be reproduced, in whole or in part, including
illustrations, in any form (beyond that copying permitted by Sections
107 and 108 of the U.S. Copyright Law and except by reviewers for the
public press), without written permission from the publishers.

Yale University Press books may be purchased in quantity for educational,
business, or promotional use. For information, please e-mail
sales.press@yale.edu (U.S. office) or sales@yaleup.co.uk (U.K. office).

Set in Electra type by Newgen North America.
Printed in the United States of America.

Library of Congress Control Number: 2023947975
ISBN 978-0-300-18729-8 (hardcover: alk. paper)

A catalogue record for this book is available from the British Library.

This paper meets the requirements of ANSI/NISO Z39.48-1992 (Permanence of Paper).

10 9 8 7 6 5 4 3 2 1

For G. Antony and Jacqueline L. M. M. Wood

CONTENTS

Acknowledgments   ix

Note on the Translation: Idiomatic and Literal Translation   xi

Translator's Introduction   1

The Caliphate   47

Glossary   215

Notes   225

Index   253

ACKNOWLEDGMENTS

Special thanks are due to all those who offered help, support, and encouragement, in particular: G. Antony Wood, Jacqueline Wood, Catharine Wood, Julia Keown, Abla Hasan, David Geraghty, John Bretherton, Marco Abel, Joy Castro, William Harris, the late Mahmoud Ayoub, Khalid Yahya Blankinship, Sidnie Crawford, Stephen Lahey, Anne Duncan, David L. Johnston, David Hollenberg, David Harrington Watt, Marcia Pascoe Keown, Scott Keown, Sara Miller, Brandon Miller, Lisa Keown, Larry Keown, Cassi Calabro, Shantel Johnson, and Bedross Der Matossian. The College of Arts and Sciences at the University of Nebraska-Lincoln provided support through an Enhance grant. I am very grateful to Bill Frucht at Yale University Press. I am also very grateful to Jaya Chatterjee at Yale for all of her assistance throughout the review and publication process. Thanks also to Amanda Gerstenfeld at Yale. Thanks also to series editor Andrew F. March, who encouraged me to take up this project. Finally, thanks are due to four anonymous reviewers—I would like to single out the person known to me as "Reader 4"—whose critiques were extremely constructive and thorough.

ix

NOTE ON THE TRANSLATION: IDIOMATIC
AND LITERAL TRANSLATION

It is rather stating the obvious to note that there is more than one way to approach a translation. Generally, drawing on the work of Lawrence Venuti, a leading scholar in the field of translation theory, it might be observed that many translators aim either to achieve *fidelity* to a foreign text or, more commonly, to *domesticate* it in a target language. This division goes back to the ancient world. Fidelity results in a facsimile or a fairly literal translation, one that, so to speak, "retains the foreignness of a foreign text." It "foreignizes." This approach has been associated with Friedrich Schleiermacher's preference for "moving the reader toward the author."[1] A focus on fidelity can mean that a translator leaves some of the "work" involved in determining meaning in the hands of the reader. Fidelity has been taken to extremes, such as when the word order of a foreign text is retained for an English translation.

Some authorities do not favor literal translation, finding that retaining or mimicking features of a foreign language does not make for good translation or convey an author's meaning most effectively. To its critics, fidelity or mimicking style or other features of a foreign text can produce awkward, unwieldy, or convoluted results. Instead, a domesticating approach resulting in dynamic equivalence and idiomatic English is preferred. This moves the author toward the reader. In some cases, the goal of a domesticating translation is to effectively answer the question: If the author had written this work in the target language rather than in the original language, what would he or she or they have said? Among religious scholars, Martin Luther is among the more influential advocates of a domesticating approach to translation.

Any translation is a compromise between these approaches. There is no such thing as a truly literal translation of any text. This translation attempts to find a

xi

balance between the two approaches, while tending toward a fairly, but hopefully not excessively, literal approach. Arabic words that have become naturalized in English (e.g., madrasah, ijtihad) are often untranslated and are not italicized. All of the endnotes to the translation are mine, except for those that begin "Rida's note," which are Rida's.

TRANSLATOR'S INTRODUCTION

Muhammad Rashid Rida (1865–1935), commonly known as Rashid Rida, the famous Syrian Muslim intellectual, wrote *The Caliphate or Supreme Imamate* (1923) during the winter and spring of 1922–23, after the Turkish National Assembly had abolished the Ottoman sultanate on November 1, 1922. Responding, he identified himself as a supporter of the Turkish leadership, and appealed to it to establish the version of the caliphate imagined in his book. By contrast, when the Republic of Turkey abolished the Ottoman caliphate on March 3, 1924, Rida would decry the move, characterizing Mustafa Kemal and the Turkish leadership as corrupt, self-aggrandizing, atheistic enemies of Islam who in campaigning against religion sought to go even further than Lenin had in Russia.

The Caliphate—as it is generally referred to—is an engaging, wide-ranging, and eclectic text that was written during one of the most turbulent periods in modern history. It is also a curious work in that it foregrounds and outlines a proposal which, it seems fairly clear, Rida had little expectation would be realized. There are multiple, overlapping angles from which it might be introduced: as a work by Rida concerning themes he had long engaged; as a work on the caliphate seen alongside others composed during Rida's era; as a work in Islamic political theory; as a work on post–World War I politics and the aftermath of the Ottoman Empire; as a work on Arab–Turkish relations; and as an anti-imperialist work whose author may here be seen alongside the likes of his contemporaries Gandhi, whom he admired, and Ho Chi Minh. An introduction could focus on any of these or other aspects. But the limits of space do not allow exhausting all of them. I have introduced the book by discussing it together with some of Rida's other postwar work, briefly touching on other stages of his career. I focus on the years leading up to *The Caliphate*.

Translator's Introduction

Against the backdrop of the postwar period, I suggest that Rida's book is continuous with his other efforts to establish independence for his people. Here, as in his career generally—commercial, legal, political—he was at heart a pragmatist and a realist. His work issued from entanglements in a changing world more than exercises in the abstract. As a result, he was prepared to make whatever rhetorical appeals and alliances would further his goals, notwithstanding apparent and even glaring inconsistencies involved in that. From that angle, some of his interventions appear tactical more than ideological, his inconsistencies more comprehensible. Similarly, in advocating communal sovereignty he took a flexible approach, aligning "community" with the exigencies of a given moment. Thus, he variously championed the rights of Muslims, Arabs, Syrians, Easterners, and global Southerners. He also saw himself as "religiously committed," in which connection he sometimes aligned himself more with certain non-Muslims than with Muslims he regarded as astray. Rida's wide-ranging efforts were not undertaken on behalf of Muslims exclusively, nor did he hesitate, where he found it apposite, to oppose Muslims he deemed oppressive. Yet it would seem that the various identities he embraced coexisted in a hierarchy in which "Muslim" was preeminent: Rida promoted non-Muslim identities, ideas, and agendas to the extent that he saw that as an effective way to advance his fundamental goal: the cause of Islam and the sovereignty of its community, the Muslim ummah.

Further, where he did draw on or appeal to the non-Islamic, he generally folded that together with Islam, at least in the material examined here. What might be emphasized is that for Rida all universal values (e.g., justice) and progressive political-legal notions (e.g., popular sovereignty) definitively originate with Islam. For Rida, this is so even where they appear to be promoted by Western non-Muslims, such as a sitting American president. By highlighting Rida's pervasive, consistent realism over his discursive shifts, or what have been regarded as such, I depart from interpretations that find him ideologically changing course. Framed by Rida's realism, what may initially appear startling becomes less so. His embrace of Woodrow Wilson's postwar vision, for instance, probably lacks the dramatic significance that it may seem to have. If Rida never genuinely embraced liberalism, *The Caliphate* with its overtly Islamic politics, sometimes sketched quite apologetically, would not represent a major shift.

If Rida did not write *The Caliphate* to set down a viable plan, why did he do so? His own answer provides a good starting point, and it is unclear that we have firm grounds to reject it. If Rida's primary motivations were those of a committed Muslim, his commentary might be taken at face value. He writes that

Translator's Introduction

he took seriously the burden that God had placed upon those with knowledge to explain matters clearly, and "not conceal" from others what he knew to be true (Qur'an 2:24). He comments that this applies particularly when confusion abounds, or people are proceeding thoughtlessly. To be sure, he found this to be the case after the abolition of the sultanate, when he began the series of essays in his magazine, *Al-Manar*, that would issue in his book. Here, it is also worth reiterating what Leor Halevi notes in his study of Rida's fatwas. Rida founded a commercially successful, independent magazine. While he had other roles, he depended upon his business for his livelihood. Rida wrote and published for consumers, an educated and somewhat elite constituency of subscribers. While roughly the first third of *The Caliphate* reviews theory, it is a topical work. Rida was here responding to events. But while his fatwas often endorsed new developments—such as the adoption of the gramophone—in *The Caliphate* he ostensibly rejects what had occurred. As well as overtly promoting a political agenda, the book has a rhetorical and pedagogical dimension. It clarifies, educates, stimulates reflection, and serves as a rallying cry: his readers should have confidence in their traditions. Continuing to work for Muslim independence, Rida here envisions achieving that through Islamic tools, drawing on the kind of discourse suited to circumstances and his purposes at the time. Thus, *The Caliphate* is very much an Islamic book. While modernizing, it also reassures Muslim readers that any solutions to their political and other problems are to be found nowhere beyond Islam. Where Rida refers to Western ideas he does so to critique them, or to show that they are not, in fact, Western at all. Here, Rida proposes a reenvisioned caliphate. Yet only once in his book does he offer anything approaching optimism on that. By contrast, he often shows that he did not expect the Turks, on whom his proposal hinges, to take up the task he sets down. Introducing Rida's book against the backdrop of his postwar politics comes at the expense of other aspects that, it might be argued, are no less important. Whether or not I have chosen the right focus, I hope I have introduced Rida's text in the manner described.

RASHID RIDA, REFORM, AND LABELING

It is difficult to capture or label Rida's political and other endeavors with any single term. One can label him a Salafi, but that may not in itself be very helpful. The word has a wide range of shifting meanings and is obscure to many. It probably would not help a nonspecialist a great deal to read that Rida was a Salafi, and could even be misleading. If not a Salafi, was he a liberal, modernist, constitutionalist, and democrat? Or was he a hardliner, an anti-Western

Translator's Introduction

Islamic exclusivist, fundamentalist, or even, as Mark Sykes described him, a fanatical Muslim?[1] Or did he at some point—during the war, or following the Paris Peace Conference or the League of Nations' ratification of mandates, or following the rise of Ibn Sa'ud—abandon the one for the other?[2] I argue against the suggestion that Rida turned course in that manner. That said, he is difficult to pigeonhole. He was a complex figure and his projects and stated views varied considerably. He was a prolific author who wrote as a scholar and cleric, and as a journalist in a novel vein. He was a publisher, a businessman, and, against the advice of his early mentor Muhammad 'Abduh, politically engaged. He advocated Syrian nationalism, Arabism, and pan-Islamism, although there is no evidence in the material examined here to suggest that the sovereignty of Muslims did not remain his ultimate concern, other causes being means to that end. He critiqued the Turks' treatment of Arabs, often forcefully, yet also appealed to them to lead the Muslim community. His positions on a number of leading figures shifted. At various points he supported and undermined Sultan Abdul Hamid II, urging recognition of his title as caliph and implying that caution should be taken in opposing him, while at other points campaigning against him, characterizing him as a despotic tyrant, and celebrating his deposition. He supported and then opposed Sharif Husayn of Mecca as a Muslim leader. His views on Mustafa Kemal's leadership also shifted. His writings dismissed the Great Powers as intractable enemies of Islam. Yet he on occasion worked with or appealed to Western representatives and institutions to secure his community's sovereignty, and the rights of modern citizenship.

Rida upheld non-Muslim rights under Islam, an unexceptional stance for a Muslim cleric in his milieu—more conservative clerics were also on board with legal equality for non-Muslims. Yet at times he also dismissed Christianity and Judaism in straightforwardly polemical terms. He lambasted 'Ali 'Abd al-Raziq for his heretical *Islam and the Bases of Rule* (1925) while publishing materials that, it might be argued, advocated a similar thesis.[3] Also suggesting a hardline profile, Rida has been regarded, rather glibly, as akin to the "godfather" of the Muslim Brotherhood. Hasan al-Banna, its founder, was one of his students, and he took over *Al-Manar* following Rida's death, although it is not clear that he had a mandate from Rida. Rida's work has also been regarded as precursor to so-called fundamentalism more broadly. While such a reading is dubious—overstating his influence over his "fundamentalist" successors—it nevertheless retains some currency. In the mid-1920s Rida became a key supporter of Ibn Sa'ud and his Saudi-Wahhabi kingdom. Yet during the Syrian Congress of 1919–20 Rida had upheld representative ideals against the autocratic ambitions

Translator's Introduction

of another monarch, Faysal.[4] In view of such variety one might conclude that Rida was completely fickle, or prone to turning course or dashing off in different directions, as some have suggested.[5]

Altogether, the work examined here shows that Rida may be labeled a reformer, political realist, and advocate for his community's rights. On the one hand, he never wavered in consistently rejecting any obstacles to the material reform of Muslim culture—Leor Halevi dubs this "laissez-faire" Salafism—and what he characterized as its hidebound intellectual life.[6] While he was here a modern figure and certainly no "fundamentalist," the Western term "Islamic modernist" does not correspond well to his self-understanding. On the other hand—here I find that the point that Mahmoud Haddad emphasized in 1997 stands unrebutted—he subordinated all other matters to political independence of Muslim lands.[7] Where that entailed changing position, he was willing to do so. Rida upheld *maslahah 'ammah*, well-being of the community. Yet as circumstances turned and turned again, his reading of what tools, agendas, and alliances best served that interest shifted on multiple occasions, as did the shape of the community he promoted. Thus, we find him recognizing and undermining the Ottoman sultan, supporting and criticizing the Young Turks, welcoming the Turks' defeat at the hands of non-Muslims, and elsewhere appealing to that same community to provide Muslim leadership. Rida heard a prophetic voice in the words of a sitting United States president, which may reflect strategy more than worldview, Rida, like Faysal, seeing an opportunity for political gain by adopting a liberal-nationalist idiom. By contrast, he also dismissed Western culture as inimical to Islam. He resisted Faysal's move to autocracy in Damascus yet embraced Ibn Sa'ud, an absolute monarch. Such shifts suggest that Rida's promotion of popular sovereignty was always tempered by pragmatism. He embraced it insofar as circumstances allowed, insofar as it lent to the more important objective. Thus, his writings uphold the ideal, but also sanction autocracy in the absence of a viable alternative. Thus, the definitive concern is Muslim independence from foreigners, not popular sovereignty specifically. That goal might be striven for through various means: a forward-looking Syrian Constitution, a reenvisioned caliphate ideally based on consent but also allowing for tyranny, or supporting an absolute monarch who appeared distinctive as a sovereign Arab Muslim ruler. In all of this, practical considerations override ideals. It would, for instance, seem unremarkable to suggest that Rida was drawn to Ibn Sa'ud by matters other than doctrine.

This may be appreciated by seeing *The Caliphate* together with writings on Wilson's postwar vision, the Arab government of Damascus (1918–20) and

6 *Translator's Introduction*

Syrian General Congress (1919–20) and its aftermath, and the Turkish War of Independence. These writings share common themes, yet vary in character. For instance, in conceiving a postwar order, Rida wrote optimistically and on a broad scale, promoting universal values, while also taking care to view events through an Islamic lens. Reflecting on his time in Syria from the fall of 1919 through the summer of 1920, he continued to stress universals such as justice, equality, and freedom. But he was also reckoning with the contingencies of engaged politics—especially the need to compromise—encountered in the effort to establish Syrian independence. Yet Rida's commentaries before, during, and after that effort again suggest that his overriding priority was the sovereignty of Muslims, which was not incompatible with the sovereignty of Syrians. Retrospective comments in *The Caliphate*, including a telling comment from a 1919 memorandum, support this reading. Rida began his book after the failure of the Syrian endeavor at the hands of European leaders who handed almost all of Greater Syria to Britain and France, essentially as colonies. As Rida highlighted, they did so in violation of their own rhetoric. Throughout all of this, there is little indication that Rida favored or even sanctioned disestablishing Islam.

While *The Caliphate*—like Rida's other religious writings—is reformist, it delineates a Muslim future in Islamic terms. Its proposals are foregrounded and framed with traditional and apologetic tropes. In that sense, it differs from his overt appeal to Wilsonian self-determination. The president's liberalism, as Rida seemingly read it during the war's last year, provided a path forward. Yet even here, where Rida appears quite "liberal," it would not seem that he actually subscribed to a Western form of liberalism. He emphasizes that what Wilson articulates originates squarely with Islam. Wilson is not credited with originality. That is due to God alone. Wilson is credited with sincerity, which carried weight given that the president, unlike so many other leaders, had the wherewithal to make good on what he said. Rida published translations and commentary on several of Wilson's wartime speeches, urging readers to embrace the president's prophet-like vision and apparent commitment to universal self-determination. Four years later to the month Rida begins his series on *The Caliphate*, now depicting Muslim self-determination through the framework of a genuine, shari'ah-based caliphate, not the shell to which the Turks had reduced it. That said, Rida's discussion does not reflect great hopes for success. His clear-eyed assessment is also seen in his predictions for the subsequent Cairo Caliphate Congress, while he supported it in principle. Following delays and on a reduced scale from what had been conceived, it convened to little effect in May of 1926. Rida had been an organizer, but did not attend, commenting positively on the attendees' efforts in *Al-Manar*. By that point he

Translator's Introduction

had embraced a Saudi-Wahhabi monarch, while still pursuing his laissez-faire agenda on reform generally.

AN ISLAMIC–AMERICAN POSTWAR VISON: DECEMBER 2, 1918

Rida begins *Al-Manar*, Volume 21, welcoming the war's end as a sign from God, confirming that those guided by His signs will gain mastery, while others will be wretched.[8] He sees in it "one of the mightiest things, a warning to humankind, to those of you who choose to go ahead and those who lag behind" (Qur'an 74:35–37).[9] Drawing on the Qur'an, Rida discusses the fate awaiting those who depend on material power at length. He asks, "what manner of power is this?" It is the power of armies, force, strategies, conspiracies, arrogance, and corruption, of those who commit atrocities. Without initially identifying any nation, he exhorts, "remind them of how God punished those who came before them," of how He set some against others.[10] Every party to a conflict, Rida notes, believes that it is rightful, or that truth and justice are found with those who hold power (*al-haqq li'l-quwah*). This sets up the discussion for what Rida deems a victory of spiritual over material power, truth over desire (Qur'an 23:71). Thus, he welcomes the demise of Germans and fellow-Muslim Turks, and the interventions of non-Muslims. In this instance, Rida promotes the vision of an American president rather than a Muslim leader.[11] He integrates qur'anic apocalypticism and reformist Islam with Wilson's delineation of universal principles, which he apparently deemed sincere.

Rida sees war illustrating the need for divine guidance, and the folly of reliance on human knowledge. Characteristically, he integrates commentary on topical events with an unwavering call for reform. Thus, he avers that guidance is found with a progressive religion, not one based on imitation and traditional custom. He sees war leading to a tipping point also alluded to in his other writings. The Western peoples of the North had risen to power through learning and industry, but Rida predicts a return to an earlier state of affairs, when the peoples of the South had "illuminated the horizon with knowledge and light" while the North lagged. Rida sees the qur'anic reference to Meccans who resisted Islam applying to the warring peoples of the North: "have they not traveled through the land, so that they have hearts to understand with and ears to hear with?" (Qur'an 22:46).[12] Rida's point is that God ultimately holds control and deals with tyrants present and past in a singular manner. Thus, at His hand "the Turks' shadow has been lifted from the lands of Arabs, Armenians, and Kurds." The corrupt Ittihadists (Unionists), like the ancient enemies of God's prophets,

8   *Translator's Introduction*

are defeated as "your Lord brought down upon them the lash of pain" (Qur'an 89:13).[13] Rida also quotes a qur'anic reference to "soldiers" or "angelic forces" (*junud*) of God whose identity is known only to Him: "no one knows your Lord's [angelic] forces except Him; this is nothing but a warning to human-kind" (Qur'an 74:31). He elaborates:

> Among the greatest examples is that God saved Europe from the Germans' aggression . . . at the hands of the great nation least inclined to make war, and farthest removed from seeking sovereignty over other nations, or from having designs on the lands of others. That nation is the United States of America. Its victory was a victory of the power of moral truth, which is more significant than the way it successfully tipped the balance of power in favor of the Allies' troops and military forces. Its president (Doctor Wilson) calls for building peace among nations on the basis of the principles that he set down: truth and universal justice, independence of peoples and nations, and equality of strong and weak, allies and foes.[14]

American intervention was an earthquake, leading to "a victory of moral over military and financial power." Here again, Rida finds qur'anic signs illuminating recent events, both affirming truth's vindication (Qur'an 7:118–19; 21:18). Know, he urges, that power is with those who uphold truth — *al-quwah li'l-haqq*, inverting the expression cited above, *al-haqq li'l-quwah*. He finds in this a definitive word on the human condition across all times and places. In *The Caliphate*, Rida will reaffirm that what is right ultimately prevails over what is strong, presenting that as a fundamentally and uniquely Islamic principle.[15]

In Rida's view, the war has made it clear to prescient Westerners that peace can only be established through abandoning the politics of secrecy, and establishing universal justice, self-governance, and an international body for resolving disputes. Achieving what is good, he finds, hinges on "the principle [of independence] that the president has called upon all warring parties to accept."[16] Those who assented but then conspired against Wilson "scheme only against themselves" (Qur'an 6:123). Rida finds that if all parties fail to heed Wilson's suggestion, the result will be strife and a return to war, quoting qur'anic references to those who plot, deceive, and are deluded by the things of this world (Qur'an 35:10; 31:33). Rida then presents four of Wilson's speeches in Arabic along with commentary from the newspaper *Al-Muqattam*, edited by Faris Nimr, a Greek Orthodox Syrian, as well as his own.[17] As historian Elizabeth F. Thompson has highlighted, a leading Muslim scholar here embraces an American president. Wilson is presented to Muslims in weak and wronged nations as a source of hope

Translator's Introduction

and trust, his ideals standing in contrast with Great Power designs. Rida quotes *Al-Muqattam*'s description of Wilson as a "prophet of truth" committed to justice and the welfare of the weak, evidencing his "genuine, sincere socialism."[18] While Wilson is credited with authoring the best *human* definition of justice, his inspiration does not in *Al-Muqattam*'s reading, or Rida's, lie in originality. Other leaders had professed the same values, albeit insincerely. Wilson inspires because of his apparent determination and ability through his nation's resources to implement what had hitherto been mere theory. Thus, *Al-Muqattam* calls upon weak nations to pray to God to enable Wilson to realize his vision of assisting the oppressed. He speaks with a prophetic voice and as successor to George Washington. The president does not engage in poetic fancy. He is a man of sincerity whose vision aligns with sound mind and sound religion.[19]

Here, I do not read Rida in quite the same manner as Thompson, whose discussion is headed "Cairo: A Sheikh Prays to an American President." In Thompson's rendering, Rida writes that Faris Nimr "was right to say that President Wilson is the one who proposed these principles of truth and justice. But he is not the first to call for them. For God had done so."[20] I think, however, that Rida wrote that Nimr "was right to say that Wilson is not the one who set them down [*laysa huwa al-wadi'*]." One does not want to glean too much from a disparity hinging on one word—"not"—and perhaps I have misread. Yet there is a different sense conveyed. Thompson finds Rida suggesting that Faris Nimr "had not gone far enough" as Wilson was not only agreeing with revealed religion but speaking the word of God.[21] As quoted above, Rida had referred to Wilson setting down the principles in question, but at this juncture he endorses the editor's qualification: Wilson was not the one. Read that way, the dramatic impact may be lessened. The different sense may be further suggested as the passage in question continues:

> *Al-Muqattam* is correct in stating that President Wilson is not the one who set down these principles of truth and justice, nor was he the first to call for them. God is the one who set them down in statements such as the following: "God commands you to return things entrusted to you to their rightful owners, and, when you judge between people, to do so with justice" [Qur'an 4:58]. Thus, God's justice applies to all people, as is supported by His statement, "do not let hatred of a people lead you away from justice, but adhere to justice, for that is closer to awareness of God" [Qur'an 5:8]. "Hatred" here means hate along with disdain. The first to call for these principles in this era and during this time of war were Russian . . . as we explained in the previous volume of *Al-Manar*.[22] . . . *Al-Muqattam* was also correct in determining that what

distinguishes President Wilson is that, following his elaboration of them, he seeks to realize these principles by utilizing the power of his nation, and further his statement that politicians in the past adorned themselves with these principles while inwardly resisting them. . . . All people recognize this now.[23]

The picture Rida paints is an odd combination. The leader embraced is non-Muslim. Yet Rida avers that when it comes to what underlies Wilson's discourse — the origins of his principles — Muslims have no need to look beyond Islam, nor to Rida's understanding is the president even the first non-Muslim to promote them during the era in question, the first being Russian. Hence, as Wilson echoes the Qur'an as well as other voices, what appears most significant to Rida is not Wilson's prophet-like voice, nor his principles *as such*. Wilson matters because he was in a position to put theory into practice and, seemingly, was sincere. Rida's appeal may be read as evidencing something approaching a genuine embrace of "liberal secularism," or, alternatively, in more pragmatic terms as reflecting a willingness to embrace powerful individuals, states, or their representatives to further his cause. One might suggest here that Rida's strategy was consistent: he attached himself to "rising stars" as and when it made strategic sense, and moved on when it did not.[24] Wilson's championing of the rights of the weak as equal to those of the strong aligned with Rida's efforts on behalf of those he regarded as having been wronged, and here Rida's categories of oppressed and oppressing do not break down along straightforward Muslim versus non-Muslim lines. Four years later, Rida would package his ideas in overtly Islamic discourse in *The Caliphate*. Yet the appeal to Wilson was not an isolated case. Following that, his work in Damascus and Geneva suggests a continued willingness to appeal to or cooperate with Western non-Muslims, while still upholding Islam and its shari'ah as integral to any proposal for establishing a postwar state in a Muslim majority land.

THE ARAB GOVERNMENT OF DAMASCUS; THE SYRIAN CONGRESS; THE CONSTITUTION OF JULY 1920

My intention is to introduce Rida's book, not to review Thompson's. Yet as Thompson has covered this territory and produced an impactful, thought-provoking narrative based on quality research, I note where I differ.[25] One aspect of her discussion may echo Rida's own reflections: the failure of Faysal's state was a missed opportunity of great significance. For Thompson its importance has been underappreciated: by destroying that state "the West stole democracy." This is not the venue to evaluate the broad thesis — was democracy there to be stolen? — but to consider Rida. Thompson portrays him as a liberal

Translator's Introduction

Islamic scholar who at one time embraced democratic, Wilsonian ideals, and who played a role in enabling the production of what was substantively a non-Islamic constitution in 1920. In this portrayal, Rida was on board with a plan that disestablished Islam and limited the jurisdiction of Islamic law. Disillusioned by subsequent events, Rida turned away from the "liberal secularism" that he had earlier embraced and "turned his attention in the later 1920s to religious matters."[26] Thompson sees that shift reflected in works such as *The Caliphate* (1923) and *The Muhammadan Revelation* (1934), which criticized how European scholars and Christian missionaries had depicted Islam. My interpretation differs. I note that Rida had always been interested in religious matters, engaging the issue of the caliphate, for instance, since the nineteenth century. He had also been critiquing European scholars and Christian missionaries for decades. In the years 1901–03, for instance, he wrote sixteen essays on that theme, later publishing them as a monograph.[27] The figure of Rida that emerges below is not one who subscribed to the disestablishment of Islam, limited the jurisdiction of Islamic law, or in any genuine sense embraced "liberal secularism" and then, changing course, rejected it.

In the spring of 1922, just over six months before he began *The Caliphate*, Rida published some reflections on the government and the Syrian Congress. His comments, sometimes idealized, sometimes sober and candid, have a different character to *The Caliphate*, while concerning the same themes: sovereignty, justice, and freedom. In two articles, "The Arab Government of Damascus" and "The General Syrian Congress," Rida discusses efforts to resolve immediate problems of postwar politics. Thus, they provide a window into another dimension of Rida's work. Authoring *The Caliphate*, for instance, he is more of a scholar and commentator than someone directly involved in events, although he does refer to his own work. For the most part, Rida surveys tradition and then applies it, at times quite speculatively, to the contemporary scene. This contrasts with his endeavors in Damascus and then in Geneva. Rida did not work in Faysal's government. He was not a government functionary, member of the Council of Directors, or member of the cabinet. Yet as a deputy and then president of the Congress — which was not technically part of the government — he engaged with and became fairly close to leading political figures, including a head of state, Faysal.

Rida had traveled to Syria in September 1919 to assist his fellow nationals in building an independent state after four centuries of Ottoman rule, and resisting Great Power designs. Proclaimed near the end of the war to encompass all of Syria, the state proved short-lived, lasting approximately twenty-two months, and had no clear boundary. It consisted roughly of Damascus and

Aleppo and their surroundings along with various other territory, some of it poorly defined. It also made claims in territories occupied by the British and French—Palestine, Lebanon, and the Syrian coast. It was terminated by General Henri Gouraud of France, whose forces easily overcame Syrian resistance in July 1920. Reflecting on its successes and failures around twenty-one months later, Rida begins by emphasizing his level-headedness. He had been aware before leaving Egypt, he writes, that the government of Damascus was weak, deficient in everything required for modern governance: "this is the reality of the situation."[28] Yet he argues that the state was nevertheless superior to those of British and French occupation. In justice, freedom, equality, and reform it surpassed those in territories occupied by states "who gave us the innovation of mandates to reform our lands, on the pretext that we were incapable of doing that by ourselves."[29] Further, it had been progressing and dedicating itself to reform, particularly following the Declaration of Independence on March 8, 1920.

Rida highlights what he characterizes as the freedoms of speech and association that the Arab government established, and how these had rendered it an object of envy, obsequiousness to the powerful in Damascus replaced by self-respect and dignity. In this particular connection he credits Faysal for the effect of his humility. Unlike Palestine and the Syrian coast, where Rida saw Zionist Jews and Christians respectively having preferential status, the government of Damascus upheld equality: "no Christian or Jew had any fear that the government or the people would be prejudicial toward them, or that they would be wronged by Muslims, and Muslims expected nothing from Muslim ministers that they did not also expect from Christians."[30] Yet Rida tempers this description by also pointing to a lack of moral courage. The government failed to discard old habits, continuing to oblige the powerful in hiring and promotion. His writings elsewhere identify such habits as a major cause of Muslim political failings, as in *The Caliphate*. Rida's critique here applies particularly to those close to Faysal. Although he notes an episode where the king was rebuffed, Rida finds the king's interference excessive and harmful to the government.

Rida's tone is contemplative. At one point he finds himself unable to grasp why his hopes in the government ended in disappointment. He identifies causes of failure in very broad terms, and notes shortcomings of Faysal and Prime Ministers 'Ali Rida Pasha al-Rikabi and Hashim al-Atassi. In sum, Rida finds that the government was not resolute, judicious, and decisive, and neglected reforms that—he implies—could have secured independence. Rida also faults its impatient and self-interested critics, and those currying favor with foreigners, seeking French rule. In what may read as somewhat idealized, Rida implies that

Translator's Introduction

if not for these shortcomings "great things" could have been achieved through the opportunity for independence, particularly after its declaration. He does not appear to address certain dynamics. Were France determined to secure a colony, the government lacked the resources to effectively resist and could not have marshaled them in any short timeframe, as events would prove. Yet Rida does show his awareness of the Great Powers' intentions. He notes his incredulous reaction when Rikabi had stated that independence was assured and would be recognized by Britain and France. Even after developments in Washington, D.C. and Europe continued to undermine prospects that what he had envisioned at the end of 1918 might be realized, Rida continued to champion representative governance. This might be a "liberal" position, and Rida averred that it accorded with all progressive principles of modern civilization. Yet it was no less an "Islamic" position, Rida stating quite matter-of-factly that it accorded with the Islamic revealed law and its purpose of ensuring human submission to God. Thus, he resisted autocracy insofar as circumstances allowed. Following Gouraud's ultimatum to Faysal of July 1920, he headed a group formed to determine how to respond. It notified Faysal of the need to replace the government of Atassi, who had replaced Rikabi two months previously. Rida relates, "Faysal replied that he does not take orders from a group, party, or congress." Not for the first time Rida pushed back: "I gave him an answer to that which was harsher than his answer."[31] The dispute became moot when French forces won an easy victory at the battle of Khan Musaylun and entered Damascus on July 25. It would take Rida some time to get back to Cairo.

In a May 1922 article Rida turns to the Congress. He describes its character in bold terms. It was, he writes, genuinely representative (*niyabiyyah*), speaking for all Syrians, who were completely united over independence. As in 1918, Rida points to Arab hopes aligning more with American than with European or other agendas. He notes that the Congress was to work with what transpired to be an American commission — the King-Crane Commission — highlighting the refusal of Britain and France to participate and consult with the Syrian people on their governance. He explicates that refusal by stressing that public opinion had unanimously rejected any foreign oversight that would undermine complete independence. Rida notes that all who met with the commission had confidence in the Congress, seeing significance in the Congress rather than a party or some other entity declaring, "We have announced the termination of the current governments of military occupation in the three areas, which are to be replaced by a representative monarchy that will be responsible to this assembly (that is, to the Congress) until it is able to convene its representative assembly."[32] With its Declaration of Independence supported throughout Syria, Rida sees

14 *Translator's Introduction*

the Congress acquiring "the character of a national constituent assembly," also highlighting how the wording authorized it to act without restraint.[33]

Rida's narrative again shows him resisting autocracy. When it was proposed that the government seek the endorsement of the Congress for its agenda, Faysal objected. While Rida noted his own ambivalence, he advised Faysal that the proposal should be implemented. The king conceded. Rida relates:

> Emir Faysal said, "The Congress does not have the right to demand that of the government because it is not a representative assembly." I said, "To the contrary, it has this right because it has a higher authority than a representative assembly: it is a national constituent assembly." He said, "I am the one who created the Congress, and I did not grant it the right to make this demand of the government, which would hamper its work." I said, "No, to the contrary, it is the Congress that made you [king]. You were one of the Allies' commanders, serving under General Allenby, and the Congress made you king of Syria. Yes, you were in a position to authorize the convening of the Congress, as you were ruling these lands in a military government in the name of the Allies. Yet once it had convened in the name of the nation it then had a higher authority. This accords with both the principles of the Islamic revealed law, through which one submits to God, and all progressive principles of this era's positive law. Furthermore, when the Congress was established, it was stipulated that this government, for which the Congress chose you as king, would be responsible to it in everything pertaining to independence. . . . Thus, I hope you do not create a crisis for us when we are at the beginning of our journey."[34]

Rida reports the incident, he suggests, not to insinuate that Faysal inclined to tyranny, but to establish the Congress's representative character. For Rida, that tendency, after all, is innate to the human soul, as he sees the recent history of the Turkish Ittihadists demonstrating. Thus, tyranny can only be curbed by revealed or positive law. Rida notes that recognizing a monarch while simultaneously restraining him through law is nearly impossible.

Given Rida's role as president of the Congress, it seems reasonable to hold that he endorsed or at least assented to the Syrian Constitution of July 1920, which upholds the notion of representative governance and freedom of religion for all confessions (Article 13). The Constitution represents the results of efforts of different constituencies—secularizing and traditional—to reach an agreement and Rida appears to have played a mediating role as president. Thompson finds that the Constitution "disestablished Islam as the state religion" because, for instance, "[n]one of the articles on individual rights, the legislature's pro-

Translator's Introduction 15

mulgation of law, or the law courts even mentioned Islamic law."[35] Thompson has also characterized the Constitution as "the most secular and democratic to date in the Middle East."[36] Yet the notion of disestablishment of Islam is not the only possible reading. There are details that may be interpreted as indicating a less Islamically or religiously neutral project. For instance, Article 14 of the Constitution shows that the government was to be in charge of regulating shari'ah courts: "Oversight of Sharia courts and religious councils that administer personal status laws and the management of public [Waqf] endowments shall be administered under laws issued by the Congress." Also perhaps complicating its characterization as "non-Islamic," the 1920 Constitution stipulated that preexisting laws would "remain in force" (Article 147)—the principle of equality of non-Muslims had already been enshrined by an Ottoman Constitution that recognized Islam as the state religion.

Granted, as Thompson notes, the 1920 Constitution does not address the role of religion in legislation. While that could be indicative of a liberal-democratic-secular project, this again is not the only possible reading. It may also reflect an urge to avoid controversy and expedite the process, kicking the proverbial can down the road. Furthermore, the Constitution did make other concessions to Islam and religion that are not insignificant. It mandated that the head of state must be a Muslim (Article 1). In a somewhat vague manner, it required the head of state to respect "divine laws" (*shara'i' ilahiyyah*), which would presumably include but not be limited to Islamic laws or *shara'i'* (Articles 5 and 6). In view of these points, together with the reaffirmation of preexisting laws, it seems plausible that the 1920 Constitution would have rendered Islam the de facto state religion in a country with a Muslim majority. That, to be sure, is speculative. Yet evidence for the alternative reading of disestablishment of Islam does not appear firm.

As for Rida, his position seems clear. It would not appear that he was ever on board with an endeavor that would disestablish Islam. While the focus here is on the postwar period, it would seem that he prioritized Muslim sovereignty over Syrian independence before, during, and after the war. One might note the following examples. The "organic law" he presented to the British in 1915 proposed not a Syrian state but an Arab federation including the Arabian Peninsula (Jazirat-el-Arab) along with "the Provinces of Syria and Irak [Iraq]," with Islam as "the official religion," a dual administrative system with a religious capital in Mecca and a political capital in Damascus, with the religious branch taking precedence over the political branch, the caliph in Mecca having the right to nominate the president in Damascus out of three candidates selected by the Parliament.[37] Here also I read differently to Thompson, who states that

Rida proposed a law for "the future Syrian Arab state that envisioned 'a sort of republic' that would separate religion from state."[38] I find it difficult to see how that description aligns with Rida's organic law, or where the phrase "a sort of republic" is found in his proposal. But even if he did not include that expression, it is clear that for Rida an Islamic state could be a type of republic. To quote *The Caliphate*, "an Islamic government is a type of republic."[39]

There are also indications that during 1919–20 Rida held to the same stance. For instance, in *The Caliphate* he quotes from a memorandum that he had written to British Prime Minister David Lloyd George in the summer of 1919. This would reflect his thinking at the very time that the King-Crane Commission was visiting the region and the drive to establish Syrian independence was at its peak. Rida wrote: "For Muslims, the greatest agitation concerns Islamic sovereignty, without which they believe Islam cannot exist. Concern for its existence flows in the blood of every Muslim's veins. That is because no Muslim can envision his religion enduring without the existence of an Islamic state, one that is independent, strong, and self-sufficiently capable of implementing the rulings of the revealed law."[40] Similarly, in February 1920, Rida argued that most Muslims—that is, most of the population—would consider a secular state illegitimate and would reject it in favor of a religious one at the first opportunity. Thus, he argued that "our shariʿah should be the main source of needed legislation, even if the government is not Islamic."[41] Elaborating on what he meant to those who disapproved of his ideas, Rida apparently made clear that he was not advocating a theocracy, which is not the only form an Islamic government might take. In any case, whatever might eventuate, Rida's preferences seem clear, as further indicated below.

Rida regarded the Constitution as informed by multiple sources, one of which was the shariʿah. Indeed, he notes that the Congress was qualified to set down a constitution and laws because its membership included those with expertise in the shariʿah together with others whose credentials rested on their expertise in positive law and their education in Ottoman and foreign schools.[42] In typical fashion, Rida divides its membership into those bound to the old, those infatuated with the new, and moderates in between. He laments an incident where Muslims infatuated with the new prevailed in a legal debate involving overturning restrictions that were based on religion. At issue was socializing between men and women in clubs and the consumption of alcohol. The incident appears to have left a mark. Rida also relates it in *The Caliphate*. Thus, while his role as president of the Congress involved mediation between secularizers and those less willing to discard religious tradition, he remained committed to Islamic morality. Indeed, he labels Muslims who jettisoned it disgraceful

Translator's Introduction

and further removed from true religion than some Christians. Referring to the matter in *The Caliphate*, Rida describes Muslims who had urged the Congress to establish a nonreligious government as heretics. He notes that most Muslim delegates along with some Christian delegates rejected that suggestion, which he clearly considered wrongheaded.[43] Thus, Rida does not show himself advocating a government void of religious influence, at least when regarding it retrospectively. His comments suggest that along with appeals to what could be regarded as liberal values and his "in between" stance, he invariably felt that the politics of civil society should not override established principles of religious morality. His approach might bring to mind the phrase from the hadith, *la darar wa la dirar* (do not inflict injury nor repay one injury with another). In a modern context, this speaks to the notion that in order to promote Muslim public well-being new laws should be adopted in cases where the shari'ah is silent or not explicit. Rather than reflecting a willingness to limit the scope of Islamic law, Rida's work may be read as informed by Islamic religious sentiment.

RIDA'S TRIP TO GENEVA

The details related above suggest that to whatever extent Rida embraced a liberal worldview he did not do so along secularist lines. Nor did he see Western conceptions supplanting those drawn from Islam. Altogether, he may never have been a true political liberal at heart. Yet France's termination of Syrian self-rule did not lead him to abandon appealing to the West to support the cause of his people's self-rule, contrary to the path Faysal came to pursue in Iraq with British support. Rida's writings convey hopes that independence could be recognized and restored by appealing to "wise," "just," "liberal," and "merciful" Europeans, and the League of Nations Assembly. For instance, in a June 1921 article entitled "The Arab Question" Rida commented, "I still hope to convince the two countries not to divide our lands and deny our rights. It is unfortunate that my previous quest was with their extremist colonialists. I hope to reach an agreement with the liberals among them. There are many of them, thank God for that."[44] Rida would unsuccessfully promote that agenda in Geneva a few weeks later. When the League Council, dominated by the Great Powers, approved the mandates the following year in a London meeting, Rida's hopes were dashed.[45] His reading is captured, for instance, in "The European Trip," an installment of his commentaries on his trip to Geneva, published in November 1922. It includes an article entitled "A Call from the East to the Liberals of the West." The intended audience, initially at least, was European, not the readership of *Al-Manar*. Rida had attempted to publish it in Geneva, hoping that its themes would be echoed in the newspapers of that "free city," and shrill in the ears of those attending the League of Nations. But his commissioned translator deemed it unpublishable, given its vehement criticisms of the Great Powers. In appealing to "European spirits" Rida positions himself as an "Easterner."

Rida characterizes his "Call" as a proof through which liberal Europeans could testify in favor of justice and truth, or, alternatively, a proof against them, should they endorse the West's continued oppression of the East. He urges liberals to rally the oppressed to rise up against leaders who embrace the politics of deception, subjugation, and theft. Failing that, Rida envisions an apocalyptic war, more evil than the preceding one, which would continue until the earth is destroyed. Positioning himself as an expert in the affairs of the East, Rida calls upon liberals to prevent this. He admonishes: Do not let the greedy use your resources, soldiers, and workers to serve injustice; do not be misled by their eloquent rhetoric. Previously, Rida finds, liberals could be excused for believing that preparations for war were deterrent in nature, and that competing in establishing colonies was a service to humanity. But given what resulted, war followed by the unjust Treaties of Versailles, San Remo, and Sevres, no such excuse remains. Liberal Europeans should know that this has taught the Eastern masses "about the need to unite and cooperate, in spite of their different religions, doctrines, and ethnicities, in order to resist colonial aggression . . . and not to fear death in the cause of freedom and independence . . . and that the colonizers lack any conception of truth, justice, virtue, or humanity."[46]

Rida sees Easterners having reversed their understanding of what "English" and "French" connote. In the past, these terms denoted what was positive and progressive. Notably, however, Eastern peoples have now come to see the Turks as more just, honest, and merciful than Europeans, and particularly the British and French. This, Rida finds, is perfectly understandable, given the deceptions of their states, their false promises of freedom, spread in myriad ways, including leaflets dropped from planes. Rida refers specifically to what had been published in the names of Sharif Husayn and Faysal. Yet the outcome was occupation of Syria and Iraq, destruction of farms and villages, and the deaths of thousands. Rida goes on to consider whether most members of the League of Nations, or "those among them who embrace truth and justice," had been misled by the Allies or the League Council—Rida notes the endorsement of the council's "subjugation of the Eastern peoples in the name of mandates." His point is to question how members could have been unaware of the Great Powers' intentions, and the discrepancies between words and actions, given what they

Translator's Introduction 19

could observe, or read in their own publications: how could they consider that what was provided to Syrians and Iraqis was "help" and "assistance"? To the contrary, Rida sees in the mandates an innovation conceived to extricate the British and French from their false principles, including the claim that that war had been fought for the principle of freedom and independence and against the German principle of rule through force. Rebutting that, he reiterates that Eastern peoples must have the right to select rulers from among themselves. He concludes by warning liberals that if the League of Nations materially supports the oppression of the weak by the strong, it will have become an instrument of evil, one serving the elimination of truth and justice. The result, he warns, will be the destruction of Europe through further war or a worse form of Bolshevism than the Russian variety, and the peoples of the East uniting to take revenge on the nations of the West.[47]

In sum, much in Rida's efforts in Cairo, Damascus, and Geneva can be read as evidencing a commitment to popular sovereignty and representation. One could argue on the basis of these and other examples—such as his initial response to the Young Turks' deposition of Abdul Hamid II in 1909—that he "believed in" such principles.[48] He worked toward implementing them through efforts that included mediation between differing constituencies on the matter of religion, along with on occasion embracing Western discourse. Where those in power, Muslim or non-Muslim, pursued a different path, he sought to hold them to account, *where doing so seemed viable*. At the same time, he never wavered in his Islamic religious commitments, and he would easily draw on, integrate, and move between different kinds of rhetoric, ranging from Islamic apologetics to championing the cause of Eastern or Southern peoples generally. There is an anger in his "Call" to liberal Europe. Rida published it at a time when the promises of liberal politics had been exposed as false, and his resentment is palpable. His response, along with *The Caliphate* and his career generally, suggests that Rida may never have endorsed liberal politics *as such* but as a means to a more important end. Where liberal politics lent to Muslim independence, he endorsed them. Yet under different circumstances Rida sanctions autocracy and tyranny. That is, representative ideals, Islamic or liberal, would always be subordinate to practical considerations. Taken in isolation, the statement, "Rashid Rida believed in popular sovereignty" conveys little of substance, his stance always tempered by circumstance. Hence, Rida was prepared to support an autocrat such as Ibn Sa'ud where that appeared to enable Arab Muslim rule of Arab Muslim subjects. Likewise, where it appeared strategically cogent, he had aligned his cause with the military successes and Muslim leadership of Mustafa Kemal, while rejecting his reading of Islam.

THE CALIPHATE

As Rida was reflecting on his work in Syria, Cairo, and Geneva, he was also engaging the issue of the caliphate, as he had throughout his career.[49] He serialized and commented upon an Arabic translation of Abul Kalam Azad's Urdu "The Islamic Caliphate," critiquing Azad's claim that the caliph need not be Qurayshi.[50] Rida also commented on pertinent events, notably the Turkish War of Independence, discussing some of the ideas he would elaborate in *The Caliphate*. A consistent theme runs throughout: subjugated peoples, or those at risk, must be united if they are to resist foreign powers. In Damascus, Rida had been part of an effort to unify Syrians, while also pointing to how they would benefit from Islamic law and governance. That may speak to another aspect of pragmatism. Syrian independence would benefit many Muslims, and was not incompatible with broader goals, such as those he had proposed in his organic law, or the ultimate goal of universal Muslim independence. When events in Turkey and the caliphate are at issue, it is Arab–Turkish unity that is to the fore, Rida suggesting how Turkish nationalist successes have ramifications for all Muslims. Thus, in the summer of 1922 he argues that any actions that would estrange Arabs from Turks would lead to the subjugation of both. Responding to a query about Turkish Islam, Rida repeats a comment by a Persian emir: "If it were not for Mustafa Kemal Pasha, every Muslim on earth would feel humiliated."[51] Hence Arab preeminence in Islam is downplayed as historically contingent rather than innate. As noted, in 1918 Rida had welcomed the lifting of the Turkish shadow from Arab lands, and in Damascus had subsequently worked for Syrian independence in place of Turkish rule. When it comes to the Turkish War of Independence, Rida gives the Turks recognition and praise. They are presented, as in *The Caliphate*, as the Muslims' preeminent temporal power. Thus, their military successes should be celebrated.

Rida found it apposite here to also comment on the Ottoman, 'Abbasid, and Umayyad caliphates and how they were at odds with theory. That is, they rested on power and partisanship (*'asabiyyah*) rather than choice. In theory, Islamic rule hinges on the role of those who loose and bind (*ahl al-hall wa al-'aqd*). This is the notoriously imprecisely defined group that is qualified and empowered to represent the community. Legitimate rule rests upon this group

Translator's Introduction

consulting one another prior to electing a caliph. Rida's point is that while this was not the case under the Ottomans, neither was it so under the 'Abbasids and Umayyads. He had highlighted the themes of consultation and consent when discussing the Syrian Congress as legitimizing its work, also finding that its embrace of those principles explained the British and French refusal to engage it. His subsequent reading of the Turkish situation again suggests that practical considerations override ideals where the two are in conflict. His commentaries on postwar Syria promulgate representative ideals, which for Rida are informed by both Islamic theory and modern civilization. With the Syrian effort failing and the Turkish experience the object of attention, Rida allows for recognition of tyrants or those whose rule he found resting on force, including Turkish nationalists and Ottoman sultans, the path to Muslim sovereignty served by celebrating Mustafa Kemal's successes, whatever his failings.[52]

This does not represent a shift in Rida's fundamental disposition. As noted, he had previously been prepared to support or recognize autocrats, tyrants, or those whose rule did not rest on popular support. He was always willing to consider tactical alliances, as with Sharif Husayn, whom he later turned against. It is well known that Rida had numerous identities: Muslim, Arab, Syrian, Syrian-Egyptian, Eastern, global Southern, and "religiously committed," where he found himself closer to "genuine" Christians than "heretical," Europeanizing Muslims.[53] As he promoted the causes of varying communities in the materials discussed here, there is no indication that the "Muslim" identity and cause was not foremost. Framed thus, Rida's stances appear less fickle. Syrian or Arab independence, for instance, lent to that cause. Those plans also involved non-Muslim minorities, and in both cases Rida sought Islamic governance along with legal recognition of Christianity and Judaism. Such recognition, it might be noted, is unexceptional.[54] Highlighting Rida's tactical mindset might also be helpful when it comes to reckoning with shifts in his attitudes toward the Western and Turkish ruling classes.

THE ABOLITION OF THE SULTANATE, NOVEMBER 1, 1922

A few months after Rida published these commentaries on Syria and Turkey, the Turkish National Assembly abolished the Ottoman sultanate. Wahid al-Din (Mehmed VI, r. 1918–22), was deposed and replaced with 'Abd al-Majid II (Abdülmecid II, r. 1922–24), who ruled as caliph rather than sultan-caliph. The institution that had theoretically held authority in the temporal realm as sultanate and the spiritual realm as caliphate was reduced to the latter, which in turn would be abolished by the Republic of Turkey on March 3, 1924.

Rida responded to the Assembly's action a few days later, in the issue of *Al-Manar* that also included his reproduction of his "Call" to liberal Europeans. In an article entitled "The Turks' Victory over the Greeks; Their Toppling of the Ottoman Throne; and Their Turning the Islamic Caliphate into a Spiritual, Moral Institution," Rida again sees modern wartime events affirming divine signs. Beginning with qur'anic verses (Qur'an 3:140–41) he sets this conflict alongside others that God has "dealt out" and in which disbelievers and believers will both suffer setbacks, as in the Muslim defeat at Uhud in 625. Such conflicts reveal true religion and bring forth martyrs or witnesses to faith. Where earlier Rida had seen divine justice underlying the Central Powers' defeat, he here sees God's hand directing the victory of the Turkish "lions," a victory not merely of one party over another, but one with universal ramifications. All Muslims, then, should celebrate, even while some of their leaders do not. Rida notes that Muslims had done so to the extent that their political freedoms allowed. The religious dimension that Rida wants his readers to see is also found in his characterization of Lloyd George as having attempted to execute a final crusade.

Rida explicates how these events bear on the caliphate. The last sultan-caliph, Wahid al-Din (Mehmed VI), had collaborated with the British. Thus, his deposition by the National Assembly—which, notably, Rida finds effectively taking on the role of those who loose and bind—is valid. The Kemalist Turks had certainly erred in reducing the caliphate to its spiritual dimension, an action with no precedent beyond the Batini Shi'ah and one that had alarmed the entire Islamic world. But on practical grounds Rida finds that all Muslims must nonetheless support them. Rida's pragmatism is also seen in his acceptance of what—he suggests without showing great confidence—might be temporary responses to unavoidable contingencies and which could later be revised and harmonized with Islamic principles. Thus, whereas a spiritual caliphate cannot be squared with Islamic teaching, its creation brought no immediate harm, nor was it *effectively* inferior to what it replaced. The temporal dimension of the caliphate had long been nominal. Therefore, nothing substantial was lost by its abolition. Its political utility had benefited the Ottoman Empire, and therefore the new state did not harm Islam by abolishing it. Prefiguring *The Caliphate*, Rida finds that the new state would benefit from the caliphate's political influence if it subsequently reestablished it in an orthodox manner.[55]

This was the context in which Rida began his series on the caliphate, the first installment appearing in the December 18, 1922, issue of *Al-Manar*. That issue also included Rida's critique of Mustafa Kemal's lengthy speech to the Grand National Assembly of November 1, in which he had justified the abolition of the sultanate. Rida's discussion, as in *The Caliphate*, walks the line of criti-

Translator's Introduction

cizing the leader's interpretation of Islam, while still identifying himself as a supporter of the Turkish state. Where Rida finds a spiritual caliphate Islamically unsupportable, acceptable only on a contingent basis, Mustafa Kemal argued that it was progressive and Islamically sound, with precedents in early Islam. Retorting, Rida deems the move part of an effort to create a purely Turkish republic based on the principle that "what is true and right rests upon power" (al-haqq li'l-quwah), the principle Rida had four years earlier found overturned by the Central Powers' defeat in the war. Rida laments that "this is the principle that shapes the politics of our era." Muslim support for the Turks, Rida reiterates, rests solely on their military prowess, which forced European foes to reckon with them as peers. Rida flatly rejects Mustafa Kemal's Islamic proofs. He writes:

> I say what I say as a faithful advisor to this power, which I support in its efforts to resist the Muslims' enemies. . . . I praised the Kemalists, preferring them to Sharif Husayn and his sons. But I say nothing that I do not believe to be true. This applies to my statement that Ghazi Mustafa Kemal erred in his intentions in his speech, in attempting to prove that the regime of caliphate is unsound, and does not lend to the common good, and that our sayyid 'Umar [ibn al-Khattab] was aware of that, and so attempted to prepare the way for a different regime by commanding that the election of his successor be based upon consultation. He also erred in attempting to use the failure of the Umayyads, 'Abbasids, and Ottomans to establish a caliphate based upon that system of consultation as proof for his argument. Likewise, he erred in claiming that most of the Companions rendered the caliphate an institution that rested upon the partisan support of an ethnic group. As a result, he erred in saying that those who prevailed over the first caliphs and stripped them of their authority, leaving them merely holders of blessed titles, did what was right and proper, and then using that as a model to be emulated by the Turkish national government. All of that is invalid, and represents an assault on the revealed law by force. . . . We wrote to Ghazi Mustafa Kemal indicating the ideal way to revive the caliphate and the benefit of doing so. That was before this last event [the abolition of the sultanate], and we hope that they may correct their error . . . after consulting with Islam's leading ulama in all lands.[56]

Some have taken Rida's expression of "hope" as indicating that at this juncture he believed the Turkish leadership could yet reestablish the caliphate in what he regarded as a sound form, following his advice.[57] On the other hand, taken together with *The Caliphate*, Rida's critique might be read as an exercise

24 *Translator's Introduction*

in due diligence. That is, it may have been informed more by his sense of duty as one of the ulama to correct a leader's misrepresentations of Islam than by a genuine hope that his words would be heeded by those in power.

RIDA'S BOOK, *THE CALIPHATE*

Rida's *Al-Manar* series on the caliphate ran through the winter and spring of 1922–23, in Volumes 23 and 24 of the magazine. He then added an Introduction and published it as the book translated here. Its full title is: *The Caliphate or Supreme Imamate: Studies on Law, Governance, Society, and Reform Offered to the Courageous Turkish People, the Party of Reform in the Arab and Indian Lands, and to the Other Islamic Peoples.* The text following the Introduction has two sections: a reprisal of theory, and a reading of the contemporary situation and proposal for reform. Aside from *Al-Manar* itself, *The Caliphate* may be Rida's most significant publication. It has been translated into languages including French, Urdu, and Japanese, and described as the most important work on the caliphate since that of Mawardi.[58] It has also been seen as a notable work in political theory and as prefiguring the idea of a modern Islamic state. The secondary literature on Rida's book is very extensive.[59] What was his intention in writing it? Ostensibly, it is a call to implement a proposal of doubtful viability: reestablishing the caliphate in a "sound," orthodox, and universal form. Rida is not consistent on the universal aspect. He implies that this would mainly concern the Muslim community, and that the caliphate would not threaten Western states. Yet he also states that it will be one for "all people."

Rida's call raises the question of how far somebody of his experience could have seen it as viable. Given the general postwar political situation, along with the establishment of mandates, it seems unlikely that he imagined a shari'ah-based, universal caliphate actually being established. His proposal hinges on the Turks, whose new state did not yet have an apparently antireligious character, taking up the task. Rida implies that Mustafa Kemal's agenda on the caliphate would prove untenable beyond the short term because his popular support rested on military successes, not genuine endorsement of his political vision. Thus, Rida finds that Muslim sentiment will preclude continued Europeanization. He also alludes to an unnamed group in the National Assembly that saw the benefits of a genuine caliphate.[60] But beyond such brief comments his book offers no evidence that the Turks, or their leaders, would be inclined to walk the path he sets down. His tentatively suggested seat of the caliphate, Mosul, was under a mandate. Neither is a mechanism for moving forward, including the matter of who would initially head the revived institution, sketched in more than general terms.

Translator's Introduction 25

Rida does not maintain a consistent tone on prospects. His discussion includes numerous apologetic assertions: the caliphate holds the key to universal salvation; it will save both East and West. But, taken as a whole, his book leaves little doubt: Rida did not expect to see his plans realized. He plainly voices misgivings about obstacles and a lack of the resolve that would be necessary to overcome them. That is so even as he continued to find that Muslims should *strive* for a revived caliphate, and supported those besides himself seeking to realize it. Some of Rida's work in the period after he published his book also suggests that he saw little prospect of success. Whereas his book appeals to "the courageous Turks," he would shortly turn to critiquing Mustafa Kemal and the Turkish leadership. Around the same time, Rida was lending his support to a different kind of Muslim leader, Ibn Sa'ud, who had established a larger Wahhabi kingdom in much of Arabia in the mid-1920s. As an absolute monarch Ibn Sa'ud was not the "caliph" delineated in Rida's book, although he would credit him for "reviving the government of the rightly guided caliphate on earth."[61] Rida's predictions for what might result from the Cairo Caliphate Congress are also suggestive of his sober assessment. He correctly discerned that it could not succeed, or elect a caliph, although he published supportively on the Congress in *Al-Manar* as the attendees' "brother."

Yet however much circumstances before and after Rida published his book might appear to render a genuine caliphate unviable, that, taking his words at face value, is what he calls for. While he had been involved in the day-to-day business of politics in Syria, his book is more of an exercise in rhetoric. Various features point to a project that is still in progress, with critical matters not explicitly resolved. How ideas would be transferred to the scene is yet to be fully worked out. At the outset Rida addresses the question posed above: why did he write his book? As he also states in other works, he took seriously the burden that God had placed upon the learned class. As one of the ulama, Rida was duty-bound to explain matters clearly and elucidate truth (Qur'an 2:42), particularly where confusion abounds and, in Rida's wording, the uninformed might be inclined to proceed recklessly, as he saw many of his fellow Muslims doing at the end of 1922. The issue of the caliphate, hitherto a "sleeper," had come newly into view. Given the resulting confusion evidenced in newspapers and elsewhere, Rida writes, "we saw that it was incumbent upon us to elucidate our shari'ah's ordinances regarding the issue . . . as the situation requires."[62] Thus, Rida defines his tasks as delineating the true caliphate and its superiority over other systems of rule, along with supporting the new Turkish government. He implies that he is not supporting that government as such, but to promote Muslim sovereignty. His support, then, is provisional and that of the Muslims should be likewise. Rida folds this together with the idea that nothing has weakened Islam more than weak blindly deferring to strong, ruled to ruling, masses to caliphs and monarchs. Hence while their military successes have rendered the Turks "Islam's sharp sword" with whom rests the best hope for sovereignty, deference to their leaders' spiritual caliphate is contingent. Muslims should stop deferring to whatever their leaders determine in the political realm. However far he felt that it was a realistic prospect, Rida expresses the hope that as the new state becomes more firmly established its leaders might be persuaded to reverse course and establish a genuine caliphate. The hope would prove short-lived.

Framed by mainstream Sunni tradition, *The Caliphate*'s main thesis overlaps with what Rida had argued across the period examined above: Islamic governance can and must be modern; modern governance can and must be Islamic. Rida consistently sought to debunk the notion that the two were in conflict. The West's rhetoric had been exposed as false, appeals to its leaders and officials not bearing fruit. Moving on from anger and disappointment, Rida continued to push for the ideals that he had associated with the efforts of the Syrian General Congress: self-determination, representative government, and popular sovereignty. Commenting on those efforts, Rida had at times integrated them with qur'anic signs. And where his discussion was conceived for a liberal European audience, as noted, he adopts a more overtly Eastern than Islamic voice, and the two are not incompatible. Responding to the Turks' action, Rida adopts a more distinctively Islamic voice. His theses emerge from tradition even where their implications may not. Rida counterpoints Islamic with non-Islamic politics, often in apologetic terms. Self-determination, representation, and popular sovereignty, along with the people's right to enact novel legislation, are again promoted, with Rida emphasizing over and again that they originate in Islam. These notions "belong" to the Muslims.

RIDA'S INTRODUCTION TO *THE CALIPHATE*

Rida introduces his book with a variety of themes: succession in the Qur'an; Muslim weakness; Islam's spiritual-political character; the historical caliphate; and a call upon "courageous Turks" not to be "seduced" by the common Muslims' deference to a spiritual caliphate. Characteristically, he commences with qur'anic verses: "God has made a promise to those among you who believe and do good deeds. He will make them successors to the land, as He did those who came before them [Qur'an 24:55]. It is He who made you successors (caliphs) on the earth and raised some of you above others in rank, to test you through what He gives you, your Lord is swift in punishment, yet He is most

Translator's Introduction

forgiving and merciful [Qur'an 6:165]." Such references to "successors," like other qur'anic references to "caliph," "caliphs," or verbal cognates, do not prefigure the institutional caliphate, or not in any explicit way. Neither did the earliest exegetes draw such a connection. No obvious evidence points to the qur'anic "caliph" as the leader who would succeed Muhammad. The Qur'an rather appears to allude to the more generic idea that the righteous will be successors to the land so long as they follow God's laws, but be dispossessed when they do not. Yet by the eighth century commentators were identifying qur'anic successors with earthly rulers, and by the time of Tabari (d. 923) Sunni commentators had merged the qur'anic caliph with the institutional caliph. While Rida's initial comments concern the generic idea, this foregrounding implies that the caliphate is canonical: it is sanctioned by the Qur'an. In this, Rida follows a mainline Sunni position.

At the same time, in his very first sentence Rida points to a conundrum facing all commentators: succession may be shari'ah-based or illegitimate, as under Umayyad, 'Abbasid, and Ottoman rule. That is, excepting—at least in theory— the rightly guided era (632–61), the caliphate fell far short of ideals. Rida then integrates the idea of the righteous as imams or leaders with a call for reform. God had granted the imamate or right of leadership to the peoples of Abraham, Moses, and Muhammad. In each case, however, wrongdoing leads to dispossession of the land. Thus, Rida implies that Muslims are dispossessed and dominated by non-Muslims as a result of their own sins. They resemble a sick person who, unaware of the illness, does not seek a remedy. In routine fashion, Rida faults his peers for dispensing with the Qur'an in favor of works of law (fiqh), and for what he deemed Sufi malpractice. Rida intimates that all of this should be a surprising state of affairs: if Muslims merely proceed upon the path that the Qur'an guides them to, they would understand. Yet, he laments, rarely do they proceed, and when they do proceed, rarely do they reflect.

From there, Rida avers that Islam is political-civil as well as spiritual, its ideals progressive and flexible. Ijtihad—namely, personal intellectual effort or independent reasoning—and judicious opinions, he argues, empower people to adjust their politics as required. Here, primarily through an Islamic idiom, Rida advocates similar notions to those he had promoted in Damascus. Thus, sovereignty rests not with ruler but with ruled, the community, whose affairs are to be arranged, as the Qur'an commands, on the basis of mutual consultation. Along with conventional Islamic vocabulary, Rida states that Islamic government "is a type of republic [*jumhuriyyah*]," although he does not explicate this modern term, or use it on any other occasion in his book to characterize Islamic government. It may be that where "republic" is a concept Rida may associate it with Islam, while where he refers to an actual republican government, such as that in Angora (Ankara), a different sense is conveyed. He deems that government acceptable on a contingent basis at most, and will soon oppose it. Rebutting Mustafa Kemal's November 1 speech, he had found the leader's Islamic "proofs" providing false cover for a purely republican agenda that he flatly rejected. Lambasting the republic's abolition of the caliphate in 1924, Rida would comment, "we do not deny that the Islamic system of rule is closer to a republic than to a pure monarchy," which may read more as a disclaimer than an endorsement.[63] This reference to *Islamic* republican government in *The Caliphate* is left hanging as the discussion goes on to reiterate standard principles, such as the notion that the caliph, in his person, has no priority over others. He merely implements the revealed law and the community's well-reasoned opinions. Concluding this sketch, Rida reiterates Islam's dual character: it concerns both what is this-worldly, public, and material, and what involves religion and virtue. In all of this, apart from the reference to an Islamic republic, Rida's terminology is traditional, his reading reformist: those are the principles of Islam, but Muslims have failed to implement them.

Rida then briefly depicts the sweep of Islamic civilization: its rapid rise and unparalleled achievements in science and the arts; its apparently—but not actually—irrevocable decline; and lastly the postwar moment, where upheaval has traumatized Muslims yet also provided opportunity and hope. Conspicuously, as some have highlighted, at this juncture Rida provides a singular Muslim example embodying such opportunity, which he also describes as its clearest manifestation: the Turks' "awakening from their hibernation" and overthrowing the sultanate.[64] After commending their strengthening of brotherhood between non-Arab Muslim peoples, pivoting to classical Islam, Rida straightforwardly states that they should reestablish the caliphate in the orthodox form set down in theological and juristic texts. While stating that this would not threaten the West, Rida's discussion is often apologetic and supersessionist. Islam and Islam alone can revive the East, save the West, universalize brotherhood, and meet the needs of all people. Thus, he urges the Turks to reject Europeanization, suggesting that a genuine caliphate would find many learned and liberal European supporters. Rida concludes boldly: "take what I am giving you and be thankful, and that is shown only by acting upon it."[65]

RIDA'S REVIEW OF THEORY

The first third of Rida's book reprises well-known details and theory. Thus, beginning with God's word, Rida then walks the reader through the caliphate's rise and derogation, theory, and, building upon that, in the remaining two-

Translator's Introduction

thirds of his book proposals for revival. In this way, at least when Rida published his essays as a monograph, his ideas may appear to emerge from orthodoxy, resting on the work of Mawardi, Taftazani, and others, with Rida on occasion addressing what he found to be notable omissions. He highlights the caliphate's absolute, canonical necessity and its provision of universal spiritual-temporal leadership. Over and again, Rida notes that the caliphate integrates religion and life in this world. For instance, he quotes Taftazani's statement that order cannot be secured by any other means. Sound Islam, then, involves obeying a caliph, and he must be learned in the Qur'an and hadith. Somebody must therefore be appointed so that people can obey him. Rida adds prescriptions on the *jama'ah*, a term he deploys scores of times and implying a self-identified mainline community as distinct from deviationists. Quoting the Prophet, Rida shows that failing to "hold fast to the *jama'ah*" removes one from Islam.

Next, Rida discusses appointment and deposition. This falls to those who loose and bind, who act on behalf of the community. He had deemed the Syrian Congress legitimate because, along with other factors, it consulted with the Syrian people. Here also consultation is to the fore: those who loose and bind consult, elect, and pledge allegiance to a caliph upon the demise of a predecessor. The membership of this group, however, is rather unclear. Furthermore, allowing for conceivable or theoretical exceptions such as in the appointments of 'Umar (634), 'Uthman (644), and Mehmed V (1909)—as Rida read it at the time—this putative group had not actually exercised its role. Rida's elaborations combine classical sources with clarifications, rebuttals, and modern applications. Noting confusion regarding those who loose and bind, he offers:

> Who are they? Is their pledge of allegiance conditional on it being made by all of them, or is it sufficient for a specified number of them to make it? Or is a number not specified? Their being named those who loose and bind should suffice to preclude disagreement, since what that suggests is that they are the community's leaders, people of high rank and in whom the great majority of the community has confidence. That is so insofar as the community follows them in obeying the one whom they appoint as ruler. Thereby, the community's affairs are ordered, while the caliph is protected from the possibility that the community would disobey him or rebel.[66]

Where the record runs counter to this ideal, Rida resolves the discrepancy through a contextual, historicist reading. He reads Abu Bakr's appointment by acclamation in this manner, deeming it an exceptional act borne of exceptional circumstance, not a precedent. In Rida's reading, the appointments of 'Umar and 'Uthman did rest upon consultation, his larger point being that those who loose and bind wield authority insofar as they embody popular will: their pledge

30 *Translator's Introduction*

has effect only if others follow. Thus, in 'Uthman's case what matters is not the council that elected him, or how many served, but that its choice embodied popular will and public interest.

As Rida discusses such matters he makes modern applications. Thus, we read well-known details about 'Umar and Mu'awiyah, who respectively upheld and corrupted the caliphate, and critiques of Mu'tazili and Ash'ari misinterpretations of leadership. Along with that, we read that modern military and other leaders are equivalent to the "leading figures" of early Islam, whose allegiance to a caliph reflected that of the people. Rida stresses time and again that consultation is the foundation of legitimate rule. This applies from the Prophet's time—"the Messenger said, 'whoever would pledge allegiance without consulting with the Muslims should not do that'"—down to his own era, authority, as such, lying with the community. The Qur'an, he notes, commands obedience not to "the one in authority" but to "those in authority" (Qur'an 42:38), who are obeyed insofar as the community has confidence in them. The community is embodied by the *jama'ah*, a term that Rida deploys to convey uprightness, whether of leaders or, more ideally, of the community generally. Rida's review is generally straightforward, and one might see in it further indications of belief in popular sovereignty—here in Islamic form. Yet where "facts on the ground"—the rule of tyranny—violate the principle, Rida follows predecessors like Mawardi in validating them.

Rida's discussion of the qualifications of those who loose and bind similarly integrates tradition—including Mawardi, Tabari, and Ibn Hajar—and modernity. After enumerating integrity, insight, political know-how, and ijtihad, Rida adds knowledge of international law and treaties, and conditions of states having relationships with Islamic lands. Stressing the political, Rida circles back to Ibn Hajar's comment that 'Umar appointed emirs for their political know-how when others were superior in religion. Rida's modernizing, historicizing take is also seen in his assertion that Abu Bakr and 'Umar are to be emulated not in their decisions but in their method: ijtihad. Thus, for instance, taking 'Umar's actions regarding taxation or non-Muslims as precedential is misguided. Rida stresses that loosing and binding is void of partisanship. What matters is not the identity—partisan or other—of those who loose and bind, but their ability to effectively discharge the legal duty. Rida finds the notions of loosing and binding, a *jama'ah*, and consensus, if applied correctly, fully at home in the modern, civilized world.

On the caliph's qualifications, Rida reprises Mawardi's list: integrity; knowledge enabling ijtihad; vitality of senses and organs; bravery; and Qurayshi lineage. He devotes several pages to Quraysh, reflecting his broader approach.

Translator's Introduction

That is, where history or tradition appear problematic, inconsistent, or potentially at odds with modern sensibilities, he again seeks to overturn the perception. Here, his task is complex, which perhaps accounts for the attention he gives to it: How can limiting the office to one tribe be reconciled with Islamic egalitarianism? Is this not similar to the Shi'i restriction of the Imamate to the 'Alids? Rida proposes circumstance and necessity as the keys to answering such questions. Quraysh are preferred not because of *inherent* qualities or favoritism but because of their unique standing at the time of Islam's rise, and likewise that of the Arabs more generally. While flatly denying that the prescription is a disputed one, Rida deems a non-Qurayshi or non-Arab caliphate resting on force compatible with Islam where the alternative might be chaos. He poses, "and how would it harm the Ottomans [to say] that their caliphate rests purely on force, when some of the jurists have said the same of all or most of the Umayyads and 'Abbasids?"[67]

On allegiance, Rida reinforces the notion, following the Prophet, that people pledge to obey insofar as they are able. He reiterates the standard position that people should rebel against a disbelieving caliph while noting that the picture is less clear when injustice is at issue. In a characteristically generalized vein, Rida finds that under an unjust caliph the people's duty is to "command what is good and avoid what is harmful" without rebelling for fear of causing strife. The people who loose and bind, however, must do whatever is most supportive of public welfare, even if by fighting. Rida relates traditions on Mu'awiyah and the Umayyads: had they not sinned against God, voiding the pledge to obey? Such traditions and Rida's comments fall short of implying that the duty to rebel applied. Even when his criticisms are damning, he reads pragmatically. Rebellion was not viable as most of those who loose and bind were in the Hijaz, a weak region lacking the resources that might have enabled rebellion. Thus, the principles of necessity and "the lesser evil" obtain. But, stressing a larger point, Rida sees the ulama erring in *perpetually* deferring to injustice, assuming but not actually determining that rebellion was unviable.

On the caliph's obligations, Rida underscores the notion of a first among equals: he may be called to account by any member of the community. He adds consultation to Mawardi's ten maxims, finding his predecessor's omission odd. The discussion again depicts the caliphate as political and this-worldly. The caliph must "personally supervise all affairs and scrutinize all circumstances, so that he may execute public policy"—quoting Mawardi. Rida again applies qur'anic and legal maxims in a modern fashion. Thus, "prepare whatever power you can" (Qur'an 8:60) involves modern weaponry, chemistry, mechanics, and natural sciences. Rida explicates consultation—the caliph's "most important duty"—in detail, debunking the notion of absolute rule. The caliph is constrained by the Qur'an, the sunnah, and the obligation to consult. Here also Rida presents Islam as progressive. A mechanism for consultation can never be fixed but must accord with circumstances. Rida critiques ulama who, rather than engaging this matter, have been preoccupied with the arcane, such as rules for ritual purity, menstruation, buying, and selling.

Rida's discussion of designation continues one of his main arguments: Mu'awiyah diverted the caliphate from the course that had been set down for it. His designation of his son Yazid was foul, unjust, and contrary to the Qur'an and sunnah. This rendered the caliphate a possession of the greedy and powerful, like property bequeathed to progeny. Rida finds that no rational person could compare that to Abu Bakr's consultation-based designation of 'Umar. Nevertheless, even while Mu'awiyah's act contradicted God's word, here following Ibn Hajar al-Haytami, Rida again intimates that there was no alternative but to endure it: one should not destroy an entire town for the sake of one castle. As throughout, Rida stresses that a caliphate such as Mu'awiyah's should be eliminated where there is no risk of discord, following his predecessors in articulating broad sentiments without specifics. How, for instance, would one determine that the risk of discord was sufficiently low to justify rebellion? While the rhetorical stance is firm, Rida offers no mechanism upon which action might be based. What his discussion does convey is familiarity with certain important materials and, perhaps on that basis, his credibility.

Next, drawing particularly on Taftazani, Rida discusses caliphates of necessity and tyranny, and explains how tyranny was established. He finds that a caliphate may be sound or based on necessity, the latter subdivided into necessity and tyranny. Necessity obtains when there is no fully qualified candidate and some of those who loose and bind elect the best partially qualified candidate. Tyranny rests purely upon force. The distinction appears abstract. Rida does not identify any caliphates of necessity. While there are intimations of possible exceptions, such as "the fifth rightly guided caliph," 'Umar bin 'Abd al-'Aziz (r. 717–20), his portrayal suggests that those who ruled from the end of the rightly guided era onwards did so as caliphs of tyranny. Rida reiterates that recognition of such caliphates is permissible, like eating dead flesh when necessary. But when it comes to the applicability of this principle, Rida again sees Muslims—or more pertinently those who ought to represent them—having profoundly erred: "It is impermissible for the people to reconcile themselves to the permanence [of this state of affairs] . . . because they were ignorant of the power that was latent within themselves, and of the fact that the power wielded by their monarchs and emirs was actually their own."[68]

Translator's Introduction

As for peoples actually wielding that power and replacing their rulers, Rida's examples are conspicuously limited to two cases: "socially aware" Europeans and, as highlighted in his Introduction, the Turks. Yet they did not overturn Ottoman rule on the basis of Islamic principles, or prompting from the ulama, but in imitation of European trends. Compounding that, "they then replaced one form of tyranny with another," misguidedly assuming that the caliphate undermines independence. Again rendering Muslim independence paramount, Rida proposes a genuine caliphate as the means to achieve it. The task he sets, persuading the Turkish leadership and Muslims generally, appears very difficult, as he acknowledges on numerous occasions. He goes on to reiterate what are by now familiar readings of such topics as apostasy, tyranny, and injustice. Rida briefly applies this to the Turks: their constraining and then eliminating the Ottoman sultans' authority was a case of those who loose and bind resisting injustice. But again, the approach of statesmen such as Midhat Pasha (d. 1884) was misguided because it followed a European rather than Islamic lead.

Providing more detail on tyranny, Rida holds the Umayyads responsible: they "replaced that [consultative and elective] principle with a materialistic one: what is powerful prevails over what is right. Thus, it was they who destroyed it, and they were followed in that by those who came after them."[69] Rida presents an ambivalent picture. The likes of Mu'awiyah, Yazid, and Muslim bin 'Uqbah are unforgivably sinful. The commander is "the enemy of God" of whom the Prophet said, "the curse of God, the angels, and all of the people be upon him."[70] Yet Rida finds the Umayyads' rise inevitable. This is due to the weakness of the Hijaz and the longstanding pattern of rule in Egypt, Syria, and Iraq, whose peoples were accustomed to being subjugated by outsiders. Here, the Umayyads are successors to Romans and Persians, their practice "the sunnah of Heraclius and Caesar."[71] The Muslims, then, had no choice but to recognize those who replaced the practice of the rightly guided caliphs with that of the caesars of Rome "as rebellion would lead to even greater ruination"—quoting Ibn Hajar.[72] Rida finds nothing distinctive in the good works of the Umayyads and 'Abbasids, which were no more than requirements of Islam. The sense of ambivalence is reinforced as Rida integrates his historicist take with prophetic tradition, quoting Muhammad's statement that a vital prophetic community later becomes corrupt. He does not suggest why that should be the case, beyond leaving the impression that it reflects a pattern of prophetic communities. What he wants to convey is that Mu'awiyah's precedent and the failure to overturn it—"the source of the corruptions and calamities that have afflicted Muslims in their religion and worldly lives"[73]—paved the path to servility to tyrants, Muslim and non-Muslim. Yet, again, nowhere does he identify a case

34 *Translator's Introduction*

where that stricture against rebellion ought not to have applied. Rida's tone shifts as he discusses multiple caliphs. Technology, he finds, fulfills prophetic traditions on the unseen, and new communications and transport might soon enable a universal caliphate. Yet here too Rida laments Muslim weakness: contrary to qur'anic commandments they have left themselves dependent on others in the technological realm.

RIDA'S PROPOSAL FOR REVIVING THE CALIPHATE

In a section entitled "The Unity of the Imamate [Caliphate] through the Unity of the Muslim Community [Ummah]," Rida shifts to the contemporary scene. Restating his basic proposition—Muslims must unify—he immediately shows his pessimism: "I do not say that this, in itself, is an impossibility. I say only that I do not know of any Muslim people or group that treats this matter with the seriousness that it requires, and pursues a viable path to it."[74] Rida finds Muslims ignorant, unmotivated, factionalized, and paralyzed, with no possibility that their independent rulers would recognize a unified Islamic government. He briefly shows why Yemen, 'Asir, the Hijaz, Najd, and Oman could not seat a unified caliphate. In particular, he rejects the usurping claims of his former ally, Sharif Husayn of Mecca, and his sons, 'Abd Allah, Emir of Transjordan, and Faysal. As noted, Rida had grown fairly close to Faysal in Damascus. Here, Faysal along with his brother and father comes in for harsh criticism for claiming the caliphate purely on the basis of lineage, excommunicating the Turkish caliphate, and, particularly gallingly, collaborating with a hostile, foreign state.[75] Rida's willingness to shift in his collaborations is seen again here. He had years earlier sought Britain's assistance on the misguided perception that it would support an Arab caliphate. Here, he presents Husayn's collaboration with that same state as truly egregious. Rida speaks favorably of Yemen's Imam Yahya, without suggesting that he could head a universal caliphate, or addressing his Zaydism. Elsewhere, he implies that Yemen lacks sufficient resources.

Rida then comments on Turkey, Iran, Afghanistan, and states under colonial rule, whose Muslim populations lack the freedom to unify, or recognize a unified caliphate. His comments on the Turkish caliphate are typically ambivalent and general. He denies that the 'Abbasids ceded the caliphate to the Ottomans, reiterating that their caliphate rested on force, also seeing no significance in the Turks naming their new institution a "caliphate"—its character, not the nomenclature, being at issue. Rida states that he will support it to the as-yet-unknown extent that it harmonizes with the revealed law. He finds that

Translator's Introduction

35

Afghans, notwithstanding their criticisms of the Turks' action, have no alternative but to recognize the new caliphate "because they are a Muslim people who ardently hold fast to their religion."[76] Yet this involves no more than recognition of an "honorific title." While Rida sees no alternative, the scale of the dilemma is seen in his comment that reducing the caliphate to mere names and titles is a mockery of Islam. Altogether, he sees no expectation of Muslims uniting in view of foreign rule and internal divisions.

This leads to a key proposal: constituting a *genuine* body of those who loose and bind and igniting their authority. Yet Rida details sobering obstacles, illustrating why those who would be expected to fulfil that role have not done so. In colonized lands, they have been coopted by foreign and national governments, who followed the practice of Muslim rulers preceding them. They have thus become complicit in their own people's subjugation, their authority contrived and mercenary. Where Muslims have risen up and established representative bodies that loose and bind, as in Turkey, a different problem obtains: these bodies do not rest on Islamic principles. Rida reiterates what he argues throughout the period examined here: governance of Muslims—whether in an Arab Federation (1915), a Syrian state (1919–20), or postwar Turkey (1922–23)—should be informed by Islamic law.

In Egypt and India, Rida suggests, the Muslim community is insufficiently developed for a group rather than individual leaders to emerge. Rida alludes to Muhammad 'Abduh and Sa'd Pasha Zaghlul, along with those languishing in Indian prisons, Abul Kalam Azad and Muhammad and Shawkat 'Ali. Rida adds Gandhi, recently sentenced to a six-year sentence, as a Hindu example— Rida was an Arab advocate of Gandhi. He depicts traditional institutions in Cairo, Constantinople, Tunis, and Deoband as effete, largely ignored by those in power. Traditionalist ulama, then, have ceded the right to loose and bind to people who generally "have absolutely no knowledge of Islam's sciences."[77] As those who actually loose and bind rarely exist, Rida asks whether the body might be formed by those having potential. He answers, "Yes, this is possible, although it is difficult. But the strength of resolve may render what is difficult easy."[78]

Rida argues that this body could be constituted of reformists, provided that their resources increase, reiterating that most Muslims were misguided Europeanizers or traditionalists. As for the Europeanized, Rida notes that while the Turks oppose a genuine caliphate they see utility in a nominal caliphate as it lends to the integration of non-Arab Muslims with the Turkish nation. Rida states that he has not "abandoned hope" of winning over the Europeanized, but without providing particular grounds for optimism. As for traditionalist jurists, he reprises his standard critique: they are unable to meet contemporary challenges, derive modern laws for modern circumstances, or manage affairs of war and peace. It is because of this, he reiterates, that other Muslims have apostatized and Europeanized. Further, he suggests, had the jurists elaborated Islam soundly many Europeans would have embraced it. Yet, regrettably, the enfeebled ulama allowed those with no knowledge of Islam to take control of the Ottoman state. Thus, Rida laments, his proposal to found an institute for Islamic "outreach and guidance" before the First World War had been rejected—he subsequently founded it in Cairo, but with the outbreak of war it proved short-lived. Rida highlights the sad state of affairs seen in Ottoman statesmen such as Talat Pasha having more influence over the Muslims' caliph than the shaykhs of Islam. His solution is to direct the ulama toward "the party of reform." Rida alludes to what would qualify as success here, and how it would be seen, only in general terms. He does stress that this hinges on Turks and Arabs cooperating, and on winning over Arab emirs and others.

Rida calls for a kind of publicity campaign. Most Muslims are uninformed about the caliphate, but should they understand it, he finds, they would embrace it. He notes that where Egyptians and other Muslims recognize the new caliphate, this has little to do with Islam or religion but is a political move designed to undermine British intentions. Similarly, India's Muslims, he notes, are unconcerned about the caliphate's Islamic soundness. Rida finds no prospect of reviving the caliphate unless such sentiments are overturned. To the contrary, such attitudes along with perpetual resignation to tyranny have led to the impression that the caliphate undermines rather than enables Muslim sovereignty. Thus, Rida calls upon reformist Muslims to publicize the true character, viability, and benefits of the caliphate, which he again sketches in apologetic terms.

He then discusses the need for Turkish–Arab cooperation, his tone at times speculative more than firm. He finds that were Arab emirs to appoint one among them as caliph, the Turks would be unable to oppose a rival. This would be so, he finds, even if the Turks were to grant the rival his due rights under the shari'ah, plainly stating, "and they would not do that."[79] He does not elaborate, albeit that, ostensibly, persuading the Turks to grant the caliph his shari'ah rights is precisely what his book seeks to achieve. Rida does not make explicit whether he deems the Turks unwilling to do that as a general rule, or in the event of an Arab emir being appointed as caliph. The comment may reflect his reading of the prospect that Turkish leadership would walk the path he lays down. As noted, only once—through an allusion to the National Assembly—does he provide any specific grounds for optimism on the matter. Rida adds that if most of the Hijaz, Tihamah, and Najd pledged

Translator's Introduction

37

allegiance to Imam Yahya, all of the ulama would be bound to follow suit. He states, "and if this imamate [caliphate] was not recognized in some Islamic lands today it would not remain unrecognized tomorrow."[80] Rida leaves such possibilities hanging, beyond intimating that Arab disunity might preclude them, and again without addressing Yahya's Zaydism. He goes on to reiterate his familiar theme that in this matter the Turks are materially preeminent, the Arabs spiritually so. The caliph must be a Qurayshi, but the Turks should supervise his election.

Rida rejects the Hijaz as the seat of the new caliphate, while seeing pros and cons in a Turkish possibility. While noting the fear that the Turkish leadership would oppose that, appealing to its government's "determination, courage, boldness, high aspiration, and tenacity," Rida still finds this possible.[81] As he considers an "intermediate" alternative, he shows both pessimism and perseverance:

> In truth, I have little hope in the Arabs and Turks. I do not see anyone among them taking the necessary steps of his own accord. I see no clear sign of their readiness to cooperate over what I have recommended. Yet when it comes to this matter I am not among those who would let a river of resignation flow into his heart. Thus, I urge the party of reform to endeavor to convince the Turks, firstly, to install the caliphate in the headquarters of the state. If they do not respond, let them assist in installing it in . . . Mosul. . . . This would be a zone of neutrality, geographically expressing the bond of a spiritual tie. Thus, Mosul would become a place befitting its name [as a place where things come together].[82]

Rida's suggestion reads as somewhat speculative, and does not engage practical obstacles, such as Mosul's status under a mandate. His proposed course of action should the Turks reject these suggestions is also unclear. In that event, he states, things should be restored "to their original state," without explicating what that would entail or how it would be achieved. On such matters he appears to be floating ideas more than establishing clear plans for action.[83]

Rida's proposed programs are more concrete. He recommends a temporary caliphate of necessity prior to the establishment of a sound one. Proposals include a work on the shari'ah "providing a basis for Islamic positive law" and "disproving the allegations of anyone who argues that the shari'ah is unsuited to civilization and progress in this era."[84] Rida emphasizes over and again that Islam not only allows but requires novel legislation. Here, some have seen Rida freeing law from religion, if not precisely or explicitly.[85] However that point might be regarded, Rida's position is clear: Islamic positive law and novel

38   *Translator's Introduction*

civil, criminal, political, and military legislation are essential. He notes that jurists have long distinguished differing objects of the law—worship and social relations—and aspects not explicitly or outwardly concerned with religion. He also finds that those who resist modern Islamic legislation misunderstand pertinent technical terms, such as *tashri'* or legislation, which has modern as well as traditional applications. Nevertheless, Rida deems all lawmaking, whatever the immediate focus, definitively an exercise in religion. He avers: "The reality is that these matters, in their entirety, are specifically concerned with religion . . . legislated to enable people to draw nearer to God through acts of worship, forsaking abominations and forbidden acts, and paying heed to people's rights and justice in social relations."[86] Nothing here suggests that Rida would consider positive law that violated shari'ah principles acceptable. Rida's description of Muslims who had shunned Islamic norms when debating the Syrian Constitution as "disgraceful" reinforces that impression.[87]

Rida proposes a madrasah for the science of ijtihad and modern subjects including international law, history, and sociology. Its graduates would include qadis, muftis, legislators, those tasked with upholding Islam, and candidates for caliph. This would void the need for dissolute or tyrannical caliphs: a qualified candidate would be elected and universally recognized. The thrust concerns the caliph's credentials as a mujtahid, his ijtihad, with standard exceptions, having public effect. Rida's proposed offices and councils provide more detail without being explicit on the issue of executive authority. Along with standard prescriptions on morality and upholding public interest, the caliph's credentials here are mainly intellectual. Some have found Rida outlining an Islamic "pope."[88] Yet when he refers to the papacy in *The Caliphate* he almost always does so to point to something unsuited to Islam, contrary to its very nature. He also contemplates whether the National Assembly had intended something in the vein of an Islamic "pope" or "patriarch" in politically motivated efforts to garner Muslim sympathy for its actions. If so, he flatly disapproves: this matter, he avers, is not one for innovation.[89] While Rida's focus on juristic-intellectual qualifications has been read as compatible with some kind of separation of powers, he does not discard the notion of the caliph as a temporal ruler, or certainly not unambiguously. For instance, the institution he heads would be responsible for "delegating to heads of government, qadis, and muftis" and "general supervision of government."[90] What manner of "supervision" is envisioned is not spelled out, but it would not appear that Rida's caliph resembles an "Islamic pope," as he himself states.

As "a religion of sovereignty and power," Rida finds Islam needing material revival. This hinges on ijtihad. Neglecting it, he avers, has led to regression,

Translator's Introduction 39

heresy, and Europeanization, which in this connection he defines as following Europe's superficial customs, but not its sciences. Rida again bemoans the prevailing Muslim mindset, where it is foreign pressure and not Islamic sentiment that has prompted some to action. Various suggestions here underline a pragmatist, laissez-faire stance on modernization. Contrary to Mustafa Kemal, he sees no utility in public statues. Muslims cannot afford such frivolous activities: "we remain poor." Yet images, alcohol, and fingerprinting are permissible where they serve a purpose, as in medicine and policing. Altogether, Rida finds that Muslims have no need to replace their culture's core values, distinctive characteristics, and revealed laws with those of other people. He proposes committees to determine which customs should be discarded and continued, where the shari'ah will prove the "strongest ally" in that endeavor, while "the laws of social evolution" must also be heeded, reiterating a central theme: what is genuinely Islamic is modern, what is genuinely modern is Islamic.[91] Rida was a notable issuer of fatwas. While he stresses that people may act upon fatwas individually, he rejects that as means to solve the Muslims' universal problems, given how much they vary. A universally recognized mujtahid-caliph who had mastered Arabic, however, could achieve that. Rida makes a point of noting that his emphasis on Arabic does not represent a partisan stance.

Continuing in a reformist, historicist, and sometimes apologetic vein, Rida overturns other wrongheaded assumptions. Many Muslims take the notion of a community's sovereign right to legislate as European. Rida locates its origins squarely with Islam, as he does all progressive features of modern civilization. Yet Rida does not merely "Islamicize" Western culture, deeming Islamic politics and law superior because they involve religious virtue. Thus, Islamic legislative methodology is superior to its Western counterpart because it is not simply majoritarian: it requires deliberation on God's revealed sources. Here, he finds the demise of Islamic legislation and administration of law intertwined with the caliphate's demise. As caliphs entrusted legal affairs to nonmujtahids, the institution squandered what any state needs to be established, sustained, and developed.[92] Where theoretically the Muslim community is sovereign and the state subordinate, these corruptions have inverted that relationship. Rida's solution, again, is new legislation. Failing that, he reprises his unelaborated, pithy statement that the caliphate should be resorted "in its original form."[93]

Rida applies his call for ijtihad to finance, Muslim socialism, and the status of women. The Muslims' ills and errors in all of these areas again rest on the habit of clinging to what is antiquated. Why, he asks, have the ulama not studied finance in their madrasahs? This has resulted in Muslims being outstripped, their wealth passing to others, contrary to basic commandments, such as that on entrusting resources to the "feeble-minded" (Qur'an 4:5). Altogether, he finds the jurists adhering to fixed, outdated rites primarily to draw a livelihood, and oblige rulers who were and are "at war with the science of ijtihad."[94] Rida emphasizes that the jurists' own imams, those whose schools they follow or claim to follow, endorsed the very principles he advocates. Ijtihad, he finds, has always been integral to Islam, while the modern era uniquely enables an ijtihad-based, unified consideration of law. As he elaborates, Rida integrates idealized hypotheses — if a true caliphate were established "even if on a small piece of land on earth, all of the Islamic world would willingly submit to it" — with critiques of arcane and partisan jurisprudence.[95]

Rida then turns to non-Muslims. His broad point is that political systems informed by religion benefit all people more than those which are not. Specifically, he argues that non-Muslims would fare better under a caliphate because — as in Yemen and elsewhere — the shari'ah provides minorities with protections not granted to heretical Muslims. Even where the law favors Muslims there is nothing to prevent exceptions. He states, "We declare in the strongest terms possible that absolute and universal justice does not exist except in Islam," deeming Islam more merciful than all other religions.[96] Rida implies that this may explain the Turks' resistance to the caliphate: if they *properly* established it they would be bound to treat with mercy the Greek and Armenian "criminals and rebels" who had assisted their enemies.[97] True Christians living in Muslim lands, Rida finds, have nothing to fear from the caliphate. It would be insupportable for them to reject it: how could it be reasonable for the wishes of a minority to overturn those of the majority? Such a stance could not be based on actual Christianity but rather on the blindly partisan or "social-political" version that underlies Europe's materialism and the horrors of its wars. As in other works, Rida contrasts this with a humble, altruistic, and genuine Christianity.[98] Overall, Rida imagines a future framed by the principles of Islam to the benefit of Muslims and non-Muslims alike, his language frequently apologetic.

Rida next discusses the colonial states. Given his discussion, it might seem surprising that during the First World War he had sought British support for the effort to establish an Arab Caliphate. Here, his depiction of the British Empire is relentlessly negative. Its representatives are misinformed, misguided, cynical, and insincere. Their solicitation of information on the caliphate from various ulama was purely self-serving. Among other errors, the British had failed to recognize that independence was the Muslims' preeminent, continual concern. Rida quotes what he had written to Lloyd George in 1919: naming Sharif Husayn "King" and recognizing the independence of Hijaz "did not have the

Translator's Introduction

impact upon Muslim hearts that the English had anticipated."[99] The Hijaz, Rida explains, is a seat of worship, not power, and thus secondary to the issue of Muslim sovereignty, without which Islam could not exist. Overall, Rida finds that the only constant in Britain's policies on the caliphate over a long period is a willingness to use force to promote its agenda: "subjugation of the entire East." Indeed, it has demonstrated that it recognizes and yields to nothing but force. This explains its attitude toward the Turkish state, whose forces defeated its Greek allies, compelling it to be on amicable terms with it. Thus, Rida finds that nothing that its leaders state should be taken at face value, nor should Muslims expect it to hold to its agreements and promises, words that in the dictionary of British politics have different meanings to those known to all other peoples. Rida again subordinates ideals and consistency to the goal of sovereignty of Muslims. He had been willing to work with British officials when he misguidedly believed that doing so would lend to that goal, enabling Arab Muslim sovereignty. In *The Caliphate*, written under different circumstances, Rida depicts Britain as the antithesis of the Muslim cause. As noted, Rida also reversed his stance on Sharif Husayn.

Rida pursues similar lines when discussing pan-Islamism, sovereignty of all Muslims, finding that England opposes all that it signifies. More generally, he sees Europe "terrorizing" Muslims, prompting some to Europeanize because "they had nobody to explain the true nature of matters to them."[100] Rida here suggests that it would be Europeanized Muslims, not Europeans, who would prevent the establishment of the caliphate. In this connection, Rida is quite candid, commenting that a caliphate to which all Muslims submit "is neither practical nor possible at this time," also pertinently noting that God does not burden the soul with an unrealistic burden (Qur'an 2:286). He further states that "we are doubtful" that the Turkish government will reestablish the caliphate," particularly given its leader's influence. Referring to what he had said about pan-Islamism in 1913, Rida leaves no doubt that he did not see his advice being heeded by the Turkish leadership. Explicating, he states that his intention was to see the state either granting the caliphate its due rights—which it would not—or delegating control over most religious affairs to independent individuals and associations. Notwithstanding his characterizations of the caliph as a temporal ruler who supervises government, such remarks raise questions about how far he considered that realistic. In this respect, his discussion again seems more of an exercise in rhetoric and pedagogy than a plan of action that he envisioned being implemented. Rida concludes by reproducing an article he had written previously which critiques Ibn Khaldun's thesis that power and success, prophetic or caliphal, issue from a partisan support base (*'asabiyyah*).

42   *Translator's Introduction*

In spite of his pessimism, he finishes with an upbeat flourish, finding that destiny has turned, the errors of Europeanization and traditionalism have become clear. Thus, "blessed be the renewers, the reformers, and woe unto the conceited traditionalists. The future belongs to the pious."[101]

THE ABOLITION OF THE CALIPHATE, MARCH 3, 1924

If Rida's response to the abolition of the sultanate in 1922 was guarded and complex, his response to the abolition of the caliphate along with the primary institutions of Islam was straightforward. He discussed the matter in an issue of *Al-Manar* that also addressed Sharif Husayn's pretentions, 'Abd al-Majid II's (Abdülmecid II's) invalid caliphate, Ittihadist (Unionist) corruptions, and English and European conspiracies.[102] He lambasts the Kemalists for their action, deeming them arrogant, disingenuous, cynical enemies of Islam who had sought to go even further than Lenin and Trotsky in their campaign against religion. He also sees foreign hands behind events. He here sees no substantive difference between Ittihadists and Kemalists, except that the latter are more audacious. He points to the name—"Kemalists"—which he describes as hated by the Turkish people, as belying their claim to have replaced personal authority with communal authority. Rida finds in the state's anti-Islamic actions nothing other than a case of those in power imposing their will through sheer force. For Rida, this represents nothing but extremist Europeanization whose proponents justify it through "dressing falsehood with truth." He depicts the caliphate's abolition as the final step in a cynical, gradualist strategy pursued over a period of years. Tracing that, Rida sees Kemalists having had no regard for the views of the people, and points to the generally quiescent or accepting stance adopted by Muslims at various stages of that gradual process. For instance, he suggests that nobody questioned the framing of the Constitution of 1921, where stipulations on legislative and executive authority were void of reference to the shari'ah. Why, he asks, had nobody questioned that and its implications for the caliphate?

In 1922 Rida's response to Sultan Wahid al-Din's (Mehmed VI's) deposition was ambivalent. While it was un-Islamic and even represented a mockery of Islam, in practical terms the act in itself brought no harm: if the sultan's temporal authority was fictitious, nothing was lost by its elimination, while there were multiple other grounds for welcoming his deposition. Rida also credited the Turkish leadership for recognizing the corrupt nature of the Ottoman state. From the perspective of May 1924, he depicts it only in unambiguously negative terms as one of the steps taken by the Kemalists in their cynical campaign against

Translator's Introduction 43

Islam. The pledge made to his successor, 'Abd al-Majid II (Abdülmecid II), was entirely invalid: nobody had pledged correctly. Arguing as he had throughout his career that Muslims bore primary responsibility for their own predicaments, particularly their weakness, he asks, "and what did other Muslims do?" Rida's point is that some supported this supposed revival of the rightly guided caliphate, even celebrating Mustafa Kemal as "the hero of Islam," while those who opposed it failed to sufficiently publicize their views. Rida relates his own thwarted efforts to change such attitudes, alluding to what he had written in an unnamed publication.[103]

Rida goes on to depict Kemalists as opportunistic, taking advantage of the people's exhaustion through war. Earlier, as noted above, he had seen in the Turks' victory a Muslim victory with universal ramifications. Here, he finds that while Mustafa Kemal was victorious in war and in the peace that followed, for the people victory in war was followed by defeat. Mustafa Kemal's success informed his vanity, self-aggrandizing, and indifference to Muslim sentiment, Turkish and other. The leader had come to see himself in the company of Napoleon, Peter the Great, Lenin, and Trotsky. Thus, he felt empowered to push through an agenda that, Rida finds, the people would never endorse. Rida also points to a foreign connection, implying that what had occurred was not an indigenous Turkish-Muslim development. Those empowered by the Kemalists, even more than under the Ittihadists, Rida finds, were rarely people of genuine Turkish lineage. Here, Rida alludes to Russian connections. For instance, "Rarely is anyone among these corruptors known to have genuine Turkish ancestry. But we know that some of them were cast from Russia to the Turkish capital in order to undertake these actions [against Islam]."[104] Altogether, Rida sees Mustafa Kemal seeking to sunder the Turks from Islam, a point he makes elsewhere.[105] He finds the Kemalists' project a purely material one. They had made a cold-hearted calculation that they would gain more by shunning global Muslim sentiment than by winning it over. They found that in political-material terms liberation from the caliphate was preferable to being attached to it. For Rida, the stunned reaction he observed not only in the Islamic world but also in Europe further reaffirmed that what had occurred was an entirely unnatural development that was indicative of the Turks' lack of freedom: "It is inconceivable that any people would over a number of days or years rid themselves of doctrines, systems, rulings, and regimes for their rulers that had been firmly rooted in their souls for centuries, and that they had esteemed generation after generation."[106] Even the most advanced Europeans, Rida notes, have seen fit to retain the idea of monarchy and state religion, as indeed have the English.

44 *Translator's Introduction*

In sum, Rida lent his support, even where he had misgivings on other grounds, to those he felt were best placed to assist the cause of his people's sovereignty. His shifting stance on Mustafa Kemal is another case in point. The comments on the Turkish leadership with which he introduces *The Caliphate* stand in sharp contrast to his reading of the situation in the spring of 1924. By that point it had become clear that support for his agenda would need to be found with a different kind of Muslim leader.

OTHER WRITINGS BEYOND *THE CALIPHATE* AND CONCLUDING REMARKS

Rida discussed the caliphate in numerous other writings following the publication of his book. These include: critiques of Kemalist works and actions; fatwas, discussions of Sharif Husayn's pretentions and 'Ali 'Abd al-Raziq's "heretical" *Islam and the Bases of Rule (Al-Islam wa Usul al-Hukm*, 1925); commentaries on the Cairo Caliphate Congress and other post-Ottoman congresses; and commentaries on his support of Ibn Sa'ud and on Sunni–Shi'i relations.[107] There is no space here for a detailed discussion of these works, yet the following may be noted. It seems clear that after the publication of his book Rida was under no illusions as to the impossibility of reviving the caliphate. This is seen, for instance, in various comments he made on the Cairo Caliphate Congress. He had written to his friend Shakib Arslan in January 1925 that the Congress was not equipped to succeed. In a brief commentary he wrote accompanying the publication of the Invitation to the Congress in March 1926, he noted that while the effort to convene the Congress was commendable, "the time is not right for appointing a caliph, the paths not paved."[108] Commenting on the proceedings two months later as the attendees' "dear brother," Rida also conveyed the view that success was unattainable, also raising the question of how, given the fragmented state of Muslim leadership at the time, it would be beneficial to appoint yet another Muslim leader.[109]

Rida had worked with or spoken positively about a variety of leaders during his career. He had attempted to assist in the creation of a unified Muslim leadership, whether of Arabian emirs or, as in *The Caliphate*, universal. He had had relationships with leaders including Sharif Husayn, his son Faysal, Imam Yahya of Yemen, and Sayyid Idrisi of 'Asir (d. 1923). As is well known, he came to place his support with Ibn Sa'ud, and claimed that his stance in that had always been consistent.[110] It is no original observation to suggest that support of Ibn Sa'ud derived from his distinctive standing as a sovereign Arab Muslim ruler, rather than from doctrinal or theological considerations. If so, that would support the

Translator's Introduction 45

suggestion advanced here that Rida subordinated all other considerations to communal sovereignty. To that end, he was willing to endorse the discourse of a sitting American president, and to support a Wahhabi emir. Rida credited Ibn Sa'ud with reviving the rightly guided caliphate, notwithstanding that there would not appear to be any obvious sense in which his new state, an absolute monarchy, embodied the ideal Rida had sketched in *The Caliphate*.

THE CALIPHATE

IN THE NAME OF GOD, THE COMPASSIONATE, THE MERCIFUL

Remember when Abraham was tried by his Lord with certain words,
which he fulfilled. He said, "I shall make you an imam to humankind."
Said he, "And what of my progeny?" He said,
"My covenant shall not include the wrongdoers."
[Qur'an 2:124][1]

God has made a promise to those among you who believe and do good
deeds. He will make them successors to the land, as He did those who
came before them; He will establish their religion which He has chosen for
them; He will grant them security to replace their fear.
"They worship Me and do not associate anything with Me."
Whoever chooses to disbelieve after that is truly rebellious.[2]
[Qur'an 24:55]

It is He who made you successors (caliphs) on the earth *[khala'if al-ard]* and
raised some of you above others in rank, to test you by what He has given
you, your Lord is swift in punishment, yet He is most forgiving and merciful.
[Qur'an 6:165]

Reading the True Book [the Qur'an] and reflecting upon human history
have led us to contemplate the issue of succession. This concerns how peoples succeed others in having sovereignty and ruling on earth. It involves how
one individual succeeds another, and how one dynasty succeeds another. Succession can occur rightfully as well as illegitimately, where the right to rule
is bequeathed or acquired unlawfully. The True Book [the Qur'an] and reflecting on history have also led us to what is the Almighty Lord's when it comes
to succession: rules of conduct, social norms, shari'ah ordinances and norms,
the pledge of the universal imamate given to some of the messengers, and the
promise given to His righteous servants that they will be appointed as successors,
as inheritors of the land.[3] These common norms include testing peoples against

others to determine which of them is most upright, just, and truthful. This becomes a proof for Him against mankind, so that He may take revenge upon the wrongdoers. Sometimes that is achieved at the hand of those who are corrupt like the wrongdoers, and sometimes at the hand of the wrongdoers' adversaries, those who do good. The future belongs to the pious.[4] The pious are those who push back against the door to failure and disappointment. In their actions they follow God's prescriptions, legal and natural. The righteous are those who avoid corruption, follow the path of integrity in their conduct, and repair the affairs of God's servants whenever they have deviated from what is right.

God Almighty pledged the universal imamate to His prophet and intimate friend Abraham and the just among his progeny, but not the wrongdoers.[5] He then promised it to Moses' people, the children of Israel, and Muhammad's people, the children of Ishmael. Regarding the first promise, the Almighty states: "But We wished to favor those who were oppressed in the land, to make them imams, the ones to inherit" [Qur'an 28:5]. Regarding the fulfillment of that promise, He states: "And We caused those who had been oppressed to inherit [succeed to] both the eastern and the western parts of the land that We had blessed. Your Lord's good promise to the Children of Israel was fulfilled, because of their patience, and We destroyed everything Pharaoh and his people had made and all they had constructed" [Qur'an 7:137]. Regarding the second promise, He states: "God has made a promise to those among you who believe and do good deeds: He will make them successors [yastakhlifannahum] to the land, as He did to those who came before them; He will establish their religion which He has chosen for them" [Qur'an 24:55]. God kept His promise to the Muslim community [ummah]. He fulfilled it as He had fulfilled His promise to the communities preceding it. Thereafter, He took from the community most of what He had given it, punishing it as He had punished other communities. He did so when it broke His covenant as they had, sinned against its Lord's command as they had, and became conceited about its pedigree and its [revealed] Book as they had. The Almighty made inheritance of the land conditional upon the establishment of what is correct, just, and righteous, along with the reform of human affairs. He excluded sinners from His covenant, and threatened that wrongdoers would be dispossessed of the land. It is incumbent upon the community to reflect upon that, and thereupon to return to proper conduct, and repent to its Lord. It might be that He will have mercy upon it, and fulfill His covenant for its current generation, just as He did for its first generation. But it has not repented yet. Perhaps it will.

A sick person who is unaware of his sickness does not seek treatment, while whoever seeks treatment from someone other than a doctor with knowledge of

The Caliphate

51

his disease will not succeed. Yet the Muslims' disease and its cure are clearly explained in the Qur'an, their revealed Book. But they failed in their duty to become acquainted with it, and act in accordance with it. They neglected to do that, favoring traditional works of law and other subjects over their revealed Book.[6] Following the path that the Book guides them to—proceeding upon the earth so as to reflect upon the affairs of nations, and contemplate God's ways with mankind—would enable them to understand that. But seldom did they proceed, and when they did proceed, seldom did they reflect and contemplate.

Islam is spiritual guidance, and the politics of civil society. In Islam, God perfected the religion of the prophets, and the norms of progress, the norms through which He elevated human society.

As for pure religious guidance, Islam brought it in a complete form in principle and in practice, in what is obligatory and what is supererogatory. This is because it centers upon revealed texts and the Messenger's explanations of them in both word and deed, God's prayer and peace be upon him. When the Muslims became afflicted by weakness, they neglected this principle. Some of them went to extremes. They added ordinances for worship, condemned things as religiously forbidden when they are not, and integrated the celebrations, incantations, and litanies of the Sufis.[7] Volumes have been written on all of this, and undertaking all of it would exhaust all available time. Incorporating it in the religion inescapably impairs the religion of the Companions and the Successors, as they lacked any of these things. Had they been occupied with such things, they would not have had sufficient time to engage in conquests, and reform the affairs of God's servants.

As for the politics of civil society, Islam set down the pertinent foundations and rules. It sanctioned the Muslim community to formulate opinions and exercise ijtihad for political, civil, and social matters as they vary across time and place, and change as civilization and the arts of learning progress. Islam's rules for the politics of civil society include:

- the principle that sovereign authority inheres in the community [and not in the person of a ruler];
- the Muslim community is to conduct its affairs on the basis of mutual consultation;[8]
- Islamic government is a type of republic;
- under the law, the Messenger's caliph has no privileges over the weakest individuals in the community;
- the caliph is rather merely the person who implements either a rule that God has revealed, or an opinion that the community has reached;

Muhammad Rashid Rida

- safeguarding both the religion and the common good in worldly life;
- combining moral virtues with material prosperity;
- preparing the path to universal human brotherhood through uniting communities' core values, both in form and in meaning.

When the Muslims became afflicted by weakness, they fell short. They failed to properly execute these rules and apply these principles. Had they executed them, they would have set down apposite methods and provisions, thereby enabling these principles to be applied in every era.

Islam's civilization arose shining from the horizon of the Qur'an's guidance. It is built on a foundation that begins with reforming man himself, thereby enabling reform in the realm of worldly and social affairs. The larger part of the rightly guided caliphs' reform consisted of establishing what is right and just, distributing resources equitably among the people, spreading virtues and overturning wrong deeds, eliminating the tyranny of kings and emirs that weighs heavily on the people, and eliminating the authority that priests and religious leaders wield over minds and spirits. With that, they achieved something very near to perfection and without precedent in the history of nations and generations. A rapidly developing civilization then followed. It combined religion and virtue, and enabled the enjoyment of good things and adornments. The sciences and arts advanced with remarkable speed. Thus, the historian-philosopher Monsieur Gustave Le Bon states in his book *People's Development* [*L'évolution des peuples*]: the talent for the arts did not take root in any nation in less than the three natural generations, except for the Arabs.[9] By the three generations he means: the generation of imitation, the generation of fusion, and the generation of independence.[10]

A period of time had come upon man[11] in which it was assumed that Islamic civilization had expired and ceased to exist, with no prospect of its resurrection, and that European civilization had acquired a state of permanence, with no prospect of its demise. Then destiny turned, and the peril of this reckoning became apparent. A growing number of Europe's sages and scholars predicted that its civilization was approaching its end due to the destructive effects of the diseases of materialism, militarism, miserly greed, and the excessiveness of carnal lust.[12] Among the prominent personalities embracing this view was the era's leading philosopher, the Englishman Herbert Spencer, founder of sociology.[13] Those embracing this view grew in number after the Great War [World War I], due to the uncountable corruptions that resulted from it. The war sowed feelings of hatred and warmongering among European peoples, and compounded financial and political corruptions and problems. Yet it profoundly shook all of

The Caliphate

the Islamic world and the East, triggering unfamiliar upheavals among its peoples, thus providing it with an opportunity for action. That opportunity is what anchors expectations and empowers hopes.

The greatest manifestation of this opportunity has been the Turkish people's awakening from their hibernation, which has toppled the Ottoman sultanate. They have strengthened the bond of brotherhood between the Iranian and Afghani states, and disseminated the call for solidarity with other non-Arab Islamic peoples. They have had success in eliminating foreign privileges and cutting back other political and financial bonds and restraints.

Our hope is that they strengthen the bonds of brotherhood with the Arab community. We hope that they cooperate with it in reviving Islamic civilization by renewing the government of the caliphate on the basis of rules stipulated in texts of systematic theology and jurisprudence [fiqh]. They should not be content with material benefits, or allow themselves to be seduced by the common Muslims' deference to what they have done in creating a spiritual caliphate. Indeed, nothing causes Muslims to ruin their worldly lives and their religion more than their common people approving of all that their governments and states do. This is to say nothing of the sentiment of Muslims who have been worn down by the burdens of colonial rule. Their sentiment is a noble one, and all that it lacks is genuine insight. The great majority of these millions used to accuse anyone opposing the desires of Sultan 'Abd al-Hamid [Abdul Hamid II] of treachery, or of straying from the religion.[14] He is the sultan who induced most of Turkey's political leaders to diminish the authority of the sultans, the one whom these millions praise today. In both of these cases their stance is not informed by learning or by any evident authority.

O living Turkish people: Islam is the mightiest spiritual power on earth. It is Islam that can revive the East's civilization, and save the West's civilization. That is because civilization only endures through virtue, and virtue is only realized through religion. No religion harmonizes knowledge and civilization except for Islam.

Western civilization endured through the centuries only through balancing the remnants of Christian virtues with the conflict between independent thought and church teaching. Communities do not discard the virtues of a religion simply because some individuals or groups come to question its doctrines. That only occurs in stages, and over a number of generations. That conflict resulted in the loss of that balance, so that both the religion and the civilization were at risk of coming to an end. Humanity's need for a civil and spiritual reform resting on firmly established pillars then grew more urgent. Such reform would eliminate the powerful's subjugation of the weak, the wealthy's disparaging of the poor, the Bolsheviks' targeting of the rich, and the practice of giving some people preferential treatment over others on the basis of ethnicity or national identity. In that way, it would universalize the bonds of brotherhood among all peoples. This will not come into being except through the Islamic form of government, whose features we broadly outline in this book. We are ready to assist by elaborating in greater detail, if God renders the effort to realize that a success.

O courageous Turkish people, among the Islamic peoples today you are those most able to realize this wish for humankind. So seize this opportunity to establish an eternal human glory, one to which your time-honored military glory could not be mentioned in comparison. Do not by any means let the Europeanized lead you into imitating the Europeans in their behavior.[15] You are a people fit to be their leader through a civilization superior to theirs. No civilization can be compared to the Islamic civilization, its rational rules firmly established on the foundations of religious doctrine. It is not shaken by speculations that impair civilization's development and corrupt the social order.

O thoughtful Turkish people, rise up by renewing the Islamic caliphate's government. Do this with the intention of serving humankind through an endeavor that brings religious guidance together with civilization. The goal here is not to establish a fanatical Islamic entity that would threaten Western states. If you do what I recommend, and prove your sincerity and the soundness of your intentions, you will find that there are people among Europe's learned and distinguished liberal spirits who will support you. They will spread your fame, and repel the accusations of opportunistic political leaders, and the goading of those who deceive and slander.

O wise Turkish people, I offer these studies to you. I wrote them to explain the following points about the caliphate:

- its true nature;
- the pertinent ordinances;
- some of its history;
- the loftiness of its station;
- how all people stand in need of it;
- how the Muslims perpetrated a crime against themselves by mismanaging it and diverting it from the course that was set down for it;
- what presently blocks the path to its revival and the means to overcoming that.

I do so in this treatise, which sets down a path and illuminates the relevant evidence. It strikes a balance between broad generalizations and detailed

The Caliphate 55

discussions. It brings the insights of those who are knowledgeable in worldly affairs together with the insights of those who understand the true nature of religion. So take what I am giving you and be thankful. And the only way to show true gratitude is to put my advice into action. "And [remember] when your Lord proclaimed, 'If you are thankful, I will give you more, but if you are thankless, My punishment is terrible indeed'" [Qur'an 14:7].

SHARI'AH ORDINANCES ON THE ISLAMIC CALIPHATE

The caliphate and the sultanate have been a trial for Muslim peoples, as government of monarchs has been a trial for peoples belonging to other communities and having other religious confessions [*milal*]. This issue had lain dormant, and then events suddenly unfolding in recent days awoke it, when the Turks abolished the Ottoman dynasty's state, and founded a republican state with a new form upon its ruins. The fundamental principles of their new state include a rejection of the notion that any individual in their new government could have authority on the basis of his title as "caliph" or "sultan," and a complete separation of religion and politics. But they designated someone from the family of the previous sultans as the spiritual caliph of all Muslims, and limited this caliphate to this dynasty, as we explained in detail in *Al-Manar*. Therefore, there have been more discussions of the issue of the caliphate and its ordinances in the newspapers. This has led to confusion, a tendency to proceed rashly, and the confounding of truth with falsehood.

Hence, we saw that it was incumbent upon us to elucidate our shari'ah's ordinances, regarding that matter with the detail that the situation requires, so that truth be distinguished from falsehood. We also saw that we needed to discuss where the system of the caliphate stands in relation to other systems of government, the Muslims' practice when it comes to the caliphate, and what is incumbent upon them in this era.

Our support for the new Turkish government is one of the reasons why we are obligated to provide the explanations and advice offered here. We support it only out of our concern for the religion's standing, and the Muslims' welfare. Nothing weakens our religion and its people more than their servility toward the strong among them. Indeed, the ulama's partiality to monarchs and caliphs became a misfortune for them and for the people. Yet God made a covenant with those who have knowledge: "You shall clearly elucidate it to humankind, and shall not conceal it" [Qur'an 3:187].[16] "Do not confound truth with falsehood, or hide the truth while you know it" [Qur'an 2:42].[17] From God, we ask for what is right, and we ask Him for wisdom and a decisive way of speaking.[18]

THE ISLAMIC CALIPHATE'S DEFINITION AND ITS NECESSITY UNDER THE REVEALED LAW

(1) DEFINITION OF THE CALIPHATE

Caliphate, supreme imamate, and emirate of the faithful are three terms with one meaning: leadership of an Islamic government that secures the well-being of the religion and life in this world.

On the principles of the religion's doctrines we cite the very learned theologian and scholar Sa'd al-Taftazani. We cite Chapter 4 of *Maqasid al-Talibin*[19] — which concerns doctrines that are based on authoritative sources.[20] He states: "The imamate is universal leadership in both religion and worldly life. As such, it succeeds the leadership of the Prophet, God's prayer and peace be upon him."[21]

In his book *Ordinances of Government*,[22] the very learned jurist Abu Hasan 'Ali bin Muhammad al-Mawardi states: "the imamate is established as prophethood's successor in safeguarding religion and administering worldly affairs."[23]

The discourses other ulama who have written on matters of religious doctrine, as well as those of the jurists in all of the Sunni schools [madhhabs], do not deviate from this interpretation. An exception is found with Imam Razi. He adds a specification to the definition. He states: It is universal leadership in both religion and worldly life that is embodied in a single person. He states: The entire community should be cautious about discharging the imam because he is dissolute. After citing and explaining this specification in *Commentary on Goals* [*Sharh al-Maqasid*], Sa'd al-Taftazani states: "It is as if by 'the entire community' Razi meant those who loose and bind, whom he regarded as leaders of others, or leaders of any individual member of the community."[24]

(2) THE RULE OF THE IMAMATE, OR THE APPOINTMENT OF THE CALIPH

The Muslim community's early generations, Sunni Muslims, and Muslims belonging to most of the other sects [tawa'if] are in agreement that the appointment of the caliph — namely, his appointment as the ruler of the community — is a duty for Muslims under the shari'ah. It is not a duty that is required only on the basis of reason, as some of the Mu'tazilis maintained. They find support for that view in matters that Sa'd al-Taftazani summarizes in *Goals*:

There are multiple issues:

(1) Consensus.

He explains in his commentary that this means the consensus of the Companions. He states:

> This is the preeminent issue. They even prioritized it over the need to inter the Prophet, God's prayer and blessing be upon him.
> (2) That what is mandatory in the way of establishing borders, protecting ports, and other such things relating to the preservation of the community's good order cannot be achieved by any other means.
> (3) That it concerns the procurement of benefit and the prevention of innumerable harms, which is agreed to be a duty.
> (4) That the necessity of obeying him, and of his being learned in the Book and the sunnah [the Qur'an and the hadith], requires that there actually is a caliph. This happens by someone being appointed to that position.[25]

The significance of the last point is as follows. They have agreed that the duty to obey him in what is recognized as good is required by the shari'ah, and that he must be learned in the Book and the sunnah [the Qur'an and the hadith], with that being among his most important qualifications. This means that appointing him is a duty under the shari'ah. In *Commentary on Goals*, Sa'd al-Taftazani elaborates at length in explaining these points, the views of certain oppositionist innovators, and the rebuttal to their objections.

He and others like him neglected to cite certain sound hadith with prescriptions on the imam's appointment.[26] These concern the necessity that Muslims hold fast to the main body of their community [*jama'ah*] and to their imam. Some of these hadith include the declaration that: "Whoever dies without a pledge of allegiance dies a death of the Era of Ignorance"[27] — related by Muslim from the hadith of Ibn 'Umar, which is "elevated."[28] The hadith of Hudhayfah, which has been firmly agreed upon, will be related presently. It includes the Prophet's statement to him: "Hold fast to the main body of the Muslim community and to their imam."

(3) WHO APPOINTS AND DISCHARGES THE CALIPH?

Sunni Muslims have agreed that the appointment of the caliph is a collective duty, and that those who bear responsibility for doing that on behalf of the community are known as the people who loose and bind. The Mu'tazilis and the Kharijis agreed with them that the imamate comes into being through the pledge of allegiance being made by those who loose and bind.[29] Yet when it comes to those who loose and bind the discourses of the ulama can be confusing. Who are they? Is their pledge of allegiance conditional on it being made by all of them, or is it sufficient for a specified number of them to make it? Or is a number not specified? Their being named those who loose and bind should suffice to preclude disagreement, since what that suggests is that they are the community's leaders, of high rank, and those in whom the great majority of the community has confidence. This is so inasmuch as it follows them in obeying the one they appoint as ruler. Thereby, the affairs of the community are properly ordered, and he is safe from the possibility that people will disobey or rebel.

In a similar fashion to other scholastic theologians and jurists, Sa'd al-Taftazani states in *Commentary on Goals*: "they are scholars [ulama], heads of the community, and people of distinction."[30] Nawawi adds in *Al-Minhaj*: "they are those who are readily able to meet."[31] His commentator Ramli explicates that this is so since "they determine matters, and other people follow their decisions."[32] This is the ultimate and well-established explanation, clearly articulated and understood. That is because if those who pledge allegiance were not in such a position that the community would follow them in that, the imamate would not come into being through their pledge.

This is based upon the practice of the Companions, may God be pleased with them, in their appointments of the rightly guided caliphs as rulers. 'Umar deemed the commencement of the pledge of allegiance to Abu Bakr precipitate [faltah].[33] The reason is that the pledge was made before the process of consultation with all of those who loose and bind had been completed, as nobody from the clan of Hashim, who were among their first in rank, was present at the Saqifah Assembly [*Saqifat Bani Sa'idah*].[34]

The sources agree that Abu Bakr, may God be pleased with him, consulted with the leading Companions for an extended period over the matter of 'Umar's nomination. None of them found any fault with 'Umar apart from his severity, although they acknowledged that it was severity born of concern for what is right. Abu Bakr responded that 'Umar regarded him as lenient, and thus he became more severe himself—this was while he was his minister—in order to achieve a balance. He said that a decision, if it fell into 'Umar's hands, would be made with leniency when leniency was called for, and with severity when severity was called for. He consulted with the leaders, foremost among them 'Ali, God bless him, until he saw that he had convinced most of them. He then announced that 'Umar would succeed him as caliph. They accepted, none dissenting.

When 'Umar was stabbed, he deemed it appropriate to limit the obligatory consultation to the six leaders with whom the Messenger, God's prayer and blessing be upon him, died pleased. He knew that no one outranked them, or opposed decisions they had agreed upon. That is because they, not others, had

The Caliphate 59

been nominated for the imamate.[35] The six were 'Uthman, 'Ali, Talhah, Zubayr, Sa'd ibn Abu Waqqas, and 'Abd al-Rahman ibn 'Awf. When 'Abd al-Rahman ibn 'Awf removed himself from the group—they had left it to him to make the choice—he consulted with the leading Emigrants and Helpers for three days, his eyes bleary from lack of sleep. When he had determined his preference for 'Uthman he summoned the Emigrants, Helpers, and the commanders [emirs] of the army. When they gathered after making the morning prayer (salat) at the pulpit of God's Messenger, God's prayer and peace be upon him, he announced his choice of 'Uthman. They all pledged allegiance to him. This account is related by Bukhari in his *Sound Collection*, and by others.

"The commanders of the armies" refers to the governors of the major regions, Egypt, Syria [Sham and Homs], Kufah, and Basrah, who that year had made the hajj with 'Umar, and visited Medina with him. When one of those governors stood alone—namely Mu'awiyah, who did not pledge allegiance to 'Ali, God bless him, notwithstanding the consensus of the rest of the Muslims on pledging allegiance to him—the well-known discord and division occurred.[36] The pledge of allegiance is valid only on the basis that the Muslims are in agreement, or that leaders who are followed by others are in agreement. Where anybody chooses not to follow them, it will be easy for them to use the power of the community to compel him to obey and comply. Among their leaders in this era are military leaders such as the ministers of war and the navy, and their top staff. When the pledge of allegiance is made in the capital, it is obligatory that the provinces follow by their governors also making the pledge of allegiance, if the people follow them in that. If not, it is obligatory for the leading figures among the people—scholars, commanders, and others—to join forces with them.

Some Mu'tazilis and jurists erred in holding that the pledge of allegiance always has effect when it is made by five people who are qualified for the imamate. They took as prescriptive what 'Umar signaled when he limited consultation to the six who were nominated.[37] All the Companions assented to that, and thus there was a consensus. Yes, that was a consensus, one based upon consultation, and a consensus of those six men in regard to that matter. It was not a consensus in regard to that being the requisite number for every pledge of allegiance. In the Ash'ari school [madhhab] they held that the imamate may come into being by the pledge of allegiance being made by one qualified person, if it is made in front of witnesses, which is a clearer error. The jurists mentioned this opinion, restricting it to cases in which the people who loose and bind are limited to one person,[38] where the community's leading figures have confidence in him and delegate their decision to him. But such a circumstance is hypothetical: it did not and still does not arise. 'Uthman's imamate did not come into being solely by 'Abd al-Rahman ibn 'Awf alone making the pledge of allegiance. Rather, the pledge was universal, not limited to him. The same point applies to 'Umar's pledge to Abu Bakr. The pledge did not have effect by 'Umar's pledge alone, but by the main body of the community [*jama'ah*] pledging allegiance to Abu Bakr.

It is beyond doubt that 'Umar rejected the view of those who claimed that the pledge of allegiance can have effect through the pledge of one person who has not consulted the main body of the community. This matter had reached him while he was making the hajj. Thus, he had intended to explain to the gathered pilgrims what pledging allegiance actually means, and what is stipulated on consulting with the main body of the community. Then some of them pointed out to him that the pilgrimage season brings together a mixture of people, including those who would not understand the teaching, and who would fly off in all directions with it. They said that it was incumbent upon him to postpone this explanation until his return to Medina so that he could then give it to people of learning and insight. So he did.

At the pulpit of the Messenger, God's prayer and peace be upon him, he said:

> It has reached me that there is someone among you who says, "By God, if 'Umar dies I will pledge allegiance to so-and-so." But then no one should be deceived by the notion that the pledge of allegiance given to Abu Bakr was a precipitate move [*faltah*], yet it succeeded, becoming an established matter of fact. Yes, indeed it was so. But God afforded us protection from the evil consequences of that action. Toward no one among you have necks been stretched out as for Abu Bakr.[39] Whoever were to swear allegiance to any man without consultation among the Muslims, his oath of allegiance would be invalid and both of them would be subject to being killed.[40]

He then discussed the story of the pledge of allegiance being made to Abu Bakr. He discussed his fear that the Emigrants and Helpers would fall into discord, had it not been for that spontaneous action of pledging allegiance and trusting that the rest of the Muslims would assent. This account is related by Bukhari.

The majority of the Companions affirmed 'Umar's action. Thus, it was the object of consensus and was settled. The principle underlying pledging allegiance is that it follows consultation with the majority of the Muslims and the choice of those who loose and bind. The pledge of others is not to be taken into consideration except when it follows theirs. 'Umar's action, may God be pleased with him, contradicted this definitive principle. Thus, it was a precipitate move

The Caliphate 61

that resulted from exceptional circumstances. It does not reflect a principle of the shari'ah which should also be implemented in other cases. Whoever tries to do something like that and pledges allegiance to someone is unfit, and so is the one to whom he pledges allegiance. Moreover, that would render them both vulnerable. It might result in them being killed, if their actions lead to division and discord in the community.

(4) THE AUTHORITY OF THE MUSLIM COMMUNITY [UMMAH] AND THE MEANING OF THE TERM JAMA'AH

Describing the faithful, God Almighty states, "they consult one another in their affairs" (Qur'an 42:38). The Qur'an addresses the main body [jama'ah] of the faithful in the ordinances that it reveals. This even applies to ordinances concerning fighting and the like, matters of a general nature not pertaining to individuals, as we have explained in our Qur'an Commentary. It commands obedience to those who hold authority [ulu al-amr] — who constitute the main body of the community — not the one who holds authority. That is because he is one of them. He is obeyed only on the basis that the Muslims who pledge allegiance to him support and have confidence in him.

Support for this notion is found in what is related in sound hadith on the importance of holding fast to the main body of the community. These hadith make clear that people obey the emir because by so doing they are in fact obeying the main body of the community. There is unanimous agreement on this point, which derives from the notion that authority inheres in the main body of the community. Take, for example, the hadith of Ibn 'Abbas, related in the two sound collections [Sahih al-Bukhari and Sahih Muslim]. From the Prophet, may God's prayer and peace be upon him, he said: "Anyone who notices something in his emir should endure it patiently, because anyone who separates from the main body of the community by the span of a hand and then dies, dies a death of the days of the Era of Ignorance."[41] As related in a widely accepted, sound hadith:[42] when the Prophet, God's prayer and peace be upon him, informed Hudhayfah bin al-Yaman about the discord that would afflict the community, he said: "What do you command me to do, should I witness that?" He said, "Hold fast to the main body of the Muslims' community and to their imam." He [Yashkuri] said, "I [Hudhayfah] said: and what if they have neither a main body nor an imam?" He said, "Then separate yourself from all factions." Etc.[43] In certain hadith one finds the explanation that the main body of the community refers to the great majority of the Muslims, namely, the great majority during Islam's early era.

Prescriptions on the community's authority, from which the principle of consensus is derived, also include the following hadith: "My community does not"—in another wording "will not"—"come to an agreement in error." In another narration:[44] "and the hand of God is with the main body of the community, and so anyone who separates himself from it does so in the hellfire." In another narration: "I asked my Lord to ensure that my community would not make an agreement in error. He granted me that request." This narration is found in *Musnad Ahmad*, Tirmidhi's *Jami'*, Tabarani's *Kabir*, and Hakim's *Mustadrak*.

After discussing disagreements about the term *jama'ah*, and the opinion that it is limited to the Companions, Tabari states: "The correct interpretation is that Muslims are obligated to hold fast to the *jama'ah*, the group that agrees on who should be appointed to rule, and then obeys him. Anybody who violates his pledge of allegiance has thereby left the *jama'ah*." He states: "It is related in the hadith that when the people do not have an imam, and thus split into parties, a Muslim, if he can, should not follow anyone into schism. He should stay removed from all parties, for fear that he fall into evil." This explanation was repeated and endorsed by Al-Hafiz [Ibn Hajar] in his *Commentary on Bukhari [Sharh al-Bukhari]*.[45]

This body is made up of the Muslims who hold authority, the people who loose and bind. When they establish a consensus it must be obeyed. They include the chief authorities and the imam's counselors. They are the people who are responsible for ensuring that the faithful fulfill their general obligations, as these are set down in the Book and the sunnah [the Qur'an and the hadith], and the Companions' statements. They are also responsible for monitoring the one who implements rules pertaining to these obligations. Reports show this issue to be a matter of consensus. They include a statement that Abu Bakr, may God be pleased with him, made in his first sermon after receiving the pledge of allegiance: "I have been appointed to lead you, and I am not the best of you. So when I act correctly, assist me; when I stray, set me straight." It is related that 'Umar and 'Uthman expressed similar sentiments. They are the ones who assigned him the status of caliph, as likewise did any average man among the Emigrants who was not the highest or the lowest among them.

In 'Adud's *Book of Stations [Al-Mawaqif]*: "The community has the right to discharge and dismiss the imam for cause. If that should lead to discord, the lesser of the two harms should be borne."[46] In his explanation of dismissal for cause, his commentator Sayyid al-Jurjani states: "That would apply when the imam's actions inescapably disrupt Muslim life, and lead to regression in religious affairs. In such a case, their right to dismiss the imam is the same as their

The Caliphate 63

right to appoint and install him for the sake of order and progress."[47] Imam al-Haramayn's opinion is similar, and will be related presently.

We related Razi's opinion previously when defining the caliphate: the right of universal leadership belongs to the community. It has the right to discharge the imam (the caliph) if it deems that necessary. Sa'd al-Taftazani explicates the meaning of this leadership in order that the matter not be obscure, so that it might be said: if leadership lies with the community, who are the led? He states: "By 'community [ummah]' he means those who loose and bind, namely, those who on the basis of their prestige and rank represent the community. Their leadership is over others, or over all individuals within the community." This second sense is sound, as is supported by Razi's explanation of the term "the holders of authority" in the Almighty's statement [Qur'an 4:58]: "O you who have faith, obey God, and obey the Messenger and the holders of authority among you." He demonstrates that "the holders of authority" refers to the people who loose and bind and who embody the community's authority. Nisaburi followed him in this interpretation, and the Master, the Imam [Muhammad 'Abduh], adopted it. We clearly explained it in our Qur'an Commentary, finding support in the Almighty's statement: "And whenever tidings come unto them, whether of security or fear, they spread it about, whereas had they referred it to the Messenger and to those in authority among them, those of them whose task it is to investigate would have known it" [Qur'an 4:83].[48] It is well known that "those in authority" who were with the Messenger—matters of peace, war, and the like that pertain to public welfare being referred to them as well as to him—were not jurists, emirs, or governors. Rather, they were his counselors among the Muslims' leading figures.[49]

(5) QUALIFICATIONS REQUIRED OF THOSE WHO ELECT THE CALIPH

The ulama stipulated certain qualifications for the body [*jama'ah*] of Muslims who constitute the people who loose and bind. Mawardi explains these qualifications in *The Ordinances of Government*:

> Insofar as the need for the imamate has been demonstrated, the duty to establish it becomes a collective duty, like the duties of jihad or pursuit of knowledge. If undertaken by someone qualified, the duty falls from others' shoulders. If nobody undertakes it, two factions emerge from the people: the electors, who elect the imam for the community, and those fit for the office of the imamate, one of whom is to be appointed.
>
> As for the qualifications required of the electors, three are recognized. One: integrity, in all of its dimensions. Two: the knowledge that enables recognition

of the person who has the right to the imamate based upon the qualifications stipulated for it. Three: the insight [ra'y] and wisdom that enable selection of the person most suited for the imamate, the most upright and knowledgeable with respect to administration of affairs. Those residing where the imam resides do not thereby have priority over those residing elsewhere. It is only custom, not[50] a requirement of the shari'ah, that because they learn of the imam's death before others, and because the one fit for the imamate is generally found where the imam resides, that they have been entrusted with appointing someone to the imamate (cf. *Fath al-Bari*).[51]

I say: these qualifications have their origin in the early Muslim generations' guiding example. Tabari states: "None of Islam's people had what the six that 'Umar commanded to consult among themselves had in terms of standing in the religion, making the hijrah, early conversion to Islam, intellect, learning, and political know-how."[52]

As for integrity—the first qualification, according to the jurists—it consists of observing duties and cultivating virtues, along with avoiding sins, vices, and whatever violates noble character. Some jurists stipulated that it should be a natural disposition, not an affectation. Yet an affectation can become a disposition if one commits to it as a duty.

As for learning, what the jurists mean here is that the electors must be learned in the religion and knowledgeable in the community's affairs and politics. When they refer to it in an absolute way what is meant is independent knowledge, which is also called ijtihad. It can be inferred from the discourses of some of the jurists that the electors are collectively responsible for ijtihad on the revealed law. This is what is stipulated. They are not individually responsible for ijtihad. The author of *Al-Rawdah* states: The basic principle is the stipulation that one of them must be a qualified for ijtihad: a mujtahid.[53]

Defined thus, learning as a stipulated qualification evolves over time. The knowledge that would entitle someone to the imamate in this era differs from the knowledge that was required in previous eras. Certain scholars have said that one of the reasons why the Companions' preference was to select Abu Bakr as caliph, may God be pleased with him, was that he was the one among them with the greatest knowledge of the Arabs' lineages, circumstances, and strengths. For this reason, he did not fear what 'Umar feared when it came to fighting apostates. Now, the imam and those who make up the body of counselors—the people who loose and bind who are the substance of his imamate and the pillars of his government—are required to be versed in the laws of war and peace, major treaties, and conditions in the nations and states neighboring and having political and commercial relationships with Islamic lands: their politics and power,

The Caliphate 65

what may be feared and hoped from them, and what is needed to avoid harming them and procure benefit from them.

Among the reports indicative of this is Al-Hafiz's [Ibn Hajar's] statement about the pledge of allegiance and 'Uthman. From *Al-Fath:* "What is apparent from 'Umar's conduct regarding his emirs, whom he appointed in the lands, is that he did not only consider the question of who was superior in religion. Rather, he also considered knowledge of politics, along with avoidance of what the revealed law prohibits. Hence, he installed, namely appointed as emir, Mu'awiyah, Mughirah bin Shu'bah, and 'Amr bin al-'As, although there were others who were superior in the matters of religion and learning, such as Abu al-Darda' in Syria and Ibn Mas'ud in Kufah."[54] The conduct of Abu Bakr and 'Umar regarding the caliphate is to be emulated, especially in regard to the broad universals known as "sunnah." This is indicated by 'Abd al-Rahman stipulating to 'Ali that it was equivalent to the Messenger's sunnah, and he did not favor 'Ali [for the caliphate] because of his uncertain response or reservation about his capability. He favored 'Uthman because of his certitude and unconditional acceptance. Their conduct is to be emulated because there is consensus on their sunnah, and because of the Messenger's statement, God's prayer and peace be upon him, "Emulate those who come after me: Abu Bakr and 'Umar," from Hudhayfah—related and deemed sound by Ahmad [ibn Hanbal], Tirmidhi, and Ibn Majah. When the jurists in the schools [madhhabs] set down the law in writing they overstepped. That is because they regarded 'Umar's actions as having provided conclusive, definitive rules for specific issues, such as taxation and treatment of the people of the pact [*ahl al-dhimmah*]. But 'Umar's actions did not set down definitive rules. Rather, they were informed by ijtihad and the principle of public welfare.

The kind of knowledge referred to in the third qualification includes wisdom and sound insight. There is no stipulation that the electors share in a strong partisan spirit. That is because it is assumed that they are the people who loose and bind upon whom the community depends for managing affairs of general interest, that ordinances of the revealed law for those affairs have authority and will be implemented, and that Muslims obey no other ordinances. They do not submit to anyone other than someone who implements them. As for people appealing to race-consciousness in their efforts to overcome others, this has nothing to do with Islam's guidance, but is a departure from it. Islam's ruling on that will be discussed presently.

From the foregoing discussion it may be appreciated that what the title—the people who loose and bind—conveys is the notion that they are authorized for the two roles, loosing and binding, in potentiality and in actuality. They are the

66   *Muhammad Rashid Rida*

leaders whom the community follows in affairs of general interest. The most important affair is the supreme imam's appointment, and likewise his dismissal, when it becomes clear to them that that is necessary. Imam al-Haramayn states that the imam who "becomes unjust, and whose unfairness and tyranny become apparent, and who pays no attention to anyone who rebukes him for the badness of his deeds: the people who loose and bind then have the right to act in concert to stop him, even if by taking up arms and instigating wars."[55] Those who imagine that for all of those described as having knowledge and prestige the imamate would come into being upon their pledge of allegiance, and that the community is then obligated to follow them in that, are ignorant of what the following terms mean: loosing and binding [al-hall wa al-'aqd]; the main body of the community [jama'ah], and consensus [ijma']. In addition, they are ignorant of the foregoing reports and statements, and the scholars' discourses on the issue, especially as they relate to the electors' qualifications.

(6) QUALIFICATIONS REQUIRED OF THE CALIPH

Sa'd al-Taftazani states:

> It is stated in our juristic works that the community must have an imam who gives life to the religion, properly applies the sunnah, brings justice to those who are wronged, upholds people's rights, and gives them due priority. It is stipulated that he be competent,[56] Muslim, just, free, male, a mujtahid, courageous, insightful, able to hear and see, well-spoken, and a Qurayshi. Should there not be any Qurayshi thus qualified, someone from the tribe of Kinana should be appointed imam. If none are qualified, then a descendent of Isma'il should be appointed. If none are qualified, then a non-Arab should be appointed.[57]

By "mujtahid," he means someone who undertakes ijtihad on the revealed law's ordinances, which is enabled by his detailed knowledge of their prescriptions. What he states on the last point—the contingency of there being no Qurayshi—represents the Shafi'i position. It is regarded as a premise for a contingency that does not actually arise. Everything he states prior to this detail accords with the views of Sunni Muslims. An exception is found with the adherents of the Hanafi school [madhhab]. Some Hanafis deem it permissible to appoint a ruler who is not one of the ulama and not a mujtahid, as he is able to seek the assistance of mujtahid muftis, as, for instance, when administering justice [qada']. In his gloss on *Al-Musayarah*, a work by his shaykh, Kamal bin al-Humam, Shaykh Qasim bin Qutlubugha states: "In Hanafi teaching,

The Caliphate

the qualifications without which the caliphate cannot come into being are: Islam, masculinity, freedom, rational mind, being fundamentally courageous, and being Qurayshi."[58] That is to say: qualifications besides these are grounds for preferring a candidate, not those upon which appointment is contingent. Mawardi elucidates these:[59]

> As for the qualifications required of those holding the imamate, there are seven. One: integrity in all of its dimensions. Two: knowledge, enabling ijtihad in the event of unforeseen circumstances, and to make rulings. Three: vitality of the faculties of hearing, sight, and speech, enabling sound assessment of whatever is perceived by them. Four: vitality of the organs, and lack of any impairment that would prevent normal movement or prompt action. Five: insight, ensuring capable tending to the people, and management of their interests. Six: bravery and courage, enabling defense of the territory of Islam,[60] and jihad against enemies. Seven: Qurayshi lineage, because of the textual prescription on that point, and because that has been confirmed by consensus. Thus, no consideration should be given to the opinion of Dirar.[61] He stands alone in declaring that it is open to all [whatever their lineage]. That is seen in how Abu Bakr the Truthful[62] remonstrated against the Helpers on the day of the Saqifah Assembly for deviating from the path set down for the caliphate. They did so by pledging allegiance to Sa'd bin 'Ubadah (that is, they wanted him to be proclaimed caliph). Rejecting that, Abu Bakr, God's prayer and peace be upon him, quoted the Prophet: "The imams are from Quraysh." Accepting Abu Bakr's narration and granting its veracity, the Helpers withdrew their claim to having a right to the imamate. They renounced their claim to share in the rights of Quraysh, one they had made by saying, "one emir will be chosen from among us, and another emir from among you." When Abu Bakr said, "We are the emirs and you are the ministers," they deferred to him. The Prophet, may God's prayer and peace be upon him, said, "Quraysh have priority over others; none come before them" — that is: you should not go before them. This text is free of any ambiguity that could lead to disputation, nor is any opinion given in opposition to it.[63]

I say: the preceding discussion concerned integrity and learning, two qualifications required of those who select the caliph. Such requirements apply with even greater force here. As for the consensus on the stipulation that the caliph be a Qurayshi, this is affirmed by narrated reports and by practice. It is related by the most trustworthy scholars of hadith. All of the scholastic theologians and jurists in the Sunni schools have drawn upon this prescription. It was implemented as standard practice, with the Helpers assenting and submitting to the tribe of Quraysh, and then the great majority of the community doing likewise in the following centuries. This even applies to the Turks, who prevailed over the 'Abbasids and effectively stripped them of their authority. Nobody among them ventured to lay claim to the caliphate, or undertook to unduly assume it, even by force, a matter that will be discussed presently. That is due to nothing other than the fact that the entire Muslim community has agreed with and religiously believed in what has been stated: the caliphs must be Qurayshis. Moreover, monarchs and sultans whose rule rested upon force used to claim that their authority derived from them, or that they were their representatives.

As for hadith on this matter, there are many. They are found in all works on the sunnah. They are cited in works on ordinances, chapters on the caliphate or emirate, works on praiseworthy deeds,[64] and works on other topics. There has been no disagreement among Sunni Muslims, Arab and non-Arab, regarding their general purport, and none of the Turkish scholars has taken it upon himself to interpret them. Some of the works attesting to their authenticity have been published in Constantinople with the permission of the Ministry of Information, even during the era of Sultan 'Abd al-Hamid [Abdul Hamid II], whose concern for the title "caliph" is equaled by none. Examples of such works include *Commentary on Goals*, which we have quoted, and *Book of Stations*, with commentary and gloss.[65]

The hadith cited by Mawardi, "Quraysh have priority over others; none come before them," was related by: Shafi'i; Bayhaqi in *Al-Ma'rifah*, where the transmitter is unnamed; Ibn 'Adi in *Al-Kamil*, in a hadith from Abu Hurayrah; Bazzar in his *Musnad*, in a hadith from 'Ali, God bless him; and Tabarani in his *Al-Kabir*, in a hadith from 'Abd Allah bin al-Sa'ib, with sound chains of transmission. An elevated [*marfu'*] hadith from Abu Hurayrah that is related in the two sound collections conveys the same point: "People follow Quraysh in this matter." We do not need to mention all of the other hadith. We mention only the hadith that Mawardi depended upon, and also that with similar wording, as he did not cite it.

As to the hadith "The imams are from the tribe of Quraysh," when it comes to its reliability—the strength of its chain of transmission—we suffice with a statement by Al-Hafiz Ibn Hajar in *Fath al-Bari*. Commenting on the chapter on praiseworthy deeds in Bukhari's *Sound Collection*, he states: "When I learned that some of the learned of the era had said that this hadith had not been narrated by anyone other than Abu Bakr the Truthful, I collated around forty lines of transmission going back to Companions." Al-Hafiz Ibn Hajar states that Abu Bakr's words to Sa'd bin 'Ubadah at the Saqifah Assembly, as in *Musnad Ahmad*, were: "I swear by God, O Sa'd, that the Messenger of God, God's prayer and

The Caliphate

69

peace be upon him, said while you were sitting [by him], 'The Quraysh hold this authority.' Sa'd said to him, 'You have spoken the truth.'"[66]

Someone who is familiar with this tradition will pay no heed to the opinions that some people have offered in this era when interpreting these hadiths, and investigating their chains of transmission. He will pay no heed to their opinion that the stipulation on Quraysh is disputed. Where some leading scholastic theologians have mentioned that opinion, they have done so in order to refute it. The reason is that it is an extraordinary and heretical deviation. They have not cited this opinion as a case where differences of opinion are healthy and inform a productive debate. So this dispute is not like disputes among the imams, who strive to serve truth by resolving issues through ijtihad. In this era, the goal of those who would contest or conceal the stipulation on Quraysh is to legitimize the caliphate of the Ottoman dynasty's sultans. In the view of Sunni Muslims, who make the stipulation regarding Quraysh on the basis of the consensus of their schools, there is no way to legitimize that except for the principle of rule by pure force [qa'idat al-taghallub]. As for the Kharijis, in their view there could never be a way to accept that stipulation. That is because they reject the notion that the imamate could ever be restricted to one dynasty. That is why they rejected the stipulation on Quraysh. And what does it harm the Ottomans if their caliphate be said to rest purely on force, when some of the jurists have said the same of all or most of the Umayyads and the 'Abbasids?

As for the underlying rationale or reason why the Prophet, God's prayer and blessing be upon him, restricted the legitimate caliphate to Quraysh, here the scholastic theologians and jurists have cited Abu Bakr the Truthful's statement to the Helpers at the Saqifah Assembly. This statement established that in their lineage and domain the Quraysh are in the midst of the Arabs, and the most eminent of them. Some of the scholars have added points that Abu Bakr the Truthful did not need to mention at that time. The most comprehensive discussion of this matter is that of Shaykh Ahmad Wali Allah of Delhi. In his book *The Conclusive Argument from God* [*Hujjat Allah al-Balighah*], some of which is contested,[67] he states:

> The reason for that is that the truth that God revealed upon the tongue of His Prophet, God's prayer and peace be upon him, was conveyed in the tongue of Quraysh, and through their customs. Most of what was imposed in the way of norms and statutes aligned with what they had, and what would prepare the way for many ordinances lay with them. Thus, they were the most upright in that, and formed the majority of the people who held fast to it. Also, Quraysh were the Prophet's people, God's prayer and peace be upon him, and his party. They had no pride but pride in the loftiness of the religion of

Muhammad, God's prayer and peace be upon him. In them, religious and tribal zeal were united. Thus, they were the people who were able to establish and hold fast to revealed laws. Also, the caliph must be of noble lineage and high social rank, so that people would not be averse to obeying him. That is because anyone who lacks a lineage will be regarded by the people as base and low. He must be someone having the qualities of leadership and eminence. His people must be practiced in gathering men and making ready for battle. They must be strong, protecting him, supporting him, and sacrificing themselves for him. These features were only found combined together in Quraysh. This was so especially following the mission of the Prophet, God's prayer and peace be upon him, with their prestige growing through him. Abu Bakr the Truthful, may God be pleased with him, pointed to that when he said, "Power belongs but to Quraysh, they are in the heart of the Arab domain, etc."

There are two reasons why he did not stipulate, for example, that the caliph must be Hashimi. One: to avoid giving the people reason to regard him suspiciously, and say that he was acting like a monarch, only seeking to establish the rule of his own house. That would cause them to apostatize. It is for this reason that the Prophet did not give the key (that is, the key to the Ka'bah) to 'Abbas bin 'Abd al-Muttalib, may God be pleased with him. Two: that when it comes to the caliphate what matters is that the people consent to the caliph's rule, be in agreement over his status, and venerate him. What matters is that he executes the hudud laws, protects the religious community [*millah*], and implements legal ordinances. These functions are only carried out by one person, followed by another. There is a sense of limitation and difficulty in the stipulation that the caliph must belong to a specific tribe. Perhaps there is nobody in that tribe who embodies these qualities, while there is such a person in another tribe?[68]

I say: God Almighty sealed His religion, and completed and perfected it with his wise Book, which He revealed "as an Arabic Qur'an"[69] and "as a judgment in Arabic"[70] through the seal of His messengers, the Arab, the Qurayshi. His wisdom required that it would spread to the lands of the East and the West through the mission and leadership of Quraysh, and through the strength of the Arabs, who safeguarded the mission with their swords. Non-Arabs who entered Islam and whose practice of it was sound followed and learned from the Arabs. This is in spite of their equal status under the revealed law's ordinances, and the illustriousness of many non-Arab clients, who had been Arabized by following the Arabs.[71] In most of their clans the Quraysh were among the most distinguished Arabs in temperament, character, fluency in the Arabic language,

The Caliphate

71

intelligence, understanding, and eloquence. Among the progeny of Isma'il they had the purest lineage. They had the most eminent of the Arabs' histories through their virtues, good deeds, and service to God Almighty's house.[72] The sum of these distinctions, which culminated with Islam, enabled them to unite the Arabs under their leadership, and the more so non-Arab peoples who entered Islam thereafter. Their status was especially established once the Messenger, God's prayer and peace be upon him, had given a prescription on that, and the Companions were in consensus on the matter.

There was a twofold rationale or reason why the Messenger, God's prayers and peace be upon him, made them successors to his prophetic leadership.

One: their abundant merits. These were merits through which the call to Islam was propagated, and which, in accordance with human nature, enabled unity, and prevented or lessened opposition and competition. And so it was. The people submitted to them, although they were divided, and although there were many among them who did not carry the burdens of the caliphate, or fulfill the duties that it mandates. The people did not seek to replace any individual or family among them, except with another from among them. The fabrications made by some non-Arabs against some of the 'Abbasids were in violation of the revealed law, and an attack on universal rights, similar to other types of attacks on property and honor.

Two: that Islamic practice be linked without interruption to the progeny of those who were first to receive, call to, and propagate it. That would ensure that the continuity of its spiritual and historical practice not be severed. And special rights of communities and nations are history's offspring and its foster child.

Do you not see that the rightly guided caliphs' conduct is considered the highest example of conduct based upon the ordinances of the Book and the sunnah [the Qur'an and the hadith]? Do you not see that the conduct of the Umayyad and 'Abbasid civil caliphs who spread the arts and sciences, and elevated civilization in the East and the West, is considered Islamic civilization's basis and support? Or, do you not see that the connection of the Islamic world to the geographic "cradle of Islam," the Hijaz, is considered second in importance, due to its connection to Islam's Book and its sunnah [the Qur'an and the hadith], such that the caliph appointed by the new Turkish state in Constantinople even gave himself the title "Servant of the Haramayn," like the sultans to whom the Hijaz submitted?

Did you not know that Islam, despite its liberality and tolerance, distinguished the Hijaz, or the Arabian Peninsula, not permitting two religions to coexist there, and that the Prophet, God's prayer and peace be upon him, decreed that at the end of his life? Has it not reached you that one of the non-Muslim historians has said: "Had the army that invaded the south of France after the conquest of Andalusia been entirely or mostly constituted of Arabs it would have taken control of all of Europe, and its people would have submitted to it"? The Europeans only fought against it because it was primarily made up of Berbers. Unlike the Arabs, the Berbers did not properly understand Islam, or adhere to its ordinances on keeping commitments, justice, and not assaulting the property and dignity of others. Can you see what would have happened if Islam had opened the office that succeeds prophethood—the caliphate—to all people, and non-Arabs had gained control over it from the first century on? In that case, would Islam and its language have been safeguarded as they were through being propagated by the Qurayshi caliphs, the virtuous and the dissolute? There is great scope for elaborating this point. But this treatise is not the right venue for that, because here we wish to keep our focus on the matter that is most pressing.

In this era, some of the learned have criticized the handing of the caliphate to Quraysh. They have said that this contradicts Islam's egalitarianism, its elimination of partisanship or the empowerment of one designated party of Muslims over others. Moreover, some have criticized it along similar lines to the criticism that some of the ulama have leveled against the Shi'ah, who restrict the imamate to the 'Alids. Namely, they have said that this opens the door for people who are not faithful Muslims to defame Islam. They may allege that the Prophet, God's prayer and peace be upon him, only established the rule of his own house. All of that is manifestly false, as we have explained elsewhere in our magazine *Al-Manar*. That is because Quraysh comprise numerous divided clans. During the pre-Islamic Era of Ignorance the enmity between these clans was similar to that between other Arab tribes and clans. Take, for instance, the enmity between the Banu 'Abd al-Shams and the Banu Hashim. This disappeared when the Prophet, God's prayer and peace be upon him, conquered Mecca and reconciled with Abu Sufyan, chief of the Banu Umayyah, and also during the caliphates of Abu Bakr and 'Umar. The tendency to give voice to that enmity rose anew during 'Uthman's caliphate. It was also seen with Mu'awiyah after him. During the era of the rightly guided caliphs, nothing new was added to Quraysh's prestige that they did not have previously, and neither during the era of the Umayyads and 'Abbasids. But the Umayyads were partisans of their own dynasty, then partisans of the Arabs. That is why the Islamic world abhorred them, and overthrew them before their rule had lasted one century.

During Abu Bakr's caliphate, the Banu Taym [clan] did not have the least privilege over any of their peers. The same point applies to the Banu 'Adi during

The Caliphate

'Umar's caliphate. Furthermore, the reason that the Banu Umayyah [clan] was able to act in ways that undermined the public welfare during 'Uthman's era was that he was weak, not that he was chauvinistic and partisan. Islamic public opinion did not forgive him for that, and it agitated the people against him. This enabled those who plotted secret conspiracies against Islam to gain ground, contributing to his killing. I refer to the conspiracies of the party of the Jew 'Abd Allah bin Saba', and the Magians [Zoroastrians], the instigators of discord in Islam.

It is related that the just and wise imam 'Umar warned 'Uthman, 'Ali, and 'Abd al-Rahman about the dangers of giving this kind of preferential treatment to relatives. It is contrary to Islam's way, and leads to corruption of affairs. When putting the matter of who would succeed him in the hands of the six counselors, he said to them: "O you three: the people will not choose anyone other than one of you. Thus if you, 'Uthman, come to have authority over the people in something, fear God, and do not empower the Banu Umayyah and the Banu Abu Mu'ayt over them.[73] If it is you, 'Ali, fear God, and do not empower the Banu Hashim over them."[74] He gave 'Abd al-Rahman similar instruction. This is related by Al-Hafiz [Ibn Hajar] in *Commentary on Bukhari*. 'Umar's statement that "the people will not choose anyone besides one of you" is based upon the rule that we have endorsed: ultimate responsibility for the caliphate lies with the community. It did not lie with those six leaders. 'Umar simply desired to use their unanimous decision as a vehicle for realizing the common will, given the esteem in which they were held for their glorious deeds.

However, in some hadiths the Prophet, God's prayer and peace be upon him, threatened Quraysh. He did so by speaking of God taking revenge, should they not implement God's revealed laws and uphold what is right, just, and merciful. Hadiths to this effect are numerous. Take, for instance, his statement, God's prayer and peace be upon him: "O people of Quraysh, you have authority over this matter so long as you do not innovate. Thus, if you make changes, God will send against you one who will afflict you as trees cut into sticks" — related by Ahmad [ibn Hanbal] and Abu Ya'la from Ibn Mas'ud with a reliable chain of transmission. It occurs in other forms with different wording and attestation. For instance: "The emirs are to be from Quraysh whenever they follow three rules: showing mercy when mercy is sought, acting equitably when dividing shares, and acting justly when rendering judgments" — related by Hakim from Anas with a good [*hasan*] chain of transmission.[75]

Yet the 'Abbasids did not bring the people under the authority of the Banu Hashim. Furthermore, they were even harsher than the Umayyads in oppressing the 'Alids, who were the best of them. They preferred Persians, and then Turks,

74   *Muhammad Rashid Rida*

to Arabs. As for the 'Alids, they were the most ascetic of the people when it came to matters of worldly life and sovereign rule over it. Otherwise, they would have made the effort required to obtain it. Anyone who truly desires something will become acquainted with strategies [*hiyal*] for obtaining it. None of them assumed responsibility for the imamate after the Prophet's grandson Hasan, peace be upon him, relinquished his right to it. An exception is found with the Zaydi imams in Yemen. They were, and still are, the most virtuous and just of "the people of the house"[76] to have taken up the imamate since the era of the rightly guided caliphs. As for the Idrisids in Morocco, they took the title "sultan." As for the 'Ubaydis [Fatimids], they were imposters with regard to lineage and also with regard to Islam.

In sum, the Shu'ubis leveled many criticisms against the Arabs and Quraysh that Ibn Qutaybah and other scholars have responded to.[77] Every people has its virtues and its faults. But the religion of God surpasses all. The only opinions or investigations that we consider acceptable are those that are supported by sound evidence, and which reflect the consensus of the community, or its great majority, during Islam's best centuries. Otherwise, nothing of our religion would remain for us. The passions of partisanship and favoritism in religion have been nothing but a source of discord for us. They have been harmful to both Arabs and non-Arabs among us, even if many of us have been unaware of that. The rationale of the lawgiver, God's prayer and peace be upon him, in making Quraysh successors to his prophecy was void of ignorant partisanship, which he forbade. It essentially concerns Quraysh's standing in relation to this religion, its Book [the Qur'an], its Prophet, its language, and the people of that language. The religion would lack a foundation were it not for Quraysh making the call to Islam, and doing so in their language. No non-Arab served Islam except those who had mastered this language. Thus, the first to serve it were Persians and others who had been Arabicized. The power of the Islamic state was subsequently revived by the Ottoman Turks, after its unity had been shredded and it had been weakened by those who preceded them. We shall explain presently what is required of us and what is required of them.

(7) THE FORM OF THE PLEDGE OF ALLEGIANCE

The imamate is a contract that, following consultation, comes into effect through the people who loose and bind pledging allegiance to the person that they have elected as the community's imam. For the imam, the basic principle underlying the pledge of allegiance is his obligation to act in accordance with the Book and the sunnah [the Qur'an and the hadith], and uphold what is right

The Caliphate

and just. For them, it is the obligation to "hear and obey" him in what is recognized as right. It is related in [Bukhari's] *Sound Collection* that in pledging allegiance to 'Uthman, 'Abd al-Rahman ibn 'Awf said, "I pledge allegiance to you, O 'Uthman, in accordance with the sunnah of God, His Messenger, and the two caliphs who succeeded him." The people pledged allegiance to him on the same basis. When the people rallied to 'Abd al-Malik bin Marwan, following the killing of 'Abd Allah bin al-Zubayr, 'Abd Allah bin 'Umar, may God be pleased with him, pledged allegiance to him.[78] He had previously refused to pledge allegiance to either of them due to the conflict and division surrounding the matter.[79] He then wrote to him: "I confirm that I 'hear and obey' God's servant, 'Abd al-Malik, Commander of the Faithful, in accordance with the sunnah of God and His Messenger, so far as I am able, and my sons do likewise."

Pledging allegiance to the Prophet, God's prayer and peace be upon him, the Companions pledged to "hear and obey" for better or worse, speak and uphold the truth so far as they were able, and not disobey him in anything recognized as right. Similarly, the Almighty states in regard to women pledging allegiance to him, "nor will they disobey you regarding what is right"[80] [Qur'an 60:12]. It has been soundly established that it was the Prophet, God's prayer and peace be upon him, who suggested that when pledging allegiance they include the proviso about acting on that pledge "so far as they were able to." They also pledged allegiance to him when it came to Islam, migrating [hijrah], jihad, patience, not fleeing from fighting, and pledged to obey him in accordance with the pledge of women referred to in the Qur'an. There are well-known hadiths on this subject that are related in the two sound collections and *Sunan* works. We especially note the hadith of 'Ubadah bin al-Samit, which has been firmly agreed upon. The version in Bukhari's "Book on Tribulations" is: "The Prophet, God's prayer and peace be upon him, called us, and we pledged allegiance. Regarding what he had thereby received from us, he said that we had pledged to hear and obey for better and for worse and on good days and on bad days. He impressed upon us that we should not come into conflict with those responsible for a matter 'except when you see open unbelief for which you have clear proof from God.'"[81] The version in the section on the pledge of allegiance in the "Book on Ordinances" is: "We pledged allegiance to God's Messenger, God's prayer and blessing be upon him: to hear and obey for better or worse, to not come into conflict on a matter with those responsible for a matter, and to uphold or speak the truth wherever we may be, and, in God's way, to not fear the reproacher's reproach." Commenting on the hadith in Bukhari on pledging to hear and obey, harking back to his commentary on the "Book on Tribulations," Al-Hafiz [Ibn Hajar] states that pledging "to not come into conflict on a matter with those responsible for it" means pledging not to come into conflict with those having sovereignty and authority.[82]

To summarize: The ulama agree on the obligation to rebel against a disbelieving imam. But they disagree on what is obligatory in the case of an unjust or dissolute imam, as there are conflicting prescriptions on that. These include the prescription on preventing the spread of discord. The generally adopted principle is that it is incumbent upon individuals to "command what is right and avoid what is harmful" in accordance with the pertinent stipulations, but to do so without rebelling against the holder of authority by force. As for the people who loose and bind, it is incumbent upon them to do what they find is most supportive of the public welfare, even if that should involve fighting. Traditions on this were cited previously in connection with the issue of the community's authority. We shall revisit this point when examining what disqualifies the imam from the caliphate.

(8) WHAT THE PLEDGE OF ALLEGIANCE MAKES INCUMBENT UPON THE MUSLIM COMMUNITY [UMMAH]

When the pledge of allegiance is completed it is incumbent upon the pledgers to obey the imam in whatever does not entail disobeying God. They must support him, and fight against those who wrong him, or seek to overthrow him. The other members of the community who follow the pledgers are obligated to do likewise. A discussion of the abode of justice and the main body of the community [jama'ah] and the pertinent ordinance, such as those on migration to that abode, will be given presently.

What needs to be emphasized most about every Muslim's duty to obey a rightful imam, and likewise an imam of necessity or tyranny, is that all who pledge allegiance, or who are obliged by the pledge of the people who loose and bind, must pay the zakat on property, animals, crops, and trade. Jihad is a collective duty, incumbent upon the community collectively.[83] It is also an individual duty, incumbent upon the members of the community, men and women, as explained in fiqh works. It is also incumbent upon them to obey those whom the imam appoints in the regions: governors, qadis, and military leaders. Muslims must obey these appointees, not other people. Appointees must defer to the imam when he limits their authority, and when he discharges them. The universal precondition for obedience is that the duty to obey is void when doing so would entail disobeying God Almighty. There are elevated [marfu'] sound hadiths to this effect, and their meaning has been firmly agreed upon.

The Caliphate

Reports and statements that are pertinent here include the following tradition, related by Muslim in his *Sound Collection:*
From 'Abd al-Rahman bin 'Abd Rabb al-Ka'bah. He said:

I entered the mosque when 'Abd Allah bin 'Amr bin al-'As was sitting in the shade of the Ka'bah, and the people were gathered around him. I went to them and sat beside him, and he said, "We were on a journey with God's Messenger, God's prayer and peace be upon him, and we stopped at a place. Some of us were fixing their tents, some competing in shooting, and some sitting where their animals were resting [*jishr*][84] when an announcer of God's Messenger, God's prayer and peace be upon him, announced, 'gather for prayer.' So we gathered by the Messenger of God, God's prayer and peace be upon him. He said, 'There has not been a prophet before me but that he was duty bound to call the people of his community's attention to what he knows is good for them, and to warn them of what he knows is bad for them. This community of yours is most vital at its beginning, while at its end you will experience trials and things that you will find unfamiliar. A number of trials will come, each one rendering the preceding one insignificant.[85] A trial will come, and the faithful believer will say, "This destroys me," and then it passes. Another trial will come, and the faithful believer will say, "This, this is the one." So for anyone who wishes to be delivered from the hellfire, and granted entry to paradise: let death come to him while he believes in God and the last day, and let him treat others as he wishes others to treat him. Whoever pledges allegiance to an imam, and gives him the clasp of his hand, and the fruit of his heart, let him obey him, so far as he is able. If another comes to oppose the imam, cut the neck of the other.'" Then I approached him and said to him, "I ask you, for the sake of God, did you hear this from God's Messenger, God's prayer and peace be upon him?" He put his hands on his ears and his heart, and said, "I heard it with my ears and understood it in my heart." Then I said to him, "This one, your cousin, Mu'awiyah: he commands us to wrongfully consume each other's wealth, and to kill one another, whereas God says, 'You who believe, do not wrongfully consume each other's wealth but trade by mutual consent. Do not kill each other, for God is merciful to you'" [Qur'an 4:29].[86] He spoke and then remained silent for one hour. Then he said, "Obey him in what thereby is obeying God, and disobey him in what thereby is disobeying God."[87]

God glorified mankind through Islam. The Book and the sunnah [the Qur'an and the hadith] mandate that under Islam there is no obedience and no submission except to God Almighty. Obeying the Messenger is a form of obeying Him. This is seen in His statement, "Whoever obeys the Messenger obeys God"

[Qur'an 4:80]. The same point applies when it comes to obeying those in authority. This is seen in His statement, "[obey God and the Messenger,] and those in authority among you" [Qur'an 4:59]. Hence, obedience is mandated to ensure that the fundamental principles or specific provisions of His revealed law are implemented. One of the Umayyad emirs said to one of the scholars among the Successors: "Has God not commanded you to obey us in His statement, 'and obey those in authority among you?'" [Qur'an 4:59]. He said to him, "Was the obligation to you"—he means: the obligation to obey you—"not removed when you opposed what is right, per His statement, 'If you are in dispute over any matter, refer it to God and the Messenger, if you truly believe in God and the last day'?" [Qur'an 4:59]. This is reported by Al-Hafiz [ibn Hajar] in *Al-Fath*, who comments that it is an admirable and noteworthy reply. However, here "those in authority" refers to the main body of the community [*jama'ah*], which effectively means the community as such, as mentioned previously.

(9) THE IMAM'S OBLIGATIONS TO THE RELIGION [*MILLAH*] AND THE MUSLIM COMMUNITY [UMMAH]

It is the imam's duty to propagate the call to what is true and right, establish the scales of justice, protect the religion from assaults and innovations, and seek counsel on all matters that lack a textual prescription. He is responsible for his actions, which any individual member of the community has the right to scrutinize and regard critically if it seems to him that the imam has erred. The people who loose and bind may call him to account over his actions. God's Messenger, God's prayer and peace be upon him, said, "The imam is the one who is the people's guardian, and he is responsible for his subjects," transmitted by Ibn 'Umar and related by the two shaykhs [Bukhari and Muslim] and others.[88]

Mawardi explicates what is incumbent upon the imam in ten universal maxims. He does not discuss consultation. This is in spite of the abundance of texts on that, and the abundance of statements by the rightly guided caliphs on consulting, and how by doing so one follows the sound practice of the Prophet, God's prayer and peace be upon him. Mawardi states:

In affairs of a public nature, there are ten duties incumbent on the imam.
(1) Safeguarding the religion by upholding its established fundamental principles, and what the community's first generations agreed upon. If an innovator appears, or someone who harbors a dubious opinion deviates from the religion, the imam will clearly show him the proof exposing the fallacy. He will explain to him what is correct, and admonish him by means of the laws and

The Caliphate

punishments that he stands in need of, so that the religion is protected from flaws, and the community is prevented from going astray.

(2) Implementing ordinances for disputation between parties, and terminating conflict between antagonists, so that justice prevails, the wrongdoer commits no violation, and people who are wronged are not weakened.

(3) Protecting territory [baydah][89] and households, so that people may proceed securely in their lives, and spread out in their travels safe from risk to lives or property.

(4) Executing hudud laws, so that things declared sacrosanct by God Almighty are secure from violations, and His servants' rights are safeguarded against abuse and misappropriation.[90]

(5) Protecting border outposts with deterrent equipment and defensive forces, so that enemies cannot unexpectedly seize the initiative and attack what is sacrosanct, or shed Muslim blood, or that of an ally.[91]

(6) Jihad against anyone who resists Islam after hearing the call to it, until he converts or enters into a pact [dhimmah] with the Muslims, so that what is due to God Almighty is established: "that He may cause the religion of truth to prevail over every other religion" [Qur'an 9:33].

(7) Collecting fay' taxes and alms, based upon what is mandated by the revealed law, either through a textual prescription or on the basis of ijtihad, and doing so without fear and without acting unjustly.

(8) Estimating payments and what is due from the treasury, without extravagance or stinginess, and being timely in their payment: neither too early nor too late.

(9) Employing those who are trustworthy and appointing those of good counsel to perform the functions that he charges them with, and take care of the funds that he entrusts them with, so that effective management of functions is ensured by their competence, and safeguarding of funds is ensured by their trustworthiness.

(10) Personally supervising all affairs and scrutinizing all circumstances, so that he may execute public policy and protect the religion [millah], not being reliant on delegating authority to others while preoccupied with pleasure seeking or with worship, as the trustworthy may betray the trust, and those of good counsel may deceive. God Almighty says:

> "David, We have made you a deputy [caliph] on the earth. Judge justly therefore among the people. Do not follow your desires, lest they divert you from God's path" [Qur'an 38:26].

God, be He glorified, is not content to delegate without supervising, nor to grant him an excuse for following his desires, describing that as going astray.

Muhammad Rashid Rida

This behavior, although required of him by the rules of the religion and by the office of the caliphate, is indeed one of the duties that politics imposes on everyone who has authority for something. The Prophet, peace be upon him, states, "Each of you is a shepherd, and each of you is responsible for his flock." The poet aptly expresses this point. Describing a statesman, he states (in the *basit* meter):

> Entrust your affairs, and your achievement is God's, to one
> Competent and artful in war,
> Unpretentious in good times, unsubdued in adversity,
> Who has learned the vicissitudes of time, conquering one day, conquered another,
> Takes hardships in his stride, and is free of pomp and servility.[92]

I say: Mawardi's delineation of the first duty is absolutely correct. The imam's duty is to safeguard those aspects of the religion that the pious ancestors [al-salaf al-salih] had agreed upon, while granting the community freedom in other aspects of the religion—matters relating to knowledge and individual worship that are to be resolved through ijtihad. As for political and judicial matters, which are affairs of government, here consulting with the learned among the people who loose and bind entitles the imam to favor some ijtihad-based ordinances over others. This applies especially if he is not personally qualified to undertake ijtihad on the revealed law. When it came to matters of government lacking an applicable and definitive text in the Book or the sunnah [the Qur'an or the hadith], the religion's imams would obey the caliphs even when doing so entailed assenting to what their own ijtihad opposed. But they did not do that when it came to the opinion that the Qur'an is created, as this is among the matters of doctrine in which their views had opposed those of the ancestors.[93]

By jihad, stipulated in the sixth maxim, Mawardi means fighting, individual and collective. This only becomes incumbent upon every fully responsible adult Muslim when an enemy seeks to seize Muslim land whose defense requires that. Otherwise, the duty is fulfilled by those the imam calls upon as needed. Jihad is also undertaken by contributing funds, and with the tongue, which includes using clear proofs to call people to Islam. It is obligatory to obey the imam's military directives, such as those on recruitment and other matters. It is incumbent upon him to threaten enemies with as much force as he can, so as to fight them with a force equal to theirs, or one surpassing theirs. This includes building battleships, submarines, military aircraft, and various types of weaponry, etc. In all of this it is obligatory to obey the imam and to offer property and life. This is seen in God Almighty's statement, "Prepare whatever

The Caliphate 81

power you can" [Qur'an 8:60]. This command is addressed to the community. Its leader is no more than someone who, through the position that he holds, unifies and organizes it. In view of that, the study of chemistry, mechanics, and all of the natural sciences is a collective duty. Whatever actions would be necessary to fulfill a duty in its absolute sense become specific and binding duties. In Islam, there is no jihad that mandates fighting with every person who holds a contrary view, even an ally [mu'ahad] or a tributary [dhimmi].[94]

(10) CONSULTATION IN ISLAM

I say: The imam's most important duty is to seek counsel on every issue for which God or His Messenger provided no prescription, or for which there is no genuine consensus that would support a decision, or for which there is a stipulation derived through ijtihad, but one that is not definitive. This applies especially to matters of politics and warfare, which rest on the foundations of safeguarding public welfare. The same point applies to the means of implementing stipulations for these matters, as they vary across time and place.

The imam, then, is not an absolute ruler, as many imagine. Rather, he is constrained by prescriptions in the Book and the sunnah [the Qur'an and the hadith], by the general example of the rightly guided caliphs, and by the obligation to consult others. Were nothing on this related except for the prescription in God Almighty's statement that the faithful "consult one another in their affairs" [Qur'an 42:38], and His statement to His Messenger, "Consult with them on the conduct of affairs" [Qur'an 3:159], that would suffice.[95] How much more so, then, when the obligation is affirmed in reports and statements, in actions and in words?

The reason underlying the command to the Messenger, God's prayer and peace be upon him, to consult when it came to the community's affairs led to that becoming a rule of the shari'ah for matters relating to public welfare. There are multiple ramifications and provisions related to public welfare that cannot be fixed permanently, and which vary across time and place. Thus, they cannot be delimited.

Some of the learned ancestors held that the Prophet, God's prayer and peace be upon him, had no need of consultation. They held that had it not been for the intention to make it a rule of the shari'ah, God would not have commanded the Prophet to consult others. It is related of Hasan al-Basri that in his commentary on the Almighty's statement, "Consult with them on the conduct of affairs" [Qur'an 3:159], he said: "God knew that the Prophet did not need anything from them. But He desired that it be introduced by him as a rule that would then be followed after him." This is supported by what is related in an elevated [*marfu'*] tradition with a good [*hasan*] chain of transmission that Ibn 'Adi and Bayhaqi report from Ibn 'Abbas.[96] When the verse was revealed, the Messenger, God's prayer and peace be upon him, said: "God and His Messenger have no need of consultation. But God has made it a blessing for my community. Those in it who consult will not be without proper conduct; those who relinquish it will not be without error." That is to say: God Almighty legislated the requirement to consult to ensure sound conduct, conduct that would uphold public welfare and prevent corruption. Indeed, to stray from the right way is to become corrupt and lost. Yet sound hadiths convey that the Prophet, God's prayer and peace be upon him, did not seek to extricate himself from the views of others. That is so except for cases concerning matters that he had received revelations about. He said: "You are more knowledgeable in the affairs of your worldly lives," related by Muslim from 'A'ishah and Anas. He said: "What concerns your religion, refer to me; what concerns your worldly lives you are more knowledgeable about," related by Ahmad [ibn Hanbal]. In a hadith of Rafi' bin Khudayj, included in Muslim's *Sound Collection*, it is also related that the Prophet, God's prayer and peace be upon him, said: "I am only a human being. If I give you a command concerning religion, carry it out. If I give you a command that reflects my own opinion, I am only a human being." This harmonizes with the Almighty's statement, "Say, 'I am only a human being, like you, who has received revelation'" [Qur'an 18:110]. The Prophet, then, is distinguished above others by having received revelation. However, in what goes beyond revelation and what revelation mandates, he is a human being with human characteristics. He stands in need of others when the ability to make the right decision depends on having certain kinds of knowledge that he may not have acquired himself. Thus, his nature as the most perfect human being does not mean that his knowledge is all-encompassing, or that he is capable of every action. God alone has those qualities. This is seen in the Almighty's statement, "Say, 'I do not tell you that I have the treasures of God, nor do I claim to know the unseen, nor do I tell you that I am an angel'" [Qur'an 6:50].

Hence, when people asked the Prophet about a command that he had given them, and where they found that an alternative would be preferable, they asked him whether it was something that he said or did on the basis of revelation from God, or whether it was on the basis of his opinion. If he said that it was on the basis of his opinion, they offered their opinion, and he acted upon it, preferring it to his own, as he did on the day of the battle of Badr.[97] The Prophet, God's prayer and peace be upon him, had arrived at a water-hole and stopped there. Hubab bin al-Mundhir said, "O Messenger of God, do you regard this place as the one that God has ordered you to occupy, so that we can neither advance nor withdraw from it, or is it a matter of opinion and military tactics?" The Prophet

The Caliphate   83

said, "It is a matter of opinion and military tactics." He said, "O Messenger of God, this is not the place to stop. Have the people go on to the water-hole nearest the enemy and halt there, stop up the wells beyond it . . . etc." The Prophet said to him, "You have given a judicious opinion," and he acted upon it.[98] In the narration of Ibn 'Abbas, according to Ibn Sa'd, Gabriel descends and says to the Prophet, God's prayer and peace be upon him, "The sound opinion is Hubab bin al-Mundhir's opinion."

The Prophet, God's prayer and peace be upon him, consulted with Abu Bakr and 'Umar, may God be pleased with them, about the captives at Badr. They offered differing opinions. The Prophet said, "If the two of you were in agreement, I would not dissent." As his opinion aligned with Abu Bakr's, that was the one that he applied. But then he received a revelation that supported 'Umar's opinion. This is the Almighty's statement, "It is not right for a prophet to take captives before he has conquered the battlefield" [Qur'an 8:67].[99] He, God's prayer and peace be upon him, then said to 'Umar, "An evil was on the point of befalling us because of our disagreement with you." There are numerous narrations on this incident.

All of this occurred before God Almighty had commanded the Prophet to consult with others. That command was revealed during the expedition to Uhud, where the opinion of the majority prevailed over that of the Prophet, God's prayer and peace be upon him, and that of many of the leading Companions, may God be pleased with them. Ibn Mardawayh (Ibn Mardawyhi) reports from 'Ali, God bless him, that the Messenger, God's prayer and peace be upon him, was asked about the word meaning "resolved" ['azm] in the Almighty's statement, "Consult with them on the conduct of affairs, but when you are resolved ['azamta], trust in God and proceed" [Qur'an 3:159].[100] He answered, "Consult with the people whose opinions are sound, and then follow them."

We have discussed the function of consultation in Islamic governance in detail in our Qur'an Commentary. We did so when commenting on this verse, which is found in "The House of Imran."[101] We also discussed it in our commentary on the verse, "Obey God, and obey the Messenger and the holders of authority among you" [Qur'an 4:58], which is found in "Women."[102] Commenting on the former verse, we explained why the Messenger, God's prayer and peace be upon him, left the matter of determining a system for consultation in the community's hands, not setting down [fixed] ordinances.

To summarize: the system differs as the conditions that affect the community's evolution, social composition, and welfare vary across time. Thus, it is not possible to have fixed ordinances for a system of consultation that would befit all times and places. Had the Messenger set down temporary ordinances for that, he would have feared that people would take what he set down—intended solely for his era—as a precedent. He would have feared that the people would have regarded those ordinances as having a religious basis, so that they were to be implemented under any circumstance and in every era, even if doing that would undermine public welfare. That is what they did, for instance, in assuming that precedent had been set with the pledge of allegiance and Abu Bakr, and 'Uthman, and with 'Umar's installation as caliph. Hence, when it came to the obligation to consult, the Prophet, God's prayer and peace be upon him, sufficed with God's revealed law on that, instructing the community to act in accordance with it. However, those who were motivated by their partisan disposition opposed what God revealed. They were driven by their desires and greed. This situation was a result of those who hold authority having fallen short in carrying out their duty. They failed to set down a system for consultation in such a manner that it could be adjusted to suit every era. That was what 'Umar, God be pleased with him, had done, adjusting it in a manner that befit his era. Moreover, rather than addressing this matter our ulama have been more interested in such issues as ritual impurity, menstruation, and buying and selling. We even see that a leading imam such as Ash'ari has said that the pledge of allegiance of just one of those who loose and bind, if witnessed, obligates the community to follow it. How could the community follow the correct path in managing its affairs if it would follow this opinion regarding its universal leadership?

As for the rightly guided caliphs' statements on consultation, these are extensive. They include what Darimi and Bayhaqi relate from Maymun bin Mahran. He relates that when Abu Bakr was faced with an issue that lacked any applicable prescription from the Book or the sunnah of the Prophet [the Qur'an or the hadith], God's prayer and peace be upon him, he would ask the members of the Muslim public whether they knew of anything relevant from the Prophet, God's prayer and peace be upon him. Perhaps a group might come to him saying, "Yes, he ruled such-and-such." Abu Bakr would accept that, and give thanks to God Almighty. If nothing resulted from asking the public, he would call upon leading and learned Muslims and consult with them. If they were agreed in their opinion, he ruled in accordance with it. 'Umar bin al-Khattab used to do likewise—and he added that, after examining the Book and the sunnah [the Qur'an and the hadith], he would also examine how Abu Bakr had ruled on a matter. That is because he would only issue a ruling on the basis of a textual prescription or consultation.[103]

Consider the difference between asking the Muslim public about a narration, and singling out the leaders and the learned for consultation—and that is because these people constitute the body [jama'ah] of those who hold authority and who loose and bind. The Book [the Qur'an] commands the faithful to obey these people, which follows from obeying God and His Messenger.

The Caliphate

On referring the community's affairs to them, He says: "had they referred it to the Messenger and to those in authority among them, those of them whose task it is to investigate would have known it" [Qur'an 4:83].[104]

They also include what Tabarani (in *Al-Awsat*) and Abu Sa'id relate from 'Ali on making rulings: "He said: 'O Messenger of God, if a matter comes to me on which there is no ruling that has been revealed, and also no sunnah, how do you command me to proceed?' He said, 'Render it a matter to be determined by consultation with people who are learned and worshippers among the faithful; do not issue a decree regarding it on the basis of your personal opinion.' "[105]

They also include what Ibn 'Abbas narrates: "The Qur'an reciters were on 'Umar's council and were those with whom he consulted, mature or young." He then relates an incident in which 'Umar deferred to the statement of someone who had reminded him of [a pertinent verse in] the Qur'an, saying that 'Umar strictly observed the Book of God, be He glorified and exalted. This is related in Bukhari's *Sound Collection*.[106]

They also include what is related in the two sound collections, and other works, on 'Umar consulting with others on the matter of an epidemic when he set out for Syria. When he was in Sargh people informed him that there was an epidemic in Syria, so he sought the counsel of the early Emigrants, and then that of the Helpers. Their views differed. Then he sought the opinion of the Qurayshi shaykhs who were present on whether to continue journeying for conquest. They were in agreement on returning and not entering the region of the epidemic. So 'Umar announced to the people: "In the morning I am riding" (that is, traveling, on a riding camel). In the morning they came to him. Abu 'Ubaydah then said, "Is this fleeing from what God has decreed?" 'Umar said, "Would that anyone but you had asked this, Abu 'Ubaydah! Yes, we are fleeing from what God has decreed to what God has decreed. Can you see, if you had camels and you came to a wadi with two banks, one fertile, one dry, is it not so that if you graze them in the fertile bank you graze according to what God has decreed, and if you graze them in the dry bank you graze according to what God has decreed?" Then 'Abd al-Rahman bin 'Awf arrived and informed him of an elevated hadith traceable to the Prophet that agreed with the opinion of the Qurayshi shaykhs.

APPOINTING THE CALIPH BY DESIGNATION

The jurists have unanimously agreed that it is sound practice for an imam who is rightfully in office to designate his successor. That is conditional on him being fit for office per the stipulated qualifications,[107] namely, those required of the rightful imam. Designating is not sound practice except when both the imam and his designee have all the qualifications required for the imamate. This is what is stipulated for an individual candidate. They found support for this position in the precedent of Abu Bakr's designating 'Umar as his successor. As for entrusting the matter to a collective, with responsibility given to a select number of those who loose and bind—who are then to consult among themselves—they have stipulated that in such a case the person appointed as imam must be one among them. Thus, there could be no basis for anyone to challenge the person they unanimously select. This harmonizes with 'Umar's action in delegating the matter to the council of six, who determined who should be imam by consulting among themselves. Mawardi states: "the consensus that it reached was the basis for the imamate coming into being by agreement, and for the pledge of allegiance being made by a number of persons who had been designated for the imamate to the one among them who had been selected by the people who loose and bind."[108]

Imams and caliphs who were unjust and who ruled purely on the basis of force and greed clung to the idea of this mode of appointment. But in so doing they did not heed what those who applied it correctly heeded: consulting with those who loose and bind, those who are knowledgeable. That is done, firstly, to gain their approval and, secondly, to convince any waverers. There are well-known narrations on this topic found in works on hadith—among the most comprehensive is *Kanz al-'Ummal* [*Treasure of the Laborers*]—historical works, and works of praise.[109]

What wise or rational person could compare Abu Bakr with Mu'awiyah when it comes to this matter? Abu Bakr designated 'Umar, striving to uphold what is right, just, and safeguards public welfare. He did so after consulting those who loose and bind, receiving their consent. Mu'awiyah designated the wanton and dissolute Yazid as his successor, doing so on the basis of the power of terror on the one hand, and bribery of leaders on the other. Then, consider what ensued. His foul example[110] was followed by others. The unjust and greedy who monopolized power bequeathed it to their progeny or friends, who then inherited it as one inherits property and goods. Are these not the partisan acts of a conquering power, acts contrary to the Qur'an's guidance and Islam's sunnah?

In *Al-Tuhfah* [*The Gift*], the jurist Ibn Hajar [al-Haytami] discusses a rightful imam's prerogative to designate a successor. He discusses both forms that this takes (designating an individual; designating a collective) and how it is confirmed. He then states: "What is recorded in historical and biographical works may raise doubts about this process. This is seen, for instance, with regard to ulama and others endorsing the 'Abbasids' designations of their successors even

The Caliphate

though they did not follow the pertinent stipulations. Moreover, the ancestors endorsed the Umayyads' designations, although they acted likewise in that. But it can be said that these were developments that were endured: they only endorsed these designations due to the prevailing dynamics of power and the fear of discord, not because of any genuine desire to do so. This much appears evident."[111]

On the designation referred to at the beginning of the discussion of this issue, Mawardi states: "The qualifications for the imamate are considered from the moment of the designation. If the designee has not reached legal maturity or is dissolute at the time of the agreement on his designation, but comes of age and turns into a man of probity by the time the incumbent dies, his succession is not valid until the electors pledge allegiance to him anew."[112] In his commentary on the hadith of 'Ubadah [bin al-Samit] on pledging allegiance, cited above, Al-Hafiz Ibn Hajar reports that: "It is impermissible to affirm the appointment of a ruler who is already dissolute at the time. The dispute about rebelling against a dissolute imam concerns the contingency of one who was just, and whose imamate was sound, but who thereafter turns and becomes unjust."[113]

From what we have said in the above discussion, it may be appreciated that designation of a successor, per the legal stipulations, depends on the endorsement of those who loose and bind. The jurists' reasoning requires that, even if they have not said so explicitly.

As for those who take power through the force of partisanship, their designations of successors are like their imamates. These are not rightful, not shari'ah-based, and do not stand in their own right. Thus, they should be discarded. Such an imamate should be eliminated and replaced with a shari'ah-based imamate when possible and when there is no risk of discord, which causes even greater harm to the community. If such an imamate should be eliminated by another that is based on pure force, Muslims are not obligated to fight for its restoration.

ONE WHO SEEKS TO RULE IS NOT TO BE APPOINTED

Islam's guiding principles include the rule that someone who seeks an appointment as a governor or emir for the sake of his prestige or wealth is not to be appointed. The Prophet, God's prayer and peace be upon him, said to two men who had asked that he appoint them as emirs: "We do not appoint to our office anyone who seeks it." Another version of the tradition is related by the two shaykhs. In Bukhari's *Sound Collection* the wording is, "We do not appoint to this office someone who asks for or covets it." In Muslim's *Sound Collection* the wording is: "By God, we do not appoint to this office someone who asks for or covets it." In Imam Ahmad ibn Hanbal's *Musnad* the narration is: "In our view, the least trustworthy of you are those who seek it." Thus, until the time of his death he never called upon those two men for anything.

The reason for this definitive prohibition, underscored by the oath, is that those seeking public office—this applies especially to the supreme governorship, the imamate, and those who covet it—love power for the sake of glory and gratification, and because power enables them to control people. It is clear that it was people such as these who corrupted the community's affairs. The Umayyads were the first party to do that. That is so even while there were some peerless individuals among them, and moreover the first among men, the unique 'Umar bin 'Abd al-'Aziz, the fifth rightly guided caliph.[114] He did not covet the imamate. If he had been able to do so, he would have handed it to the 'Alids.

In his commentary on the hadith cited above, Al-Hafiz [Ibn Hajar] relates a word of truth from Muhallab: "It was coveting the role of governance that led to people fighting over it, such that blood was shed, property and honor violated, and corruption spread throughout the land."[115] Other hadiths convey the same point.

Had the Muslims heeded what the revealed law sets down for the caliphate, and which was established during the era of the rightly guided caliphs, they would have been spared those episodes of discord and corruption. In that case Islam would have spread throughout all lands. Indeed, while in Constantinople a German scholar said to a nobleman from the Hijaz: "We should erect golden statues of Mu'awiyah in our capitals. That is because if had he not deviated from the path that the revealed law set down for caliphal authority, the path that the rightly guided caliphs followed, the Arabs would have seized all of our lands, and fashioned them into an Islamic-Arab domain."

(11) THE IMAMATE OF NECESSITY AND THE IMAMATE OF TYRANNY

Ulama who have investigated the matter have unanimously agreed that it is impermissible to pledge allegiance to someone as caliph unless he has all of the qualifications required for office, especially integrity, capability, and Qurayshi lineage. In the event that some qualifications are lacking the law of necessity becomes applicable, with necessity limited by the extent of the need. At such a juncture, the duty is to pledge allegiance to the one among those who have some of the qualifications who is best qualified, and who, together with that, strives and works to acquire the qualifications that he lacks. In *Al-Musayarah*, Kamal bin al-Humam states:[116] "According to the law of necessity, the functions

The Caliphate

89

of one who takes power through imposing himself by pure force may be recognized as sound. This applies, for instance, when there is no candidate who is a Qurayshi and who has integrity. Or, it applies when there is such a candidate, but tyranny has prevailed, rendering it impossible to appoint him."[117] He states this in response to his party, the Hanafis, arguing that integrity need not be stipulated as one of the imam's qualifications. They had made that argument on the basis that some of the Companions had given recognition to Umayyads who were sinful, such as Marwan. They recognized their status as governors, assented to their rulings, and prayed with them. By "functions" he means those of qadi, emir, and ruler. *Al-Musayarah*'s commentator states likewise.

In *Commentary on Goals*, Sa'd al-Taftazani states:

> There is a point to be investigated here. It concerns the contingency of there being no imam qualified as such. A group of the people who loose and bind then pledge allegiance to a Qurayshi who has not all but merely some of the requisite qualifications. But his rulings are not implemented, and his commands are not obeyed by the people at large. He lacks the kind of authority that would enable him to proceed as he wills when it comes to securing the welfare of God's servants, and to appoint and discharge whomever he wills. Would doing that be an effective discharge of the duty? Would it then be incumbent upon monarchs in different regions who have great power and are described as having sound politics and integrity, and as acting equitably, to vest their authority entirely in him, standing in relation to him as do the rest of his subjects? Here, one may take recourse to God Almighty's statements, such as the following: "Obey God, and obey the Messenger and the holders of authority among you" [Qur'an 4:58]. The statement of the Prophet, God's prayer and peace be upon him, also applies here. He said, "Anyone who dies without recognizing the imam of his age dies a death of the Era of Ignorance." That is because the obligation to recognize and obey the imam means that there must actually be an imam so that the people can recognize and obey him.[118]

That is to say: doing that is incumbent upon them.

In this conception, it is only stipulated that some of the people who loose and bind pledge allegiance to the imam. That is because if all of them—including the monarchs that he mentions—were to pledge allegiance, his power would be complete, his status as ruler definitively established. This proved so for some of the Umayyad and 'Abbasid caliphs who lacked integrity or the learning that is essential for ijtihad. The majority took the view that they must be obeyed and that, as a matter of necessity, their imamates must be recognized as sound. That

Muhammad Rashid Rida

is because there was no easy way to pledge allegiance to a more ideal candidate for the position, even if such a person actually existed.

According to the Hanafis, the principle to be adopted is that their imamates be recognized as absolutely sound. That is because they hold that recognition of an imamate does not depend on an imam having learning and integrity, as mentioned previously. In *Al-Musayarah*, the Hanafi scholar Kamal bin al-Humam, following Ghazali, states:

> Principle Ten: If it is not possible to find knowledge and integrity in someone who puts himself forward for the office of the imamate — such as when somebody who is ignorant of the pertinent ordinances or is dissolute seizes it by force — and dismissing him is likely to precipitate unendurable discord, our rule is that his imamate is recognized. In that way, we avoid putting ourselves in a position like that of somebody who destroys an entire town in order to build a single castle. If, out of necessity, we recognize that the decisions of rebels have effect in the lands they control, how, when faced with the prospect of universal disorder, can we not recognize the soundness of the imamate by decreeing that it has not come into being? If anyone seizes power from that tyrant, and takes his place, the one is dismissed and the other becomes imam.[119]

In *Commentary on Goals*, after discussing the qualifications required for holding the office of the imamate, the last of which is Qurayshi lineage, Sa'd al-Taftazani states:

> As for when there is no Qurayshi fit for office, or an imam cannot be appointed because those who are in error, unjust, and astray have seized power: in such cases there is no debate about legitimacy when it comes to the functions of the qadi, the implementation of ordinances, the execution of hudud laws, and all of the other functions that depend on the authority of an imam who is in power. The same point applies when there is an imam who is a Qurayshi but who is dissolute, unjust, or ignorant, to say nothing of the requirement that the imam must be a mujtahid. To summarize what we have said about the imamate: it rests upon free choice and agency. As for cases involving incapacity and constraint, or sinners, unbelievers, and the dissolute taking control, or strong tyrants imposing their will and dominating: in these cases worldly leadership becomes that of pure force. Religious ordinances depending on the imam rest upon that force as a matter of necessity. In such cases learning, integrity, and other qualifications required for holding office are lacking. The requirement that the imam must have those qualifications is not heeded. Here, necessity renders what is forbidden

permissible. Complaints about misfortunes are for God. Our hopes for the removal of what causes pain are with Him.[120]

The difference between this caliphate and the preceding one—aside from the fact that both are permissible in cases of necessity—is that the first caliphate comes about through the people who loose and bind selecting the most worthy candidate, when none of the candidates has all of the required qualifications. Thus, the scholar Taftazani makes it a duty to appoint a Qurayshi, as Quraysh are always numerous. He asserts that obeying him is obligatory, even if he is weak. As for the second caliphate, it is that of a usurper who seizes the caliphate using partisan force. He is not in power because he has been selected by the people who loose and bind and there is nobody better qualified than he is. Thus, the one caliph is obeyed out of choice, the other out of necessity.

This means that the rule of tyranny is like eating dead flesh or pork when that is necessary. It occurs under compulsion, and is permissible because it is less harmful than the alternative of chaos. It is required that the effort should be made to eliminate it whenever possible. It is impermissible to reconcile oneself to it as a perpetual state of affairs. Nor should people allow power to become like a ball that tyrants can kick back and forth between themselves, and receive from each other. Those living in nations who have been wronged allowed that to happen, assenting to that because they were ignorant of the power that was latent within themselves. They did not realize that the power wielded by their monarchs and emirs was actually their own. Have you not seen those among them who enlightened themselves by learning how human societies are organized: how they rose up to bring down their unjust governments and despotic monarchs? The most recent to do so was the Turkish people. But they overturned one kind of tyranny and replaced it with another kind of tyranny, hoping that it would be better. They did that for no other reason than to follow the example of those proud nations. That is because most of the ulama in Turkey, India, Egypt, and elsewhere had mandated that they obey the Ottoman caliph-sultans so long as it was clear that they were not unbelievers or apostates from Islam. They mandated such obedience regardless of how much that should lead to injustice, corruption, destruction of the land, and oppression of God's servants. In doing that they followed the principle adopted by the jurists, but did so without reasoned reflection or ijtihad. Taking this uninformed approach is the primary reason that many of them believe that the authority granted to the caliphate, as this is defined under the shari'ah, undermines rather than promotes the preservation

Muhammad Rashid Rida

of sovereignty and political independence. We will elaborate presently, and explain what would be necessary to remake government in a form that is shari'ah-based and Islamic.

(12) WHAT DISQUALIFIES THE CALIPH FROM THE IMAMATE

After explaining the imam's duties, as quoted above, Mawardi states:

> If the imam grants the members of the community their due rights, as we have discussed, he will have accomplished what is due to God Almighty regarding their rights and duties. He then has two rights in relation to them: that he be obeyed and supported, so long as he remains fit for office. Two changes in his state will disqualify him from the imamate. The first is that his integrity is impaired, the second a physical impairment. As for his integrity being impaired, there are two ways that this can happen. The first is that he becomes driven by lust. The second is that he holds a dubious opinion.[121] As for the first, it concerns actions: he commits sinful and forbidden acts, driven by his lust and subject to his passions. This is a moral deviation that would preclude him from taking up or continuing with the imamate. Thus, if this befalls someone who has already taken up the imamate, he is disqualified. If he regains his integrity, he cannot regain the imamate except by a new appointment.
>
> As for the second, it pertains to doctrine: his manner of interpretation being dubious and contrary to the truth. The ulama have differing opinions about this. One group maintains that it precludes him from taking up or continuing with the imamate, that it disqualifies him from office ... etc. (P. 16)[122]

After detailing the dispute on this issue—innovation in interpretation—he discusses the second category of what would preclude his taking up the caliphate, physical impairment. He discusses three categories: impairment of the senses, the organs, and the capacity to act freely. He also discusses other categories. He explicates the pertinent ordinances at length. What is at issue here requires quoting his comments on impairment of his capacity to act freely. He devotes a section specifically to this matter. He states:

> As for impairment of his capacity to act freely, there are two kinds: wardship [hajr] and coercion [qahr]. As for wardship, this occurs when one of his aides comes to dominate him, and autocratically takes charge of affairs, without outwardly appearing to sin, or commit an act of disobedience. This does not prevent him from continuing to hold the office of the imamate, nor does it diminish the legitimacy of his rule. But the actions of the one who has taken charge of his affairs should be investigated. If these are in accordance with

The Caliphate

93

the religion's ordinances and the requirements of justice, it is permissible for them to be endorsed and implemented, lest the religion's affairs be interrupted, and the community be corrupted. If, however, his actions run counter to the religion's ordinances and the requirements of justice, it is impermissible for them to be endorsed, and the imam must seek the assistance of others to overcome him and end his domination.

As for coercion, this occurs when the imam becomes the captive of an overpowering enemy force, and is unable to free himself. This precludes him from being appointed to the imamate. That is because he is incapable of conducting the Muslims' affairs, regardless of whether the enemy is a polytheist or a rebel Muslim. The community has the purview to choose someone other than him from among those who have the capacity to act. If he becomes captive after he has been appointed to the imamate, it is incumbent on the entire community to try to rescue him, because the rules for the office of the imamate make that a binding duty. He continues to hold office so long as there is hope of his release, either by force or by ransom. If there is no hope for him, consideration must be given to whether his captors are polytheists or rebel Muslims. If he is the captive of polytheists, he is disqualified from the imamate, and the electors should make the pledge of allegiance to someone else.[123]

Here, he discusses the issue of appointing someone else to the imamate, what is sound and unsound in relation to that. He then states:

If he is taken captive by rebel Muslims, and there is hope of his release, he retains the imamate. The designation of his next in line [*wali al-'ahd*] is endorsed, even if he should not become imam. If there is no hope of his release, the rebels will necessarily be in one of two situations: they appoint an imam for themselves or they do not. If there is chaos and they have no imam, the captive imam retains his imamate, since their pledge of allegiance to him is still binding, and their obedience to him is still obligatory. Thus, his status with them is the same as it is with those who are loyal [*ahl al-'adl*] when he has been placed under wardship. The electors must appoint someone to substitute for him, unless he is able to do so himself. If he is able, he has more right to do that than they do. If the captive renounces his office or dies, the one who had been appointed as his substitute does not become imam, as he was substituting for an imam who was still in office. Thus, that role ceases when that imam is no longer in office.

If the rebels have appointed their own imam, pledging their allegiance and obedience to him, the captive imam is disqualified from the imamate once any hope for his release is lost. That is because they have established an abode of independent rule in which they have abandoned obedience, effectively separating themselves from the main body of the Muslim community [*jama'ah*]. Thus, those who are loyal may no longer rely on them for assistance, and the captive imam no longer has any power. It is incumbent upon the electors in the abode of justice to appoint to the imamate the person they have agreed upon. If the captive imam is freed or escapes, he may not be reinstated to the imamate as he has been disqualified from it. (Pp. 19–20)[124]

It is a given that all of this detail concerns a rightful imam, one who has all requisite qualifications, and who discharges the obligatory duties. As for the imamate of tyranny, it proceeds entirely in accordance with the rule of necessity discussed above (Section 11).

What he says about an imam being deposed because he is dissolute is a matter of dispute. The established position, endorsed by the majority, is that it is impermissible to appoint someone who is dissolute. But if he becomes dissolute after being appointed that does not absolutely invalidate his imamate. Some elaborate on this point. In *Commentary on Goals*, Sa'd al-Taftazani states: "If an imam rules on the basis of coercion and tyranny and then somebody comes and subjugates him, he is deposed. The subjugator then becomes imam. It is impermissible to depose an imam (that is, a rightful imam) without cause. If he is deposed, the deposition is not to be enforced. If he deposes himself: if that is because he is unable to execute affairs, he is deposed, otherwise he is not. The imam is not deposed because he is dissolute or faints. But if he suffers from insanity, blindness, deafness, being mute, or an illness causing loss of memory, he is deposed."[125]

Those who hold that an imam is to be deposed for unbelief, but not for sinning, find support for that view in a hadith of 'Ubadah bin al-Samit on the pledge of allegiance. According to the two shaykhs [Bukhari and Muslim]:

> He said: "The Prophet, God's prayer and peace be upon him, called upon us and we pledged allegiance to him. Regarding what he had thereby received from us, he said that we had pledged to 'hear and obey' when alert and when tired, in ease and hardship, and to obey the ruler and grant him his rights, even if he did not grant us our rights, and not to fight against him 'unless you find in him clear unbelief, for which you have a proof from God.'"[126]

Commenting on the statement, "unless you find in him clear unbelief," Al-Hafiz [Ibn Hajar] mentions narrations in which the words "sin" [*ma'siyyah*] and "misdeed" [*ithm*] are used instead of the word "unbelief" [*kufr*]. He then states:

> In the narration of Isma'il bin 'Abd Allah, which is included in the works of Ahmad [Ibn Hanbal], Tabarani, and Hakim, narrating from Abu 'Ubadah:

The Caliphate

"After me, your affairs will be administered by men who will instruct you to do what you reject, and rebuke you over what you know to be right. No obedience, then, is due to those who disobey God." According to Abu Bakr ibn Abi Shaybah, from the transmission of Azhar bin 'Abd Allah, from 'Ubadah: "You will have emirs who command you to do what you do not recognize as right, and what you reject. You have, then, no obligation to obey them."[127]

Commenting on his statement, "for which you have a proof from God," he states:

That is to say: a qur'anic verse or a sound tradition that is not open to interpretation. This means that it is impermissible to rebel against them so long as their actions are open to interpretation.

Nawawi states: "What is meant by 'unbelief' here is 'sin.' What the hadith means is that you should not challenge those who hold power, contesting their right to rule and opposing them, except when you see them doing something that is definitively forbidden, something you are able to recognize as such on the basis of Islam's rules. If you see that, disavow them, and speak up for what is right, wherever you may be."

Other authorities state that what is meant by "misdeed" here is "sin" and "unbelief." Thus, the sovereign cannot be opposed unless he clearly falls into unbelief. It is evident that the narration referring to unbelief may be applied to the matter of contending: one may not contend with him in a manner that impeaches his right to rule except when he apostatizes. The narration referring to sin concerns matters other than rule. Thus, if his right to rule is not challenged, one may still contend with him when it comes to his sins. That can be done by condemning him in a gentle way, to the point where one shows him what is right, but does not resort to violence. If one is able to do so, that is the appropriate course of action. And God knows best. Ibn al-Tin reported from Dawidi that he said: "The ulama hold that when it is possible to depose an unjust emir without causing discord or oppression that is obligatory. Otherwise, patient endurance is obligatory. Certain ulama regard appointing someone who is already dissolute as impermissible. As for the case of an emir who had ruled justly then turns and becomes unjust [*jawr*], they disagree on whether that constitutes grounds for rebellion. The sound opinion is that this is prohibited, except when he apostatizes, in which case rebelling against him is obligatory."[128]

Explanations of this issue and the works of those who have investigated it have been given above. To summarize: it is incumbent upon those who loose and bind to struggle against oppression and injustice and, through their actions,

96 Muhammad Rashid Rida

to reject those who embody that, eliminating the power that they unjustly wield. This is even to be done by fighting, when it is clear to them that the benefit outweighs the harm. An example of this is eliminating the personal, autocratic form of authority, as in the Turks' elimination of the Ottoman dynasty's authority. Those belonging to this dynasty were unjust, even though they laid claim to the Islamic caliphate. In most of their ordinances they followed a path that in this era people refer to as that of "absolute monarchy." Therefore, the Turks began to constrain them through a constitution [al-qanun al-asasi] that was based on the laws of European nations. The reason for that is that those who effected that, such as Midhat Pasha and his partisans, were ignorant of the Islamic revealed law's ordinances.[129] Thereafter, the Kemalists definitively brought down this state, and rejected the notion of personal authority in all of its forms and aspects.

(13) THE ABODE OF JUSTICE AND THE ABODE OF INJUSTICE AND TYRANNY

The concept of the abode of Islam and what stands opposed to it, the abode of war, is well known. There are many ordinances pertaining to both. We have often referred to the abode of justice when relating what the ulama have said about the caliphate's ordinances, and this is the abode of Islam, whose imam is rightfully appointed and properly establishes the scales of justice. It is referred to as such when another abode stands opposed to it: the abode of rebellion [baghy] and injustice [jawr], the abode of rule through pure force (tyranny), the abode of those whose power rests solely on the support of their own partisan group and in which shari'ah ordinances and stipulations on the imamate are not observed. Those who reside in the abode of justice are referred to as the jama'ah: the main body of the Muslim community. All Muslims are obligated to follow them and their imam, the imam they have chosen. They are not permitted to follow those who oppose the jama'ah, except out of necessity. These two abodes may exist simultaneously, or one may exist without the other. There are ordinances pertaining to each.

As for the abode of justice: in this abode it is obligatory under the shari'ah to obey the imam in what is right, outwardly and inwardly. It is impermissible to disobey him, except when he gives a command that involves sinning against God Almighty. Its characterization as sinful must be explicitly affirmed by a prescription in the Book or the sunnah [the Qur'an or the hadith]. It cannot be dependent on ijtihad, or the opinion of a scholar. It is obligatory to fight Muslims who rebel against the imam, or who use force to spread oppression and corruption in his lands. The obligation to fight here is the same as it is for

The Caliphate

97

other kinds of fighting that are obligatory under the shari'ah. Anyone residing in the abode of war and the abode of rebellion who has been wronged—for instance, by being oppressed or prevented from practicing his religion—is obligated to migrate to the abode of justice. The same duty to migrate applies to those who are needed in the abode of justice to safeguard it, and protect it from unbelievers and oppressors. The same duty also applies when it comes to maintaining public welfare, where fortifying the religious community [*millah*] depends upon migration. As for the abode of rebellion and injustice, in this abode obedience is not, in itself, an obligatory act of piety under the shari'ah. Rather, this is a matter where the rule of necessity applies—necessity determined according to the extent of the need—as elaborated above.

One kind of oppression that would make it obligatory for those who are able to do so to migrate from the abode of rebellion and injustice to the abode of justice, if it exists, is when tyrants compel their subjects to fight so that they can expand their own partisan realm, and install governors in Muslim lands. It is then obligatory for those capable of migrating to do so. What is commanded always hinges on the rule of pursuing the lesser of two harms. Clearly, there is a distinction between cases in which tyrants fight people who are just—in such cases it is impermissible to obey them under any circumstances—and cases in which they fight against others like themselves, such as other tyrants who rule purely on the basis of force. There is considerable detail to be elaborated on this matter, but there is no space for that here. As for jihad, under the shari'ah this is an obligatory duty even for those who are subjects of unjust imams. For instance, jihad is obligatory in defense of such imams when they are attacked by unbelievers.

> The Messenger of God, God's prayer and peace be upon him, said: "Whoever renounces his obedience separates himself from the *jama'ah*, the main body of the Muslim community, and dies in that state: his death is that of the days of pre-Islamic ignorance. Whoever fights under the banner of a people who are blind [to their cause] is bloated with pride for kin, or calls on people to fight for kin, or supports his kin, and is killed: his death is that of the days of pre-Islamic ignorance. Whoever attacks my community, fighting its righteous and its wicked, not sparing the faithful, and not fulfilling the obligation to those who have been given a pledge of security: I have nothing to do with him and he has nothing to do with me."

> In a different narration: ". . . who is bloated with pride for his kin, and fights for his kin, does not belong to my community"—a hadith of Abu Hurayrah related by Muslim and Nasa'i.[130]

Muhammad Rashid Rida

The word *'ummiyyah*, which means "blind," has two pronunciations. It may be pronounced with a "u" on the letter *'ayn*: *'ummiyyah*. Or, it may have an "i" on the letter *'ayn*: *'immiyyah*. The letter *mim*, "m," is doubled. Authorities have understood it to refer to being bloated with pride and going astray. It connotes extreme force, violence, and tyranny, where people are motivated to fight by something other than a desire to establish what is right. For that reason the Messenger explained it as being bloated with pride for one's kin. This happens when a man's people are roused: they band with him, and he teams up with them. With that, a man becomes more vehement and severe. In a different narration the word used is *'asabiyyah* [partisanship for one's kin], which is cognate to the word *'asabah* [kin].

You know now that what enabled—and enables—tyrants to rule is nothing but the partisan support of their own kin. Tyrants are motivated purely by a desire for power. Their aim in fighting is not to glorify God's word, nor is it to establish the scales of truth and justice for all people. This community has had its affairs corrupted and its power stripped by nothing other than:

- people assuming that obedience to unjust and violent rulers is an absolute obligation under the shari'ah;[131]
- people assuming that the rule of tyranny is lawful under the shari'ah;
- people assuming that the rule of a tyrant has the same legal validity as the rule of a rightful imam, an imam whose rule rests on a pledge of allegiance given by those in authority and those who loose and bind who elected him;
- every unjust tyrant restricting authority and power and might to his own family by asserting that the right to appoint his son, or someone else among his kin, is his entitlement under the shari'ah, and a principle to be observed in and of itself;
- the failure to see how Mu'awiyah's designation of his son Yazid as his successor differed from Abu Bakr the Most Truthful's designation of 'Umar bin al-Khattab. Yazid was a dissolute wrongdoer, and Mu'awiyah's designation of him was rejected by the Muslims. 'Umar, the just imam, was a man of great virtue. Abu Bakr consulted with the people who loose and bind, persuading them and receiving their consent before designating him.

(14) HOW TYRANNY CAME TO BE ESTABLISHED UNDER THE CALIPHATE

The reason that the Umayyad dynasty prevailed over those in the community who loose and bind is that during the era of its rule the power of the great Islamic community was diffused throughout the lands that the Muslims had

The Caliphate

99

conquered, and throughout which Islam had spread with remarkable speed. Those lands are Egypt, Syria, and Iraq. Those residing there had been raised generation after generation under the subjugation of their colonial rulers, the Romans and the Persians. Thus, when control of their affairs fell into the hands of rulers who were Arabs like them, Mu'awiyah, the one who established the evil practice of tyranny in Islam, was able to take advantage of that history to incline them to yield to his authority. He did so by selecting people among them who would support him, and appointing them as governors. These appointees preferred the acquisition of wealth and prestige to following Islam's guidance, and applying its principles of justice and egalitarianism. Most of those qualified under the shari'ah to loose and bind resided in the two noble towns, Mecca and Medina, and they were in a weak position when compared to the people of those great and affluent lands, which supported and fed the Hijaz.

Mu'awiyah used coercion and bribery to obtain pledges of allegiance to his dissolute son Yazid. The only place where he met any noteworthy resistance was the Hijaz. Bukhari, Nasa'i, and Ibn Abi Hatim relate a report with different chains of transmission in which Marwan, Mu'awiyah's governor of Hijaz, makes a declaration in Medina.[132] In his Qur'an commentary Ibn Abi Hatim relates: "Marwan said, 'In his son Yazid, God has shown the Commander of the Faithful a good decision. If he appoints him as his successor, Abu Bakr and 'Umar have previously been appointed as successors.'[133] 'Abd al-Rahman bin Abi Bakr responded: 'This is the sunnah of Heraclius and Caesar. By God, Abu Bakr did not hand it to one of his sons, etc.'" A different version of the report makes reference to the sunnah of Abu Bakr and 'Umar. In another version the wording is: "This is the sunnah of Khosrau (Chosroes) and Caesar.[134] Abu Bakr and 'Umar did not hand it to their sons."

Mu'awiyah then made the hajj to lay the ground for the pledge of allegiance being made to Yazid in the Hijaz. He spoke with the leading figures among those who loose and bind, the sons of Abu Bakr, 'Umar, and Zubayr. They resisted his plan. They threatened him with consequences, should he not determine the matter of succession by consulting with the Muslims. But he ascended the pulpit, and claimed that the Muslims had heard, obeyed, and pledged allegiance to Yazid. He threatened with death anyone who denied the truth of what he had said. Tabarani reports from Muhammad bin Sa'id bin Zamanah that as death was taking him Mu'awiyah said to Yazid: "I have prepared the lands and people for you. I hold no fears for you from anyone except for the people of the Hijaz. If you suspect anything of them, send Muslim bin 'Uqbah to them, because I have experience with him, and approve of his counsel." He states: "So when they then opposed Yazid as they did, he called on and dispatched Muslim bin 'Uqbah, and he fought them for three days. He called upon them to make the pledge of allegiance to Yazid and to unquestioningly obey all of his orders." Abu Bakr bin Khaythamah relates a report with a sound chain of transmission going back to Juwayriyyah bint Asma': "I heard the shaykhs of Medina saying that as Mu'awiyah was dying he called Yazid and said to him, 'You will have a day with the people of Medina. If they move, send Muslim bin 'Uqbah against them, because I approve of his counsel, etc.'" Al-Hafiz [Ibn Hajar] cites this report in *Al-Fath*.[135] The enemy of God fought the Messenger's city for three days. Thus, he was deserving, he and his army, of the universal curse in the statement of the Prophet, God's prayer and peace be upon him, which he made when giving Medina the same sanctification as Mecca: "Anyone who causes trouble in it, or supports anyone who causes trouble: the curse of God, the angels, and all people is upon him. On the day of resurrection God will accept neither repentance nor ransom [*la . . . sarfan wa la 'adlan*] from him." That is to say: neither obligatory nor supererogatory deeds. This hadith has been firmly agreed upon. How forcefully would it apply to someone who seeks to appropriate the city's blood, honor, and wealth??

Hasan al-Basri states: "The people's affairs were corrupted by two people: 'Amr bin al-'As on the day that he advised Mu'awiyah to hold up copies of the Qur'an" (he discusses how the arbitration was corrupt) "and Mughirah bin Shu'bah" (he discusses the story of Mu'awiyah dismissing him from the governorate of Kufah, and then bribing him, making it easy for him to acknowledge Yazid as his designated successor by reappointing him). Hasan states: "For this reason, Muslims have pledged allegiance to these people's sons. Had it not been for that, the principle of determining matters through consultation would have been applied until the day of resurrection." From *History of the Caliphs* [*Tarikh al-Khulafa'*], abridged.[136]

This statement by Hasan al-Basri, one of the Successors' imams, harmonizes with what that German politician said to one of the Hijazi nobles: "If not for Mu'awiyah Islam's government would have continued to operate in accordance with Islam's fundamental principles, and Islam would have spread over all of Europe," referred to above.

People who are governed by their passions have been confused about this. This is also so for people whose knowledge of Islam—its true nature and how it evolved—is limited to what one finds in the reports of historians. These are of uneven reliability. Only the *huffaz*, the eminent scholars of hadith, have been able to discern which are sound and which are weak, which are true and which are false.[137] Thus, we find that among such people there are some who are

The Caliphate

favorably disposed to the Nasibis or the Kharijis, and there are some who side with the extremist Shi'ah.[138] Our master Shaykh Husayn al-Jisr used to recite:

Whoever reads history without	holding fast to sound doctrine
Becomes a Shi'i; else say	he deviates from the straight path
	of right guidance.

For this reason, we find Egyptians and other Muslims affiliated with the Sunni schools [madhhabs]—despite their common people going to extremes in glorifying the House of the Prophet—who are Nasibis, who prefer the Umayyads to the 'Alids, and claim that they invigorated Islam and properly applied the religion. The fact of the matter is that Islam's conquest of many lands during their era, which was their greatest achievement, was required by the very nature of Islam, and by the reform that it brought to rescue mankind. None of them performed any unique act in properly applying the religion, except for 'Umar bin 'Abd al-'Aziz. In that regard they did not perform any act that was distinctive to their empire, so that one might say: had it not been for them, Islam would have regressed in knowledge, practice, or conquests. Their good deeds in these matters were also performed by those who came after them and who were like them, the 'Abbasids. Both were followers, not followed: in matters of religion they followed rightly guided caliphs. As for matters of civil affairs following the Islamic conquests, both dynasties performed some actions. The Umayyad's only unforgivable sin is what they enacted when it came to the principle upon which Islamic government is based. That principle was originally elective, meaning that government rested upon electors consulting one another. These electors were those who loose and bind and who were in a position to make their choice freely. The Umayyads replaced that elective principle with a materialistic one, meaning that what is powerful prevails over what is rightful. Thus, they are the ones who destroyed that principle and they were followed in that by those who came after them.

Anyone who is familiar with the prophetic tradition—works on the sunnah—knows that God Almighty informed His Messenger about his community's future, and that what transpired resulted from human nature and accorded with God's decree and His way. Some of the Messenger's Companions spoke of this, sometimes intimating, sometimes speaking plainly. Among them is Abu Hurayrah, who narrated a number of hadiths and reports on this matter that are included in sihah, sunan, and masanid works.[139] He related that he sought refuge in God from the rule of young boys and from the commencement of the year 60 [A.H.], the year in which Yazid was appointed (he died before that). He used to say: "If I say to you that you will burn the house of your Lord, and kill the son of your Prophet, you will say, 'Nobody is a greater liar than Abu Hurayrah.'" He was referring to the death of Husayn, which indeed occurred after his lifetime. Bukhari and others relate the following from 'Umar bin Yahya bin Sa'id bin 'Amr bin Sa'id bin al-'As the Umayyad:

> He said:
>
> "My grandfather said to me: 'I was sitting with Abu Hurayrah in the Prophet's mosque, God's prayer and peace be upon him, and Marwan (bin al-Hakam bin Abi al-'As, Mu'awiyah's governor in Medina) was with us.[140] Abu Hurayrah said, "I heard, the trustworthy one, the one who is to be believed [the Prophet], God's prayer and peace be upon him, saying, 'The annihilation of my community will occur at the hands of youth of Quraysh.'" Marwan said, "God's curse be upon them, the youth." Abu Hurayrah said, "If you wish that I say 'the sons of so-and-so and the sons of so-and-so,' I can do it."' I used to go out with my grandfather to [the lands of] Marwan's sons when they were ruling Syria. When he saw youth belonging to that family he said to us, 'Perhaps they are among them.' We said, 'You know best.'"[141]

They ruined the community through nothing but corrupting its government so that it no longer conformed to the shari'ah, or served to reform human society. Had they not corrupted it in that way they would have been unable to seize control of it with partisan forces.

Commenting on this hadith, Al-Hafiz [Ibn Hajar] states:

> Ibn Battal states: This hadith is a proof for the opinion given previously: one should not rebel, even when a sultan is unjust. That is because he, God's prayer and peace be upon him, informed Abu Hurayrah of the names of those people. But he did not command him to rebel against them, even though he informed him that the community would be ruined at their hands. But rebellion leads to an even greater ruination. Annihilation is more likely to result from rebellion than from obedience. Thus, he chose the lesser of the two corruptions, the easier of the two options.[142]

We say: the rule cited is sound. But the manner in which it is applied is unsound. The people of the Hijaz resisted and were overcome. The sound explanation of what occurred is the one that we have given previously: those Muslims who were learned and just — the people who make up the body known in Islam as the *jama'ah* — were dispersed throughout the lands, and those remaining in the Hijaz were weak relative to the new Islamic state's strength. For that reason, the only viable kind of rebellion was a partisan rebellion, one enabled by people rallying in support of their own kin in the manner of the Umayyads and the 'Abbasids. Most of the ulama applied the rule as they did

The Caliphate

because they were subservient to the Umayyads and 'Abbasids. By doing that, they effectively smoothed the path to oppression and injustice. The facts of this matter have been given multiple times. ·

Al-Hafiz [Ibn Hajar] then states: "It is odd that Marwan cursed the youth who are mentioned, when it is apparent that they include his offspring. It is as if God Almighty made that statement issue from his tongue to make it a stronger proof, so that they might take heed. Hadiths are related on Marwan's father, Hakam, and his sons being cursed. These are reported by Tabarani and others. The validity of most of them is subject to contention, while some are excellent. Perhaps the intention is to single out the youth who are mentioned."[143] The comment about "his offspring" applies to all of them. Yet it is to be emphasized that when Abu Hurayrah referred to the youth, the first person he had in mind was Yazid bin Mu'awiyah.

To summarize: our intention in this investigation has been to explicate:

- how the Islamic caliphate was diverted from the course that Islam set down for it;
- how it became an institution that fell under the control of partisan groups or those who ruled through tyranny;
- how the corruption of the caliphate led to other corruptions and calamities that have afflicted Muslims in their religion and in their worldly lives.

We have made our points repeatedly so that they may be committed to memory and not forgotten.

One of the most remarkable developments is that Muslims have fallen behind those in other religious communities [*milal*] that they had previously surpassed in learning and in practice. Yet not one of them has undertaken any action to restore Islam's government to its original state. Rather, Muslims have reconciled themselves to factionalism and division, and to the unjust and disparaging actions of anyone who seized control of one of their lands. They adopted that posture to such an extent that they then found it easy to reconcile themselves to receiving the same kind of treatment from non-Muslims. They were like those we have described in these lines:

> Whoever is led by the whip of injustice
> easily accepts injustice, wherever it is found
> whoever is weak cares little for his people,
> his property, and his religion, whose weakness he accepts

Has the news of the papacy's actions not come to them, of how it organized the religious societies and accumulated riches in order to restore its religious authority? Yet we imitate others only in what is harmful. We do not imitate others or act independently in pursuit of what is beneficial. The Islamic caliphate has essentially been eliminated, and only remnants remain. Yet there are still Muslims among us who are striving to eliminate even those remnants! They imagine that allowing the caliphate to endure in any form weakens the Muslims. But the opposite is the case: eliminating the caliphate is what has weakened the Muslims. Where we do still invoke it we do so to support autocrats. That is a falsehood, one that slanders Islam and the Muslims. Had we held fast to the caliphate's firm bond, we would have become masters of the world. This is acknowledged by many foreign scholars, but not by any of our own political leaders.

(15) SINGLE AND MULTIPLE CALIPHS

A fundamental principle of the revealed law is that the head of government, the imam, is one person. This notion is a point of consensus in all communities, as it is for Muslims. The reason is well known: business of government takes priority over all other business. It has multiple branches, and this requires pursuing a single line so as to maintain order and prevent anarchy. The two Kamals, the author of *Al-Musayarah* and the author of the commentary upon it, state:[144] "More than one person may not be appointed" to the imamate. This is seen in the statement of the Prophet, God's prayer and peace be upon him, "If the pledge of allegiance is made to two caliphs, kill the second of the two." Related by Muslim, a hadith of Abu Sa'id al-Khudri. As the ulama have clearly explained, the command to kill is to be understood as applying when killing him is the only way to repel him. If he persists in his claim, he is a rebel. If the only way to repel him is to kill him, he is to be killed.[145] The rationale for prohibiting multiple imams is that it would undermine the imamate's purpose: unifying Islam's people and preventing discord. Having more than one imam would entail putting people in the situation of having to obey contradictory ordinances.

> Al-Hujjah—Hujjat al-Islam al-Ghazali [The Proof of Islam Ghazali]—states: "If more than one person described as having these required qualifications is nominated, the imam is the one to whom the majority's pledge of allegiance has been made. The opponent is a rebel. It is a duty to bring him to yield to what is right." The discourses of other Sunni Muslims are only concerned with who has precedence. The duty is then to bring the one who is second to yield.[146]

The Caliphate

The prescription that the majority follows is the one stipulated in the hadith.

Mawardi states (p. 7.): "If two imams are appointed to the imamate in two lands, the imamate of neither is valid, because it is impermissible for the community to have two imams at one time, even if there are people who would allow that. Their views are exceptional."[147] I say: those who permitted that only permitted it in cases where unity is impossible. The dispute on this matter is what 'Adud is referring to in *Book of Stations* when he states: "It is impermissible to appoint two imams in a narrow region. As for lands that are extensive, such that it is not possible for one imam to manage it, that is a contingency to be resolved by ijtihad." His commentator, Sayyid al-Jurjani, adds, "that is because this issue is a matter of dispute." Permissibility is supported by the gloss of Fanari, one of the famous ulama of the Byzantines or the Turks.[148] As for cases where unity is possible, we do not know of anyone among the ulama whose knowledge is worthy who deems multiple imams permissible. The opinion of those who permit multiple imams in cases of necessity—when both of the imams, or more than two, have all requisite qualifications and establish justice—is stronger than the opinion of the majority who permit the imamate of a tyrant in cases of necessity. If the one entails division, it is without hostility and enmity. The other entails iniquity and oppression and might corrupt the religion and worldly life together, and that, in fact, is indeed what happened.

Sayyid Siddiq Hasan Khan Bahadur endorses and elaborates this opinion at the end of his book *Al-Rawdah al-Nadiyyah*.[149] He states:

> If the Islamic imamate is conferred upon one person, and all matters are referred to and tied to him, as was the case during the days of the Companions, Successors, and those who succeeded them, then the revealed law's rule for a second imam, who comes after the confirmation of the first, is that he is to be killed unless he repents and gives up his claim. As for when the pledge of allegiance is simultaneously made to each, and each has his own group of supporters, in such case neither has precedence over the other. Rather, it is incumbent on the people who loose and bind to assist both, until command is handed to one of them. If the two persist in disagreeing, it is incumbent upon the people who loose and bind to select the one who will deliver the greater benefit to the Muslims. The means for determining who deserves priority are not unknown to the people qualified to do that.
>
> As for after Islam had spread out, its terrain expanded and its borders extended, it is known that in each land, or in each of the lands,[150] governance was transferred to an imam or a sultan. For some, their commands and prohibitions had no effect outside of the land or lands under their jurisdiction. Thus, having multiple imams and sultans is acceptable. It is obligatory that

each be obeyed, following the pledge of allegiance, by the people of the land in which his commands and prohibitions have effect. The same point applies to those who have command in other lands. If someone should then rise up and contend with him in the land in which he has been firmly established as ruler, and whose people have pledged allegiance to him, the applicable ordinance is that the contender is to be killed, should he not repent.

People in other lands are not obligated to obey him, nor are they his subjects, because of the distances separating lands. Information about the imam or sultan may not reach distant lands. It may not be known who has been appointed or who has died. In such cases, commanding obedience is commanding what is untenable. This is known to anyone who is acquainted with the circumstances of people and the lands in which they live. The people of China and India do not know who governs the land of Morocco, let alone are they able to obey him, and vice versa. Likewise, the people of Transoxiana do not know who governs Yemen, and vice versa. Be aware of this, as it corresponds with the principles of the shari'ah, and conforms with what the prescriptions stipulate. Set aside whatever is said contradicting it, because the difference between Islamic governance as it was at the beginning of Islam and what it is now is clearer than the daytime sun. Whoever denies that is stupefied and does not deserve to be addressed with proofs, as he is incapable of comprehending them. And God is the Helper.[151]

This is the best-founded elaboration on the permissibility of multiple imams in cases of necessity. It is a distinguished ijtihad. According to some, the issue of multiplicity here is similar to that of multiple Friday prayers being made in one town. A fundamental principle of the revealed law is that all of the people residing in a town gather in a single mosque, as the lawgiver gave a clear rationale for gathering together. If prayers are made more than once the prayer of the one who prays first is valid, while the prayer of the one who prays later is not. When it is known that the prayer has been performed in a mosque, it is impermissible that it be performed a second time in that mosque, or in another mosque in that town. The prayer of those who perform it will be invalid and they will be in sin, their duty of performing the midday prayer unfulfilled. Yet those who were most strict in prohibiting prayers being made more than once out of choice permitted it when that was deemed appropriate due to necessity.

The sense conveyed by the discourses of the majority loosens the prohibition on having more than one rightful imam. It excuses Muslims who are unable to follow the main body [jama'ah] of the Muslims' community and their imam in the abode of justice due to problems created by great distances and impracticalities of communication. They are permitted to form a government unique

The Caliphate

to their land. The ruling that applies here is the same as the ruling applying to those who converted to Islam but were unable to migrate to the abode of Islam to support the imam. Their abode is not equal to the abode of justice and the imamate's main community, which properly applied the revealed law before them. Rather, it is incumbent upon them to avail themselves of all means to join and unify with it. They should do that even by drawing on its power in support of their own actions. They must support its imam and the main body of the community by fighting those who fight them whenever possible. Similarly, it is incumbent upon the main body of the community to support them when they are attacked. If it is true that their case is like that of those who did not migrate to the abode of Islam, then the ruling on assisting them is found in the Almighty's statement: "As for those who believed but did not emigrate, you are not responsible for their protection until they have emigrated. But if they seek help from you in the matter of religion, it is your duty to assist them, except against people with whom you have a treaty" [Qur'an 8:72].[152] According to the adopted view, this verse concerns political jurisdiction generally. It is not limited to jurisdiction over the inheritance of estates.[153]

To summarize: The majority of Muslims agree that it is impermissible for the Islamic imamate to be multiple. Accordingly, an Islamic government that arises out of necessity, and which is excused for not adhering to the main body of the Muslim community, is a government of necessity. It is to be regarded as provisional. Its ordinances are implemented, but it is not equivalent to the principal imamate, even if it fulfills the requirements of the imamate as it does. According to another opinion, which is regarded as exceptional, if it fulfills the requirements it is a sound imamate. That would be genuine multiplicity. But no two people disagreed on the point that it exists out of necessity: if the necessity is eliminated, unification becomes obligatory. There are numerous ordinances on these issues, but there is no space to investigate them here.

However, it is important to investigate how firmly the necessity has been established. This is because great distances between lands and the infeasibility of the communications upon which the implementation of ordinances depends are among the things that differ across time and place. It is unsound for there to be a perpetual excuse for a rift in Islam's unity. In this era of ours, the time is approaching when what is related in certain hadiths about events hidden in the innermost recesses of the unseen will be realized. Distant lands have been connected with each other across land and sea by ships and railways, and thereafter by air transportation (planes and dirigibles), which transport mail and people across distances of hundreds or thousands of miles in one or more hours. This is to say nothing of electronic transmission of news from one end of the earth to the other in a matter of minutes. Had these means been available during the era of our ancestors, they would have gained mastery over the entire world. This is what some nations aspire to today, the peoples of northern Europe, who have dominated most of the peoples of the South and the East. Between the two is the greatest gap in civilizational development on earth.

But Muslims have fallen short in regard to these means. Some of their lands are entirely bereft of them, while in others they depend on Europeans for them. This is in spite of the fact that there are many reasons why acquiring them is a religious duty under their revealed law. The most important reason is that the performance of many duties and obligations depends upon them, or cannot be completed without them. Take, for instance, the duty to maintain and defend sovereignty, and prepare against the Muslims' enemies as much force as is possible, as our Book [the Qur'an] commands us to do. Their seizure of most of our lands has imposed this duty on us individually. For men and women, the individual duty comes into effect when an enemy seizes a small village. This is to say nothing of the indispensability of ensuring that power is unified by submission to one imam who can establish what is right and just for us, implementing our revealed laws' ordinances.

Coming before the duty of unifying under a single imam are numerous others that Muslims neglected. They did so because they acceded to ordinances that legitimized the rule of tyranny and squandered most of the reforms having to do with government — its form, characteristics, and so forth — that Islam brought to mankind. Which of these duties do they need to fulfill so that they may then seek to undertake that duty?

(16) UNITY OF THE IMAMATE THROUGH UNITY OF THE MUSLIM COMMUNITY [UMMAH]

Unity of the imamate follows from unity of the community. Islam united the Islamic peoples through faith in one Lord, one God, one Book [the Qur'an], submission to the rule of one revealed law, and through the religion, rules of conduct, and other things having been received in one language. That unity was subsequently torn apart by people affiliating themselves with the schools of law [madhhabs] in a partisan manner, and then by the way that people identified with others who belonged to their own ethnic group. How, then, can the Muslims have a single imam today when they are not a single community?

I do not say that this, in itself, is an impossibility. I say only that I do not know of any Muslim people or group that treats this matter with the seriousness that it requires, and pursues a viable path to it. That is because the Muslims are at their very lowest. They are ignorant, unmotivated, and factionalized by

The Caliphate   109

their affiliations to the schools of law and their ethnic prejudices. They lack resolve. This paralyzes them, preventing them from attaining Islam's high ideal of religious and social perfection. Using military force to compel Islamic lands with independent governments to submit to a single head is something that cannot be achieved in this era. There is also no way to convince these lands' governments to adhere to one among them, to do that readily and as a matter of free choice.

The independent governments today are those of Turkey, Persia, Afghanistan, Najd, and Upper Yemen—the highlands and their surroundings—Lower [southern] Yemen, and the Hijaz. Some Islamic lands under tsarist Russia, such as Bukhara and Khiva [Uzbekistan], have obtained their independence. But their independence is not yet firmly established, although it is acknowledged by the Turkey–Afghanistan Treaty.[154] The same applies to Azerbaijan, and to a lesser degree to Kurdistan. The Turkish state proclaims that it will dominate these smaller governments and incorporate them in its Turanian union, and will likewise incorporate the Islamic peoples of the Caucasus region.[155] None of these governments is able to lay claim to the religious caliphate. Hence, our discourse concerns the Arab governments and the three non-Arab states.

As for the people of Upper Yemen, they believe:

- that the sound imamate, as defined under the shari'ah, has been restricted to them for 1,000 years or more;
- that it is sound because their imams are selected through a shari'ah-based process that makes provision for all required legal qualifications stipulated by Sunni Muslims, while it also complies with the stipulations of their Zaydi school [madhhab];
- that complying with Zaydi teaching does not entail violating the teachings of the Sunni schools;
- that they rule in accordance with the revealed law and enforce the hudud laws;
- that when it comes to the specific provisions of the law, their school is that of the way of the Prophet, and is rarely in conflict with the four Sunni schools, especially the Hanafi madhhab.

Thus, there is no way to convince them to follow others. The Turks fought them for a number of centuries, but were unable to eliminate their imamate. But their Arab neighbors, like other Muslims, do not recognize their imamate or call people to it, and they do not wish to see its authority universalized. Its soundness was recognized by the most eminent of the learned hadith scholars, the chief qadi of Egypt, and leading shaykh of his era at Al-Azhar, Al-Hafiz Ahmad Ibn Hajar al-'Asqalani. He did so when commenting on the following hadith in Bukhari's *Sound Collection:* "Quraysh have command, so long as two of them remain."[156]

As for Sayyid al-Idrisi, although he is an independent ruler, an 'Alid lord, an Azhari jurist, and a Sufi guide, he did not, as far as we know, lay claim to the office of the caliphate.[157] He did not call upon his emirate's leaders to make the pledge of allegiance to him. Yet his family and his community believed that he had a more rightful claim to it than did the sharifs of the Hijaz, and they gave him the title "The Sayyid, The Imam." Some of them gave him the title "His Hashimi Majesty." Some trustworthy people have reported to us that King Husayn tried to incline him to acknowledge dependence on the Hijaz in matters of foreign policy, if only nominally.[158] But he was unsuccessful, as he was unsuccessful in his effort to convince Imam Yahya to do that.[159] Both found this effort strange. It has been related to us that in matters of foreign affairs affecting his lands Sayyid al-Idrisi's preference was to recognize the Turks' political supremacy, so as to escape European conspiracies and strengthen Islamic ties.

As for the government of the Hijaz, it is new, and it is not thought to be organized well. The king of the Hijaz embodies the government in all respects. The people of Mecca pledged allegiance to him as king of the Arabs. Moreover, others in Syria and elsewhere pledged allegiance to him as caliph and emir of the faithful, at the time when his son Faysal was in Syria before the announcement of independence in Damascus. In that respect they resemble others in Syria and Egypt who have pledged allegiance to the new caliph in Constantinople. It is clear that his sons, King Faysal of Iraq and Emir 'Abd Allah of Transjordan, are resolved to bring all of their influence to bear to see him installed as caliph and, when the opportunity presents itself, receive the pledge of allegiance to him from Syria and Iraq.[160] In *Al-Qiblah* newspaper, articles have been published, recent and old, that delegitimize the Turkish caliphs' caliphate in Constantinople, excommunicating them along with their government.[161] There was a dilapidated mosque in 'Amman, and the emir, 'Abd Allah, had it renovated. His qadi, Shaykh Sa'id al-Karmi, memorialized its renovation in lines inscribed on a marble plaque set above its door.[162] In the first lines, he states:

> Husayn bin 'Awn built up the glory of 'Adnan[163]
> he became Commander of the Faithful with no equal
> God has returned to him the right to the caliphate
> which had long been prey to the Ottomans

This qadi made Husayn's construction, which he named "The Glory of 'Adnan," a reason for his becoming "Commander of the Faithful" with no equal

The Caliphate

in Islam's lands. Yet he did not build up the glory of 'Adnan. Neither does the glory of 'Adnan entitle one to the caliphate. The poet said that for no other reason than to please his emir, who was and is still striving to make his father caliph. But he did not only slander the caliphate of his enemies, the Turks. He slandered the imamate of Yahya Hamid al-Din, whose friendship his emir and the father of his emir, the king, had tried to win. And nobody could compare Imam Yahya to any of the sharifs of the Hijaz and others who resemble them in deeming themselves qualified for the imamate solely on the basis of their lineages. In addition to having an unbroken Hashimi 'Alid lineage, and being unambiguously free of suspicion of having committed acts of enslavement contrary to the shari'ah, Imam Yahya was chosen because he was an 'alim, a mujtahid, a man of courage, a statesman having the valor and vigor with which he preserved his lands' independence. The pledge of allegiance has been made to his imamate for scores of years. Those who recognize his imamate number more than the residents of the Hijaz, and moreover more than all of the people of Syria, and also of Iraq.

Our purpose here is not to discuss the claims and intentions of these people, or those of others. Rather, it is to explicate the reality facing the independent Islamic lands. This is that the king of the Hijaz and his sons believe that they are entitled to the caliphate on the basis of their lineage and social standing in the Hijaz. They believe that with the assistance of the British state they will be able to lay claim to it successfully. One of them, Emir 'Abd Allah of Transjordan, stated in Alexandria, "The caliphate is ours." The Egyptian newspapers reported his statement, and in some of them it was rebutted.

As for the people of Najd, they are Hanbalis and Salafis. They call their emir "imam," not "caliph." I have not heard that he lays claim to the universal caliphate. But they believe that he is the only Muslim emir who has properly applied God's religion as He revealed it. They believe that their lands constitute the abode of justice and the *jama'ah*—the main body of the Muslim community—and that migration to it is obligatory in keeping with the legal stipulations on that. Thus, there is no expectation that they would follow others in this matter. They have been accused of creating a new school [madhhab] for themselves, alienating others. But they do not care about what is said about them. They do not call upon anyone to follow them, except for the neighboring Bedouin, who know nothing of Islamic doctrine or practice. Thus, they call on them to take up the religion, relinquish Bedouinism, and recognize their Islamic government. They claim that their government properly applies God's revealed law and executes its hudud laws in accordance with the school of Ahmad bin Hanbal, the imam of the sunnah.

This summarizes what we know about conditions in the independent Arab lands. We omitted a discussion of Oman's Ibadi government, as the influence of the English over it is extensive. Its people are unable to find a way to build relationships with others. Most of them follow the Ibadi school. Thus, their character is that of the Kharijis, whose school does not stipulate that the caliph has to be Qurayshi. I learned from the previous sultan of Muscat that he hoped to join with the Ottoman state.

As for the independent non-Arab states, Turkey is foremost. It claims that the caliphate was transferred to its sultans when the last of the 'Abbasid caliphs ceded it to Sultan Salim, who captured him in Egypt and transported him to Constantinople. According to this interpretation, this transfer has remained in effect down to the events of the present day through a chain of caliphs designating and appointing their successors. It is said that Sultan Muhammad Wahid al-Din [Mehmed VI], deposed, still lays claim to the caliphate, which passed to him through the system of inheritance.[164] We have explained the truth of the matter previously. The 'Abbasid caliph captured by Sultan Salim did not actually hold office. He was not in a position to cede the role, even to someone with a rightful claim. That is because he was not able to act freely, which is a legal requirement for that action to be valid. The same point applies to Sultan Wahid al-Din [Mehmed VI] today. Thus, no consideration should be given to the possibility of him abdicating in favor of the king of the Hijaz, which some people have anticipated. The Ottoman Turks' caliphate rested on force. Thus, there is no substantive difference between choosing Emir 'Abd al-Majid II [Abdülmecid II] now, after the chain of designation and appointment of successors has been cut by Muhammad Wahid al-Din's [Mehmed VI's] deposition, and choosing Muhammad Wahid al-Din before him on the basis of that system.[165] This is if Angora's (Ankara's) government had made him the "caliph" in terms of what that title is known to signify under the shari'ah.[166] But it has invented a new form of government and another form of the caliphate. For the former, it set in place a constitution with which we are familiar. For the latter, it has not set down laws [qanun] that would enable us to discern its nature. If it is a spiritual caliphate, one with no authority over the community's politics and governance, it is not the imamate whose ordinances we have explicated. Still, we welcome anything that they set down for this caliphate that harmonizes with the revealed law. But we reject whatever they set down that runs counter to the revealed law. It does not particularly concern us that the new institution has been named "caliphate," and using the title in such manner is common among those belonging to the brotherhoods. There is no disputing the need for reform. At each juncture, we will explain what Islam makes incumbent upon it.

The Caliphate

The second non-Arab state is Iran, which is Imami Shi'i. According to Imamis, the imamate is held by Imam Muhammad, the awaited Mahdi.[167] They do not recognize the imamate of any other imam. It is tied to other Islamic states through political alliances.

The third non-Arab state is Afghanistan, which is Sunni. According to the treaty contracted between it and the new Turkish government in Angora (Ankara), it recognizes that the Turkish state is the state of the caliphate. But it recognizes no Turkish sovereignty over Afghanistan. Rather, the treaty between the two is one between peers.[168]

The text of the third article of this treaty, composed in Angora (Ankara), subordinates the Afghani state to the Turkish state. The following is a translation of it that was published in the Egyptian newspaper *Al-Akhbar* by its reporter in Kabul, capital of Afghanistan: "On this occasion, the state of Afghanistan declares that it is guided by Turkey, which performs great services and carries the banner of the Islamic caliphate." That is to say: it affirms and acknowledges it as an exemplar.

The correspondent stated that Afghanistan's emir did not accept this text, and moreover changed it as follows: "The state of Afghanistan is not guided by the supreme Turkish state, but acknowledges that it is the state of the caliphate." This occurred before the last Turkish upheaval. In some newspapers it was reported that the Afghans criticized the Turks who had made the caliphate a spiritual institution, having nothing to do with politics or legal ordinances. What this matter comes down to is that they do recognize the Ottoman Turkish caliphate as sound under the shari'ah. Thus, they have no alternative to recognizing the caliph, as they are a Muslim people who ardently hold to their religion.

But it is clear that Muslims who are not subjects of the Turkish government but who nevertheless recognize the Ottoman Turks' caliphate are thereby recognizing nothing more than an honorific, and a caliph who has some spiritual influence in other states. The fact that a man is the Muslims' "caliph" cannot mean anything more. This differs from a situation in which the caliph is actually and genuinely the Muslims' imam: their leader in religion and the head of their government. In such case, they must obey him. Should they fail to do so, rebelling and seeking independence from his rule, it becomes permissible to shed their blood. This accords with well-known stipulations set down in works of law [fiqh]. As for a tyrant who is only obeyed on the basis of coercion, it is impermissible for anybody who is not coerced to recognize his caliphate. It is a mockery of Islam that its supreme imamate be rendered nothing more than a title praising and honoring the one who holds it.

This describes the situation in the independent states. As for the Islamic lands that remain under the yoke of foreign control, such as Egypt, other North African lands, Syria, and Iraq, their peoples have no sovereignty, and no control over their religion. These lands lack any organized group [jama'ah] capable of addressing these problems and taking up the roles that we know as loosing or binding.

If heads of government and the people in one of these lands—if not for foreign control these people would be those who loose and bind—wanted, for example, to make a sound pledge of allegiance to a caliph in the Turkish or Arab lands, one subjecting them to his authority, commands, and prohibitions in their general affairs, and obligating them to assist him against anyone who fights against or wrongs him, they would be unable to undertake or implement that without the permission of the foreign state dominating them. That state would not grant such permission. This is so even where a foreign state claims that it does not stand in the way of what Muslims determine when it comes to affairs of their own religion, and that it leaves the matter of the caliphate in their hands.

As for the individuals and groups who lack the leadership or influence to guide the people, and who are unable to obey when they make the pledge of allegiance, or fight when they are asked to fight, or assist when they are asked to assist, in some of these lands they are permitted to speak freely, and in others they are not. In each of these lands the opinion of the great majority of the Muslims is contrary to the opinion of the state dominating it. Take, for instance, the pledge of allegiance to the new Turkish caliph made by certain individuals and groups in India and Egypt. If the people of Tunisia and Algeria wanted to do likewise, that would not be permitted of them. This is in spite of France, the power dominating them, being aware that their subservience to the Turkish government would not result from a pledge of allegiance. France understands that the Turkish government is itself not subordinate to its caliph. To the contrary, it sees him as its subordinate, as its employee. It is the government that determines his role and his functions.

The essential point being made here is that Islamic peoples living under foreign rule have no control over their own affairs, except for what the foreigners subjugating them allow them to do. They are unable to assist in the effort to unify the community, which is a prerequisite for unifying the imamate, except by spreading the call to Islam and providing material support. As for those Muslims who are independent, there is currently no expectation that they will unite. There is no expectation that they will relinquish their partisan affiliations with the schools of law [madhhabs] and their tendency to align themselves

The Caliphate

with others who share their ethnic identity, and, building upon that foundation, erect a strong, sound caliphate. In that case they would live under a unified government. A more realistic possibility is that treaties of friendship or military-political alliances be contracted between them. The non-Arabs have begun that undertaking. As for the Arabs, they have scarcely been found unified down to the present day. Should God smooth the path to that, it would then be possible for them to unify with others. That, in turn, would prepare a path to the creation of a universal imamate uniting all Muslims.

Who are the people capable of calling for the restitution of the Islamic community, its ties loosened and its joints broken? Who can call for the reestablishment of the institution of the caliphate in the form that the Lawgiver set down for it? The people who loose and bind—the people who loose and bind. Who are they, and where are they today?

(17) THE PEOPLE WHO LOOSE AND BIND IN THIS AGE AND WHAT IS REQUIRED OF THEM IN REGARD TO THE MATTER OF THE MUSLIM COMMUNITY [UMMAH] AND THE IMAMATE

We have covered everything that we wanted to explain about the ordinances for Islam's supreme imamate. We follow that by explaining what the endeavor to implement these ordinances requires: the reconstitution and unification of the community, and the appointment of its rightful imam, which, as we explained in Section 2, is the community's duty under the shari'ah. The community in its entirety is in sin if that duty is forsaken, its life and death reckoned that of the days of pre-Islamic ignorance in view of its loss. The community in its entirety is accountable and responsible for the matter, as we explained in Section 4. Those who are to undertake this action, then, are those who represent it, the people who loose and bind, as we indicated in Section 3. The people who loose and bind are accountable for all matters pertaining to the community's general welfare, and in particular the matter of the supreme authority.

We have said that the people who loose and bind are at the head of the community, its leaders and chiefs. They are those who hold its confidence in theoretical and practical matters, and in what promotes the common good. These are the things upon which the community's vitality depends. Their decisions regarding matters of religion and worldly life are to be followed by others. This is among society's necessities for all of mankind's peoples. Stable social life depends upon it. Our Arab poet states:

> People cannot thrive when in chaos, without leaders. And there are no leaders when the ignorant prevail.

When this class of people in the community is righteous, the community and its government are also in a righteous state. When they are corrupt, the community and its government are corrupt. Thus, Islamic reform requires that the people who loose and bind in Islam are those who have an independent mindset when it comes to the shari'ah, and likewise the political, social, legal, administrative, and financial matters that affect the community's welfare. Hence, they must have integrity, insight [ra'y], and wisdom, as we explained in Section 4. These are the qualifications required of the people who elect the caliph.

The people who loose and bind have been mentioned multiple times in relation to the caliphate's ordinances. Yet we did not use that expression—the people who loose and bind—as a title for any section except this one. This section was composed specifically to discuss them: where they are found today, and what they are obligated to do to serve their community in this era. Foreign and national governments that are illegitimate under the shari'ah work to corrupt the leaders of the people whom they despotically rule. As a result, those leaders then become complicit in that despotism. Whenever these governments find that their efforts to turn a leader against his own people through enticements or intimidation have failed, they conspire against him, or ostracize him. Thus, except in free nations, people who loose and bind who genuinely act on behalf of the community are rarely found. In subjugated nations, most leaders act on behalf of their rulers. It is their rulers who entrust them to supervise certain functions, and thereby to maintain public welfare. Thus, whatever authority they have to loose and bind is a mercenary authority. The community might be deceived by some of those who wield this authority, and it may come to regard them as unfaithful and deserving of punishment. There may also be trustworthy people among them, and the community may recognize this, or be unaware of it. If the community does not voice its contempt for the machinations of despots because of internal divisions that occur during times of subjugation and humiliation, it voices them when the people unite in agitation and revolution. In recent years the Egyptian revolution has clearly shown us the community hating and disdaining some individuals among the leaders whose role is to serve the public interest in worldly life and religion, and entrusting other individuals to lead it.

What signals that this is a contrived and mercenary leadership, that actual leadership lies with the government, is that when someone in a position of leadership leaves that position, you find most of the community disregarding him, not considering him its leader, and perhaps viewing him with contempt and scorn. In these doomed years we have seen foreigners who have unjustly seized some of our lands directing some of these leaders, whom they have corrupted

The Caliphate   117

against or empowered over the Muslim community, to the capitals of their lands, conspiring with them to establish their authority there (namely, authority over the community). They have engaged some of them, seeking their assistance in colonizing lands. This is the same as what sultans and emirs used to do, winning the favor of ulama and notables by conferring ranks, decorations, and gifts. Then the Turks and the Egyptians rose up, seeking to reclaim the community's sovereign authority through representative parliaments [*majalis al-nuwwab*]. These parliaments signify what the group [*jama'ah*] of people who loose and bind signifies in Islam, except that Islam stipulates that those belonging to this group must have certain specific intellectual and moral qualifications. But in the current era Europeans and their Muslim imitators do not make similar stipulations for their representatives.

The members of the National Assembly in Angora (Ankara) became, in effect, those responsible for loosing and binding, despite there being a sultan who combatted them and wound up disgraced and deposed. They took the place of the Chamber of Deputies, the Council of Ministers, and the figure of the sultan, one and all. This reminds me of what Ghazi Ahmad Mukhtar Pasha told me in Constantinople when I asked his opinion on constitutional government. He said: "We have a council, but we do not have a sultan, yet both plates of the scale are required for balance."

As for the lands subjugated by foreign occupation such as Egypt and India, their peoples lack the scope to undertake the like of what the Turks undertook. Until the Muslim community in those places reaches maturity only solitary individuals will emerge.

The Master, the Imam [Muhammad 'Abduh], attained a position of leadership in this Muslim community, as well as the status of being one of the people who loose and bind in matters of religion and worldly life, political and nonpolitical. Moreover, he was near the point of becoming the entire Islamic community's leader. But the potential for that was not realized, as the Muslim community had not developed sufficiently to walk the path that he had set down for it. Hence, he used to say, "Woe to the man who does not have a community." The emir of his lands used to isolate and shun him, yet he used to defer to him on matters of importance, and to resolve problems.

During these recent years his disciple[169] Sa'd Pasha Zaghlul attained a position of political leadership as his people's consciousness developed. When he strove to empower them, he was rewarded by exile followed by exile.[170] In this era, some Muslim and Hindu men in India rose to positions of leadership in their community, as developments revealed their abilities and high determination. Now they languish in the darkness of prisons. Among them are Gandhi, for the Hindus, and Abul Kalam,[171] Muhammad 'Ali, and Shawkat 'Ali for the Muslims.[172] There are also their organizations, such as the Wafd for us in Egypt, and the Khalifat Movement for them in India.[173]

As for the older organizations, like the council of eminent ulama at Al-Azhar in Egypt, and at the Fatih and Suleymaniye Mosques in Constantinople, the Zaytunah Mosque in Tunis, and the Deoband Madrasah in India, the community's majority trusts that their statements accord with God's commands. But most of the Europeanized — most of the political authorities, commanders, and political parties — rarely attach importance to them, except for those whose dignity or wealth lends them a certain prestige. None of the Sunni ulama have attained, collectively or individually, the leadership and following among the people that the mujtahids among the Shi'i ulama have attained, especially the mujtahids of Najaf, who are truly their school's [madhhab's] leaders.[174] It is said that they recently issued a fatwa prohibiting the election of the National Assembly. King Faysal's government had ordered that it be constituted so that the treaty between Iraq and the British state could be ratified. This fatwa was obeyed by the Bedouin and by the urban Shi'ah. Mirza Hasan al-Shirazi, God Almighty have mercy upon him, issued a fatwa forbidding tobacco. All of Iran's people obeyed it, relinquishing its use and cultivation, and as a product of their lands it is as cotton is to Egypt. The person who prompted him to issue this fatwa was the rouser of the East, Sayyid Jamal al-Din al-Afghani, may God sanctify his spirit, as the government of Iran had granted a concession [*imtiyaz*] for the tobacco trade to an English company.[175] The government was forced to rescind the concession, compensating the company 500,000 English guineas. Had that company not been dissolved, what happened with the English Leather Company in India would have happened in Iran, its home nation, Britain, seizing lands and annexing them to its empire.[176]

I have said that autocratic governments strive to corrupt those who emerge as leaders among the peoples they rule. Yet prior to that they had been concerned with how to prevent the emergence of leaders from among the people. They corrupted and supervised their education, and alienated the religion's ulama from matters of politics and government. Thus, most of their people and supporters came to be constituted of those who were ignorant of the shari'ah. These people took on responsibility for education, and for using it to prepare people for work in government. And as they did that the ulama for their part withdrew, seeking refuge in the corners of their mosques or the interiors of their homes, not demanding their rights. They did not equip themselves to meet the challenges facing them in the manner that the era's circumstances and the very nature of civilization require. They did not know how to maintain their role of leading the Muslim community by informing people of their rights, and pro-

The Caliphate

viding the kind of leadership that would enable them to demand them. For this reason they lost their right to be regarded as those in the Muslim community who loose and bind. They yielded that role to those holding official positions and those belonging to political parties and associations. For the most part, these are controlled by people who are completely unlearned in the religious sciences, and who have not received even the disordered remnants of religious education that some Muslims still receive.

Thus, if I wish—in this circumstance—to endeavor to undertake the duty under the revealed law of establishing a true, just, and universal imamate, it is necessary to first endeavor to constitute a group of people who loose and bind who have the qualities stipulated for that role, as discussed in Section 5. This is because it is they who have the right to appoint the imam on behalf of the Muslim community, and to support him by prompting the Muslim community to obey him. But what is required before a supreme imam can be appointed, an imam for the entire Muslim community or for those living in the independent Muslim territories, is for the people in those territories to unite. For that to happen they would have to stop letting their various differences—their affiliations with the schools of law, ethnic identities, and languages—become a barrier to unity and concord.

We ask here: Are there people who loose and bind in the Islamic lands who have the capacity to undertake this task? If there are no people who have sufficient influence to actually achieve this, are there not people who have the potential to do so? Then, is it not possible for the Muslims to set down a program for turning this potential influence into an actual influence? Yes, this is possible, although it is difficult. But strength of resolve may render what is difficult easy, and strength of resolve follows from the strength of the one who makes the call to action. From whom is it hoped that they will set down a program and put it into practice? None but the party of moderation and Islamic reform.

(18) THE PARTY OF MODERATION AND ISLAMIC REFORM

It may be appreciated from what is stated above that those who have the ability to unify the Islamic community as much as possible are limited to two great peoples: the Arabs, the root of Islam, and the Turks, its sharp sword. The independent Arab territories are in the hands of their imams and emirs. Thus, what takes precedence over all else is that they unite. We say here:

Those in the Islamic lands beyond the Arabian Peninsula who take up the task of providing political leadership and placing themselves in the position of the people who loose and bind fall into three categories: those who imitate what is set down in various works of law [fiqh]; those who wish to imitate Europe's laws and systems; and the party of reform. This party brings an independent mindset to bear on the religion and the ordinances of the Islamic revealed law. It takes the same approach when it comes to European civilization in its essential nature.[177] It is this party that has the capacity to eliminate division within the Muslim community, and undertake the action necessary to revive the institution of the imamate, provided that its support increases and its resources and membership grow. Its middle position enables it to appeal to those on both sides who stand ready to revitalize the Muslim community. This is the party that we named the party of the Master, the Imam [Muhammad 'Abduh], in the third of the articles on the civil character of laws that we published in *Al-Manar*. That was during the time when *Al-Manar* was preparing a path for him to lead reform in all of the Islamic territories. We know individuals who embrace moderate reform in different territories, and especially the Arab, Turkish, and Indian territories. We attest that the hope for strengthening this party with resources and members generally lies more with India's Muslims than with others. But they cannot act unless the rationally minded among them unify with the rationally minded in other lands. This would enable a body [*jama'ah*] of people who loose and bind to be formed, one that would coalesce around an agenda that they had agreed upon. Its function would be to lead public opinion and convene an emergency conference charged with determining the actions to be undertaken now.

There had been silence on the issue of the caliphate, and then the recent Turkish upheaval made it one of the most pressing issues in need of discussion. Were it not the case that most of what has been written about it has only added to confusion and misled public opinion, we would have preferred silence to discussion, along with endeavoring to follow what we find to be the best course of action. Yet it is necessary to prepare for that by explaining certain facts, although these have already been the object of investigations and controversies resulting from people's differing opinions and desires.

It suffices us to call the party of reform's attention to the obstacles that will be presented by parties of traditionalism and fanaticism, and to the principles and proofs that should guide its actions.

(19) THE PARTY OF THE EUROPEANIZED

In the third of our articles on the civil character of laws we explained:[178]

- what we mean by "Europeanization" and those who embrace it;
- that the Europeanized include apostates who openly declare their unbelief as well as those who keep it secret;
- how the Europeanized conceive of Islam's government and shari'ah.

The Caliphate

We also state here:

The Europeanized heretics believe that the religion in this era does not harmonize with politics, science, and civilization. They believe that a state that is effectively constrained by religion cannot attain glory, strength, or equality with the powerful states. Many people educated in Europe and in schools in which European languages and modern sciences are taught hold this view. Most of them are of the opinion that government must be free of religion. This group is strong and organized among the Turks, disorganized in Egypt, and weak in places like Syria, Iraq, and India. They view it as a duty to eliminate the institution of the Islamic caliphate from the state, weaken the Islamic religion in the community, and utilize all means to replace Islamic religious ties with national and ethnic ties. Among them, the Turks are the strongest opponents of establishing the sound imamate in the Turkish state.

In Anatolia, the cradle of Islamic pride, their organizations spread the call to blind partisanship. They did so in ways that left the masses unaware of their intentions. We pointed to some of these previously. They had the desired effect: if asked about his identity, a Turk in that place would say: "I am a Muslim, thanks be to God." In that way, he distinguished himself from Greeks and Armenians. As for now, he answers, "I am a Turk." He had understood the obligation of military service as nothing but obedience to his caliph and his sultan, jihad in the way of God. Then, the notion of fighting in the way of the Turks, their nation, and their glory was instilled in him. In recent days, we have come upon a story, A *Shirt of Fire*, by an author of Israelite lineage whose politics and ideology are Turkish: Khalidah Adib, the minister of education in Angora (Ankara). She composed it to demonstrate the character of the nationalist movement in Anatolia, which was established to oppose the authority of Constantinople, expel the Greeks, and secure the lands' independence. We find it typifying what we have discussed: in this story we do not see a single word suggestive of the notion of Islamic jihad, or the religious spirit with which we are familiar.

There is, however, a faction of the Europeanized who can see that in political, moral, and other terms there is utility in seating the caliphate in Turkey. This applies if it is a nominal or spiritual caliphate with no authority to legislate or implement legislation. Its influence would be limited to that of political propaganda that it promotes on behalf of the state in the guise of religion, its authority resembling that of the pope, patriarchs, and missionary societies. Most of these people are partisans of Turanian ethnic identity who, in certain respects, have a similar attitude to the proponents of pan-Islamism [*al-jami'ah al-islamiyyah*]. That is because as they seek to form a great nation constituted of non-Arab Muslim peoples of the East by rendering all of them "Turks," as none of them have a codified scientific language—with the exception of

Persian for the Iranians and Afghans, and likewise the Urdu language for India's Muslims—though the Turkish language is spread throughout most of Iran's lands. Those who cannot be integrated with the Turkish nation in the name of Turanian unity and the tie of the Turkish language may be integrated with it by recognizing the Islamic caliphate. Those people's offspring would then be raised and educated as Turks, following government policy. The party of those who promote an exclusively Turkish ethnicity opposes the party of those who promote a broader Turanian ethnicity. That is because they fear that the Turks would fade under a broader Turanian identity, as, according to their argument, under pan-Ottomanism or pan-Islamism. It is not our purpose here to evaluate or critique these perspectives. Rather, it is to call people's attention, in as few words as possible, to how they stand in the way of the rightful Islamic imamate's establishment. We have not abandoned the hope that we may convince many of them that it is possible to combine national and Islamic identities.

There is a faction of the Europeanized—some of whom are devout—and others who hold the view that in this era it is impossible to establish the Islamic caliphate in a civil state, and to appoint as head of state the rightful imam who upholds Islam. This is because only two possibilities are seen. Either: it would be the case that under the Turkish state the caliphate is nominal, as under the Ottoman state. Whatever possible benefit would be derived from it, while the evil of the caliph's tyranny would be guarded against. The government would be absolutely free from the restriction of having to adhere to ordinances of the revealed law that cannot be implemented in this era. Or: it would be the case that the caliphate is dispensed with entirely. The party of reform will find winning the favor of these people easier than winning the favor of others.

(20) THE PARTY OF INFLEXIBLE TRADITIONALIST JURISTS
[HIZB HASHWIYYAT AL-FUQAHA' AL-JAMIDIN]

All of the religion's ulama, along with the masses who follow them, desire that their government be purely Islamic. The Turks would even prescribe that it adhere to the Hanafi school of law's [madhhab's] fiqh, while some among them see no barrier to drawing on the other Sunni schools' [madhhabs'] fiqh for certain ordinances. They are unmindful of how doing that would impair this era's civilization. Yet these ulama are incapable of writing military, financial, and political laws that are derived from traditional fiqh, and refuse to allow unrestricted ijtihad for all civil transactions. Were the matter of governance entrusted to them and placed in their hands, they would be found completely incapable, unable to manage affairs of war or of peace.

The Caliphate 123

How often have we explained in our magazine *Al-Manar*: the Muslim ulama's deficiencies in explicating Islam's true nature and defending it in the manner that this era's circumstances require is the primary reason that many Europeanized Muslims have apostatized from it. Had they explicated it, as is their duty, many of the Europeans themselves would have embraced it, and in greater numbers than those of the Muslims who have left it due to Europeans enticing them to do so. The reason for that, or the primary reason, is that Muslims lack an imam or a group [*jama'ah*] that has a program and the resources necessary to undertake that task, as does the Catholics' imam, the pope, and the patriarchs, bishops, and missionary societies in Christian lands. Yet sultans, emirs, and their followers have corrupted the ulama, voiding their role as the Muslim community's leaders, except when it comes to supporting their injustice and their tyranny, as we have discussed previously.

If the Muslims had had a caliph who carried the burdens of the supreme imamate, he would not have neglected to defend Islam and call people to it. It was such neglect that led to increased apostasy, and enabled those with no knowledge of Islam to take control of the Ottoman state. Is it not remarkable that when I set out a project for outreach and guidance so that these duties — the primary duties of the Muslims' imam and of the community's main body [*jama'ah*] — could be undertaken, not one minister or leader of state dared to endorse that name? And that those who approved of the proposal agreed upon entitling the association charged with implementing it "The Society for Science and Guidance"? Yes, in my presence the advisor to the office of the grand vizier said to the grand vizier, Haqqi Pasha, "If we implement this proposal will we not face opposition from the Great Powers?" He answered him, "The Bulgarian state has a school here that graduates Christian missionaries. Can it be that the state of the caliphate has less religious freedom in its own capital than the state of Bulgaria?"[179] But this grand vizier did not implement the project, and did not provide us with the least assistance. We took advantage of the opportunity to obtain official endorsement of the project that was presented by his travel to Italy, and also that of the minister of the Interior and leader of the Ittihadists, Talat Bey, to Adrianople (Edirne).[180] I was assisted in that by the convening of a Council of Deputies under the leadership of the Shaykh al-Islam, Musa Kazim Efendi, one of its supporters.[181] I did not cease imploring him — God have mercy upon him — until he issued a decision on implementing the proposal from the council. Then Talat Bey returned and destroyed the project.

He whom the people call sultan (and caliph) was imprisoned in his cage, his power of command wrested from him, incapable of rousing from his intoxication. The Islamic shaykhs did not seek anything from him in word or in deed in this matter, or in any other matter. Why was the influence of the like of Talat [Pasha] and [Doctor] Nazim over him greater than that of the Shaykh al-Islam, and the shaykhs of the Dar al-Fatwa? Is this not because of the impotence of the shaykhs and their assistants? Is this not due to their inability to administer affairs of state, demonstrate the shari'ah's relevance and applicability, and affirm the fundamental principles of doctrines and the practices based upon them, rebutting all specious criticisms? Is this not because in their intellects, political know-how, competence [*kifayah*], and fitness [*kafa'ah*] they are not marked by the qualities that the imams of the revealed law have stipulated for the people who loose and bind?

The religious scholars [ulama], however, have more influence in the Turkish lands than in places like Syria and Egypt. But their opponents among the Europeanized are stronger than they are in Syria and Egypt. Each of the two parties considers the other the cause of the state's weakness and the community's regression. The truth is that the sin is shared by both. The goal of appointing the rightful imam and making the Turkish state the guardian of the office of the caliphate cannot be realized unless the party of reform unites the divided Muslims. It can do that by drawing to itself most of the people of influence, to the point where all of those who have the qualities required of the people who loose and bind would be its supporters. The only way to achieve that is to guide the ulama among them away from the inflexibility of traditionalism and partisan affiliations with the schools of law (madhhabism). Additionally, the Europeanized Muslims' criticisms of the religion and the revealed law must be debunked, and the problems created by ethnic prejudices explained. If it is not possible to convince the great majority of these points now, then this party of reform gaining ascendency over the parties may be regarded as a sufficiently successful outcome at this juncture. We will explain how it can lay the ground for that.

Islam provides spiritual guidance, and a social-political bond. The person who is complete in their practice of Islam will also be complete in these two respects. The person who falls short in their practice of Islam will be weak in either or both. The heretics among the partisans of extreme ethnic prejudice lack both. There is no possible treatment for these people: not in the view of the caliphate's supporters, nor in the view of others. But what is possible is elucidating Islam's true nature along with its maxims and ordinances, the things that enable people to reach the highest levels of civilization and prosperity, together with avoiding all of materialistic civilization's evils and corruptions. We will indicate the way to do that in these investigations of ours. This can weaken them and halt their progress. Moreover, it may guide those individuals among them whose hearts are not sealed.[182] It would, however, be more apt to guide many others, and the success of our call to them is a higher priority.

This suffices to indicate what the endeavor to undertake this action requires in relation to the Turks. As for the Arab people, it is not possible that the sound imamate could be formed without their involvement. They are Islam's foundation and root, and without their language Islam has no life. Islam's pillars are incomplete without the hajj. This is the only social pillar that brings all of Islam's peoples together, and it is a duty undertaken in Arab land. The Arabs in their entirety are a religious people, their peninsula free of heresy or Europeanization. Their only bane is being ignorant of the means to develop their lands and culture, and of the sciences and arts upon which preservation of independence and the glory of the religious community [*millah*] depend. There is also the mutual enmity that exists between emirs, and the conspiracies of enemies. The party of reform has no greater obligation than that of convincing the Arab emirs of what is needed to enable unity, and assisting them in preparing ways to develop material and cultural strength. Here, we are those calling its attention to programs of action that may be publicized, how to argue the case, and what needs to happen to prepare the Muslims for this great undertaking.

(21) PEOPLE'S INTENTIONS REGARDING THE CALIPHATE; THE PARTY OF REFORM'S OBLIGATIONS

Affairs are what people's intentions make them, and when it comes to the caliphate people's intentions differ. It is rare to find among the people someone who has the intention of establishing the caliphate in a sound, shari'ah-based form, the caliphate whose true nature and ordinances we have explicated. That is because the majority of the people do not understand it, while the minority who do understand it believe that it is impossible to establish it. They believe that there is no alternative to being reconciled to a caliphate of necessity, one in which not all legal requirements are heeded, nor all that is required of the caliph and the main body of the Muslim community [*jama'ah*]. Then, they disagree on the extent of this necessity. The reason is that opinions and desires range widely in this matter, so that their views, in effect, are not greatly different from the views of those who are ignorant of the true nature of this institution and the benefits that it brings. If the great majority were aware of these things, they would wish to have it. Were a program for its establishment set in place, and were they called to it, they would respond, giving themselves to working for it, so far as they were able.

I have discussed this issue a great deal with educated Egyptians, turbaned and unturbaned. I found them agreeing that what underlies support for the new caliphate, an innovation created in Constantinople by Angora's (Ankara's) republican government, is the intention to leave the British state disappointed in its conspiracies. These conspiracies were designed to bring this lofty Islamic institution under its control, to turn it into an instrument that it could wield to further its agenda. That is seen in its endeavor to win over King Husayn in Mecca and Sultan Wahid al-Din [Mehmed VI] in Constantinople, and in what wound up with it bringing the two of them together, after it helped the latter find refuge in Malta. Not a single one of the Egyptians has intended to convey through their actions that the new caliph was recognized in their land as the Muslims' rightful and supreme imam. They showed their support through giving congratulations or pledging allegiance. But that does not mean that they recognized that he had authority over their government. It does not mean that it would assent to whatever decisions he saw fit to make in matters such as appointing and dismissing emirs and rulers, levying taxes, enlisting soldiers for jihad, and other functions of the caliphate discussed by Islam's ulama. This, as you can see, is a political objective. A spoiling effect is intended. It is motivated by a roused universal Islamic consciousness born of foreign pressure, born of this state's attempt to subjugate Islamic peoples who have retained remnants of their independence, especially the Turks and Arabs. Striving to realize this political objective does not require that there is a sound caliphate, an imam who holds office rightfully, or that the main body of the Muslim community has been properly constituted. Rather, it is comparable to the public demonstrations supporting the political leader Sa'd Pasha Zaghlul, yet less powerful. For this reason, Egyptians are not concerned with what has been stipulated for this caliphate and its functions. Africa's other Muslims are similar to them in that respect, as are other Muslims who, like them, have been humiliated by foreigners. Yet these people desire to adhere to the Turkish state, even while knowing that that is impractical. But none of the Egyptian political leaders hopes for that.

India's Muslims are more concerned with this matter than all of the other Muslims on earth. Their support of the Turkish caliphate has positive and negative dimensions, not merely negative dimensions. They are not reconciled to a spiritual caliphate, one that lacks command or authority. Their conception of necessity may lead them to laxity over some of their legal school's [madhhab's] stipulations for the caliphate—and they are their school's strongest partisans. But they are not lax when it comes to its fundamental objective and the purpose for which it was founded: proper application of the Islamic revealed law's ordinances for worship and for civil, political, and other worldly transactions.

The Caliphate

They regard the caliph—even if he is a tyrant—as the Islamic government's supreme leader. But beyond that, they do not question whether or not he actually executes the revealed law's ordinances. This is seen in their ardent support of 'Abd al-Hamid [Abdul Hamid II], who placed himself above both revealed and secular law, and was tyrannical in all matters. The same point applies to their support of Muhammad Rashad [Mehmed V], who lacked any authority—and thus the Ittihadists, who wrested all authority from him—and then for Wahid al-Din [Mehmed VI], who, on bad terms with his own people and with the rest of the Muslims, took flight with foreigners.[183]

If this remains their ultimate purpose, a sound caliphate will not come into being through their endeavors, and there will be no need to form a party or an organization beyond what they already have. Under this state of affairs it would be possible to satisfy them with a spiritual caliphate through linguistic artifice. An example of that is when the actual government states that the person it calls its "caliph" has delegated all authority to it, meaning authority over rulings, or what in today's legal terminology is known as legislative and executive authority. Yet he and the rest of the people understand that somebody can only truly delegate something if he has authority over it. Only somebody who is able to act freely and of his own volition can delegate. That is not possible when the person who is supposedly delegating has no right to supervise and reproach his delegate, or even to dismiss him if he should violate prescriptions of the revealed law or stray from the path of justice. Moreover, this role of supervising ministers, emirs, commanders, and judges is one of the duties of the Muslims' imam. In undertaking that duty, and the other responsibilities that come with it, he is constrained by his obligation to adhere to the revealed law's texts and consult with the people who loose and bind. He is, therefore, no autocrat.

If Muslims remain in this condition there will be no imamate and no imam. It is high time for them to recognize that turning the rule of necessity, which is applicable to a caliphate of tyranny, into a fixed, enduring principle is what has destroyed the imamate's structure. It has also eliminated the community's sovereign authority, which is embodied in the main body of the community, known as the *jama'ah*. This has led to factionalism and weakened both the religion and the state. In addition, it has enabled beliefs and practices based on innovation to prevail over those based on the prophetic tradition (sunnah). Indeed, conditions reversed and ignorance spread to such an extent that thousands of Muslim leaders—eminent rulers, commanders, and those who lead Muslims in other aspects of their worldly lives—came to suppose that, rather than empowering Muslims, the institution of the caliphate and Islam's ordinances have weakened them. Thus, they came to feel that the Muslims will not become a mighty and rich community by holding fast to the caliphate and Islam's ordinances. But the truth of the matter is the complete opposite.

The treatment that can cure this disease, the medicine that can eliminate this epidemic, is the revival of the institution of the caliphate. The way to do that is to restore the sovereign authority of the people who loose and bind, the group referred to as the *jama'ah*. That would enable the establishment of a genuinely Islamic government, which is the best form of government. It enables Muslims to thrive, and beyond that humankind generally. It does so by combining justice and equity, maintaining public welfare, preventing corruption, and "commanding what is good and forbidding what is evil."[184] It safeguards minors and the disabled, and through the Muslims' alms provides sufficiently for the poor and people in need. Thus, it provides remedies for all of the social corruptions found under civil governments, corruptions that have compelled numerous groups to turn to Bolshevism and anarchism.

If a government were established on the basis of these foundations and rules, one with a sound structure, it would soon become a prototype. It would inspire those who live in free nations and who have control over the forms of their governments. The worst criminals would then be unable to beguile the people, to alienate them from it and lead them astray. God will then fulfill his promise to us, as he fulfilled it to those who came before us, in keeping with the Almighty's statement: "God has made a promise to those among you who believe and do good deeds: He will make them successors to the land, as He did those who came before them" [Qur'an 24:55].

The first priority for the party of reform that we have conceived is to direct all of its energy and resolve toward delineating the most ideal form of the Islamic caliphate and its government. That form entirely befits the current era, and it is by enabling the creation of such a government that this era is distinguished over others. Then, this party should attempt to convince people of influence who reside in the Islamic lands where there is hope that such a government could be established of the following points:

- how it would safeguard public welfare;
- how it would enable the provision of services and prosperity;
- how it is superior to every other type of government in the world;
- how its establishment is feasible;
- how the doubts of Europeanized Muslims and those who have given up hope are unfounded.

All of this is straightforward, as we ourselves have found by experience.

The Caliphate

(22) THE CALIPHATE'S RELATIONSHIP TO THE ARABS AND THE TURKS

Then, this party should be aware that success in this depends upon the Arabs and Turks joining together, uniting, and being in agreement on the matter, if only in broad terms. It should heed how the tendency people have toward identifying with others who belong to their own ethnic group has increased in this era, and consider how to ward off the harmful effects of that as much as possible. The same point applies to how those belonging to the Zaydi sect identify with their school of law [madhhab] in a partisan manner. This is not only because creating unanimity and uniting the Muslim community are among the caliph's most important functions. It is also because success in this matter depends upon the two peoples cooperating. The reason is that revitalizing the institution of the caliphate in a sound form depends upon revitalizing the religion and the shari'ah. This can only be achieved by bringing an independent mindset—also known as unrestricted ijtihad—to bear on the religion. That requires command of the Arabic language, which enables one to comprehend the Book and the sunnah [the Qur'an and the hadith]. The relationship of the caliphate to the Arabs' language, history, and lands, then, is clearly apparent. All of the following are found with the Arabs: the site where revelation descended, the place where true Islam was manifested, its qiblah and ceremonial shrines, and the site where the duty of performing its universal, social pillar is fulfilled. Anyone who would contest the stipulation that the caliph must be of Qurayshi lineage—a stipulation upheld by all of the Sunni schools of law—could not possibly contest any of these facts. The same point applies to anyone who would contest what the Shi'i schools [madhhabs], especially the Zaydi school, stipulate on the imam's lineage, namely, that he must be a descendant of 'Ali and Fatimah.

The Arabs constitute a great power that could be harnessed with a view to revitalizing the caliphate. But their power is not organized or unified like the Turks' power. The governments ruling the independent Arabian Peninsula and its peoples are seen to observe the shari'ah more fully and completely than what one observes in the Turks' lands. But these governments are presently not able to show the world the true nature of Islamic civilization. Neither are they capable of calling people to Islam correctly, doing so in way that would attract attention and align with what some of the theologians have stipulated. If it was possible to persuade the Turks to establish a true imamate by following the straight path that has been set down for it, they would then be more able than the Arabs to achieve the first of these goals, and able to marshal more resources in support of the second. Thus, in this matter it is possible for each of the two peoples to bring to the table what the other lacks. Along with that, each would act independently in the administration, politics, and governance of its lands. Each of their independent governments—and likewise the governments of other Muslims—would be directly tied to the seat of the caliphate by consent and as a matter of choice. The tie to the caliphate would, on the one hand, require them to adhere to the rules of revealed law, and, on the other hand, enable them to benefit at all times from how that lends to Islamic unity.

Were heads of government in the Arabian Peninsula to agree on appointing one among them as the Muslims' caliph and, along with the ulama, qadis, and commanders in their lands, make the pledge of allegiance to him, the Turks would be unable to oppose them by announcing the installation of another caliph in Constantinople, even if they were to grant him the rights that are due to the institution of the imamate under the shari'ah—and they would not do that. Moreover, were the people of the Hijaz, Tihamah, and Najd, or most of them, to agree to make the pledge of allegiance to the imam of Yemen, known for his knowledge, integrity, and talents, and he announced that in his imamate he would follow the rules for ijtihad, and validate all of the schools of law [madhhabs], so that everyone was free to follow his own school, none of Muslim ulama, Arab or non-Arab, would be able to defame his caliphate. Neither would they be able to favor another caliphate, except for the case of someone who simply follows his own desire, and whose opinion is of no value. This would be so especially if this imam enacts religious reform in the Hijaz and in the Arabs' other lands, and manages the imamate's resources in the manner that the era's circumstances require. This is not a difficult proposition. If this imamate was not recognized by the people in some of the Islamic lands today it would not remain unrecognized tomorrow, following the dissemination of the call to Islam, even if only during the pilgrimage season, and the religion is their supporter and helper. However, the greatest disaster afflicting the Arabs is factionalism and love of power.

In this matter, Egypt comes next in standing, following the Arabian Peninsula. This point applies if it were independent and desirous of establishing a sound, shari'ah-based caliphate. But the Europeanized Egyptians are like the Europeanized Turks and most of them reject that, and ignore its value. The British state is the enemy of the caliphate and the Arabs, and opposes the one and the other with all of its power. The assistance it gave the Turks against Muhammad 'Ali was motivated by its fear of the revitalization of Islam's youth under an Arab state.[185] It believes that the Turks would never revive and enliven the caliphate in a sound form, or spread the call to Islam. This was one of the reasons underlying its support for them and their caliphate generally.

The Caliphate

Everything that has been said about the English endeavoring to establish an Arab caliphate in Egypt or the Hijaz before the Great War [World War I] is pure falsehood. If Egypt had established such a caliphate the Hijaz would definitely have adhered to it, and likewise Syria, if it were able to do so. Moreover, these countries aspire to follow Egypt even without the caliphate being established there. And perhaps Sunni Muslims and many of the Shi'ah in Iraq would not reject this Arab unity, if it were realized.

Some people suppose that there is something more important than these defects that diminishes the Arab lands: their weakness and loss of the power that enables people to protect the caliphate and the seat of the caliphate, to say nothing of the strength that enabled the Turks to undertake jihad and conquest. This supposition is false, as Yemen alone preserved its independence and the institution of its imamate for over 1,000 years. The Turks fought Yemen's imams for over four centuries, but were unable to eliminate their imamate, or seize all of their lands. This is in spite of there being many people in those lands who supported the Turks because they followed a different school of law.[186] Had it not been for Yemen's strength, the English could have occupied it long ago. As one of its governors of Aden plainly stated in the presence of a Hadrami Arab chief: If not for this imam—who has half a million fighters who would obey him if he told them to throw themselves into the fire—we would have occupied the entire Arabian Peninsula without having to engage in any significant combat.

Yet the Arabian Peninsula has nobody to fear besides the English. And they do not attempt to conquer it with swords and gunfire because there are many factors forming obstacles to that. These include: the point that they would not fight a strong, militaristic people in rugged territories with many mountains and valleys, lacking railways and other means of transportation. These also include: the point that fighting the people in these territories would bring great expense and little profit, and moreover no profit at all unless seizing the lands were to become easy, and millions in currency were spent on their development for the sake of a delayed profit. What they hope for, however, is to take control by winning the friendship of its emirs and leading figures with schemes and money, making gradual encroachments through business and by way of commercial privileges.[187] In this vein, they have paid great sums to the Arabs' leaders—except for Yemen's imams—and they are still paying. But they have not received in return anything of substance that would correspond to what they have paid. They have been unable to win the friendship of any of those emirs by this means. The king of Hijaz and his sons are an exception, and from today onwards they will be unable to achieve anything on behalf of the

British because the Arab nation has recognized the nature of the crime that they were committing against it. Thus, the British state's continued clinging to them avails it and them nothing but the hatred of the Arabs and the rest of the Muslims.

We say, moreover, that the principle underlying British policy is not that of conquest purely through the use of military force. And it was not the Ottoman state that prevented the English from conquering these territories prior to today. The state was unable to send any armed forces to them, except by sea. And when has it had a fleet that could equal one of the British fleets, so that it would be possible to send soldiers and ammunition to Yemen to protect its coastline—and likewise the state's other coastlines—from the English in the event of war breaking out between them? And why did it not protect Egypt from the English, or expel them from it?

As for the people of the Arabian Peninsula having a nature that renders them unable to undertake jihad for conquest as do the Turks—and some among us who have investigated the matter prefer the Turks here—on this point it may be said that, thanks to God's grace, there have never been foreign peoples of differing ethnicity or religion in the Arabian Peninsula who scraped up against the Arabs, which would have facilitated conquest of their lands. When it comes to the Turks and their lands, it may be said that they have not found a policy that grants them greater security than that of safeguarding themselves from mutual friction and its ill effects by expelling peoples who have a different ethnicity and religion. They will not venture to fight any of their neighbors for the purpose of conquering his lands—all of their wars during the previous centuries were fought to defend against invaders or defeat rebels. None were fought to expand the domain of their rule or spread the religion. They are the people who are most in need of a respite from conflict. They need to turn their attention to their lands' development, along with the sciences and arts pertinent to that. Those of them who advocate expansionism seek only to unite with eastern Islamic peoples whom they are able to assimilate on the basis of their linguistic identities, such as the Kurds, Circassians, Tatars, and the other peoples of Turanian nationality.

As for calling people to Islam without fighting, here the Arabs are more capable than the Turks. They are a people whose very nature is to call people to Islam. Millions residing in Africa and islands in the southern ocean converted to Islam upon the call of traveling Arab traders and dervishes.[188] Freedom of faith, which in this era is guaranteed by most governments, frees the Muslims' caliph from the obligation of having to fight to protect the call to Islam and freedom of religion, as was the case for the first Arab caliphs.

The Caliphate

In spite of our awareness of all that has been mentioned, we hope that the Turks and Arabs will cooperate over the revival of the institution of the caliphate. We will call attention to the ways in which the Turks surpass the Arabs in this matter. The purpose in doing that is to demonstrate that each of the two peoples is incapable of taking action if it stands alone. Yet each is strong enough to take up the burden of this great reform if it stands with its brother. This reform can alter the world order, saving both East and West from annihilation. The means we recommend for achieving cooperation and concord pertain specifically to plans that may be made, plans for realizing the goal of establishing a genuine caliphate, one that will endure. This goes together with our silence on the well-known divisions that exist between the two peoples under current conditions. That goal can be achieved by ensuring that those who are raised and educated to be nominees for office come from families of Qurayshi sharifs and sayyids. After consultation, one of them will be chosen through a shari'ah-based election process. The Turkish state should be responsible for preparing for this process. It should supervise all matters connected to it. That would serve to minimize any possibility that the two peoples compete with each other, and ensure that reviving the institution rather becomes the primary reason that they unify and cooperate. If the Turks then wish to seat the caliphate in their lands, it is incumbent upon the party of reform to convince the Arabs to assent to that. We can see, however, that a plan to seat it in an intermediate zone, located in between the two people's lands, is more likely to meet with approval. We will detail this presently.

There are three places that might be designated as the seat of the caliphate: a location in the Arabs' lands, or the Hijaz specifically; or in the Turks' lands, or Constantinople specifically; or in a shared intermediate zone.

(23) OBSTACLES TO MAKING THE HIJAZ THE SEAT OF THE CALIPHATE

From what has been discussed above we can appreciate that the Arabs' lands—and more so the Arabian Peninsula, and even more so the Hijaz—are the Islamic lands most worthy of being home to the Islamic caliphate. This becomes more apparent when one considers the religious reform that it is the caliph's duty to undertake in this era. But today there are obstacles blocking the possibility of the genuine caliphate that Muslims desire being located in the Hijaz. Given its present condition, people in other Islamic lands would not agree to adhere to it. What, then, if it were desired that it govern all of the Arabs' lands, or manage the other Islamic lands' affairs? What if it were desired that its government become an archetype of the most perfect government, without which there can be no hope of reforming the human condition? Here, we discuss the points that are most important when it comes to these obstacles and present conditions in the Hijaz:

(1) In order to maintain his power the king, who has imposed his rule on the Hijaz in this era, depends on a non-Islamic state. This state has subjugated many Muslim peoples, and it wishes to subjugate others, especially the Arabs. He has entangled himself with it through treaties and ties by which he has recognized that the Arab community stands in relation to that non-Islamic power as does a minor in relation to a guardian, and that it is responsible for the community's development and for securing it internally and externally. This even means that this non-Islamic state is entitled to enter his lands with military force to curb internal disorder. Anyone who wishes may consult what we published on this subject in *Al-Manar*, Volume 23, pages 612–24.

(2) This king has given himself the title "King of the Arabs." He wants to be recognized as the Arab community's greatest leader. He wants to be regarded as the representative of all of the independent Arab governments. That would mean that they are also debased, bound, and burdened by those treaties, and stripped of their independence. However, all the Arab governments neighboring him are in all respects stronger and more righteous than his government, and they have not bound themselves by treaties that deprive them of their independence.

(3) He assented to making his two sons, who serve as leaders in certain Arab lands that are under the domination of the aforementioned foreign state, subservient to that state's Colonial Office. In that respect they resemble many national leaders who serve in that state's colonies. By doing that, he and his sons became the first to help a non-Muslim, foreign state in colonizing Arab lands.

(4) His government is autocratic and dictatorial. It lacks any restraint. He does and he rules as he wishes. We know this through things that we hear of and read about in its newspaper *Al-Qiblah:* reports of seizures of property, official penalties, and other things that, so far as we are aware, have no basis under the Islamic revealed law. As for positive law [*al-qawanin al-wad'iyyah*], he forbids it and declares those who act in accordance with it to be unbelievers!!

(5) This government opposes all of the sciences that would support religious and this-worldly reform.[189] In addition to its hatred of the modern sciences and arts, even geography, it bans many works on Islamic law from the Hijaz. These include works by Islam's two great reformist shaykhs, Ibn Taymiyyah and Ibn Qayyim, as well as works by others.[190]

The Caliphate

(6) It has been established through various lines of evidence that the members of this dynasty covet the caliphate, the emirate, and power, even if that should be under the patronage of a foreign authority rather than an Islamic one. As stated above, one who seeks the role of governance should not be appointed to it.

(7) The members of this dynasty lack the most important qualifications that are stipulated for the caliphate, especially knowledge of Islamic law. We see evidence of this in what we read in the king's official publications and his government's statements: errors of language; qur'anic verses that have been distorted; hadiths whose ascription to the Messenger, God's prayer and peace be upon him, is fraudulent; and interpretations of texts that are contrary to what the wording actually conveys and what has been the object of the consensus of both exegetes and nonexegetes. Further, we see these errors continuing rather than being corrected. This indicates that not a single one of the Islamic ulama in all of the Hijaz has dared to correct a mistake—relating to a qur'anic verse, a hadith, or a rule of Islamic law—published in their newspaper, which is a symbol of ignorance. We will refrain from mentioning what we have come to know through our own experience, and from trustworthy people's reports of their experiences.

(8) Most of the Islamic world loathes the current government of the Hijaz. We see it defamed in the papers in Egypt, Tunisia, Algeria, Java, Turkey, India, and elsewhere. Yet many of these papers' editors and writers do not know everything that we know about its bad condition.

(9) Those who seek to revive the institution of the caliphate in Islam aim to realize three goals by doing that. (1) The establishment of a consultative Islamic government, one that accords with what God prescribed so that it becomes a proof for all of humankind, as mentioned previously. (2) The resuscitation of Islam's civilization through developing the sciences, arts, and industries that enable strength and prosperity. It is a civilization that combines the material blessings of worldly life with religious and spiritual virtues, and loosens the knots of all social problems. (3) Religious reform through eliminating superstitions and innovations, reviving the prophetic example, uniting the people, and fortifying the ties of Islamic brotherhood and the other human virtues. The government of the Hijaz lacks the will to pursue these high goals. There is no hope that its ruling dynasty would consent to the theoretical and practical means upon which this great reform depends.

(10) The Hijaz lacks the power and prosperity upon which the caliphate's establishment depends. It lacks the strength to stand independently. How, then,

136 *Muhammad Rashid Rida*

could it carry the burdens of this great office? None of the Muslim Arabs in the lands neighboring it would agree to adhere to its weak and autocratic government. How, then, would other Muslims assent to that?

(24) ESTABLISHING THE CALIPHATE IN THE TURKS' LANDS: CONS AND PROS

The obstacles to establishing a sound caliphate in the Turks' lands fall into two broad categories. (1) The most important obstacle is the fear that most of the political and military leaders would oppose that because the caliphate unifies all authority in the person of the caliph, and depends upon the Arabic language's revival in the Turks' lands. The reasons for their opposition and its ramifications are well known. (2) The second obstacle is the opposition of the Arab nation, especially in the Arabian Peninsula and the adjacent lands. Yet this opposition would not be influential, or firm, except in the event of the caliphate being rendered in a nominal form, as it was, or a spiritual form, as it is now. Had the Turks not wanted to render it a tool of government, one that could disseminate propaganda on behalf of the Turkish state, perhaps they would not have selected Constantinople for it. It is a city of vain luxury and fleeting grandeur, one that came to be on the periphery of the Islamic lands, threatened by sea and land. If it is unfit to be the Turkish state's capital, all the more so will it be unfit for the Islamic caliphate.

If those Turks who are responsible for the matter were to agree to revive the institution of the true caliphate, the expectation is that its three goals and purposes would be more completely and more easily realized. Upon that, the Arabs would be inclined to lend their support, unless the Arabian Peninsula's emirs agreed to make the pledge of allegiance to one among them. But that is not anticipated, as explained above. The prevailing sentiment, then, is toward supporting the caliph established in office by the Turks. This is for the following reasons.

(1) Turks are presently caught between the ossification of traditionalism and the ambition to Europeanize. This ossification is that of the Arabs of the Arabian Peninsula. As a result, the religion has been fashioned in such a manner that it has effectively become an obstacle to progress, an obstacle to the development of the sciences and arts that would enable the community to advance in its civilization and material prosperity. Similarly, it undermines rather than promotes the state's might and power. The ambition to Europeanize brings a desire to eliminate what from a historical and religious perspective have been the Islamic community's core values and distinctive characteristics, and replace them with those of another community. Islam's

The Caliphate 137

civilization and the caliphate's government represent moderation. They stand at a midpoint, in between the extremes of traditionalist ossification on the one hand and the Europeans' materialistic civilization on the other. That civilization is being destroyed by microbes of corruption and diseases of destruction. Thus, it is apt to perish. What, then, is the nature of someone who blindly imitates it, when his own community in its very nature and its doctrines resists that?

(2) The new Turkish government's evident determination, courage, boldness, high aspiration, and tenacity can, by God Almighty's grace, guarantee its success in executing this Islamic reform, and beyond that a greater reform of humankind, by establishing the government of the caliphate. This combines material strength with human virtue, and protects humankind from the dangers of Bolshevism and anarchism. That is because it guarantees everything that people seek when they embrace moderate socialism: the establishment of equity, and redress of the injustices caused by capitalists' selfishness. Having these characteristics makes it more able to block the ruses of Islam's enemies, who resist the caliphate with all of their strength.

(3) The new Turkish state is the Islamic state that excels in the art of modern warfare. It may be hoped that if it is successful in its goal of acquiring the means to wealth and prosperity, its resources would then enable it to dispense with importing weapons and other kinds of military equipment by manufacturing them in its own lands. That would enhance its ability to protect its government and lands, and enable it to become a model for its neighbors, as well as their teacher.

(4) If the Turks were to be responsible for the seat of the caliphate, or if it were located in their lands, that would strengthen religious guidance in this great Islamic people. It would prevent Europeanized heretics and those who embrace extremist forms of nationalism from succeeding in detaching it from the body of the Islamic religious community. It would continue to be a shield for Islam, and a leading member of its most excellent community.

(5) During the previous era, the Arabs and Turks may have been ignorant of the concept of the caliphate and how it functions. That applies especially to how the caliphate unites the Muslims. Their ignorance of that was one of the reasons why they became mutually estranged, at odds with each other. That wound up with the fall of the Ottoman sultanate and foreign occupation of a significant portion of the Arabs' lands, preparing the way for the occupation of the remainder. If that is so, then what we are endeavoring to achieve will, if God wills, be one of the main factors that brings them together and inspires them to cooperate in reviving Islam's sciences and civilization. Along with that, both

138 *Muhammad Rashid Rida*

parties would administer their own lands independently, while also drawing authority from the caliph-imam. He would be a mujtahid, qualified in the sciences of the Islamic revealed law, and elected by the people who loose and bind. That group would include Arabs, Turks, and other Islamic peoples. They would elect the caliph after consulting with each other, following a method established for that purpose.

(25) ESTABLISHING THE CALIPHATE IN AN INTERMEDIATE ZONE

In truth, I have little hope in the Arabs and Turks. I do not see anyone among them taking the necessary steps of his own accord. I see no clear sign of their readiness to cooperate over what I have recommended. Yet when it comes to this matter, I am not one of those who would let a river of resignation flow into his heart. Thus, I urge the party of reform to endeavor to convince the Turks, first, to install the caliphate in the headquarters of the state. If they do not respond, let them assist in installing it in a zone in between the territories in which Arabs, Turks, and Kurds predominate, such as Mosul, which Iraq, Anatolia, and Syria contest, and to which neighboring lands contested by Syria and Anatolia may be annexed. This would be a zone of neutrality, giving geographical expression to the bond of a spiritual tie. Thus, Mosul would become a place befitting its name.[191] If they are skeptical about the outcome of this great undertaking, let them put it to the test. Let them entrust the party of reform to set down a program for establishing the supreme imamate in this location, along with implementing its ordinances and embracing the means it provides for purifying Islam. Then, nobody in the surrounding territories would adhere to it except voluntarily and as a matter of free choice.

Were the Turkish state to assent to this, on condition that it would have the role of guardian and protector, the hope is that the Arabs and Kurds in this and the neighboring areas would assent to it, and that all of those in the surrounding regions would agree to respect it. It would then perpetrate no injustice, and nor would injustice be perpetrated against it. Otherwise, the obligation is to endeavor to restore things to their original state and establish them in their proper place, after removing all obstacles and preparing all means of action. If it is initially incomplete and weak, it will become complete, and strong. Indeed: "Verily Islam started as something strange and it would again revert to being strange, just as it started, and it would recede between the two mosques just as the serpent crawls back into its hole."[192] "A group of people among my followers will remain obedient to God's orders and they will not be harmed by

The Caliphate

anyone who will not help them or who will oppose them, till God's order comes upon them while they are still on the right path"[193] — stated by the Prophet, as affirmed in sound hadiths.

(26) MODELS OF PROGRAMS REQUIRED FOR THE CALIPHATE

The first duty for the party that wishes to direct its attention toward undertaking this great reform is to:

- set in place a basic program for bringing the government of the caliphate into being in its most complete form, which, under present circumstances, is required to guard the state's religion and politics, or that of the Islamic states, and to reform the Muslim community;
- set in place a plan enabling this program to be implemented as quickly as is viable;
- produce a work on the fundamental principles of the shari'ah that would provide a basis for Islamic positive law. This work would disprove the allegations of anyone who argues that in this era the shari'ah is unsuited to civilization and progress.

After a comprehensive program for establishing the imamate upon its foundations has been set in place, enabling its roles and functions to be carried out, a temporary program for an imamate of necessity could be set in place, with implementation of the programs commencing simultaneously.

A specific example of an action based upon this broad outline: founding an advanced madrasah whose graduates would be trained to hold the office of the supreme imamate and undertake ijtihad in the revealed law. The following would be selected from its graduates: those working in the special office of the caliphate, qadis, muftis, and those whose role is to formulate common law and programs for calling people to Islam, defending Islam, and eliminating the innovations and superstitions that Islam's people still cling to. Topics studied in this madrasah would include principles of international law, religious communities and sects (heresiography), universal history, sociology, and the study of how religious institutions — such as the Vatican, patriarchates, episcopates, and their affiliated associations — are organized and function. Then, when individuals graduate from this madrasah with all of the qualifications required for the caliphate — most important, competence in the science of ijtihad and integrity — the need to install a caliph who is ignorant and dissolute will be no more.

One of the graduates of this madrasah would then be freely elected by people qualified for that task. Care must be taken to ensure that they include representatives of all Islamic lands, especially those that are independent, in accordance with a program set in place specifically for that purpose. The rest of the people who loose and bind, in whom the entire Muslim community has complete confidence, would then pledge allegiance to him. When this happens it stands as a proof for every individual, group, or people that he is the rightful imam. He is the representative of the Messenger, God's prayer and peace be upon him, in religion and the politics of worldly life. Obeying him in everything pertaining to public welfare that does not involve a definitive sin, firmly established as such by a text in the Book or the sunnah [the Qur'an or the hadith], is then a duty under the revealed law. It is impermissible to disobey him in anything related to that on the basis of ijtihad that is contrary to his ijtihad, or by following another mujtahid. That is because his ijtihad takes precedence over the ijtihad of others in matters of public welfare, if he is qualified for ijtihad, and it is required that he is. Each man follows his own personal ijtihad, or a fatwa that issues from his heart and puts his conscience at ease, only in matters of personal affairs. Those are matters on which the ulama's ijtihad has produced varying results, such as differing views on whether or not such-and-such is licit.

Every Muslim is permitted to call the caliph to account when his actions run contrary to a text. The people who loose and bind are permitted to call him to account over his opinion and ijtihad when implementing that would undermine rather than promote public welfare. In what is at issue here, the caliph's ijtihad can be said to have effect as does the ruling of a judge who resolves a dispute on an issue—where that issue is one that is subject to ijtihad. But if someone knows that he is not actually entitled to what has been adjudicated in his favor, it is not religiously permissible for him to accept it. That is because his knowledge of the facts takes precedence over the qadi's opinion, where the qadi uses his ijtihad to make a ruling, or to determine how a rule should be applied in a given case, as related in sound hadith. However, the Hanafis hold that a judge's ruling has effect for both what is known and what is not known. In their view, it is thus religiously permissible for you to accept what a qadi adjudicates in your favor, even if you know that it is not rightfully yours.

That said, I call the [reform] party's attention to the most important programs and organizations upon which accomplishing what we propose depends: (1) a program for establishing an advanced madrasah whose graduates would be caliphs and mujtahids; (2) a program for electing caliphs; (3) program for establishing the caliphate's administrative and financial offices and its councils:

(a) a council for general consultation;
(b) a council responsible for fatwas, works on religion and the shari'ah, and for supervision of publications;

The Caliphate 141

(c) a council responsible for investiture, and delegating to heads of government, qadis, and muftis;

(d) a council responsible for the general supervision of government;

(e) a council responsible for calling people to Islam, and for those who make the call;

(f) a council responsible for preaching in mosques, exhortations, religious guidance, and the office of the *hisbah*;

(g) a council responsible for the zakat, which is obligatory under the shari'ah, and its disbursement;

(h) a council responsible for the hajj and the Haramayn;

(i) a council for correspondence.

(27) THE MUSLIMS' RENAISSANCE AND ITS DEPENDENCE ON IJTIHAD ON THE REVEALED LAW

I do not see the utility of publishing all of my knowledge and detailed opinions on the ways to renew the supreme Islamic imamate, along with the purposes and benefits of doing so. That is because I fear that Islam's enemies would find a way to turn what I wrote to their own advantage. That would make it easier for them to block our path, while we would not draw any benefit from it ourselves—and that would be required to justify a decision to publish. Indeed, our readiness to undertake this reform remains very weak: the Muslims have grown fond of injustice, afflicted by weakness and reconciled to humiliation. None of the Muslim peoples demonstrated any resolve in regard to what is good or what is evil prior to this current era, which saw this new development among some of them. The primary cause of that development was the force of foreign pressure bearing down on them. It was not caused by Muslims returning to their religion's guidance. Nor was it stimulated by them coming to realize the truth of the matter, which is as follows. By forsaking religious guidance, the Muslims were losing what they had acquired by following the path it sets down for them. Had they applied the revealed law correctly and obeyed God's command in the Almighty's statement, "Prepare whatever power you can" [Qur'an 8:60], nobody would have outdone them in producing guns, bombs, and other instruments of war, nor in building great ships that float in the sea like mountains.[194] No one would have surpassed them in the sciences and arts upon which these activities depend. No one would have surpassed them in the things that give expression to a civilization, the adornments of worldly life, and the good things in life. What they read in their revealed Book [the Qur'an] speaks clearly and decisively to this point: "Say, 'Who has forbidden the beautiful things of God which

Muhammad Rashid Rida

He brought forth for His servants and the good things of sustenance?' Say, 'They are for those who believe during the life of this world: they will be theirs alone on the Day of Resurrection'" [Qur'an 7:32].

Had this renaissance been brought about by people following Islam's guidance—which is fit to enable something even more advanced—they would have progressed faster in developing their civilization, and made more progress in achieving their goals. In that case, reviving the institution of the caliphate would not require great effort or persistence, or the formation of a party. Yet Islamic sentiment is among the most potent spiritual forces that may be harnessed in the effort to bring about a renaissance. This is so even if some of those working toward that renaissance are entirely lacking in Islamic sentiment and are, moreover, its enemies. But most of them appreciate that the great majority of the people continue to hold to it. Hence, they recognize that they must show deference to it and indulge those who embrace it, and continue to do that until they find themselves able to raise an entirely new generation, instilling in its youth a purely ethnic sentiment that is then broadly adopted by the people.

This is what we know from experience regarding the renaissance in Egypt and among the Turks. Besides that, we have been told that the Afghans' recent renaissance has a civil rather than a religious character. They are the most religious and least Europeanized of the rising Islamic peoples. Indeed, it is accurate to say that they are quite void of Europeanization. We use that term to refer to an infatuation with blindly imitating Europeans in the superficial aspects of their lives, customs, and politics—their form of government. But Europeanization does not mean following them when it comes to the sciences, arts, industries, and programs that they have developed in this era. Furthermore, this follows long centuries during which we had greater claim in these domains. We were more qualified, while they were bereft of the necessary knowledge and skills. The best of the news that has reached us from the Afghans is that in this renaissance of theirs they are taking care to acquire the arts of agriculture and industry from Europe, but not its ethics and legal sciences. That is because what they have in Islam's ethics and shari'ah makes that redundant. This point applies especially if here they follow the path of independent knowledge, the path of ijtihad. The reason is that Islamic progress depends on that: Islam depends on it for its renovation as it depended on it when it first emerged. We have made this point repeatedly. It is necessary to repeat oneself a great deal when discussing subjects such as this. If the Afghans were closely tied to the Arabian Peninsula, and made Arabic their official language, they would be the Islamic people most worthy of taking the lead in reviving the institution of the caliphate. Yet there is great hope that they will revive Islam's civilization

The Caliphate   143

in the East, and small wonder, since the rouser and leader of the East in this era emerged from their lands.[195]

Muslims will be unable to revive Islam as a religion of sovereignty and power, bringing its guidance together with its civilization, except by undertaking ijtihad on its expansive and flexible revealed law. That is because neglecting ijtihad is what led some Muslims to regress to Bedouinism, which had been eliminated, or to something approaching it. Such neglect led other Muslims to stray to Europeanization, heresy, and efforts to distance themselves from religion.

An example of this is seen in the Turks appointing as caliph someone who is adept in the arts of painting and music, including playing stringed instruments. Yet according to the teachings of all four schools of law [madhhabs] both of these activities are forbidden, and lead to the loss of integrity. The strictest on this point is the Hanafi school, which the Turkish people follow, and the shari'ah court in Egypt recently rejected the testimony of a professor of music. In both of these matters, however, a solution could be found through ijtihad, as we will indicate in this investigation. During his recent travels in Anatolia Ghazi Mustafa Kemal Pasha was asked about the production of statues and their erection in the land: is this not forbidden under the revealed law? It was related that the people were going to erect a statue of him in Angora (Ankara). He gave a fatwa stating that this is not forbidden today as it was forbidden at the time when Islam began, a time still close to the pagan era. He declared that the Turkish nation should busy itself sculpting statues, as that is among the indispensable arts of this era's civilization. He invoked statues he had seen in Egypt, finding support for their permissibility in that.

He issued a fatwa on behalf of himself and the government on the issue of women and men fraternizing and working together. Moreover, he established a new norm here when he married a young Europeanized woman in Izmir. She appeared in person in the marriage hall, and stood facing him. The qadi asked her about her consent to having him as her husband. She answered in the affirmative, and he registered their marriage. After that she traveled with him dressed in the attire of a rider, and stood with him in the company of the men that he met. What he declared on the issue of women and their place in the new Turkish nation would be unacceptable to religious leaders and to those having a religious disposition. He continues to be asked about the community's religious affairs and responds with fatwas based upon his opinions, sometimes erroneously, sometimes soundly. What is needed to resolve these kinds of issues is to adopt a middle position, in between blindly rushing into the new and the inertia of rigid adherence to the old. That can only be achieved by acting independently and embracing ijtihad, not by *taqlid*, blindly imitating others.

Mustafa Kemal Pasha is intelligent and eloquent. But he is not versed in the rational principles of the revealed law, nor is he a jurist [*faqih*]. He feels empowered to deliver fatwas on these kinds of religious issues on the basis of his acquired status in the military realm, and the conceit of his political prestige. The masses yield to what he commands, while jurists dare not challenge him. Yet it will not be possible for his government—the government of an Islamic nation—to continue on this path on the basis of a single personality's influence. Thus, it must choose one of three options:

Either: follow what the jurists of the Hanafi school of law [madhhab] have prescribed, proceeding in accordance with the most widely recognized opinions found in fatwa collections. Nobody who seeks a modern civilization, whether they pursue that in a moderate or an extremist fashion, would assent to this option.

Or: they can eliminate the government's Islamic character, advocating the separation of religion and state. This is what the Europeanized freethinkers hope for. But there is no viable path to that, as the community's great majority are Muslims, and it is they who hold power and whose opinions will be dominant in the National Assembly.

There remains only a third option: the path of independent knowledge, the path of ijtihad, which we have commended. This is the option that can prove the following to this government, and to the entire world:

- that the Islamic form of law, the shari'ah, is the most comprehensive and complete;
- that its fundamental principles include forbidding everything proven to be harmful, permitting everything proven to be beneficial, and making everything necessary a binding duty;
- that what is prohibited by its texts may become permissible in cases of necessity;
- that what is prohibited in order to prevent corruption may become permissible when maintaining public welfare presents a more pressing need.

(28) EXAMPLES OF THE TURKS' NEED FOR IJTIHAD ON THE REVEALED LAW

We have already broached the main points that need to be discussed here. As for making images, this was prohibited for a well-known reason: blocking a path that might lead to paganism and imitation of God's creation. If images are necessary because of a need in the realm of science that outweighs that prohibition, they are permissible under the revealed law. That permission rests on

The Caliphate   145

the condition that there is no suspicion that they would be used for worship, or that there is any intention to imitate God's creation. Examples of this include images of bodies that are used to facilitate precision in the sciences of medicine and surgery. Images can also be used in identifying birds and animals with precision, and purely for the sake of improving the accuracy of language. They can also be useful when it comes to questions about the application of the revealed law that may arise from that, such as questions about what may and may not be eaten where eating predatory animals is forbidden. Images can also be used in relation to numerous other scientific, military, and administrative matters—such as in photographing spies and criminals. All of this is permissible under the revealed law. We have explicated this in detail in *Al-Manar*'s fatwas.[196]

This is one of the matters that Mustafa Kemal Pasha treated in a perfunctory fashion. He gave a fatwa permitting it without any restrictions and from all angles. Yet it is not something to be allowed without any restrictions. His reasoning—erecting statues of leading men is permissible because the Egyptian government has done so—resembles his reasoning that stripping the caliph's authority now is sound because the 'Abbasid caliphs were stripped of their authority. But this has nothing to do with the religion because the Egyptian government is not restricted by the revealed law when it comes to justifying all of its actions. It did not erect these statues on the basis of a fatwa issued by ulama at Al-Azhar or other ulama. Were it to request a fatwa from them they would not give one. That is not only because the erection of statues is forbidden in Islam, but also because it entails spending a great deal of the community's money on something that brings no public benefit. They do not accept the specious claim of those who hold that erecting statues of great men animates the community, instilling a desire to imitate them, and perform actions like theirs. That is because they are absolutely certain of the following: that it has not occurred to any Egyptian that he should be like Muhammad 'Ali Pasha, Ibrahim Pasha, or the Frenchman Sulayman Pasha, whose statues are in Cairo and Alexandria; that statues of those who set a bad example might also be erected; and that this is one of the Europeans' traditions of ornamenting their civilization, one requiring a great expenditure and which only rich nations with vast wealth could undertake.[197]

Even if this were absolutely permissible under our revealed law it would be worthier for us not to do it. There are two considerations that would outweigh its permissibility. (1) We need to economize because we remain poor peoples. (2) We need to avoid blindly imitating the Europeans when it comes to distinctive features of their civilization that have seduced us, as these are among the things that have caused us to glorify them and disparage ourselves. Indeed, our Prophet, God's prayer and peace be upon him, prohibited us from copying others so that we could remain independent and moreover, be an example for them. This is an important social issue, and we have outlined the harms that may result in detail and on many occasions.

Mustafa Kemal Pasha's statement that the community must perfect the skills of manufacturing and sculpting statues may be rebutted by noting that the community has neglected many industries that are mandatory under the revealed law. These are all things upon which people's livelihoods and their ability to fulfill essential duties depend. They include industries for clothing, weaponry, airplanes, warships, and other things. Thus, it is unsound for someone to neglect essential things and everyday needs, being content to depend on foreigners for them, and instead take great interest in a matter that is purely one of ornamentation, even if it is not something that is harmful to the religion or to worldly life!

As for the question of music, those who prohibit it do not have at their disposal sound texts comparable to the hadiths that prohibit making images, pictures, and statues. Rather, this is a disputed question. In *Al-Manar*, we have discussed the arguments of those who forbid listening to singing and stringed instruments. This discussion involved narrations, analysis, and derivation of law. We determined that the fundamental principle here is that musical activities are permissible, but forbidden when they lead someone to commit another sin, such as when listening to music causes someone to be tempted to drink wine, or commit some other depravity. We also determined that pursuit of musical activities should remain within reasonable bounds, otherwise it is reprehensible . . . etc.[198]

As for the issue of women, here Islam's ordinances are the most elevated, just, and superior of all ordinances. Most of what the wise and learned criticize concerning urban Muslim women who wear hijab, and rightly, has to do with social custom. And if those who wish to change social customs are seeking guidance on how to relinquish those that are harmful while retaining those that are beneficial, they will find that the Islamic revealed law is their strongest ally in that endeavor. Distinguishing the harmful from the beneficial on this and similar questions is no easy task. Rather, it requires careful scrutiny and investigation. That is because people have offered a variety of different opinions on this matter, which results from their differing sentiments and educational backgrounds. This may be seen in the following example.

A professor from one of the official madrasahs in the region accosted a married woman, tempting her. He spoke to her while she was walking in the street, saying something in the vein of how her beauty made it impossible for him

The Caliphate

147

to sleep at night. Her husband filed suit against him in the national court.[199] He did so in efforts to see the professor punished for tempting his wife and attempting to corrupt her against him. The qadi of the Court of First Instance ruled that the professor was innocent. He justified his behavior on the basis that it was informed by a praiseworthy instinct, love of beauty, and evidenced a sound sensitivity. How, then, could it be considered a sin punishable under the law? But the qadi of the Court of Appeal considered his action a sin, and ruled that he be punished.

In this era, the Muslims of Egypt and Turkey—and others like them—are educated in shifting and confused ways that vary greatly. Some of them are extremists in their promotion of Europeanization. They want to allow immoral behaviors, and incline toward libertinism. They are a minority, thanks be to God. Some of them hold rigidly to all of the old traditions, the good and the bad, especially those traditions that may be ascribed to the religion—even if they are ascribed erroneously. Between the two are people who embrace moderation and balance. They include religious scholars and modern scientists.[200]

What is needed is to refer the matter of all of the community's customs where there is a desire for change to committees comprised of these moderates. They would be responsible for exploring every angle in investigating what is beneficial and what is harmful. They should then set in place a program for implementing the changes that they determine are required. When doing that, they should give due consideration to the laws of social evolution. They should also be wary of the dangers of hasty and impulsive action. That can lead to chaos, and cause great disharmony between individuals and groups in the community. Indeed, the present generation is the previous generation's progeny and heir in its instincts, actions, passions, and customs. Beyond that, its roots go back to the preceding generations. Were the present generation tasked with relinquishing certain practices or customs, that would only prove easy where it aligns with people's desires and what brings them pleasure. That would not prove easy when it comes to changes based on the dictates of reason, or that are needed to maintain public welfare.

They would, then, face opposition from a large section of the community. This follows the workings of human instinct, as love of creating the new and love of preserving the old are both products of that instinct. Thus, the one love will be manifest in one people, and the other love in another people. This accords with what God—the Wise, the Just—has decreed. Otherwise, people's lives would follow a single, unchanging pattern, like those of bees or ants. Or, each day they would be living in the new, but never maintaining it. Thus, no generation would resemble any other generation.

Whoever imagines that he can destroy a community by abolishing its core values — its doctrines, instincts, and ethics — and its distinctive characteristics — its morals and customs — and then resurrect it anew in the span of a single generation: he is deceived. Whoever thinks that that could be achieved by changing a community's positive laws and the form of its government, and then prevailing upon it to accept those changes in speeches, poetry, and newspapers: he is deceived. The coercive force that would impel it to do that is only found under a despotic government.

To be sure, change is possible and does indeed occur. The path to it is well known. God Almighty guides us to that path in His statement: "God will not change what is in a people until they change what is in themselves" [Qur'an 13:11]. A people can only systematically change "what is in themselves" through raising and educating people in a unified and consistent manner. Sociologists have determined that the things that would induce a people to change its condition only have effect after three generations. These are the generation of deference and imitation [jil al-taqlid wa al-muhakah], the generation of fusion [jil al-khadramah], and the generation of independence [jil al-istiqlal], and as it reaches maturity the capacity for change is completely developed. Peoples move through these generations similarly to individuals passing through the stages of primary, secondary, and advanced education. Some peoples might excel in certain talents in the way that some individuals excel by virtue of their exceptional intelligence. This enables them to master talents at the outset that an unintelligent person has not acquired by the end of his development. In his book *People's Development* [*L'évolution des peuples*], the famous French philosopher and sociologist Gustave Le Bon determined that the ability to acquire the sciences did not take root in any community on earth in less than the three stipulated generations, with the exception of the Arabs.[201] They stood alone in being raised with this ability. It was their lot to give it distinct expression, beginning with the first generation to be raised under Islamic civilization. Therefore, wherever a change is desired for the community the matter should be referred to committees of specialists. They would be charged with studying and clarifying the matter. They would determine which changes would promote the Muslims' communal welfare, and how to implement them while remaining true to their shari'ah.

Elaborating this point is not our intention at this juncture. That would be a digression from our purpose here: bringing the discussion of the issue of women, and likewise similar issues, back to the fundamental principles of rational science. Confusion over this matter prevails in our lands, as also in the Turkish lands. Take, for instance, how we see what some people regard as a clear-cut harm being regarded by others as beneficial and essential. Those

The Caliphate

149

who blindly imitate the Europeans here resemble those who inflexibly cling to what is old. They lack guidance and insight. The Europeans' wisest sages and leading scholars are dissatisfied with the condition of European women. Indeed, we have been told that when the German emperor was in Constantinople during the war, and witnessed Turkish women behaving immorally and appearing in the presence of men dressed like European women, he censured Talat Pasha, the Ittihadist grand vizier.[202] He said: your religion provides you with a restraining influence when it comes to women, and this bears on the things that we complain about in Europe, moral and economic problems that we cannot remedy. How, then, could you discard this of your own volition? You have erred in this matter.

On some issues Muslim scholars of jurisprudence [fiqh] cling to positions that are at odds with the needs of modern civilization and the maintenance of public welfare. A noteworthy example is found with the liquid called alcohol or spirits. They claim that it is an impurity whose use by doctors, pharmacists, and other workers who consider it essential to their industries is forbidden in all instances. Indeed, in recent months a group of jurists [faqihs] in India issued a fatwa to this effect. We responded with a lengthy rebuttal in which we affirmed that this liquid is something pure and a medical disinfectant. It is a necessity that is essential for many purposes, and a necessity generally speaking. Yet the fundamental principle concerning fatwas issued by individual ulama is that they may be acted upon when someone is convinced of the soundness of the evidence upon which they are based and has confidence in the expertise of the issuer. That point applies where a fatwa is supported by evidence indicating that it is in keeping with the way of the ancestors, the way that we have followed in *Al-Manar*. An alternative view, embraced by Muslims who take a traditionalist approach, is that someone may act upon a fatwa when the issuer is affiliated with his own school of law [madhhab]. Thus, let it be known that issuing fatwas does not solve problems of a general nature. Rather, it keeps the Muslim community in state of confusion. That is because of the incompatible differences seen in fatwas and opinions given by the ulama. Only the supreme imam, the caliph, can solve these problems and unify the Muslim community, provided that he is a mujtahid, as discussed above.

(29) IJTIHAD ON THE REVEALED LAW DEPENDS UPON THE ARABIC LANGUAGE

As we have established above, combining this era's civilization and arts with safeguarding Islam can only be realized through ijtihad on the revealed law. Thus, the caliph—the rightful imam whom it is a duty to obey, who is able to spread the call to the religion, safeguard it, resist innovations, and eliminate disputes within the Muslim community over social and civil issues that affect the public—cannot be someone who is not a mujtahid. Ijtihad depends upon command of the Arabic language, its idioms and distinctive constructions, and being well versed in a specialized field of learning. This enables comprehension of the texts of the Book and the sunnah [the Qur'an and the hadith] which constitute the high apogee of the Arabic language. In all of the schools of law [madhhabs] ulama who study the principles of the revealed law have determined that having personally mastered the Arabic language is a requirement for ijtihad, along with being learned in the Book and the sunnah [the Qur'an and the hadith]. Moreover, some of the ulama's imams declared that knowledge of this language is a duty that is incumbent upon every Muslim. That even applies to a *muqallid,* namely, someone one who is not qualified to formulate independent opinions and thus defers to someone who is so qualified. Were it not that all of the ancestors of the Muslim community had subscribed to this view, Arabic would not have spread during the best centuries in every land in which Islam spread, without organized madrasahs administered by governments or societies. Is there any reason for that, other than belief in the religious duty? Among the indications of that are that we see the ulama across all eras and in all locations being in consensus on the need to perform all of the acts of worship that are spoken in this language. Examples include the recitations of the Qur'an in the prayer, and the litanies of the prayer, the hajj, etc. They even persist in using this language for preaching the Friday sermon, not merely for glorifying God, the two testimonies of faith, recitation, and supplication [*du'a'*]. However, some translate the sermon following the prayer. It has been reported to us from Constantinople that on the first Friday on which the new spiritual caliph attended the prayer the sermon was delivered in the Turkish language. It is known as a matter of course that in Islam we show our devotion to God by reflecting on the Qur'an and taking lessons and warnings from its verses, and by taking cognizance of the recitations and litanies in the prayer. All of that depends on knowledge of the Arabic language. The shortcomings of some Muslims in fulfilling this duty are like their shortcomings in numerous other duties that have led them to squander their religion and their worldly lives.

It is not our purpose here to call on non-Arab Muslims to learn the Arabic language. Our purpose is only to draw the party of reform's attention to the strong connection between the institution of the caliphate and the Arabic language. This is a point that most of its supporters are not unaware of. Our reason for highlighting this point is that the party will face strong resistance when it

The Caliphate
151

comes to the issue of the language. But it has a strong proof. Without the language, ijtihad on Islam's ordinances, and indeed the life of Islam itself, is impossible. Without it, it is impossible for Muslims to become acquainted with one another and unite to the maximum extent possible. That is because in every region in which Muslims reside, and in every city in which Islam remains alive, there are people who know Arabic. It is possible to become acquainted with them, and promulgate what, through their efforts, has been determined as the best way to support the religion.

Linguistic ties are a kind of ethnic tie, and Islam forbids ethnic partisanship. That is because it divides the Muslim community, destroys fidelity and unity, and replaces friendship with enmity. The Prophet, God's prayer and peace be upon him, forbade blind and ignorant partisanship, and absolved himself of responsibility for anyone who calls for it or fights for it. Islam's religious and social reforms include unifying people through language. It did so by making the language of this universal religion a language for those belonging to all of the different ethnic communities that are guided by it. The religion was safeguarded by the language, and the language was safeguarded by the religion. Thus, if not for Islam the language would have changed, as did other languages, and as it had changed before the coming of Islam. If not for the language minds would have become estranged from other minds over how to comprehend Islam, which would have broken up into religions whose followers would have accused each other of disbelief. Its followers would have been without comprehensive principles that they could appeal to as they sought to understand and apply what is right, and forsake their passions. The Arab race, the descendants of Ya'rub bin Qahtan, then, was not singled out in having Arabic language bestowed upon it. Rather, it is the language of all Muslims, and the language of other non-Arab peoples, and of non-Muslim Arab communities.

No non-Arabs have served Islam but to the extent of their knowledge of its language. Nobody of Arab descent has made a distinction between Sibawayh, the Persian, and his teacher Khalil, the Arab, in regard to their merits and ijtihad in service of the language, nor between Bukhari, the Persian, and his Arab teachers, Ahmad ibn Hanbal and Ishaq bin Rahwayh, in regard to their service to the prophetic tradition (sunnah).[203] Moreover, prior to this era it had not occurred to anyone in the Muslim community, neither its ancestors or its later generations, to disdain showing a preference for numerous non-Arabs over their own Arab peers and teachers regarding their distinguished service to this religion and its language. We do not know of anyone among the non-Arab ulama who has served Islam in some way who does not know its language. Had

Muhammad Rashid Rida

the religion's ulama among all of the Islamic peoples not persisted in agreeing to show devotion to God by reciting the Qur'an, a miracle for humankind, in its Arabic style, and to perform the litanies of the prayer and other things in Arabic, and to study qur'anic exegesis and hadith in Arabic, then Islam would have been squandered among the non-Arab Islamic peoples.

Had the Ottoman state given new life to the Arabic language in the lands that it conquered from Europe, Islam would have spread there, then throughout the neighboring lands, and a very deeply rooted Islamic civilization similar to the Arab civilization of Andalusia would have been established there. But it did not do that, and it did not make its language, Turkish, a language of the sciences and arts. Rather, it depended solely on the power of the sword to maintain its rule. Among the consequences of that—which are numerous—was that all of the peoples subject to its command and authority preserved their own languages, even the Muslims among them. Thus, when linguistic partisanship cropped up anew in this era and the Ottoman Turks made their language a language of science, they sought to force all Islamic peoples under their authority to relinquish their own languages in favor of the state's language. But they all resisted them. Those speaking languages unsuited to science—such as the Albanians, Kurds, and Circassians (Jarkas)—began to address that, as the Turks had done, so that their own languages became fit for the sciences and arts. The state fought the Albanians, its greatest opponents in Europe, over the issue of language. They chose to fight it, rebelling over the issue of relinquishing their language. Had it been content to make Islam's language its own language, and then called them to it, they would not have refused. This issue is the one that has divided Turks and Arabs, a division whose ill effects we have referred to numerous times in this investigation. We attempted to repair it before the gravity of the dangers it posed grew severe. But our attempt was not successful. How can it be rational for Arabs to accept Turkish as a replacement for Arabic, which God has exalted above all languages in his Book [the Qur'an], which, in addition to its other distinctions, is a miracle for the benefit of human beings and His proof against them until the day of resurrection? We note here the case of the Tatars. They are brothers to the Turks, given their shared Turanian roots.[204] Yet they refuse to relinquish their own language and replace it with Turkish, which is superior to it.

We now face, then, circumstances from which there is no escaping. Everything that we strive for is aimed at preventing their harmful effects. In addition, we aim to reconcile the effort to unite communities through Islam with the effort to unite communities on the basis of ethnicity and language. That is achievable through the means we have detailed, which would see Arabs and

The Caliphate

Turks cooperating in establishing the true Islamic caliphate. If God grants this venture success, it will enable unity and then happiness in this world and in the afterlife, which results from that.

(30) ISLAMIC LEGISLATION [*ISHTIRA'*] AND THE CALIPHATE

By "legislation" we mean what in our Islamic terminology is referred to as derivation of law and ijtihad, and what in contemporary terminology is referred to as *tashri'*, legislation in the modern context (although some of our ulama have used that term as a synonym for revealed law [*shar'*] in theological contexts). It refers to setting out the ordinances that the government requires to establish justice among the people, preserve internal security and order, protect borders, promote the public welfare, and prevent the emergence of corruption. These ordinances vary across time and place, because people's religious and civic circumstances vary across time and place. As the just Imam 'Umar bin 'Abd al-'Aziz, may God be pleased with him, said: "New rulings are introduced for the people in proportion to whatever new outrages [*fujur*] they commit." This principle also applies to other unprecedented acts, both the harmful and the beneficial. Thus, these ordinances are subject to change, even though they all have a single goal, which we have noted above: the establishment of justice, etc.

A civil government cannot operate effectively unless it legislates. It is not possible for any people to ascend the steps that lead to civilization unless it has stable government. That is achieved through ensuring that its legislation is just, speaks to the people's needs—which are conditioned by their particular historical experiences—and sets them upon the highways and byways that lead to advanced civilization. It is unfitting for any people to adopt the law of another people that differs from it in its core values, distinctive characteristics, and historical experiences. In the same way, it is unfitting for one language to adopt the rules of another language with respect to morphology and syntax. Exceptions to that occur when a people wishes to merge and unite with another so that the two become one. That was the case when many different peoples unified through Islam, becoming one people with one law. Then there are those who adopt the laws of others [without any revision]. They do not use independent judgment or ijtihad to determine how to transform the adopted laws so that they harmonize with their own beliefs, morals, and welfare, the things that form the basis of a people's independence. When this happens, it is not long before corruption and confusion begin to spread among the people. Their national cohesion and independence weaken, thus creating an obstacle to political independence and all that derives from it. The law of a people is the symbol of its glory and honor, and the spirit of its life and its growth.

The strangest thing that has afflicted some of the Islamic peoples is that they abandoned a shari'ah that has a firm foundation in truth, and has universally applicable principles that guarantee justice and equality, and replaced it with the inferior laws of other peoples. As a result, they were left without an imam of their own when it comes to their own legislation. Instead, they are taking certain individual Europeans as exemplars, and blindly deferring to them. As a result, they are losing their community's religious revealed law. That law forms the basis of its most important and core values, gives greatest expression to their honor, and constitutes their noblest historical achievement. It is also the foundation of positive human legislation, which is developed through ijtihad.

This brief synopsis, which we present in this treatise, is insufficient to fully explicate all forms of government, past and present, their modes of legislation, and where the Muslims stand in relation to that. We only wish to draw attention to how our Arabic newspapers in this era have expressly declared, time and again, that the most modern principle of legislation is that the right to legislate belongs to the people. Those who write this, along with the majority of those who read their words, believe that:

- this principle was established by Europeans;
- Islam does not grant human beings the authority to legislate because its shari'ah is derived from the Qur'an, whose civil and political rules are few and limited, and from the hadith (sunnah), whose additions to what is in the Qur'an are few and suited to the Muslims' circumstances during the early days of Islam, and not subsequent eras, and most especially this era of ours;
- consensus and ijtihad, because of their dependence on the Book and the sunnah [the Qur'an and the hadith], no longer have effect as sources of law, their doors closed, as is acknowledged by the vast majority of Sunni ulama in all of the Islamic lands; and
- this is why Islamic governments who adhere to the religious shari'ah are lagging, and why the only two civil governments, the Turkish and the Egyptian, were compelled to supplant some laws of the Islamic shari'ah with European laws, first through imitation, and then through explicit positive legislation.

These are the beliefs of those who are ignorant of the Islamic shari'ah's fundamentals and the grounds it provides for legislation, those who do not distinguish between the juristic and modern senses of the word *legislation.*

The Caliphate

155

The word's differing technical senses have blinded them to reality. That is because the words *religion* [*din*] and *revealed law* [*shar'*] are often used interchangeably, even though one is more general than the other.[205] The Muslim jurists regularly use the term *revealed law* specifically in the context of judicial or practical rulings, to the exclusion of the fundamentals of doctrine, wisdom, and ideal conduct that constitute the universal principles of religion and form the basis of prosperity in this life and the life to come.[206] They thus divide jurisprudence [*fiqh*] into two broad divisions: ritual devotions and civil transactions. The jurists for this reason distinguish in this context between religious and judicial decision making, stating, for example, that such-and-such is valid and binding from a judicial perspective, but not from a religious one. Practical rulings are referred to as "religion" in consideration of the fact that accountability to God is maintained through them. Thus, they are regarded as binding in the spirit of submitting to His commands and prohibitions. It is on the basis of this consideration that the word *lawgiver* [*shari'*] is applied to God Almighty unrestrictedly, and to the Prophet, God's prayer and peace be upon him, insofar as he conveys and elaborates the revealed law. Some ulama believe that God Almighty gave him permission to legislate rules of revealed law, but the [vast] majority hold the view that he was the conveyor and elaborator of what was revealed to him, and that revelation as a concept is not limited to the Qur'an.

Upon due consideration, however, the reality is that these matters in their entirety are specifically concerned with religion, with what was legislated to provide people with ways to draw nearer to God. They do that through performing acts of worship, forsaking abominations and forbidden acts, and paying heed to people's rights and the need to act justly when it comes to matters of social relations. This purifies the soul and prepares it for the afterlife. There are some aspects of social relations that have religious implications. Examples of these include the obligations to: respect people's lives, honor, and property; deal with people in good faith; and forsake sin, injustice, aggression, cheating, treachery, and unjustly appropriating the property of others. As for everything else, matters having to do with administration, the judiciary, politics, taxation, and defense—things that, beyond being informed by pure intention, are not specifically constituted for purposes of devotion or drawing nearer to God—the Messenger, God's prayer and peace be upon him, legislated for such things in his time using his ijtihad. God had commanded him to consult the Muslim community on that, and particularly those people having authority. These were individual members of the community—the learned, commanders, and other leading figures. They held the people's trust when it came to decisions affecting public welfare, and their role as representatives of the community. This role of the Prophet was then entrusted to those very individuals after his demise. They chose somebody as their imam, a leader who would embody unity and serve as the Prophet's caliph, namely, as his successor.

God Almighty's statements in the Book [the Qur'an] that speak to these points include:

- His statement: "they consult one another in their affairs" [Qur'an 42:38];
- His statement: "obey God and the Messenger, and those in authority among you" [Qur'an 4:59];
- His statement: "Whenever news of any matter comes to them, whether concerning peace or war, they spread it about; if they referred it to the Messenger and those in authority among them, those seeking its meaning would have found it out from them" [Qur'an 4:83].

Sound hadiths that speak to these points include those referring to:

- what the Prophet said regarding how the Muslim community would not come to an agreement in error;
- what he, God's prayer and peace be upon him, did in making affairs of war and other things pertaining to people's welfare in this world the object of consultation;
- how he permitted the use of ijtihad and opinion to resolve cases that lacked a pertinent text in the Book [the Qur'an] or a pertinent prophetic tradition (sunnah), and the hadith on this point is well known.

The rightly guided caliphs' practices included consulting with those who were learned and insightful on administrative, judicial, and military matters. They also established councils, created taxes, and performed other actions that were not based on any explicit text in the Book and the sunnah [the Qur'an and the hadith]. The notion that the consensus of the Muslim community and the ijtihad of the imams carry authority as sources of law is a fundamental principle of Islamic jurisprudence. All of this falls into the category of what in the terminology of legal science is called legislation [*tashri'*], which is the mujtahids' broad sphere of activity. This represents the practice that was followed during the best centuries.

This clearly establishes:

- that in Islam there is legislation that is authorized by God Almighty;
- that legislation is entrusted to the Muslim community and determined through a process that involves people who have learning, insight, and leadership qualities consulting one another;
- and that authority, in its ultimate sense, inheres in the Muslim community.

The Caliphate

Were it possible for the Muslim community to hold a referendum on a given matter and be found to be in consensus over it, there would be no escaping it. The caliph—to say nothing of authorities subordinate to him—has no right to nullify its consensus, nor to oppose it, nor also to oppose its agents and representatives among the people who loose and bind. The agreement of these people, when they are of a determined number and on condition that they are qualified for ijtihad, is referred to as a "consensus" by ulama whose work concerns the fundamental principles of revealed law.

As for when they disagree, in that case their duty is to resolve their dispute by referring to the two fundamentals, the two foundations, the Book and the sunnah [the Qur'an and the hadith]. They are then to act in accordance with what is supported by evidence from both of them, or one of them. This is in keeping with the Almighty's statement, which follows the command to obey God, and obey the Messenger and those in authority: "If you are in dispute over any matter, refer it to God and the Messenger, if you truly believe in God and the Last Day: that is better and fairer in the end (in interpretation)" [Qur'an 4:59]. This means: it is better in terms of outcomes and results than other options, such as the option of deferring to the majority of the community's representatives and endorsing legislation that blindly imitates European law. That course of action cannot be reconciled with our revealed law.[207] Among the ways in which our law is superior to others, and leads to better outcomes, is that disputation within the community is brought to an end by making the Book and the sunnah [the Qur'an and the hadith] arbitrators in disputes. All of the community's representatives will be agreeable to what the evidence shows to be superior. Thus, no scope for rancor and disputation will remain. What we have discussed at the outset of these investigations (see Sections 3 and 4) suffices to explain authority in Islam, how it inheres in the community and is embodied in the people who loose and bind. For detailed comments on these two points refer to our commentary on the command to "obey God and the Messenger, and those in authority among you" [Qur'an 4:59] in *Tafsir al-Manar*, Part 5.[208]

Legislation—in Islamic terminology referred to as *ishtira'*, *tashri'*, or derivation of law—is a necessity of human society. Islamic law provides ordinances for cases of necessity. Among them: what God Almighty has forbidden being made permissible. After referring to His explanation of forbidden foods, He grants permission to eat them in His statement: "except for what you are forced to do" [Qur'an 6:119]. Among them: removing difficulty and distress from the religion, whose absence from the domain of social relations is more apposite than their absence from the domain of worship, in which it is reasonable that cultivation and purification of the soul should involve a form of hardship, since such cultivation is incomplete without the burden of some hardship and effort. This is eased by the idea that carrying this burden is informed by the intention of drawing near to God, and that through this means one strives for a reward. The underlying goal is to safeguard people, property, and honor against unrightful violations. Thus, someone who is not restrained from that by the fear of being punished by rulers in this life is restrained from it by the fear of God's punishment in the afterlife, if he is a believer in God and in what His Messenger brought, God's prayer and peace be upon him.

From this, it is clear that there are extensive prescriptions for civil, criminal, political, and military legislation. Among them are rules for cases of necessity, removing difficulties, and preventing harms. Thus, had it not been stipulated in the Qur'an that the faithful are to determine their communal affairs through consulting one another, and had it not been mandated that, following obedience to God and His Messenger, obedience is due to those who hold authority, and had it not been mandated that the community hand responsibility for these affairs to them, and entrust them with the task of deriving applicable ordinances for them, and had the Prophet, God's prayer and peace be upon him, not granted Mu'adh permission to use his own ijtihad and opinion in cases that came his way and that lacked an applicable text in God's Book [the Qur'an] and for which there was no example from his Messenger to be followed:[209] had all of this along with other evidence that conveys the same notion not been related, the rule of necessity would have sufficed to provide a shari'ah-based principle enabling derivation of law, which in this era's terminology is referred to as legislation.[210] In addition, consider the community's practice during Islam's early era and its best centuries. Then consider what followed during the Middle Ages. In that era the caliphate, safeguarder of communal affairs, deviated from the path of independent reasoning, the two ending together because they were mutually dependent.[211]

The caliphate is the anchor of unity, the source of legislation, the path to order, and the guarantor that ordinances are implemented. Its pillars are the people who loose and bind, who conduct their affairs through consultation and whose leader is the supreme imam. It is stipulated that all of them be qualified to legislate. Under our system's fundamental principles that is accomplished by means of ijtihad and derivation of law. The first corruption to befall the system of the caliphate, cracking its pillars, occurred when it was rendered an inherited institution held by people whose authority rested purely on force and the support of a partisan group. The first shortcoming that would afflict the Muslims befell them because they did not follow their duty and establish a system for maintaining its foundations. That duty was established in the command given to the community: follow the guidance of the Book and the sunnah [the Qur'an

The Caliphate

and the hadith], and adhere to the rules they set down. The first harm to result from the one and the other was that the caliphs stripped authority from the people who loose and bind—the people who represent the community—and became dependent upon people whose power rested upon partisanship, the elimination of which had been one of the most important reforms that Islam had brought to human affairs. Thus, the condition of the community—righteous and corrupt—depended upon the extent to which the caliph and his assistants were righteous. But these assistants belonged to the caliph's own partisan group. They were not representatives of the whole community. They lacked learning and insight, and were not motivated by the feeling that they should care for the community and be earnestly concerned for its welfare. They did not hold the people's confidence.

As a result, the caliphs felt that they could dispense with learning, or that they had no need for it. They felt no need to relinquish the enjoyment of frivolous pleasures and devote themselves to the scientific method so as to become proficient in ijtihad. They saw that they could seek assistance from ulama who had assumed roles as viziers, qadis, and muftis, in addition to other roles that require one to derive rulings. In this way, they did not act in a rational, scientific manner. That led them to become ignorant of the ulama's true value. They began entrusting the ulama's functions to people who were as ignorant as they were themselves. They were able to find among such people someone who would deliver a fatwa stating that the capacity to reason independently (the capacity to exercise ijtihad) was not a qualification required of the Muslims' imam, nor of a qadi, as both may seek the assistance of a mufti, who can only be a mujtahid. Ignorance then became widespread, and the caliphs began to seek fatwas from people who were ignorant like themselves—that is, from people who were not mujtahids. These ignorant people, who came to monopolize the offices of the state and its finances, then declared that the gate of ijtihad was closed and could not be reopened. They obligated everyone—themselves and the community—to follow and associate with designated individual ulama, and thereafter began to follow anyone who was affiliated with them. This is in spite of the legal consensus on the point that it is impermissible to follow a *muqallid*, namely, somebody who is personally incapable of formulating independent opinions on legal questions. In this way, the science of legal norms was squandered, the talent for legislating and deriving law gradually lost, while the community remained unaware of developments. Thus, as governance fell into the hands of the ignorant, the shari'ah and the institution of legislation were squandered. Public order was disturbed. The Muslim community fell into a state of disorder and its power declined. All of these developments resulted from the failure to adhere to what is sound, namely, Islam's fundamental principles and specific provisions. And yet the ignorant reckon that they resulted from adherence to Islam's teachings!!

In his book *Universal History* [*Jami' al-Tawarikh*], Qadi Abu 'Ali Muhassin al-Tanukhi states:

> Abu al-Husayn bin 'Abbas said to me: The first aspect of the political system that we observe falling into decay during the 'Abbasid dynasty's era is administration of the law. That is because Ibn al-Furat (the famous vizier) undermined it by giving people positions as qadis as a reward, even though they lacked the requisite learning and qualifications.[212] Hence over the years it became debased, those unfit for the role assuming responsibility for it, until in the 330s Abu al-'Abbas al-Asfahani al-Katib assumed responsibility for Muttaqi's vizierate. He was extremely servile and shameless.[213]

He goes on to state: "The vizierate's fall was followed by the caliphate's degradation, and it acquired the condition that we can observe. Thus, the 'Abbasid dynasty's state decayed as a result of decay in administration of the law. Ibn Furat's first action in that connection was putting Abu Umayyah al-Ahwas al-Fulani al-Basri in charge of it." He states that he put him in charge for no other reason than as a reward, one that he had promised him when he sought refuge with him and hid at his place during the days of his ordeal.

I say: Ibn Furat was among the most able viziers, and among the most knowledgeable in affairs of politics and power. His conduct was excellent. He dared do such a thing only because of the caliph's ignorance and devotion to diversions and amusements, and furthermore his reveling in excessive pleasure seeking. That is because he was appointed caliph at the age of thirteen. Al-Hafiz al-Dhahabi states: "The system was greatly disturbed in the days of Muqtadir as a result of his young age." Disorder had set in before his time, during the days of Mutawakkil bin al-Mu'tasim, due to the worsening misconduct of the Turks, whom Mu'tasim had relied on extensively, recruiting them to guard and protect the caliphate.[214] Thus, it was they who destroyed its structure and toppled its pillars. The primary factor underlying all of that was the innovation of designating a successor, which the caliphs had justified on the basis that Abu Bakr had designated 'Umar, may God be pleased with him, as his successor. Every caliph then became entitled to designate his successor, a mechanism that functions purely on the basis of power. That was so even for a tyrannical caliph, one who was not regarded as the rightful imam and who had not heeded what Abu Bakr had heeded when he consulted with the people who loose and bind. We explained how this is illegitimate in Section 9 of this treatise.

The Caliphate

From this brief discussion it may be appreciated that the establishment of tyranny led to laxity over certain requirements that are essential for the caliphate to function properly. These include independent reasoning, integrity, and consultation—those who are qualified consulting one another on the imam's appointment and his manner of conduct. This laxity led to the end of the legislative process—derivation of law—without which a state cannot be established, sustained, developed, and advanced. This is what caused the state's weakness, which then caused the community's weakness. That is because instead of the state being subservient to the community, the community became subservient to the state. This intertwined corruption of the state and the community led to multiple changes in social conditions and the affairs of daily life. As a result, there is a need for new shari'ah-based ordinances, ordinances other than those through which affairs were previously managed. Otherwise, what is needed is the reestablishment of the genuine imamate in its true form.

We thank God that it became clear to the pillars of the Turkish state, which arrogates to itself the institution of the caliphate, that the Ottoman state was corrupt, and that after laying claim to the caliphate it did not improve in comparison to its previous condition. Rather, it was not long before defects and weaknesses relating to every aspect of religion and worldly life gradually infected it. That occurred to such an extent that many of those belonging to its Europeanized generation began to declare that it was Islam that was the cause of these harms, and that the rule of the caliphate is a corruption and an obstacle to good living. We then had the opportunity:

- to explain for the benefit of the Turkish state, and likewise the Islamic world generally, most of which was enamored with it, that the state had not been established in accordance with the shari'ah's fundamental principles;
- to explain the true nature of the caliphate, the form of a genuine Islamic government, and how most members of the Grand National Assembly's members had erred in their opinions and actions regarding the matter. We have provided evidence that shows how the fundamental principles of Islamic government are superior to those of other peoples' governments. This is because it combines the prevention of corruption with the safeguarding of material benefits, and combines what is right with what is just, along with the virtues that enable humanity to advance culturally and mankind to attain perfection;
- to call on this Turkish Islamic nation to establish Islam's government as God commanded, and likewise His Messenger and the rightly guided

caliphs, and create the best community ever raised among peoples, even though the Europeanized are opposed to that. "So that those who were to die might die after seeing a clear proof, and so that those who were to live might live after seeing a clear proof. God is all-hearing and all-seeing" [Qur'an 8:42].

(31) LEGISLATION [*ISHTIRA'*] AND THE MUSLIM COMMUNITY'S [UMMAH'S] CONDITION: DISPARITY AND CONFORMITY

Islam sets down general principles for various types of civil and worldly transactions. These principles enable religious guidance to be maintained, and include the stipulation that under Islam government should ensure that virtues are upheld and vices avoided. The right to derive law—to legislate—that Islam grants to those in authority is not completely unlimited. It comes with restrictions. This ensures that they do not corrupt the community's morals through making an error in ijtihad or, if they had themselves become corrupt, by following their passions. It forbade usury, which was common in pre-Islamic Arabia. That is because of how it involves harshness, stinginess, and greed, which lead a person to seek profit in the needs of people who are wanting. Similarly, it forbade fraud and deceit. It made the members of the community guarantors of each other's welfare through the duty it imposed of spending in support of relatives, and through the zakat, which addresses the needs of the poor and the feeble, and other things that are necessary for the maintenance of public welfare. It made a rule that every woman has a guardian who is responsible for her affairs: a husband or relative, or otherwise the supreme imam or his representative. This ensures that she is not forced to earn a living, which, together with her special roles of pregnancy, delivering, nursing, and raising children, would be difficult for her. Forcing women to live self-sufficiently would cause a lower birthrate, in addition to other corruptions.

Among the effects of Islamic peoples and governments being weak in the matter of religion was that both neglected to heed what those principles mandated, and to adhere to rules based upon them. As a result, both had a need to become involved in forbidden practices such as usury, either out of necessity or, where the benefit of doing something appeared to outweigh the corruption it would cause, out of choice.

This is a need that prompts someone who has it to commit a forbidden practice, if he cannot find a way to avoid doing so, and being in the position of lending differs from that of borrowing. An effect of this is seen in Muslims being unable to find anyone to lend to them besides non-Muslims, either *dhimmis*

The Caliphate   163

[those living under Muslim rule and having a pact with the state], or foreigners such as *mu'ahads* [those having a treaty with the Muslim state], who were sometimes *harbis* [those from beyond the realm of Muslim rule]. This leads to Muslims' wealth being passed to others, to say nothing of it passing to their enemies, and their becoming dependent upon them for the most important aspects of their welfare. This is another cause of corruption.

The jurists then discussed issues related to usury at length. What they introduced had not been considered legitimate during the era of Islam's revelation. Most of them provided only a limited number of ordinances for financial contracts. By contrast, the nations with whom the Muslims had dealings invented numerous types of contracts and transactions. Economic sciences and financial practices were developed to such a degree that those who followed the rules and norms they set down came to surpass others in wealth, power, and sovereign command. All of these factors held Muslims back and elevated others above them, even in the Muslims' own lands. Moreover, the clearest cause of what enabled non-Muslims to strip Muslims of their power, while dominating them in places where they retained remnants of their sovereignty, lies in this set of circumstances. It is also what led those who have become familiar with these powerful nations' sciences and practices, but ignorant of Islam's fundamental principles, to believe that the cause of the Muslims' weakness lies in Islam itself. That is because they believe that Islam's revealed law requires Muslims to cling to antiquated ordinances for finance and social relations that impoverish those who adhere to them, and lead to all that poverty brings with it in the way of people being humiliated, weakened, and losing their power.

I began by discussing the issue of finance because it is an example of what befell many Islamic lands as a result of people neglecting to act in accordance with the venerable shari'ah's ordinances, as the livelihood of nations and states in every era rests on finance. In this era, it has acquired an importance that it did not have in any previous era, especially the era of the Prophet, God's prayer and peace be upon him. In that era, the Muslim community had few needs, and its livelihood was not tied to its dealings with other nations. But He who knows the unseen, the Mighty, the Wise, revealed His statement during that era: "Do not entrust your property to the feebleminded. God has made it a means of support for you" [Qur'an 4:5]. In this statement, He advises us of the importance of resources to the livelihood and organization of communities, how they cannot be sustained without them. He exhorts us to guard them, and not enable the feebleminded to act without restraint in how they use what they have. Similarly, in other verses He commands us to be provident, and forbids excess and waste. He criticizes that in the same way that He criticizes gambling, the devourer of wealth, by advising us that it is prohibited—all forms of gambling are prohibited in the religion. Could it be said, then, that this religion's revealed law requires its people to be poor? Could it be said that their livelihoods and the glory of their community and state depend on what lies in the covetous hands of people in other nations? If the answer to both of these questions is no, how can it be that scholars whose field of expertise is the revealed law are their lands' most unlearned people when it comes to the financial sciences and their political implications? Why have they not studied these sciences alongside the other subjects that they examine together in their religious madrasahs? The explanation lies in the fact that none of them live under an Islamic government that has tasked them with doing that to enable it to apply ordinances and arrange budgets in ways that align with the revealed law.

Give them another example: the tendency of some Muslims in Egypt and some among the Turks to embrace socialist teachings, and beyond that to establish socialist parties and call upon people to support them. This either has to do with their infatuation with imitating Europeans, or with how they have become aware, as have Europe's socialists, of the impact of capitalist selfishness on workers and other poor people. Were the Islamic shari'ah implemented, with its guidance for commoners and elites, not one of Islam's people would feel a need for socialist teachings. Moreover, socialists in other nations would see that it provides means for resolving social issues, and on that basis many of them would be guided to embrace Islam, and call others to it.

Why do I not include among my examples of this issue the call of many women and men in such lands for women to be raised to be independent, men's equals in all respects, with men not responsible for them in any regard? Islam preceded all other religions in establishing equality between men and women in domestic affairs, except in the degree referred to in the Almighty's statement: "and women have rights over men as men have rights over them, in accordance with what is recognized as fair, and men are set a degree above them" [Qur'an 2:228].[215] This refers to leadership. God explains this in His statement: "men are the managers of the affairs of women in that God has preferred some of them over others, and in that they spend of their wealth" [Qur'an 4:34]. Thus, the reason He sets down is that men are set above women on the basis of their ability to earn, protect, and defend, and because of how He obligates them to provide for them through the dower and adequate support. Do you see: if Muslim individuals and their rulers correctly applied this shari'ah men would thereby make women equals to themselves in everything other than the role of leadership. That means leadership in the household as well as in the

The Caliphate

public domain, which includes things like the supreme imamate and leading the prayer. They would respect them as the Messenger, God's prayer and peace be upon him, exhorted. Would women then feel the need to ready themselves to earn and take on other arduous roles of men? Or, would they prefer to live in comfort and ease, enjoying the earnings of men under their maintenance and under the guarantee of the shari'ah implemented by their government? In that way, they would be able to enjoy what their men do not enjoy. The woman eats what the man eats from what the man has earned, and prepares his food. But she has greater provision than he does when it comes to the clothes that she wears and the jewelry that adorns her. If there is any injustice in this, it is the man who is wronged.[216]

To summarize this point: failing to act and rule in accordance with the shari'ah in some matters leads to failing to do so in other matters. Or, it creates a situation in which it becomes impossible to adhere to the shari'ah, as what was originally a source of pure benefit has become a cause of corruption. That then affects the community's thinking, morality, and customs, until it is transformed through great changes in its core values and distinctive characteristics. Evil and good, falsehood and truth: each emboldens and supports those of its kind. The Islamic community forsook what would have protected it from declining and falling in that manner, and built the steps to progress for it. It forsook what would have enabled it to derive ordinances from the shari'ah's rules that befit its condition in every era, and attain a state of perfection.

That is because the art of deriving law—namely, the art of legislating—has been lost. That art is permitted to those Muslims who hold authority, and was lost because they lost their cohesion as a group [jama'ah]. Another reason is that there ceased to be a genuine imamate, one that would implement laws that they had derived, as discussed in Sections 3, 4, 5, and 17 of this treatise. The great majority of those [jurists] who did remain engaged in the science of the Islamic revealed law's ordinances did so by studying books composed in previous eras. In those eras the abode of Islam was independent and strong. It had a rich treasury that was sufficient to provide for the needy, the indebted, and other expenses that obtain under the shari'ah. Thus, these people were incapable of delivering fatwas in anything that deviated from the rules set down by the authors of those books, authors who had written for the eras in which they lived, and for their governments, who undertook to implement the rules they had set down. Moreover, when it came to stipulating requirements for issuing fatwas, they circumscribed that process by determining that set provisions in certain prescribed works had to be adhered to. They determined that anything going beyond that would constitute a form of ijtihad, even if undertaken within the auspices of a school of law [madhhab], and they prohibited that as they prohibited unrestricted ijtihad.

Where government desires to act in accordance with the shari'ah's ordinances, the most that might be hoped for from these [jurists] is that they derive some specific provisions pertaining to the maintenance of public welfare from the reliable works of the schools of law [madhhabs]. They could then provide these to the government. That is because those who forbade them ijtihad—not allowing them to derive law from the shari'ah's fundamental principles and draw directly from the sources—obligated them to follow prescribed schools. As the author of *Jawharat al-Tawhid* states: "It is obligatory to follow one of their scholars," meaning one of the renowned imams of jurisprudence [fiqh].[217] Thus, they relied on a conception of what is forbidden and what is allowed that they had received from people who were unqualified in that matter. They only allowed someone with sufficient knowledge to follow mujtahids other than the four [eponymous founders of the Sunni schools of law] in strictly personal matters, not permitting him to issue fatwas on that. As one of them states: "It is permitted to follow those other than the four in matters other than issuing fatwas, and in this is ample scope."

An example of this scope, which concerns fundamental principles of civil transactions, is that according to most of the renowned jurists the starting principle for contracts is that they are fundamentally invalid. Thus, none are valid except those shown by the revealed law to be valid. Others hold the opinion that contracts are fundamentally valid, except for those shown by the Book and the sunnah [the Qur'an and the hadith] to be invalid, in keeping with the Almighty's statement at the beginning of "The Feast" [Al-Ma'idah], the final chapter of the Qur'an to be revealed: "O you who have faith, fulfill (your) contracts" [Qur'an 5:1]. Here, "contracts" refers to what people have mutually agreed upon. This is the best-founded and most judicious opinion, the one that provides people with the most guidance as they make their way. That is because of the flexible approach it enables people to adopt. It is the opinion preferred by Hanbali scholars.

Did you not observe that when the two governments, the Ottoman and the Egyptian, wanted to deviate from certain rulings of the Hanafi school [madhhab] on marriage, divorce, and annulment under certain conditions, and to rely in these matters on what is stipulated in the other schools of law, the scholars of jurisprudence [fiqh] responded to their request? They provided laws on these matters, some drawn from the other three schools of law. Perhaps, if for certain rulings the two governments wanted to embrace opinions traceable to the Companions, the Successors, and the imams of the Prophet's family,[218]

The Caliphate 167

instead of opinions of ulama belonging to four schools of law, they would not refuse to oblige them. That is because the practice of rigidly adhering to a prescribed school resulted from nothing other than the jurists' eagerness to satisfy the desires of emirs and sultans, and draw a livelihood from the endowments that they controlled. Hence, the sin here is shared. It is shared between rulers and the jurists who found that arrangement benefiting them personally. What these people who study jurisprudence do not venture to do is deduce law that is based on the Book and the sunnah [the Qur'an and the hadith] and their general principles. These include the principle of necessity, which renders the forbidden permissible, and that of utility, where what is forbidden to block the means[219] that would lead to prohibited acts becomes permissible for the sake of a greater benefit. This is so even though the imams whom they claim to follow expressly endorsed these principles. The reason for this is that they view that as a form of ijtihad, which they regard as prohibited.

The truth is that independent reasoning (ijtihad) was not and will not be discontinued in this Muhammadan community. Otherwise, God's proof over humankind would not have effect because there would not be anybody able to take responsibility for it, call people to it, and defend it. In that case, the infallible one's[220] report on the impossibility of the community coming to an agreement in error would be unsound. The same point applies to the report on how the community will always include a party responsible for defending the truth, until the time when God's will is realized. But in every era in which ignorance prevailed, these independent ulama would turn to the schools of law that they were affiliated with before they would venture to undertake ijtihad. There are two reasons for this. One: they were unable to find a means of livelihood besides the endowments set aside for those working in these schools of law, one that would have enabled them to devote themselves to the pursuit of knowledge. Thus, they were compelled to teach and compose works for these schools. By doing so, they were able to lawfully enrich themselves through the funds that had been endowed. Two: monarchs, rulers, and their assistants embodied the posture of those referred to as *muqallidun*. In this context, that term labels those who were, and still are, at war with the science of ijtihad, those left exposed, their ignorance and straying plain for all to see. Hence, if a courageous Islamic government desirous of reviving the science of ijtihad were found, such as the current Turkish government, the place where it could find the assistance that it would need to achieve that now is the madrasah for ijtihad that we have proposed (see Section 26). That madrasah could provide it with what it lacks and requires in the way of ordinances, along with pertinent advice. Yet no sooner does the government seek something from the followers of the

168 *Muhammad Rashid Rida*

schools of law but that we find one of them providing them with a fatwa, albeit one that is far-fetched and deviates from sound teaching.[221]

The Islamic community, then, cannot extricate itself from the lizard's hole into which it has crawled except through ijtihad, the existence of mujtahids, and along with that the realization of a valid consensus, which the majority recognizes as one of the sources of law. You may, if you wish, say that it is legislation's strong pillar. Without it, no community can develop, and no government be organized well, as we stated at the beginning of this section. Furthermore, the existence of the genuine imamate depends on this ijtihad, as seen in what is stated above. In this era, the way for mujtahids to gather has been prepared and made easy. It is possible for people to become acquainted with them and call upon them to gather in one place, or present them, wherever they may be found, with issues for their consideration. This was not possible in the era of Abu Hanifah, Malik, Shafi'i, Ahmad [ibn Hanbal], and those who came after them. Thus, one of the scholars said: to know the consensus, even if it exists, is not possible.[222]

(32) THE IMAMATE'S INFLUENCE ON REFORM IN THE ISLAMIC WORLD

The Islamic world is in a state of grief over its religion and its shari'ah's ordinances. It is pulled back and forth by the passions of its rulers, who differ in the matter of religion and in their ambitions, by the opinions of its ulama and guides, who follow different schools of law [madhhabs] and subscribe to different positions, and by the assaults of those who are its enemies in religion and worldly life. It lacks a universally recognized source of general guidance that it could refer to when it comes to what it is blinded from. Whenever a reformer has appeared within it, corrupt individuals governed by their desires have risen up to block him, slandering his religion and knowledge. There is no treatment for these corruptions and deviations except for reviving the office of the imamate, and installing a rightful imam, one who has the qualifications stipulated by the shari'ah, and who, along with the people who loose and bind, carries the burden of the prophetic caliphate. That is because he is the one to whom every Muslim submits, as it is a duty to obey him, as far as possible, by embracing any general reforms that he promulgates for the common good. He is the one whose guidance every Muslim prefers over the guidance of others when it comes to specific matters.[223] That is because he is more capable of explaining them with clear proofs. If the imamate is not of this nature then under the revealed law the imam's authority is viewed as resting purely on force [*taghallub*]. And obedience to one who rules through force [*mutaghallib*] is not

The Caliphate 169

a duty under the revealed law, even where doing that would be in harmony with the religious law, except for those people over whom he has direct authority.

Indeed, Sultan 'Abd al-Hamid [Abdul Hamid II] laid claim to the caliphate. But as he did not have the stipulated qualifications and discharge the stipulated duties, the Muslims of Afghanistan, Yemen, Najd, and Morocco did not recognize the legitimacy of his caliphate, nor did they believe that it was their duty to obey him, such that their governments adhere to his state. Moreover, the people of Egypt, who were under his political authority and recognized his caliphate, did not recognize that he had any right to issue them with commands or prohibitions. They recognized his caliphate only in its formal, spiritual aspect, drawing on that aspect in their efforts to resist British domination of them, as that is the Egyptians' [main] concern. The same point applies to other Muslims who recognized the recently created nominal caliphate in Constantinople, and whose attitude is similar to that of the Egyptians, as we have explained at the appropriate juncture in this discussion. This recently created caliphate is a caliphate resting upon force. Those who innovated it did not grant it the right to issue their government with commands or prohibitions.

As for what we have suggested and the path we have provided toward establishing a genuine imamate: if this were effected, even if on a small piece of land on earth, all of the Islamic world would willingly submit to it, a spiritual submission informed by religious belief. None of the Islamic governments would be able to find a way to slander it. There would be no means for any servant of the foreigners to refuse to recognize it. Every Islamic people would then endeavor to maintain it. People who are unable to adhere to the rightful imam's government because they are subjugated by a strong state may strive and make their best effort to adhere to the main body of the Muslims' community [*jama'ah*] and their imam, as God and His Messenger commanded, in matters concerning which their government has no authority over them. Such matters include providing youth with a religious upbringing, Islamic education, and ordinances for matters of personal status. Moreover, every government that dominates an Islamic people (or more than one) is compelled, to the extent that it finds that people unified and its public opinion united, to win its favor by being on good terms with its Prophet's caliph, and permitting it to receive religious guidance from him, as do Catholics from the pope.

Perhaps the Turks had intended something in this vein when creating the role of a spiritual caliph, a role similar to that of the Christians' pope and patriarchs. But this issue is one of religion and the shari'ah: it entails compliance. It cannot be resolved successfully through new conventions and innovations, even if that is what many of those who prioritize politics over religion desire. Some of those who voiced approval of the Turkish action were ignorant of this point, while others disregarded or neglected it. All of them supposed that this action would sufficiently enable what they sought: vexing and irritating Islam's enemies, and supporting and strengthening the Turkish people against them. That is the supposition of those who are ignorant of world affairs and the politics of the Great Powers. The extent of their practical experience is reflected by what we elaborate in what follows below.

We are perhaps among the best-informed people on the matter of how the establishment of a genuine imamate would lead to reform in the Islamic world. That is due to our practical experience, and the abundance of letters and questions that we have received from various lands. One of the most recent questions sent from an Islamic land concerns what would be minimally required for an ignorant non-Arab to become a Muslim. This is an issue because the people in that land are more ignorant and farther astray than the Muslims of Bangkok, Siam, whose poor condition was described to us by someone who asked us about the soundness of their Islam—we published this in Al-Manar previously.[224] In each of these lands there remained a remnant of people who claimed to be learned and who had preserved ijtihad-based rulings from the school of law of Imam Shafi'i, may God be satisfied with him. They obliged people to adhere to these rulings, which concerned the Friday prayer, and other matters. That led to the Friday prayer being abandoned, and it led some people to abandon congregational prayer. It even led those who found it difficult to memorize "The Opening" with correct pronunciation and doubling of the consonant to abandon the prayer. This applies particularly to the ya' in iyyaka na'budu wa iyyaka nasta'in: You alone do we worship, and You alone do we beseech for help [Qur'an 1:5]. The reason is that, according to the Shafi'is, the prayer is invalid if the ya' is pronounced without being doubled.

Another recently received question comes from a person of learning in Java. It concerns the ruling regarding their practice, which follows what their Muslim rulers have commanded, of requiring everyone who marries a woman to divorce her after the marriage has been contracted if he should fall short by insufficiently providing for her, or by striking her, or by being absent from her and by leaving her without provision. The reader will find this explained in Al-Manar's section on fatwas.[225]

Many people of learning in various countries who seek to improve the Muslims' circumstances proceed in accordance with the religious truths supported by detailed prescriptions that we have published in Al-Manar. Some of them have asked us about rulings for contingencies that have arisen, but which they have not found addressed in it. In certain lands, these people, and

The Caliphate

those who are like them, find that they meet opposition from those who follow the schools of law. That is because those who follow the schools oppose whatever goes against the teachings of their school. Yet they do not make efforts to spread their schools of law and bring them to the people. Rather, they leave them lost in the matter of their religion, unconcerned that they forsake duties, or commit great sins. They are concerned only with opposing certain things that contradict the teachings of their school of law. An example is their opposition to the performance of the Friday prayer by fewer than 40 free, mature men who permanently reside within the walls of a town, even if such opposition leads to the prayer being entirely forsaken.[226]

If the Muslims were to have an imam and a group [*jama'ah*] that was constituted of people who are competent in the science of ijtihad and who have integrity, those calling for reform would strive to benefit from their learning and seek their guidance. It would then not be long before that spread to Muslims in all lands.

We have previously—in the first volume of *Al-Manar*—provided suggestions regarding the types of reform that the holder of the official Islamic caliphate could undertake. These apply even if that caliphate should have been one that rested upon force, because our lands were subject to his rule. We desired that he apply what is right so far as he could. Our reward for making such a suggestion was the banning of *Al-Manar* from the Ottoman lands, and the harming of our people and friends in the Syrian territories.

And no wonder, as that caliph was himself ignorant of the religion's fundamental principles and specific provisions. He was ignorant of what enables Muslims to live righteously and what leads to corruption. His assistants were ignorant, governed by their desires, and did not make such suggestions to him. If they did mention them, they distorted them, twisting their truthfulness into falsity, their purity into corruption. He believed them, not trusting the report of anyone besides them. Anyone who lacks something cannot convey it to others.[227]

To summarize: the harms of ignorance, which afflicts most Muslims, and partisanship for the schools of law, which divides those who have a religious education, cannot be brought to an end in a short period other than through the establishment of the prophetic caliphate in such form that it would not be easy for anyone to openly resist it. To that end, it would suffice for the great majority of Muslims to accept its validity due to it being in harmony with the teachings of their schools of law. This majority includes those affiliated with the Sunni schools of law, the Zaydi school of law of the Shi'ah, and the Ibadi school of law. The Ibadis are a remnant of the Kharijis, and if they have not stipulated that the imam must have a certain lineage, as do Sunni Muslims and Zaydis, neither do they stipulate the absence of that. In this matter, why do we not adopt the position of a school of law that depends on others, like the Zaydi school of law depending on the Sunni and Khariji schools of law, the particular on the general, the restricted on the unrestricted?

This indeed is a statement of truth, and Islamic public welfare may be secured by pursuing the course that it outlines. Any alternatives represent nothing but dross and will avail nothing useful. Such alternatives are embraced by those who follow all of those bleaters whose motivations are purely political, their stances informed only by the political considerations of the current moment. This statement enables one to appreciate how what the government in Angora (Ankara) has determined is inherently invalid, and will not bring the least benefit to the Islamic world. Rather, from now on it will cause division among the Turkish people, most of whom prefer Islamic guidance to secular legal theories and European traditions. There is a major party in the Grand National Assembly which sees that the interests of public welfare require that the caliph be installed in accordance with the requirements of the shari'ah, such that he is head of government and the one who implements ordinances. Yes, the party of Ghazi Mustafa Kamal Pasha insists that in the supreme Turkish government every form of personal authority is to be rejected, whether that be on the basis of the title "caliph" or some other title. But the reason for this has to do with the influence of that man and his party of military officers over the people, and that derives from the favor in which they are held for saving the state from disaster. It is not the case that this actually represents the Turkish nation's opinion. If the nation were asked its opinion in a free referendum it would oppose this party on this issue. This is the truth.

The Islamic world will come to know that we have given this explanation in accordance with God Almighty's command to urge one another to truth and urge one another to steadfastness, acting in good faith toward God, His Messenger, and the Muslims' imams and common people.[228] Those who oppose our opinion today may come to take recourse to it, as they took recourse to our opinion regarding Sultan 'Abd al-Hamid [Abdul Hamid II], and then our opinion regarding the Committee of Union and Progress. And the future belongs to the pious.

(33) NON-MUSLIMS' RESISTANCE TO THE GOVERNMENT OF THE CALIPHATE

Someone says: non-Muslims residing in lands regarded as Islamic (because the great majority of their people are Muslim) would be averse to the government of the caliphate being established there. This applies especially to

The Caliphate

Christians. They can see that the weakness of Islamic authority, legislation, morality, and traditions is only due to the strength of the Europeans' authority, legislation, morality, and traditions—and likewise their languages—and that as a result the core values and distinctive characteristics of the community [in these lands] align more with Christianity than with Islam. Those who do not [genuinely] believe in Christian doctrine, nor in the gospel commandments to love one's enemies, hate wealth, and offer the left cheek to one who strikes the right, hold more strongly to the specifically social-political dimension of Christianity than do those who actually have the deepest faith in the gospel. It is this false, social-political form of Christianity—not the ascetic, submissive, humble Christianity of the gospel characterized by the altruism that they call "self-denial"—that formed the basis for materialistic European civilization and which stimulates partisanship and hatred for everything Islamic.

If Europeanized Muslims embrace this stance of disliking religious government, and opposing the revival of the institution of the caliphate, do Europeanized Christians not have even greater reason to do so? If the matter is thus, how could we revert to renewing a religious government that is disliked and shunned by many of its subjects?

The answer here requires detailed elaboration. We suffice with what is essential. We say: if it is correct to attribute such views to the nationals discussed here, views that align with their persuasions and the effects of their upbringing, then someone who carefully examines the facts of the matter and does so with an eye to the public welfare, whether he is one of them or not, would come to a different conclusion.

The government of the caliphate is Islamic and civil. It rests upon the foundations of justice and equality in rights, excepting that it grants non-Muslims personal freedoms not granted to Muslim apostates and hypocrites, who would prefer Islam to be rendered purely as a national and cultural bond. That would enable apostates and hypocrites to share in all of the rights granted to Muslims by the shari'ah, custom, and positive law under an Islamic government, even if they plainly declare that they do not have faith in God or His creed, or adhere to His pillars and rituals. Yet they are aware that in no respect would an Islamic government grant them that, and even a woman who learns from her husband that he has apostatized from Islam is forbidden to stay with him or remain married to him. The ordinances for apostates are well known. Their case is more serious than that of pagans, to say nothing of People of the Book, whose sacrifices Muslims may eat and whose virtuous women Muslim men may marry. An Islamic government does not punish non-Muslims for doing anything that their own religion permits—even if what they do is not permissible in Islam—except for what is harmful to others. Moreover, an Islamic government does not call them to account over their personal conduct, provided that it does not harm Muslims or its other subjects, even if it violates their own religion's prescriptions. But it calls Muslims to account, and punishes them with the hudud penalties and various forms of censure, such as scolding and imprisonment. That is because Islam's fundamental principles include safeguarding morality and virtue, and preventing immorality and what is forbidden. God describes the Muslims in His statement: "Those who, when We establish them in the land, keep up the prayer, pay the zakat, command what is right and forbid what is wrong" [Qur'an 22:41]. And He says of them: "you are the best community ever brought forth for humankind, enjoining decent conduct and dissuading indecent conduct" [Qur'an 3:110].[229] The legal rulings on apostasy and the *Hisbah*[230] are well known in Islam.

From this, it may be appreciated that Muslim heretics and Muslims who are heedless and dissolute have greater reason than non-Muslims to forcefully resist implementation of shari'ah rulings, as that would impose upon them what it would not impose on others, and punish them for things that it does not punish others for doing. Some of these heretics suggested to the group convened at the General Syrian Congress in Damascus that they should determine to render the Syrian government a nonreligious one.[231] I do not remember any of the Christian participants agreeing to that suggestion. Rather, some declared their opposition to it, as did most of the Muslims. During that congress it was suggested that in the article on personal liberties in the Constitution these liberties should be restricted by the requirement that public morality not be violated. Some of those described as Muslims rejected this suggestion. Justifying that stance, some of them declared that this restriction would result in it being possible for the police to prevent a man from sitting with a woman in a place of amusement or a public coffeehouse to drink wine (??). The rejection of that suggestion was the ugliest disgrace to come out of that congress, even though some of them justified it on the basis that laws on public morality were not needed, as any needed stipulations could be added to existing laws. Some religious and moral people were deceived by that. They should not have been deceived. I say, moreover, that most of the Christian participants in that congress were closer to those Muslims who closely adhere to Islam's ordinances than to those Muslims who strive to extricate themselves from the religion. That is so even where these Muslims who were striving to remove themselves from Islam attempted to gain the favor of these Christians, and take their side, when doing so aligned with their desires to go against the religion's universal guidance.

The Caliphate

Of the two, experience shows that those who are not committed to religion become more hateful and cruel toward each other in practice when they disagree for political or other reasons than those who are committed to religion. That is because a religiously committed person, even if he should go astray, remains closer to mercy than does a materialist. Take as an instance of that the cruelty seen in the Balkan War, and also in the Great War [World War I], that of the Europeans themselves, and Armenians, Greeks, and Turks influenced by Europeans through their upbringings.

Consider another example. A Greek doctor said to a group of Syrians who were showing their joy and happiness with the Ottoman Constitution after its announcement: the rule of the shari'ah is better for us Christians than the rule of the Constitution, which takes from us much of the privileges that the shari'ah grants us, and subjects us to obligations from which the shari'ah exempts us. His sentiment was supported by the intensification of enmity between the Turks and the Greeks, Armenians, and others following the Constitution, which was followed by these people being wrested of much of what they had had since the time when rule was solely that of the revealed law.

I add to this statement the comment that the shari'ah ordinances most upsetting to Europeanized Turks are those that grant wide freedoms to non-Muslims in the lands of Islam. They see that had it not been for these freedoms these lands would have become home to a single religious community [*millah*], as in Europe's lands, which lack any such freedoms. They feel that they would then have been saved from the enmities and discord that the Christians of Rumelia and then Anatolia roused up against them through Europe's conspiracies, to the point that that became one of the causes of the Ottoman sultanate's dissolution.[232] This is their opinion. It is odd that many of the Europeanized Christians in our lands agree with them about this supposition. They say: if only the Muslims had compelled our ancestors to convert to Islam during the period of Islam's conquests and strength. In that case, we would have become part of a single community with a single religion in our homelands, and thus free of the misery of this discord and the trials destroying the lands.

Evaluating this opinion of the issue is beyond the scope of this treatise. Yet it is not difficult to show the error of those who believe that treating the state's Christians in accordance with the Islamic shari'ah's justice and freedoms is what provoked them against it. Nor is it difficult to demonstrate that what provoked and agitated them was the state's leaders being negligent and inattentive when faced with Europe's conspiracies involving these peoples, conspiracies seen in what they disseminated in their schools and churches! Our point in mentioning this is to make clear that the Islamic shari'ah is better for Christians living in Muslim-majority lands than civil government, whose people are not bound by the shari'ah's fundamental principles—as during the era of the caliphate under the Arabs, and likewise under the Ottoman sultans. The true difference between the two kinds of government is that under the shari'ah the Muslim majority is not permitted to follow its desires when it comes to religious legislation, nor to implement anything found to be unjust to a non-Muslim minority. This is because God Almighty has definitively prohibited injustice, allowing no laxity or excuses. His command to uphold justice is absolute and universal, allowing for no partiality of any kind. He warns in a special way against forsaking justice in cases that involve any faction—whatever faction that may be—hating or disliking others. This is found in the Almighty's statement: "Do not let hatred of a people lead you away from being just, but adhere to justice, for that is closer to awareness of God. Be mindful of God: God is well aware of all that you do" [Qur'an 5:8]. That is: do not be led by some people's dislike of you, or by your dislike of some people. Some commentators hold that this statement refers to unbelievers. The correct interpretation is that it has more general application—do not let [hatred of others] lead you away from being just with them, but adhere to justice with them, as you would with others—the wording conveying a general meaning. That is: be absolutely and universally just regarding the believer and the unbeliever, the righteous and the profligate, friend and foe, etc. He says in another verse: "You who believe, uphold justice and bear witness to God, even if it is against yourselves, your parents, or your close relatives. Whether the person is rich or poor, God can best take care of both. Refrain from following your own desire, so that you can act justly—if you distort or neglect justice, God is fully aware of what you do" [Qur'an 4:135].[233] That is: in regard to ordinances and other matters you should uphold justice in the most complete manner—as the exaggerated form indicates—bearing witness to God in acting upon what is true.[234] It is God's right that in fulfilling his duty to Him the believer does not distinguish himself, his parents, or the people closest to him over others, because making such distinctions would mean holding himself or his relatives above His Lord, be He exalted, for Whom he testifies. It is God's right that in fulfilling his duty to Him the believer not distinguish the rich man from the poor man by being partial to the rich man out of a desire to benefit from his generosity, or be partial to the poor man out of mercy for him. God followed this command by prohibiting its opposite, which is following the passions of the soul due to a hatred of justice, and by banning alteration or distortion of testimony, or turning away from it, or turning away from ruling in accordance with what is right. He threatened one who does that, advising that He is well aware of his case, that nothing can be concealed from Him. This is

The Caliphate

177

to say nothing of directives related in the prophetic hadith that pertain specifically to non-Muslims who have a treaty or a pact with Muslims [*ahl al-'ahd wa al-dhimmah*].

If not for this, strong Islamic governments would have done what other governments did to those who followed a different religion. They would have annihilated some, exiled others from their lands, or forced them to convert to the religion of Islam, or enacted special laws designed to subjugate and degrade them. In Ottoman history we see that Sultan Sulayman sought a fatwa from the Shaykh al-Islam, Abu al-Sa'ud al-'Imadi, originally from Damascus, on forcing Christians to convert to Islam or leave. He refused to give him a fatwa sanctioning that. He explained to him that the shari'ah would not permit this, and he yielded. He had wanted to do to them as the Spanish Empire had done to the Muslims of Andalusia.[235]

There is another difference between the Islamic revealed law and human legislation, wherein government is not bound to religion. This also concerns non-Muslims' welfare. It is that every Muslim believes that shari'ah-based rule is divine rule. Hence, obeying it is an act of piety through which a person draws nearer to God and for which he is rewarded in the afterlife, and that disobeying it is disobeying God, for which he is punished in the afterlife. This is so whether or not a judge rules in accordance with it. But the judge's decision resolves disagreements between the schools of law [madhhabs], so obeying it is indispensable. This provides a guarantee for a non-Muslim, as a Muslim's stance on a ruling will be informed by an internal, religious principle. The Muslim has no similar advantage when he is involved in a dispute with a non-Muslim.

Were it said: everyone who has a religion calls himself (or his conscience) to account in accordance with what he believes is incumbent upon him. We say: this notion is universal and shared. What we are concerned with is more specific: respecting shari'ah-based rule, and the necessity of obeying the judge when he makes a decision in someone's case, regardless of whether or not one accepts its soundness, and even if one were in a position to save himself from the government's punishment through trickery.

To summarize: the shari'ah lacks any unfairness toward the non-Muslim that would justify hatred of it. It makes the weakest non-Muslim—a *dhimmi* or ally [*mu'ahad*]—equal to the strongest caliph when standing before the qadi, as well as in terms of established legal rights. Testimonies to this from the era of the rightly guided caliphate and the period following are abundant. We declare in the strongest terms possible that absolute and universal justice does not exist except in Islam. What occurred with some of the Muslims' rulers deviating from the correct path by treating some *dhimmis* unjustly occurred only at the hands of those who were the least knowledgeable and the least guided by the religion. Furthermore, such deviations did not affect non-Muslims exclusively. There is nothing that merits criticism of the just imams and the rightful caliphs, except for criticism of those who ignored the fact that certain exceptional actions taken during the era of the Islamic conquests were temporary, military expedients, and sought to render them permanent. However, in this connection Islam was more just and more merciful than [the religions of] all other peoples, such that one of the fair and wise Europeans said: history knows of no conquest more just and merciful than that of the Arabs.

We do not concede to them that in the ordinances implemented by all of the Islamic states there is any violation of the shari'ah principle of equality, except for the case of revoking a non-Muslim's testimony in favor of a Muslim's testimony. And this is a case for which there is no prescription that would support a doctrine that does not allow for any exceptions. Rather, there is a solution to this derived from the Book and the sunnah [the Qur'an and the hadith] and the shari'ah's fundamental principles. The Almighty says in the chapter entitled "The Feast," among the last revealed in the Qur'an and lacking any abrogated rulings: "You who believe, when death approaches any of you let two men of integrity from among you act as witnesses to the making of a bequest, or two men from another people" [Qur'an 5:106].[236] What the wording initially suggests, and the interpretation that most of the ancestors and later generations have followed, is that "another people" refers to people other than those addressed in the verse, who are Muslims. Some of the ulama single out the People of the Book, but there is no prescription supporting such singling-out. Some of the ulama restrict its application to the like of the situation in which the verse was revealed. This is based upon the fundamental principle that the testimony of someone other than a just Muslim is to be rejected, per the Almighty's statement, "Call two just witnesses from among your people" [Qur'an 65:2].

We have explained in detail that attempting to use this verse to find evidence that would support an explanation of the verse from "The Feast" is defective. This explanation includes the point that this verse concerns the command to call witnesses in regard to the issue of divorced Muslim women during their period of waiting, not in regard to testifying in all circumstances, nor in regard to every case of calling witnesses.[237] In regard to calling witnesses in cases involving property, the Almighty says, "when you give them their property, call witnesses in" [Qur'an 4:6]. He did not restrict this calling of witnesses to their being people of integrity among the believers, as He did in regard to the specific issue of Muslim women. In that manner, we explained the weakness of using the two verses to infer absolute from restricted, given difference in their

The Caliphate

subject matters, and the difference between testifying and calling witnesses. In the same manner, we have demonstrated through qur'anic evidence that the opinion that a non-Muslim cannot be just or have integrity is weak, since the Qur'an relates: "There is a group among the people of Moses who guide with truth, and who act justly according to it" [Qur'an 7:159]. The Qur'an also includes God's statement, "Among the People of the Book are some whom if you trust with a great weight [of precious metal], they would restore it to you" [Qur'an 3:75].[238]

In the same manner, we also demonstrated the weakness of that opinion on the basis of evidence found in the conduct of human beings, known to experience and the rational mind. This shows that no community has existed that is void of sincerity and integrity, such that none of its people are honest. We also explained why some jurists prefer a Muslim's testimony over that of a non-Muslim in terms of four factors. The most important concerns the early Muslims' practice: their piety, sincerity, impartiality, and adherence to the religion's injunctions—some of the pertinent qur'anic verses have been related previously. Additionally, there is what stands opposite to that and which the historians have concurred upon: how corrupt morality prevailed in the other nations, the nations whose lands the Muslims conquered.

The fundamental principles of the shari'ah include further support for a non-Muslim's testimony: its inclusion in the totality of the evidence if in the qadi's opinion his sincerity is well established. This is because the term *evidence* [*bayyinah*] refers to everything through which truth becomes evident. The scholar Ibn al-Qayyim explains this notion in detail in his work *I'lam al-Muwaqqa'in*.[239] We published this in *Al-Manar*, and we explained that everything that has cropped up newly in this age relevant to various types of offenses, such as fingerprints, is to be included in the totality of the evidence. Whoever requires more detail may consult *Al-Manar* and *Tafsir al-Manar*.

This explanation, in spite of its brevity, leaves non-Muslims who dislike the prospect of the revival of the just Islamic shari'ah with no excuse for that attitude. They dislike it either because they are blindly partisan, or because they prefer foreigners' legislation to that of those whose homeland they share. It is neither right nor just that a community be expected to forsake the virtue of the best legislation, and an ideal government such as this, in order to satisfy a small group who would receive no benefit from pursuing that course. Their dislike is motivated only by a purely partisan attitude toward the great majority of the people in their own homeland. This is to say nothing of the hatred sown between Anatolia's Muslims and the Greeks and Armenians who revolted against the Turks during their ordeal, and assisted their enemies in their war against them.

The object of the discourse here concerns the establishment of the caliphate in the Turkish lands. That is because if the Turks were to assent to that, and treat these criminals and rebels with the shari'ah's justice and mercy, it is inconceivable that if they are rational they would dislike that, or prefer something else. I fear only that this very matter is among the factors discouraging many of the Turks from adhering to and implementing the shari'ah, which would prohibit them from following their desires when it comes to the question of how to treat these ferocious criminals who destroyed their lands with gunfire and gunpowder, while they watched with their own eyes as they turned into piles of ashes and ruins.

The governments of the Arabian Peninsula are purely Islamic. They lack secular law or European legislation. The oldest is the government of the imams of Yemen. There are many Jews there, and they are satisfied with the government of a shari'ah-based imamate, not complaining of any injustice or oppression from it. They have not indicated a preference for replacing it with a different government. If the poison of colonial politics had reached them through education or by another means, the imperialists would have alienated them from their government and incited them to rise against it and seek their own national homeland in that land. Those who poison their souls promise to help them in achieving that out of love for humankind. But what actually underlies their promises is a love of corrupting humankind. They want to incite hatred between peoples who differ in religion, nationality, or language, some against others, so as to obtain sufficient power to subjugate all of them. "Learn from this, all of you with insight" [Qur'an 59:2].

(34) THE CALIPHATE AND THE COLONIAL STATES

It is obvious that the establishment of the Islamic caliphate would displease the leaders of the colonial states, and that they resist that with all means and all force available to them. In this, the most avid is the British state. The only people who are more ignorant than those who imagine that it was attempting to form a caliphate within the Arab community before the war are those who believe that it wants to establish an Arab state or Arab states today. Had it wanted to do this previously the most viable way to achieve that would have been to support the imams of Yemen who were its neighbors in the region of Aden, supporting them against the Turks with weapons and finance for building their army and occupying the Hijaz. That is because the government of the imamate in Yemen is strong, just, ancient, and firmly established, its history going back to the third century after the Hijrah. The Ottoman Empire struggled against it

The Caliphate 181

for around four centuries in order to overthrow it, but was unable to do that. But the British government was lying in wait for it, and continues to plot against it, seeking through conspiracies and sowing discord to involve itself in its affairs, and through that means to reach the point of being able to conquer it. But it has been unable to do that. And God will not provide it with a path to do that.

It has become well known to all men, high and low, that the British Empire was a supporter of the Ottoman Turkish caliphate. The only reason for that lies in its recognition that the caliphate was nominal, and that showing friendship to it would be to its advantage. The British Empire's artful leaders were most aware that decay had crept into the body of the Ottoman state, that it was on a path to annihilation and extinction. They were attempting to sustain it only so that it could serve as a protective bulwark between the Russian Empire, the speed of whose development and growth had raised fears, and the Mediterranean Sea. That effort rested on the condition that this bulwark would not rest on its own power but on Britain's support. We have explained this in *Al-Manar* previously, [the Ottoman scholar and statesman] Ghazi Ahmad Mukhtar Pasha agreeing with us that the rule informing the British Empire's Ottoman policy was that the Ottoman Empire should neither expire nor thrive. We also explained that this rule shifted as British–Russian relations concerning their affairs in the East shifted, and as they divided the lands of Iran between themselves before the Great War [World War I]. We explained that it did not become inclined toward establishing a nominal Arab caliphate that would be a tool in its hand until after the Great War [World War I], when it was in a position to deceive the sharif of Mecca, and exploit him for its own benefit. We thank God that He made our work one of the reasons for the failure of that effort, such that it was unrealized.[240]

Since the beginning of this war, the British Empire has given attention to investigating the matter of the caliphate. Its leaders have asked the Muslims' ulama and leaders in Egypt, Sudan, India, and elsewhere their opinions about it. They did that to gain insights that they could harness toward realizing their empire's goals and nullifying the impact of the Ottoman caliph's announcement of a religious jihad. They did so by claiming, on the one hand, that his caliphate lacks legitimacy, and, on the other hand, that this war lacks any religious dimension. One of the hypocrites in India wrote a paper in English for them on that matter. Its publisher sent it to us so that we could translate it into Arabic and publish it in *Al-Manar*. We were amazed at his ignorance and hypocrisy. We would have rebutted it, had it not been for the harsh censorship of the press in general and *Al-Manar* in particular in those days. We have become acquainted with what certain Egyptian ulama wrote for them about the caliphate, copied from *Commentary on Goals* [*Sharh al-Maqasid*] and other sources on the topic. We have also learned that certain ulama have provided them with some facts in writing. These concern the nature of the caliphate.

Discussions on the Arab issue took place between us and some of their leaders. These required us to write memoranda for them pointing out the errors of their policy on the matter. In the first memorandum, which we presented to them at the beginning of 1915, we explained that most Muslims remain loyal to the Ottoman Empire, along with its caliph, because it represents the strongest of the Islamic governments. We explained that Muslims fear that if the Ottoman Empire were annihilated that would lead to the elimination of the rule of Islam from the earth, and that for Muslims this is a more important issue than that of the holy places remaining undamaged and preserved. Beyond that, we also explained that its call for jihad was shari'ah-based, and that the reason for its weak impact in countries such as Egypt is the belief that it would prevail because of its alliances, and thus was not in need of more assistance.

I came back to discussing the caliphate in the final memorandum, which I sent to Minister Lloyd George in the middle of 1919.[241] Explaining how England could appease the Muslims, I said:

> The Minister appreciates that recognizing the Hijaz's independence, and naming the Emir of Mecca "King," did not have the impact upon Muslim hearts that the English had anticipated—and that is because the lands of the Hijaz are the poorest of the Islamic lands, the weakest in all respects. This is a seat of worship, not of power and authority. Muslims were not agitated by a fear that the holy mosques would be destroyed, or that people would be prevented from making prayer in them, making the hajj to them, and visiting them. Rather, the greatest agitation concerns Islamic sovereignty, without which they believe Islam cannot exist. Concern for its existence flows in the blood of every Muslim's veins. That is because no Muslim can envision his religion enduring without the existence of an Islamic state, one that is independent, strong, and self-sufficiently capable of implementing the rulings of the revealed law, without opposition or foreign domination. This is the reason why most of the Muslims on earth remain ardently loyal to the Turks' state, and regard it as the one representing the prophetic caliphate, notwithstanding that, aside from strength and independence, it lacks the special qualifications stipulated for that role. Otherwise, they would recognize the caliphate of the Imam of Yemen, given the nobility of his lineage, his knowledge of the revealed law, and given that he has the other qualifications stipulated for the caliphate. That is because qualifications are considered secondary to the fundamental objective. An example of that kind of approach is also found with the Egyptian government. It stipulates that its employees

The Caliphate   183

be Egyptian nationals, fluent in the Arabic language, and holders of special certificates. But when it requires an employee for a technical role that no Egyptian knows how to perform, it sets aside those stipulations, as one having stipulated qualifications is only given priority over others if he is actually capable of performing the essentials of the required task.

Our goal in this was that being aware that the Turkish caliph lacks the qualifications stipulated for the caliphate should not cause the British to be misled. Also, they should not be misled regarding their goals in making the sharif of Mecca the caliph, after he had acknowledged for their benefit that the Arab community's relationship to England is that of a minor—someone childish, or an imbecile—to a guardian, assenting to their protection of himself and the community. In this memorandum, we explained to the minister that the way for his state to satisfy the Islamic world would be to leave the Arab, Turkish, and Persian Islamic peoples alone, free and independent in their lands. Further, it should leave the issue of the caliphate as it is, until it becomes possible to convene a general Islamic congress to resolve it. We also explained that in addition to facing the enmity of the Islamic world, this state risks facing the same sentiment from all of the East. Thus, it should not be deceived by the Muslims' weakness and disunity. It should not scorn their enmity, with their number in the hundreds of millions, as they will not be less potent than the "microbes" that cause epidemics. We will publish this memorandum at the appropriate time.

This minister did not heed the advice of this memorandum. He continued the policy of destroying the Turkish state and subjugating the Arabs, until God abandoned him, and his people also abandoned him, bringing down his ministry. However, one of his strongest supporters remained in the ministry that followed it. He is Lord Curzon, who is more fanatical, and has more enmity for the Muslims than him. Thus, nothing in the state's policy on the Islamic issue changed, excepting that it was compelled to be civil to the new Turkish state after it routed the Greek army, which Lloyd George's ministry had sought to entice to destroy what remained of the Turkish force in Anatolia. In that way, it demonstrated that it only yields to strength. As for truth, justice, and holding to agreements and promises: in the dictionary of its politics these things have meanings other than what is known to other peoples and in other languages.

(35) THE CALIPHATE AND CLAIMS MADE ABOUT PAN-ISLAMISM

The primary reason that the British state is the greatest, strongest, and most forceful opponent of the Islamic caliphate is that it fears that it will enliven Islam, and realize the notion of pan-Islamism, and thus prevent its subjugation of the entire East.[242] We have published numerous statements by European political leaders on this issue in the volumes of *Al-Manar*. Among the most important is what we published in Volume 10 (1325), Cromer's opinion, given in his annual report on Egypt and Sudan for 1906. Most important was his statement:

> The broad purpose of pan-Islamism is to bring Muslims throughout the entire world together to defy the powers of the Christian states, and to resist them. Considered from this angle, it becomes incumbent on all the European nations that have political interests in the East to monitor this movement extremely closely, as it may stimulate scattered incidents through which the fires of religious fanaticism might be ignited in different parts of the world.

He goes on to say that pan-Islamism has other significations that are more important than the primary one:

1. in Egypt, yielding to the sultan and promoting his objectives . . .;
2. the consequent incitement of racial and religious hatreds, except in rare cases . . .;
3. the effort to reform Islam in accordance with an Islamic manner (!!). In another formulation: the effort in the twentieth century to reestablish principles that were set down over 1,000 years ago to serve as a guide for a natural and primitive society.[243]

He mentions that the defect of these principles, practices, and laws is their incompatibility with people's opinions in the current era when it comes to relations between men and women. There is an additional matter. He states that there is something "more important than all of that, and it is the framing of civil, criminal, and financial law within a single framework that admits of no change or alteration." He states: "This is what has prevented the advancement of the lands whose people profess the religion of Islam."

He then followed his warning to the Europeans about pan-Islamism by warning them about nationalism, so that it not conceal the former, "which is the most significant regressive movement."

We rebutted Lord Cromer on each of these issues. Others also refuted him. These discussions include remarks that disprove his conception. Our purpose here is to clearly expose the intensity of English interest in: opposing pan-Islamism in all that it signifies; inciting all Europeans and Christians against it and those who take up the task of establishing it; and instilling fear of it among the Muslims.

The way that Europe terrorized Islamic peoples and governments led them to becoming fearful and leery of everything that Europeans hate in them.

The Caliphate   185

It led them to crave everything that Europeans call upon them to embrace. They proceeded accordingly. Thus, many of them came to believe that whatever these European slanderers deemed good for them was good for them, and that whatever they found detestable in them was detestable. That is because they had been raised under that conception, while they had not found anyone who would explain the truth of the matter to them. This made it easier for the Europeans to deprive these Islamic peoples, deceived and terrorized, of their independence in some lands, and render their influence ascendant over that of the government in other lands, such as in Egypt and the Ottoman Empire. Men of government in these lands fell victim to weakness and cowardliness. As a result, Ottoman state authorities dared not grant us permission to establish an Islamic madrasah named Dar al-Da'wah wa al-Irshad [The Institute for Outreach and Guidance] in the capital, as mentioned previously. Yet not all of them were ignorant of the points that I have discussed here. Rather, the Shaykh al-Islam, Husni Effendi, God have mercy upon him, said to me: We have a general rule when it comes to Europeans. It is: whatever they seek to interest us in is harmful for us; whatever they seek to turn us away from is beneficial for us. At issue here is nothing but the cowardliness of some leaders, and the corruption of the beliefs of others. Cowardliness is nothing but a veil of delusion that prevents the eye from discerning things clearly. This veil has been lifted from the eyes of Anatolia's Turks: after being in the Great War [World War I] and losing those extensive territories, they were able to see that they had emerged stronger and more powerful than they had been during the previous two centuries, when the state's lands had been shrinking, its borders receding, while the influence of foreigners in the state's capital exceeded that of its caliph and sultan.

For this reason, thousands upon thousands of Muslims pin their hopes on the government of Anatolia reviving the office of the caliphate, thereby reviving the glory of Islam along with its distinguished shari'ah. This is in the hope that through Islam's revival the glory of humankind will be renewed. Thus, humankind may embark upon a new era, one in which people live free of the corruptions of materialistic civilization. These are corruptions that threaten to destroy not only the civilization of the East, but moreover European civilization itself.

I do not imagine that it is fear of opposition from the colonizing European states that prevents the Turks from establishing the Islamic caliphate, as this is the form of our government, and the requirement of our religion. Following the war, these states frequently declared that they had no interest in interfering with Muslims when it comes to the matter of the caliphate. As for pan-Islamism, which they fear, that is a separate matter. Every state with Muslim subjects is entitled to rule them in a way that it finds consistent with its interests. Yes, it will not be the Europeans who prevent the establishment of the caliphate. The only people who will prevent that from happening are the Europeanized Muslims, they and not others, as we have previously explained.

Politically speaking, it is understandable those who colonize Islamic lands would cast aspersions on the idea of a union based on religion. They suppose that that would lead the people in those lands to rise up against them. They fear that a genuine caliphate would lead to the realization of such a union. It is understandable that for that reason they disparage the Islamic shari'ah, and seek to alienate Muslims from it. Christian missionaries also disparage it for that reason. They also do that because it lends to their goal of converting Muslims to Christianity. This fear of the caliphate being established becomes more intense where the motivation to establish it is pure politics, whose partisans sanction any action in pursuit of their interests. The fear lessens where the motivation for establishing it is the purely religious one of practicing Islam in the way that God Almighty legislated it. It is not stipulated that all Muslims must be under the caliphate's authority. We are aware that this is neither practical nor possible at this time. The burden of requiring what is impossible is prohibited in Islam: "God does not burden any soul with more than it can bear" [Qur'an 2:286]. Moreover, we are aware that in some lands the opinion that prevails is opposed to reviving the caliphate. That is why we urge the current Turkish government to revive it. But we are doubtful that it will respond favorably. That is because its leader, the one with the most influence in its most powerful party, declares in his statements that this government's authority belongs to the community. He declares that the Grand National Assembly represents the community in a manner that has no conditions or limitations placed upon it. This means that no individual could be designated as someone having any influence over it on the basis of a title that he holds. This is so no matter what that title may be, namely, whether that individual is called "the caliph" or "the sultan."

When the Ittihadists announced their intention to establish an Islamic university in Medina, and draw up a register of those seeking prophetic intercession there, and it was stated in the newspapers and elsewhere that their intention in that was to revive pan-Islamism, I wrote an article on this subject that I published in *Al-Manar*, Volume 17 (1332).[244] Therein I stated the following:

> As for my opinion, of which I have advised the state, it is that for its political class to take up the task of establishing the pillars of pan-Islamism would harm the state a great deal, while benefiting it only a little. These statements that have been made on this issue — in spite of their weak impact — are at the

The Caliphate

187

point of prompting Europe to become strongly biased against it, as we can see. In this circumstance, I suffice with a maxim that Imam Ghazali states repeatedly: "Be a true Jew, else do not play games with Torah."[245]

In saying this, my desire is that the state must do one of two things:

One: establish an Islamic government that is free of European traditions and laws, except for those that lend to the maintenance of order, conform to the revealed law, and regard all peoples in the same manner, not treating some differently to others. The state should grant the institution of the caliphate its due rights to revive the call to Islam, apply the hudud laws, and uphold religious freedom. It would then not be unable to satisfy those of its non-Muslim subjects who are not politically motivated, or involved with foreign states. Moreover, satisfying them, should it want to do that, would then be easier for it than it is presently.

If I had any expectation that it would listen to this opinion, or make it the object of reflection and research, I would explain that in more detail. I would discuss all of the internal and external problems and obstacles that block the path to its realization that I am aware of, and explain how to overcome them. I would then discuss what would result from that course of action, how the state would be enlivened and protected from peril. That is so even while many people apparently hold the view that it would create a perilous situation. They suppose that Europe would hasten to destroy the state if it became aware that it had set in motion an Islamic renaissance, knowing that doing that lays the path for a genuine revival of the caliphate. And some independently minded Europeans have recognized how that would indeed lead to such a revival. However, most of those belonging to their political classes have done nothing but instill fears of the caliphate by misrepresenting it, and deceiving people about it.

Two: Beyond its official responsibilities the state should leave everything having to do with religious affairs to the free religious associations and to individuals who are motivated by their willingness to serve. When it comes to functions related to religion, it can assist whatever merits assistance by providing protection. Likewise it can assist by providing financial aid drawn from the Muslims' charitable endowments (this is if it wishes to retain control over the general endowments, and not grant the request of those seeking reform to entrust the endowments to those who administer them), while keeping them separate from politics and those engaged in it.

Were this not my opinion, when I proposed the project on Outreach and Guidance I would not have stipulated for statesmen and the Committee for Union that it was to be entrusted to an independent society with no political affiliation, and not receive any assistance from the state treasury. Rather, its support was to derive from various kinds of assistance that it was able to

188   *Muhammad Rashid Rida*

organize by itself, and from what it might receive from the Muslims' charitable endowments. "You will remember what I am saying to you now, so I commit my case to God: God is well aware of His servants" [Qur'an 40:44].

This is what we wrote at that time. In the volumes of *Al-Manar* we have elaborated many times on Europeans' opinions on pan-Islamism, how those opinions are deluded, and what is incumbent upon the Muslims.

(36) THE TESTIMONY OF TWO LORDS ON THE ISLAMIC SHARI'AH

Not all of the Europeans who speak about Islam and its shari'ah speak on the basis of sound knowledge, while not all those with knowledge say what they firmly believe. Some of them are driven by politics to speak on behalf of their state's interests. Some of them are partisans who do not investigate any aspect of Islam except for what can be used to slander it, so as to cause Muslims to doubt their own religion, or to provoke their enemies against them. One can, however, also find Europeans who speak the truth about Islam and its shari'ah, when circumstances require them to do that.

LORD CROMER'S STATEMENT ON THE SHARI'AH

Lord Cromer is one of them. He greatly defamed the shari'ah, agitating Egypt and throwing her into a state of turmoil. He was then compelled to turn course and treat the shari'ah fairly. He qualified what he had declared when defaming it, using language that no rational Muslim could dispute, as in a statement he once made to the Master, the Imam [Muhammad 'Abduh] in which he treated it fairly. We published the one and the other in Volume 10 of *Al-Manar*, when he was in Egypt.[246] In the context of rebutting his defamation, I said that the Master, the Imam, may God Almighty have mercy upon him, told me that he had spoken to him about the issue of reforming the shari'ah courts. This was during the period when the people and the government were engaged in the matter, and some of the ulama had been opposed to reform. The Master provided Cromer with proofs demonstrating that Islam calls for every reform and befits every era. The Lord then said to him what may be translated as follows: "Could you think, Master, that I believe that a religion that established a new civilization through which it founded great states does not have justice as its foundation? This is impossible. But I am aware that this opposition (that is, opposition to reform of the courts) is an ecclesiastical matter." That is: it concerns the traditions of the Islamic religious class, which are similar to church traditions for Christians.

The Caliphate 189

This statement impelled me to send the following letter to the Lord:

Cairo, 20 Rabi' I, 1325 AH [May 1907]
A letter from the editor of *Al-Manar* to Lord Cromer
Honorable Lord,

I greet you as befits your rank, although I have not yet had the honor of becoming acquainted with you. I hope that you will honor me by giving me a few minutes of your precious time to answer the following question. It concerns me because I am the editor of an Islamic periodical that defends the religion and investigates its philosophy. It is:

In what you stated in your last report on rule by the Islamic shari'ah "which was set down one thousand or more years ago," did you mean the Islamic religion itself, which consists of the Wise Qur'an and the prophetic tradition (sunnah)? Or did you rather mean Islamic jurisprudence [fiqh], which is set down by the jurists? If you meant the latter, it is something set down by human beings in which their opinions became mixed with what they derived from the former, and in which some demonstrated the errors of others. The Muslims' rulers themselves have relinquished the requirement to act in accordance with a great deal of it. Those Muslims who seek reform are critical of many of the juristic opinions that have been set down in all of the schools of law [madhhabs].

If you meant the former, then this humble individual is ready to explain to Your Excellency that most of the religion's judicial and political rulings take the form of general principles. These support the maintenance of human welfare in every era and in every place. That is because they rest on the foundation of preventing corruption and procuring benefit, achieved through a process of consultation. Rulings having to do with particulars (which constitute the majority of rulings) are informed by those general principles.

I end my letter bidding Your Excellency farewell with greetings and respect.
Founder of *Al-Manar* in Egypt
Muhammad Rashid Rida

He replied to us with the following letter in Arabic, signed and dated in Latin letters.

LORD CROMER'S LETTER TO *AL-MANAR*'S EDITOR

The Respected and Very Learned Scholar Shaykh Rashid Rida, Editor of *Al-Manar* Magazine:

In answer to your letter, I say that in what I wrote I meant the collected Islamic laws [*qawanin*] that you call jurisprudence [fiqh], as that is what ordinances are based on. I did not mean the Islamic religion itself. Thus,

I have spoken in this last report, and in other reports, of the importance of assisting the Islamic party that seeks reform, proceeding upon the path that leads to modern civilization, but without infringing the religion's fundamental principles. Perhaps the wording I used in my report was too brief, and thus did not completely fulfill its purpose.

Respected master, please accept my boundless respect.

Cromer

May 4, 1907

LORD KITCHENER'S STATEMENT TO SAYYID AL-ZAHRAWI

Sayyid 'Abd al-Hamid al-Zahrawi visited Egypt after being appointed as a member of the Ottoman Senate. He stayed as a guest of his friend, the editor of *Al-Manar*. He visited Lord Kitchener, the British consul-general at that time, as recommended. I was with him. What the Lord said to him in Arabic included the following:[247]

> The Ottoman Empire will not prosper if it borrows laws from us, the people of Europe, as they do not suit it. These laws only became appropriate for us through a process of gradual development lasting a number of centuries. We changed and replaced them as our circumstances changed. You have a just shari'ah, one that harmonizes with your beliefs and social conditions. Thus, the state's duty is to work with that shari'ah, abandon Europe's laws, establish justice, preserve security, and exploit its fertile lands. In my opinion, this is the only way it can prosper.

This statement is true, even if one allows that the speaker is ignorant and incorrect in his supposition regarding Europe's laws not being suited to us. We know that everything found in those laws in the way of truth and justice had previously been established by our shari'ah. This point may be appreciated from what is discussed above, but detailed elaboration of that point is a task for another occasion.

(37) THE CALIPHATE AND THE PAPACY, OR SPIRITUAL LEADERSHIP

Islam is the religion of freedom and independence. It honored human beings and elevated their nature by freeing them from the slavery of serving anyone besides God Almighty, including people's leaders in religion and worldly life. Its first fundamental principle is that worship, transcendence, holiness, and personal obedience are reserved for God, Lord of the worlds, and that messengers, prayer and peace be upon them, are but guides and informers: "We sent

The Caliphate

messengers only to give good news and to warn" [Qur'an 6:48; 18:56].[248] Thus, messengers have no power over peoples' consciences, nor any right to compel or coerce, or to call people to account over what is in their hearts and thoughts, or to forgive sins and crimes, or to block their entry into paradise or send people to the hellfire. Rather, all of that is reserved for God, the One, the All-Powerful, the Pardoner, the Forgiving. The Almighty says to the seal of His messengers:

> Remind them. All you can do is be a reminder. Over them you have no power [Qur'an 88:21–22].[249] We know best what the disbelievers say. You are not there to force them [Qur'an 50:45]. Nor are you their keeper [Qur'an 6:107; 39:40; 42:6]. You are in no way accountable for them, nor they for you [Qur'an 6:52]. Say: "I have no control over any harm or good that may befall you" [Qur'an 72:21]. . . . You cannot guide everyone you love to the truth; it is God who guides whoever He will [Qur'an 28:56].

Obeying the Messenger is only mandatory in what he conveys and explains on the authority of God Almighty and which pertains to the matter of religion, and in what he implements of His revealed law. That is not the case when it comes to what the Messenger deems correct on the basis of his own suppositions and opinions in matters pertaining to life in this world. The essence of obedience, then, is that obedience is due to God alone. Hence, the Almighty says, "Whoever obeys the Messenger obeys God" [Qur'an 4:80]. Thus, obeying the Messenger and then those who hold authority in the Muslim community follows from obedience to God, which He mandated to ensure that public welfare is maintained and the shari'ah implemented. Nevertheless, the Messenger is infallible when it comes to conveying and establishing the religion. God made him a good example for his community. On this basis, the Companions used to consult the Prophet, prayer and peace be upon him, regarding his opinion on matters of public interest, such as matters of war and peace, and gave their own opinions. He would take recourse to the opinion of one of them, rather than his own, if it appeared clear to him that it was correct. For instance, he took recourse to Hubab bin al-Mundhir's opinion on the day of the battle of Badr. Following consultation, he would take recourse to the opinion of the majority, even if it did not appear clear to him that it was the most correct opinion, as he did on the day of the battle of Uhud. He said, "I am only a human. If I command you to do something that concerns your religion, follow it. If I give you a command to do something that is based upon my opinion, I am only a human"—related by Muslim, from Rafi' bin Khudayj. He said, "You are more knowledgeable in the matters of your worldly lives"—related by Muslim, from 'A'ishah.

He, God's prayer and peace be upon him, was aware that there were hypocrites among his followers. He knew the identities of some of them, but not others. Yet he treated them as he treated the faithful. That is because a fundamental principle of the shari'ah is that people are to be treated on the basis of their manifest deeds, while the matter of hearts and consciences is delegated to God Almighty. A man who saw the Prophet giving allowances to men who were among "those whose hearts are to be reconciled to Islam" said to him: "O Messenger of God, fear God." The Prophet said, "Woe upon you. Am I not among the people of the earth the one with the greatest claim to fear God?" Then the man left. Then Khalid bin al-Walid said, "Shall I cut his neck?" In another narration: Umar said, "O Messenger of God, permit me to cut his neck." He said, "Do not do that, he might be making prayer." Then Khalid said, "and how many a person when making prayer says with his tongue what is not in his heart?" The Messenger of God, prayer and peace be upon him, said, "I was not commanded to search into the hearts of people, nor to open their chests"—related by the two shaykhs [Bukhari and Muslim], from Abu Sa'id al-Khudri.[250]

If this was the stance of the Prophet, prayer and peace be upon him and his family, how could caliphs and emirs, no matter how great their prestige, have the right to call people to account over what is in their hearts, or to claim to have any authority over them in regard to their understanding or practice of the religion? Perhaps some people are more knowledgeable in the religion than they are? No. The caliph in Islam is nothing more than a leader of government whose powers are limited. He has no authority or control over people's spirits and hearts. He is but the one who implements the revealed law. The duty to obey him is restricted to that. This means obeying the revealed law, not obeying him personally, as mentioned and explained previously in Sections 1, 6, and 8.

But non-Arabs corrupted the imamate and caliphate. This resulted from what the Batinis instilled in the minds of the Shi'ah, the doctrine of the infallible imam.[251] It also resulted from the excesses of the Persians, Turks, and those who followed their example in praising the caliphs in an exaggerated manner—such excess is discussed in the historical survey that follows. They did that to such an extent that they effectively opened the door for the caliphs, enabling them to adopt a subjugating posture and force the Muslim community to be subservient and yielding. Thereafter, every exaggeration wound up resulting in its opposite. Thus, non-Arabs' exaggerated praise of the 'Abbasid caliphs contributed to the fall of their caliphate. Thereafter, the hallowing of the Ottoman caliphs was a cause of their state's destruction. The Turks retained the title "caliph," void of its legal and political dimensions, for one among them, as mentioned previously. But that did not prevent people, especially the editors of the newspapers,

The Caliphate

from describing him as saintly, or as master of the throne, and from lauding him in other ways in both word and deed. The Muslims have increasingly discussed a spiritual form of the caliphate, one that is cut off from the realm of temporal political authority. Non-Muslim discussions of such a caliphate have grown in a similar fashion. We have explained the truth of the matter in this investigation, yet we find that we can provide further clarity by relating what the Master, the Imam [Muhammad 'Abduh] wrote about it in his book *Islam and Christianity between Science and Civilization.*[252] He, may God have mercy upon him, said:

Islam's Fifth Principle

Overturning Religious Authority

I turn to one of Islam's principles, and what a lofty principle it is: abolishing religious authority and uprooting it from its foundation. Islam destroyed the structure of that authority, and erased its traces. Thus, for most of Islam's people no name for it or vestige of it remained. Aside from God and His Messenger, Islam did not recognize any person as having any authority over what another person believes, or any control over his faith.

Yet the Messenger of God, peace be upon him, was a conveyer and a reminder, not a dominator or a controller. God Almighty says: "Remind them. All you can do is be a reminder. Over them you have no power" [Qur'an 88:21–22].[253] He did not grant anyone the right to loose or bind, not on earth and neither in heaven.[254] Rather, when it comes to what is between the believer and God, the Islamic faith frees him from the control of any guardian except for God alone. It relieves him from any kind of bondage, with the exception that he is bound to worship God alone. A Muslim, however high his seniority in Islam, has no rights over any other Muslim, however diminished his standing in Islam, except for the right to advise and guide. Describing those who are delivered, God says: "they counsel one another to the truth, and counsel one another to patience" [Qur'an 103:3].[255] He says, "Let there be of you a community that calls to the good, enjoins honorable conduct, and dissuades from dishonorable conduct. These are indeed prosperous people" [Qur'an 3:104].[256] He says, "Out of each community, a group should go out to study the religion, so that they can teach their people when they return, and so that they can guard themselves against evil" [Qur'an 9:122].

Thus, Muslims give advice to each other. Thereupon, they establish a community that calls people to what is good. They watch over it, and guide it back to the straight path if it should have deviated from it. That community has no rights over the people except for the rights to call them to God, and to remind, exhort, and warn. It is impermissible for the community, or any individual belonging to it, to investigate the faults of any person. It is not allowed for a strong person or a weak person to reconnoiter anyone's belief. It is not a

Muslim's duty to draw his faith or to derive the fundamental principles that are the basis of his practice from anything other than God's Book and the Messenger of God's sunnah [the Qur'an and the hadith], prayer and peace be upon him. Every Muslim has the right to learn about God from God's Book [the Qur'an], and about His Messenger from His Messenger's words, without making anyone among the ancestors or following generations a mediator.[257] Before that, his duty is only to acquire the knowledge that would enable him to comprehend. This includes knowledge of the following: the Arabic language's grammar, and its rules and idioms; the circumstances of the Arabs, especially during the era of the Prophet's mission; the factors that affected the people during the time of the Prophet, prayer and peace be upon him; events occurring at the time when revelation descended; and some knowledge of abrogating and abrogated traditions. Aside from that, if his condition does not grant him the ability to reach a correct understanding of the sunnah and the Book [the hadith and the Qur'an], he has no duty but to inquire of those who are knowledgeable in them. When he receives an answer to a question he has asked he has the right, and indeed the obligation, to demand supporting evidence. That is so whether the question concerns a matter of faith, or a rule having to do with practice. Thus, what people refer to as "religious authority," viewed from any angle, is lacking in Islam.

Authority in Islam

However, Islam is a religion and a revealed law. Thus, it set down the hudud laws and determined people's rights. Not everyone who outwardly appears to believe in a principle follows it in his actions. Desires come to prevail, and craving takes control. This leads to rights being infringed or transgressions of limits set by God. Thus, the benefits of the wisdom underlying legislation will be unrealized unless there exists a power to execute the hudud laws, implement qadis' rulings in accordance with what is right, and maintain order in the community. That power cannot be disorganized by being given to many different people. It must be held by a single person: the sultan or caliph.

For Muslims the caliph is not infallible, nor is he regarded as somebody who receives revelation. He has no exclusive right to explicate the Book and the sunnah [the Qur'an and the hadith]. Yes, it is stipulated that he be a mujtahid. That is: it is stipulated that he has sufficient knowledge of the Arabic language and the pertinent sciences, as mentioned previously. That enables him to easily comprehend the Book and the sunnah [the Qur'an and the hadith] so that he may derive whatever he requires for ordinances, by his own efforts able to distinguish true from false, sound from corrupt. This also makes it easy for him to rule justly, which both the religion and the community require of him.

The Caliphate

195

His situation is thus: when it comes to comprehending the Book [the Qur'an] and having knowledge of ordinances, the religion does not distinguish him as superior to others. Nor does it elevate him to a distinct status. Rather, he and all of those who seek understanding are equal. They outdo one another only in terms of the purity of their minds and soundness of their judgments.[258] He is then to be obeyed so long as he acts rightly and follows the path set down by the Book and the sunnah [the Qur'an and the hadith]. Muslims watch over him. If he deviates from the path, they lead him back to it. If he becomes crooked they straighten him by giving counsel and exhortations.[259] "No obedience is owed toward a created being when that would entail sinning against the Creator."[260] Thus, if in his actions he departs from the Book and the sunnah [the Qur'an and the hadith], their duty is to replace him with someone else, so long as replacing him does not bring a corruption that outweighs the benefit of removing him.[261] It is the community or its representative, then, that appoints him. The community is entitled to exercise its authority over him, and discharge him when it finds that befitting its welfare. Hence, he is in every respect a civil ruler.

It would be inadmissible for someone who reflects soundly on the matter to conflate the Muslim understanding of "caliph" with what Europeans refer to as "divine authority." That is because in their understanding someone having "divine authority" stands alone. He receives revealed laws from God, and he alone has the right to legislate. He has the right to be obeyed as a requirement of faith, and it is the people's responsibility to obey him. This differs from a situation in which obedience rests on an oath of allegiance along with what that entails, including the requirements that a ruler must have integrity and safeguard what people rightfully hold. A believer, so long as he is a believer, cannot oppose somebody who holds "divine authority." That is so even where he deems him an enemy of God's religion, and his eyes behold him performing acts that cannot be reconciled with what he knows about God's revealed laws. That is because the actions and statements of someone who holds religious authority, however that authority is manifested, effectively constitute religion and revealed law. Such was the authority of the Church in the Middle Ages, and the Church still lays claim to this kind of authority, as indicated previously.

The achievements of modern civilization include separating religious authority from civil authority. This left the Church with the right to control beliefs and actions when it comes to the servant's relationship with his Lord. She legislates and abolishes as she wills, supervises and calls people to account as she wills, and forbids and grants as she desires. It granted civil authorities the right to legislate when it comes to people's civil transactions, along with the right to control what enables social cohesion in people's worldly lives, as distinct from what concerns the afterlife. Europeans have regarded this separation of powers as a source of ultimate goodness.

Islam's [European] critics, then, were operating under an erroneous assumption. They accused Islam of mandating that the two kinds of authority be united and embodied in a single personality. They imagined that—as Muslims understand the matter—Islamic teaching conveys the notion that the sultan is the one who determines the religion's nature and content, and the one who sets down and implements its ordinances. They imagined that faith is a tool in his hand. This enables him to proceed as he wishes, subduing hearts and prevailing upon minds as he does so. Thus, for the sultan mind and consciousness are but a commodity. On that basis, they formed the notion that a Muslim's religion subjugates him to his sultan. Furthermore, based on their experience [in Europe], they assumed that a state of war exists between religious authority and science, and that the former seeks to protect ignorance. Pursuing this line of thought, they concluded that as long as the Islamic religion includes the principle that the sultan's installation is a duty mandated by the religion, it will not be easy for Islam to embrace science with an open mind. To you, it is plain that all of this is purely erroneous, and far removed from reflecting a sound comprehension of what the fundamental principles of Islam actually require. You have learned that in Islam there is no empowerment of religious authority except for the authority to give good counsel, call people to what is good, and prevent what is evil. It is an authority that God granted to the most humble Muslims. This authority authorizes them to strike at the pride of the most distinguished Muslims. In the same way, He granted the most distinguished Muslims the right to draw on this same authority in their dealings with the most humble Muslims.

From this, the magazine *Al-Jami'ah*[262] may appreciate that the issue of authority is not something that constrains Islam and impedes it from being favorably disposed toward science. References to the good works of the 'Abbasid caliphs and Andalusian Umayyads when it comes to science, and how that related to the ulama, have been given previously. Perhaps we will revisit this point in due course.[263]

They say: "If the caliph does not hold that religious authority, should not the qadi, the mufti, or the Shaykh al-Islam hold it?" I say: "Islam did not grant these people the least authority over beliefs and the determination of ordinances. The authority that each holds is a temporal authority established by the Islamic revealed law. It is not warranted for any of them to claim the right to control anybody's faith or his worship of his Lord, or to contend with him over his manner of thought."

The Caliphate

CONCLUSION

A SOCIOLOGICAL AND HISTORICAL SURVEY OF THE CALIPHATE AND THE ISLAMIC STATES[264]

We have made some of them a test for others, such that they say,
"Is it these men that God has favored among us?"
Does God not know best who are the grateful ones?
[Qur'an 6:53]

Introduction: Those who came before us included warners and messengers who were sent to guide the people. There were also kings and rulers who assumed responsibility for ordinances and political matters. Some of the prophets were kings, and some of the kings were followers of the prophets. Power and leadership were a test for both kings and subjects, leaders and led: "We have made some of you a means of testing others—will you stand fast?" [Qur'an 25:20].[265]

Religious leaders who were not prophets would often enter into partnerships with leaders in the domain of worldly life, people such as kings and emirs. They did so because they were seduced by the prospect of fortune and glory. Some of them supported these worldly leaders, helping them to subjugate their people, savoring the fortunes and honors they received for doing that. People would submit to these religious leaders. They did so because they were motivated by their religious beliefs, coerced by those who wielded power and authority, or for both of these reasons. Perhaps some of them were unable to endure the injustices meted out by some of the kings. They then destroyed their thrones and appointed to command a group of leaders who had risen up to resist injustice and coercion through their own efforts. Yet as command passes to that group, acting as a clique they turn course. They become even more unjust and unfair than a single king, who, without the support of assistants like them, lacks the capacity to act wrongly or do harm. People remain oppressed by the spiritual control that religious leaders have over their consciences, and by the control that both religious and worldly leaders have over the outer and material aspects of their lives.

> When one day they took refuge in the shade of justice
> They were burned for many days by the fire of injustice
> When they taste the sweetness of mercy
> It is followed by drinking from the bitterness of harshness, painfully.

Thousands of them suffer so that some living in luxury may savor pleasure, thousands deprived of good living while a band of prodigals savors the fruits of their work. People were still living thus until God sent the seal of His messengers as a blessing to all people. What enables a good quality of life and right guidance in religion came to them through him.

He brought guidance to humankind, setting down fundamentals that included a religion of the middle path, a just revealed law, and a consultative state, wherein people are required to conduct their affairs on the basis of mutual consultation.[266] He eliminated the haughtiness, selfishness, and arrogance of a sovereign from government. He set down the role of a leader who embodies unity, and who, for the benefit of the community, brings order together with justice in the state. This leader is selected by leading figures in the community, those having insight, integrity, and learning, and who hold the people's confidence. He made this leader responsible for the people, and equal to the most humble member of the community under all ordinances of the shari'ah. He bound the people to obey the leader in what is right, in what aligns with truth and justice. He prohibited them from obeying him when doing so would lead to sins, injustice, and oppression. He made the motivation to obey a religious one, so that obedience would be realized in hearts and in deeds, as obedience in its true sense is due to God alone. Authority inheres in the main body [jama'ah] of the community, with the leader nothing more than somebody who embodies its unity. Thus, in the verse on the pledge of allegiance, the revealed Book addresses the Prophet who was sent to the people in this religion: "they will not disobey you in what is right" [Qur'an 60:12]. The Prophet was commanded to consult with others on affairs. He, God's prayers and peace be upon him, established these fundamental principles by acting in complete accordance with them. Thus, he would consult with others and defer to their opinions over his own. During the illness that led to his death he invited whoever he might have treated unjustly to seek redress from him. Subsequently, his successors, the rightly guided caliphs, followed this example (sunnah) of his. This is one of the main reasons why the following occurred: the religion of Islam was received well by the people, and gained ascendancy over all of the religious communities [milal] and religions; its command, laws, and language gained supremacy in the East and the West; numerous nations submitted to it consensually and voluntarily; and its dominion expanded from the Hijaz, within one century reaching farthest Africa and Europe to the west and the lands of India to the east.

If those who succeeded the rightly guided caliphs had followed their example and adhered to the guidance set down in the Book and the sunnah [the Qur'an and the hadith], Islam's guidance would have spread to the entire world. In that case, those enslaved to fame and desire would not have rushed to seize the role of leadership, which succeeds the leadership of prophethood, pouncing upon

The Caliphate

199

it with the support of their own partisan groups. That is because leadership in Islam has nothing to do with savoring bodily desires or glorying in the power that comes with tyrannical rule. The Companions allocated to the first caliph and his family support that was similar to the support that any average man among the Emigrants—neither the highest or the lowest—would receive. Yet the Prophet and the rightly guided caliphs who succeeded him chose lifestyles that were more humble than the lifestyles embraced by the typical members of their communities.

As for the aggression directed against 'Umar and his killing, that was not due to the Muslims envying or hating him, nor to the ambition of someone who wanted to succeed him. Rather, it was due to a group of secret Magians [Zoroastrians] taking revenge on him for having conquered their lands and destroyed their empire. As for the aggression against 'Uthman and his killing, that was due to the conspiracies sown by the Persians and 'Abd Allah ibn Saba', the Jew. Had it not been for these two episodes of strife, the split between 'Ali and Mu'awiyah would not have developed to the extent that it did. Anybody who examines history carefully will appreciate this.

The rule and dominion of Islam spread, and its opponents grew in number. These opponents were leaders of religious communities [*milal*] and peoples. Islam had eliminated their glory. No longer would they take relish in ruling their lands. Islam equalized their rights with those of their slaves, and all of their peoples were their slaves. The religious motivations of those who embraced Islam was not the same as it was for those Arabs who had genuinely understood it. Further, not all of the Arab clans were like those who preceded them, the original Emigrants and Helpers. It was not easy to organize the caliphate in such a manner that all of these communities and peoples in the East and West would yield to its authority, given the great distances and difficulties of communication involved in that. Thus, it was easy for the Sabaeans and Magians to propagate discord affecting Islam and the Arabs, and for Mu'awiyah to form an army in Syria (Sham) with which to fight the rightful imam, the Commander of the Faithful. Following that, he rendered the prophetic caliphate a tyrannical monarchy, one resembling the monarchies of the ancients.

THE RULE OF TYRANNY AND ITS CONSEQUENCES: NON-ARAB CORRUPTIONS OF ARAB ISLAMIC RULE

Mu'awiyah opened the door to tyranny for the powerful, and they went rushing to it. Yet the Umayyads, having done that, would not see their rule stand firm for one full century. As Islam had abolished Arab ethnic partisanship, the 'Abbasids needed to turn to the Persian nation for a partisan support group, deploying it against the Umayyads. The heretics and hypocrites among those people harbored secret conspiracies. They wanted to see Persians prevailing over Arabs, Mazdaism prevailing over Islam. To that end, they sowed division among the Muslims. They did so by disseminating exaggerated ideas about the family of the Prophet. They strove to slander most of the Companions in order to sunder the Arabs' unity, and alienate them from Islam's consultative (democratic) fundamental principles. They also sought to establish an autocratic government, holy or worshipped, by handing leadership of it to those belonging to the prophetic household who claimed infallibility. That would make it easier for them to reestablish Chosroism and Mazdaism.[267]

When the 'Abbasids discovered their plan they turned to the Turks for a partisan support base. Thus, Mu'tasim used their young men as his soldiery, obtaining them from their own lands as well as from other provinces. He granted them unlimited freedoms. He along with his successors prepared the path to power for them, unaware of how states are constituted and develop. These Turks that they had empowered proved ignorant, harsh, corrupt, and oppressive in the lands. They perpetrated multiple injustices and hostile actions against the people, to the point where they began to kill the caliphs themselves while they were on their thrones, or deposed them and replaced them with others, following their desires. Thus, their corruptions disrupted the social order, and turned people away from their duty to obey, a duty that is motivated by Islam. Thus, it became easy for their brothers, the Tatars, to overthrow the 'Abbasids' empire, laying waste, destroying, killing, and torturing. The power of the Batinis, the Carmathians (Qaramitah), and others grew dangerously.[268] The Turkish soldiers, then, stood in relation to the 'Abbasids as the Janissaries subsequently stood in relation to the Ottomans: initially their supportive force, they thereafter became a force that worked against them and corrupted their empire.

The non-Arabs, then, corrupted the rule of the 'Abbasid caliphs. They did so through laudations and glorifications that Islam rejects, and that are unknown to the Arabs. These were more damaging than their actions that were hostile toward them and overwhelmed them. An example of this is seen in what Sultan 'Adud al-Dawlah did, putting on that strange performance for Caliph Ta'i'.[269]

Suyuti states in his biography of Ta'i' li-llah in his *History of the Caliphs*:

'Adud al-Dawlah asked Ta'i' if he could add "Crown of the Religious Community [*millah*]" to his titles, bestow a robe of honor upon him, and crown him. Ta'i' acceded to the request. Ta'i' sat on the throne, around him 100 men with swords and finery, before him 'Uthman's Qur'an, on his shoulders the Prophet's mantle, in his hand a scepter, adorned with the sword

The Caliphate

of the Messenger of God, God's prayer and peace be upon him. A drape was hung that 'Adud al-Dawlah had sent. He requested that it be used as a curtain for Ta'i' so that no eye of any soldier before him should fall on him. The Turks and the Daylamites entered, not one of them armed. The sharifs and men of rank stood on either side. Then 'Adud al-Dawlah was given permission to enter. The drape was lifted, and 'Adud al-Dawlah kissed the ground. Ziyad, conducting, was alarmed by that and said to 'Adud al-Dawlah, "What is this, O king? Is this God?" He turned to him and said, "This is God's caliph in His land." (!!) He then continued walking, and kissed the ground seven times. Then Ta'i' turned to his servant Khalis and said, "Let him approach." Then 'Adud al-Dawlah rose, and kissed the ground twice. Then Ta'i' said, "Approach me." He then approached, and kissed his foot. Then Ta'i' placed his right hand on him and commanded him to sit, and he sat on a chair, this was after he had repeatedly been commanded "sit" as he was begging his pardon, prompting him to say to him, "I swear, you will sit." So he kissed the chair and sat down. Then Ta'i' said to him, "I see fit to entrust you with command of the people in the East and West, and with all aspects of administering the land, except for my court and finances. So take charge of that." He said: "May God help me to obey and serve the Commander of the Faithful." He then put the robe of honor on him and departed.[270]

The historian then discusses the consequences of this. He discusses how it affected the caliphs' standing with the sultans, as they came to resemble any other notable who belonged to their retinues. What that ignorant, flattering king used to do, and anything resembling it and everything else that he discusses in relation to that state of affairs, is rejected in Islam. That is because kissing the ground shows greater servility than bowing and touching the forehead to the ground. There are sound hadiths that prohibit imitating non-Arabs in their vainglorying and pridefulness, and even in standing at the side of their kings, or before them.

THE MUSLIMS' DISARRAY OVER THEIR GOVERNMENTS

As for what caused Muslims to be in such a state of disarray and for such a long period, it is that social changes inevitably resulted from what took place, from how people proceeded in such an unchecked and unrestrained manner when it came to determining the form that their Islamic government would take. In those times, it was not possible to establish a form of government that would be guaranteed to develop in accordance with the example (sunnah) set down by the rightly guided caliphs, or the path that the first Umayyads and 'Abbasids followed. That would have ensured that life in this world was glorious and that religion was righteous. By the time circumstances would have enabled that, the religion had been weakened. All of the Islamic peoples found that the weakening of their religion led to the weakening of their government and their civilization. For this reason, Muslims were not guided to the path that the Europeans were guided to, a path that led Europeans to annihilate monarchical tyranny, one people after another. Some Europeans irreversibly eliminated monarchical government. Some limited the authority of their monarchs, leaving them with no authority beyond certain grandiose symbols of their status which might prove useful under certain conditions. Thus, European monarchs were left without any right to unilaterally issue commands and prohibitions on behalf of a government.

That is because everyone who is given free reign over something must be responsible for his conduct with it. Under monarchy, the adopted traditions for authority involve the notion that the monarch is set above the rest of the people. Thus, they are unable to rise to his high station so as to question his actions. This is a notion that Islam abolished by regarding the Muslims' imam in the same manner as any other person under all ordinances of the shari'ah. In his statement, the Prophet, God's prayer and blessing be upon him, stipulated that he is responsible for his actions: "Each of you is a shepherd, and each of you is responsible for his flock. The imam is a shepherd, and he is responsible for his people. The man is a shepherd for his family and he is responsible for his people. The wife is a caretaker in the house of her husband, and she is responsible for her people. Etc."—a hadith narrated by Ibn 'Umar that has been firmly agreed upon.[271] The Muslims would keep the rightly guided caliphs in check. They would rebut their statements and opinions, and take recourse to a correct position when it appeared to them that the caliphs were in error. Even 'Umar ibn al-Khattab, may God be pleased with him, was shown by a woman to be in error regarding an issue. Hence, he said from the pulpit: "A woman was correct and 'Umar was in error," or, "and a man was in error."

Muslims have been heedless of this. They left the caliphate in the hands of people whose actions were motivated by their partisanship, by their partisan affiliations with their own groups. And they gave these people free reign. This is the free reign of heredity monarchs. They would claim that God had favored them—themselves and their families—over the rest of mankind, and mandated that the people must obey and yield to them in all things. None of the leading figures who loose and bind found a way to set down a shari'ah-based system for the caliphate, meaning what in contemporary terminology

The Caliphate

would be referred to as a system based upon constitutional law [*al-qanun al-asasi*]. Had they been able to do that, they could have used the revealed law's stipulations to limit the caliph's authority, and require him to consult with them on how to manage the people's affairs. While they did compose lengthy works on ordinances for politics, administrative matters, taxation, the functions of the qadi, and warfare, they did not produce a work that they had composed specifically for this purpose. Such a work could have been fortified by the prescriptions of the Book and the sunnah [the Qur'an and the hadith], and the example of the rightly guided caliphs. It would have prohibited hereditary rule, restricted the method of choosing a caliph to consultation, and explained that authority inheres in the community and is exercised by those of its members who loose and bind. Had they done that, and required people to implement those fundamental principles, we would not have fallen into the predicament that we find ourselves in.

As for the rightly guided caliphs, may God be satisfied with them, they trusted in following the path of striving to achieve what is right and just. Standing in the Messenger's place on his pulpit, God's prayer and peace be upon him, they expressly declared that the community had authority over them. As Abu Bakr said: I was appointed to rule over you and I am not the best of you. If I am right, assist me. If I deviate, correct me. As 'Umar said: Whoever among you sees me deviating, let him correct my deviation. As 'Uthman said: My commands follow your commands. The statements and actions of 'Ali on consultation are well known. This is in spite of the disarray and discord that arose during 'Ali's time, along with the deaths of many distinguished people of learning, and the factionalist tendencies of some of the people. They did not in their era embark upon a process of writing things down, and setting down systems and rules.[272] They had not felt any pressing need to do that because righteousness was abundant and the community held fast to the religion, restrained by its requirements.

The era of writing things down only came about when the caliphate had been transformed into a kind of monarchy by Mu'awiyah's two great innovations: making the capacity to rule dependent upon having a powerful group of partisan supporters, and rendering the caliphate an inheritance, transferred from the one who reigns to his son, or someone else among his kin. The people were distracted from the evil of these two innovations as the discord sown by the Sabaeans and Magians was calmed, discord that had presented the Umayyads with an opportunity that they took advantage of. Then, people were distracted by what followed that, unity, the end of bloodshed in the interior, and return to conquest along with the dissemination of Islamic guidance and leadership in the exterior. That is because when corruption descends upon great righteousness its effects do not become apparent, except very gradually.

IBN KHALDUN'S PRINCIPLE OF PARTISANSHIP IS CONTRARY TO ISLAM

Many have been misled by the conduct of that monarch, Mu'awiyah. This even applies to our sage, the sociologist Ibn Khaldun. He was mistaken. He took as normative the practice of establishing sovereignty, and managing the people's affairs generally, on the basis of partisan affiliations, on the basis of support received from one's own partisan group. He applied that norm to cases where it does not fit. Moreover, he applied it to cases that clearly refute it, such as the mission of the messengers, peace be upon them. For Ibn Khaldun, those missions revolved around the messengers' ability to wield power over people, which was enabled by the prestige and partisan support they received from their own clans. He relied on a hadith that is contradicted by numerous qur'anic verses, and by reliable accounts of the messengers' lives. Deceived about this matter as he was, he then drew connections between the institution of the caliphate and the institution of prophethood.

But the truth is the opposite of what Ibn Khaldun supposed. The institution of prophethood, and likewise its successor, the caliphate, eliminated the principle that the right to rule can legitimately be established on a partisan basis. These institutions established the rule of law, and the principles of self-restraint and voluntary submission to the Lord's shari'ah. These stories of the messengers in the Generous Qur'an contradict what would support Ibn Khaldun's interpretation. Some of them include a declaration about a lack of strength and power, as in what the Almighty states when relating the story of Lot, peace be upon him: "He said, 'If only I had the strength to stop you or could seek refuge in some powerful support'" [Qur'an 11:80]. Or, one might ask: The mission of which of the messengers was based upon the partisan support of his people? Abraham, the intimate friend of God? Or Moses, the one spoken to by God? Or Jesus, the beneficent spirit? Or the seal of the prophets, prayer and peace be upon him and upon them?

Were most of the distinctions of the Hashimi Qurayshis not moral rather than military virtues? Was it not the case that most of the opposition to the Prophet and efforts to block him from conveying his Lord's call came from the leaders of Quraysh? Were they not the ones who forced him to make the migration [hijrah]? Were they not those about whom God revealed: "Remember when

The Caliphate   205

the disbelievers were scheming against you, to take you captive, or kill you, or expel you" [Qur'an 8:30]? Thus, the Prophet made the migration hidden from view. God Almighty called his migration an expulsion—that is, an exile and a deportation—with the like of His statement: "They have expelled you and the Messenger simply because you believe in God your Lord" [Qur'an 60:1]. Thus, God Almighty granted him victory through the agency of humble people, the Emigrants and Helpers. Most of the Quraysh did not believe until after God granted him victory over them and left them forsaken in their wars with him.

Yes, some of Ibn Khaldun's discourse on the rationale for reserving the caliphate for Quraysh is sound. This concerns their high standing during the Era of Ignorance and the Era of Islam, a standing that no one among the Arabs has challenged. It is with all the more reason that non-Arabs professing Islam do not challenge them over that. That is among the reasons for the unity of the Muslim community. Abu Bakr the Truthful, may God be pleased with him, pointed to this when remonstrating with the Helpers.[273] As for how a group's partisan cohesion empowers them in a martial sense, that ramification of partisanship does not in any way, partially or wholly, explain why the caliphate was reserved for Quraysh. That is because Islam abolished this aspect of partisanship, which is one that belongs to the Era of Ignorance. Ibn Khaldun, like others, acknowledges this. Thus, he was unable to characterize it as one of the principles that underlies Islam's sound and revealed law, which centers upon the principle that what is strong is subordinate to what is right. This runs counter to the practice of all of those among mankind who are astray. They empower what is strong over what is right, so that either what is right is subordinated to what is strong, or what is strong annihilates it before it annihilates what is strong.

From this brief explanation, the blemishes of falsehood in the rest of Ibn Khaldun's discourse may be appreciated. This is seen in the way he employs his principle to justify Mu'awiyah's actions, even his installation of Yazid as his successor. He deems Mu'awiyah a mujtahid who erred when he fought the Commander of the Faithful, 'Ali, may God honor him. But he finds him acting soundly when installing Yazid as his successor, Yazid who had been rejected by the leading and wisest Companions. Hence, he achieved that through deceit, coercion, and bribery. Ibn Khaldun claims that Mu'awiyah was cognizant of the principle that he elaborates—the public's affairs cannot be effectively managed other than through power that rests upon the support of one's own group of partisans—and recognized that among the Arabs only his own people, the Umayyads, had a partisan disposition. He claims that an alternative to establishing an Umayyad caliphate—handing responsibility to those who loose and bind, the most distinguished Qurayshis, those known for their learning, integrity, and competence, who would consult one and another and then elect a caliph—was not deemed viable. All of this is false. Ibn Khaldun's own discourse includes testimonies to its falseness. We do not wish to lengthen the discussion by explicating that here.

We suffice by noting that it is incorrect to say that the only case where one finds the Arabs showing a partisan disposition is in the support given to the Umayyads, either on the basis of their military prowess, or because the community had confidence in their integrity and competence. It is rather the case that the Umayyads were able to take advantage of 'Uthman's timidity and weakness. Thus, they were able to seize positions of authority and power in Islamic lands, positions that constitute the structure and strength of the state. They recruited people who belonged to other Qurayshi clans and who loved worldly life, along with others who they knew would oblige them. Most of these people had little more than a superficial understanding of Islam, and they stood ready to respond to any call from somebody belonging to the ruling class. In that way, the Umayyads used these people to establish a practice that belongs to the Era of Ignorance. With that, they destroyed the true caliphate, namely, an institution that is based on the shari'ah, and succeeds the institution of prophethood in proper fashion.[274]

Had Mu'awiyah wished to base the caliphate on a process of consultation he could have done so. Some of the leading Companions, may God be pleased with them, had advised him to do that. Then, his own people as well as other people would have supported a caliph who had been selected through a shari'ah-based process, one in which people qualified for the task of choosing the caliph consulted one another on the matter. Nothing prevented him from doing that but love of life in this world and the seduction of power. However, 'Umar ibn 'Abd al-'Aziz was subsequently unable to put the principle of consultation into effect, as Umayyad power had grown excessively and dangerously, the Umayyads having gained full control over the one among them who held power.

In the "Book on Tribulations" in Bukhari's *Sound Collection* it is related that while in Basrah the noble Companion Abu Barzah was asked about the dispute over the caliphate between Marwan, Ibn Zubayr, and the Kharijis, which had resulted from Mu'awiyah's conduct. He responded:

> I leave it with God that I have become angry with the people of Quraysh. O Arabs, you were in a condition that you are well aware of, humiliated, poor, and astray. God delivered you from that through Islam and Muhammad, God's prayer and peace be upon him, so that you came to acquire what you see, and the life in this world that has corrupted you. The one who is in Syria

The Caliphate

(Sham) is, by God, fighting but for the sake of life in this world, and those who are among you are, by God, fighting but for the sake of life in this world, and the one who is in Mecca is, by God, fighting but for the sake of life in this world.[275]

By "those who are among you" he means the Kharijis, those whom they call "the readers." Hence in another narration there is an addition: "those claiming that they are your readers."

Yes, the first Umayyads and 'Abbasids utilized the nature of monarchical authority as a way to realize the caliphate's goals, such as spreading Islam, its language and its glory, conquering lands, and generally establishing justice among the people. Exceptions to actions taken in pursuit of such goals include taking revenge upon those who were suspected of coveting the caliphate, and acting without restraint when it came to the treasury. After detailing this issue, Ibn Khaldun states:

It has thus been shown that the form of government came to be that of monarchy, while traits characteristic of the caliphate still persisted, people remaining intent on the religion and its ways, and proceeding upon the path of truth. The change that became apparent was only one of motivation. Initially that had a religious character. Then, it shifted as people came to be motivated by their partisan affiliations and by the sword. This was the case in the era of Mu'awiyah, Marwan, his son 'Abd al-Malik, and the first 'Abbasid caliphs down to Harun al-Rashid and some of his sons. Then, the characteristic traits of the caliphate were lost. Nothing remained but its name. The form of government became purely monarchical. Tyranny reached the ultimate limit of its nature, and was employed for realizing the goals of subjugating people, gratifying desires, and pursuing pleasure. That was the case for the sons of 'Abd al-Malik, and also for the 'Abbasids after Rashid. The title "caliphate" endured under their leadership because Arab solidarity had endured. Across the two stages the two concepts, caliphate and monarchy, became mixed with each other. Then, the traces and influences of the caliphate were lost as the Arabs lost their solidarity as a group, their era came to an end, and their power was destroyed. Government remained in a monarchical form, as was the case with the non-Arab rulers in the East. They professed obedience to the caliph in order to enjoy blessings, while monarchical authority with all of its titles and attributes was theirs, the caliph having no share in it. It is thus clear that the caliphate originally existed without monarchy. Then, the characteristic traits of the two kinds of government became mixed and confused. Then, monarchical authority came to exist alone, when its spirit of partisan solidarity with one's own group became detached from the spirit of the caliphate.[276]

208 Muhammad Rashid Rida

This overview by Ibn Khaldun points to the soundness of our opinion, which we have repeated many times. It is that the Umayyad and 'Abbasid caliphs combined monarchy's augustness, comforts, and opulence with the caliphate's goals of propagating religion, truth, and justice. Corruption came upon them gradually. It continued to afflict them until over time it destroyed their power. Most Muslims have no awareness of the historical background to the social circumstances affecting their lives. The minority that does have an understanding of that lacks the ability to eliminate corruption and make amends until the ultimate conclusion is reached, and the Muslim community stands in complete ruin.

The institution of the caliphate, properly constituted, provides the only means to eliminate corruption. This institution has been lent to invalid forms of Islam, and oppressive states have been propped up in its name. In view of that, how could utilizing it to guard and preserve what is rightful, true, and as firmly rooted as the mountains possibly be unviable? I swear by the highest truth, the truth above which nothing rises: were the Muslims to devote to restoring the caliphate in its proper form a tenth of the attention that the Batini groups have devoted to corrupting it, it would come back stronger than it was before. Thereby, Muslims would become masters of the entire world.

This is indeed the situation. But what eluded the Muslims in the Middle Ages should not elude them in this era. Today, mankind has become aware of what people were previously unaware of when it comes to God Almighty's ways with human society, the benefits of social order, and the ordinances that serve to maintain it.

THE OTTOMAN TURKS, THE CALIPHATE, AND EUROPEANIZATION

The Muslims best placed to proceed in this matter were those belonging to the Ottoman political class. This applies especially to those residing in Constantinople and in Rumelia in Europe. They witnessed European peoples advancing, developing sciences and arts, and building ordered societies. But their state was not well suited to sciences and arts because, with the exception of the previous century, they had lacked a scientific and codified language befitting that. Further, aside from a few traditionally minded scholars [muqallidin], they did not take up the task of familiarizing themselves with Islam's sciences. For this reason, they gave their sultans personal and absolute authority, even after they had been endowed with the title of "caliph." Thus, when they subsequently started to study Europe's history, laws, and revolutions, revolutions that

The Caliphate

eliminated absolute monarchy from her governments, they imagined that the only way to restrain despotism and prevent oppression was to replicate the European form of government, limited monarchy. Then, in this era they came to favor the republican form of government. That is because they felt that making the sultan a holy figure who was not held to account—as they had done in their Constitution—would not achieve the desired result. Had they studied the shari'ah in the independent spirit with which they studied positive law, they would have found it providing a superior and more comprehensive solution. That is, the shari'ah would have provided them with more effective ways to realize their goals than anything previously afforded by the Constitution, and likewise anything currently afforded by the spiritual caliphate and the government of the National Assembly.

Midhat Pasha and his assistants established the Ottoman Constitution. But Sultan 'Abd al-Hamid [Abdul Hamid II] broke them apart, dismantling their unity and trampling upon their Constitution for a third of a century in which he was the absolute ruler. Nobody was able to resist his commands or challenge his authority. Revealed and positive law were both under his control. He arrogated to himself the position with which the Lord of Glory distinguished Himself over His creation in His statement, "He shall not be questioned about anything He does, but they shall be questioned" [Qur'an 21:23]. People in the Ottoman Empire, Egypt, Tunisia, and India say: "the great caliph says and the great caliph does." And if one of the Ottomans who has been wronged—wronged personally, or seeing his community wronged in its own homeland—says that he has been unjust and sinned, they curse him, and accuse him of being disloyal or an unbeliever.

This was a reason why these Europeanized Turks believed that the institution of the caliphate itself is an obstacle blocking the path that they seek to follow, imitating Europe in establishing a limited form of government. That results from the notion that obedience to the caliph must be absolute, that it is impermissible to disobey him or use positive law to limit his powers. It is also due to the belief that the caliph's position as head of state obliges the state to adhere to the Islamic shari'ah's ordinances on politics, administration, justice, and education, and that this makes learning the Arabic language obligatory, as understanding the shari'ah depends on that. These restrictions stand in the way of what they seek to do, imitating the Europeans so as to realize the independence of their Turkish nation, and grant it authority over governance and state, authority that is not in any way restricted by the laws or languages of other peoples. This is what they refer to as "national sovereignty" [al-hakimiyyah al-milliyyah].

THE REVIVAL OF THE TURANIAN NATIONAL IDENTITY

These Europeanized people resolved to revive the notion of a Turkish-Turanian nation, and make it completely independent in its sovereignty, legislation, beliefs, and morals, unrestricted by anything derived from another community. Moreover, I say in clear, formal language: unrestricted by the Islamic shariʿah or the Islamic religion. They prepared the path to that with the books and treatises that they composed toward that end, and with poems and songs that they composed. The Ittihadist authority obliged them in this. But most of the Turkish people — those for whom, by whom, and within whom they sought that revival — resisted their agenda. They are a people who profess Islam, and their sultan is recognized by most of the earth's Muslims as the caliph of the Prophet, God's prayer and peace be upon him. The Europeanized have found that, thanks to him, their state has some spiritual influence over Islamic peoples. This has lent it a certain standing in its political dealings with the Great Powers. That was beneficial on the one hand, and disastrous on the other. That is because the Great Powers were compelled to show deference to their state in certain matters so that their own Muslim subjects would not agitate against them, and accuse them of being hostile to the state that is the seat of the caliphate. They were compelled to accept every excuse it offered along the lines of it being impossible to grant a request because what had been sought could not be seen issuing from the Muslims' caliph. For this same reason, they then became united in being hostile toward the state, conspiring against it, and striving to weaken or annihilate it. They did that so as to be freed from the influence that the institution of the caliphate had over their Muslim citizens. This is why the belief that the caliphate's harm outweighed its benefits spread among these Europeanizers. Some of them had this belief shaken from them following the War of Tripoli.[277] Although the Ittihadists have a tendency to act precipitously, they have been hesitant on this matter, vacillating between inaction and acting decisively, and elevating the dominion of the Turanian nation above the dominion of Islam.

HOW THE EUROPEANIZED INTEND TO TERMINATE THE RELIGION

The obstacle stood in the path of the requirement. Thus, they adopted means to eliminate the obstacle.

These means include: spreading deviant ideas and denial of God's attributes in the official schools, especially the military schools, and among the people generally. To that end, they produced books and treatises, composed in various styles.

The Caliphate

These means include: utilizing schools and the army to instill a partisan nationalist spirit in the modern generation, and substituting that spirit in place of religious sentiment. To that end, they made it the nation's highest ideal. Thus, they celebrated its well-known historical figures, even those who were corrupt and destructive, instead of celebrating Islam's leading personalities, the rightly guided caliphs and other pious ancestors. They have numerous poems and songs for that purpose that are sung by students, soldiers, and others.

These means include: gradually erasing everything having an Islamic character from functions of government, and weakening the authority of the Islamic shaykhs. This even involves wresting control of the shari'ah courts from them, and setting in place a civil code with ordinances for matters of personal status.

These means include: weakening religious education, even limiting the number of graduates from the religious madrasahs, setting that at a low number, insufficient to ensure preservation of the religion and the revealed law.

These means include: fashioning the caliphate and the sultanate such that it has the character of a temporary expedient. The one who holds office lacks authority to issue commands or prohibitions, while his title is retained. The title remains useful as people would accept actions taken in the name of the caliph that they would not accept if they were taken in somebody else's name. It even became a matter of public knowledge that they used to promulgate decrees with Sultan Muhammad Rashad's [Mehmed V's] signature without his knowledge.

These means include: acting to corrupt Islamic morality and ethics. Thus, they permitted Turkish women to remove the hijab, flaunt, and behave licentiously. Moreover, they permitted them to practice prostitution. Previously, only non-Muslim women had been permitted to do that. Relating from the Grand Vizier Talat Pasha, Emir Shakib Arslan told me in Geneva, Switzerland, that when the German emperor visited Constantinople during the war and saw Turkish women unveiled and flaunting their beauty he had reproached him.[278] He spoke to him about moral corruptions and economic harms that result from that, harms from which Europe is suffering and cannot escape. He said to him: You have in your religion the means to prevent all of these problems. How is it, then, that you would destroy it with your own hands?

THE END OF THE AUTHORITY OF THE CALIPH AND THE SHAYKH AL-ISLAM

The institution of the caliphate, whose title the sultan holds, did not prevent the Ittihadists from undertaking any of the actions intended to efface the religion, and erase any trace of it from the state, and then likewise from the community. That is because the caliphate was nothing more than a formal title, one that did have some effect externally, beyond the borders of the state. Examples of that include the Great Powers having some respect for it, and their Muslim subjects along with other Muslims under their influence being attached to it. As for the situation internally—the matter of the caliphate's status within the state itself—the state had no special office for the caliph that had an organization and procedures that the caliph could use to carry out any functions of government. These include functions such as upholding the revealed law, safeguarding the religion, and attending to the Muslims' welfare. The caliph-sultan lacked any such thing.

There was only a member of the cabinet who was designated as the Shaykh al-Islam. He had an abode called *bab al-mashyakhah al-islamiyyah*, the seat of those who held the title shaykh and who were responsible for issuing fatwas, and administering shari'ah courts and religious education.[279] But it had been weakened to such an extent that they were incapable of carrying out these functions, functions that had been entrusted specifically to them. The Shaykh al-Islam was unable to prevent the Ittihadist government from wresting control of the shari'ah courts from him and placing them under the control of the [Ministry of] Justice. Neither was he able to stop the government from pursuing its agenda of cutting back religious education. How, then, could he have been capable of preventing it from permitting Muslim women to commit adultery or other vices? The most important reason for this weakness is that the office of those with the title shaykh was purely official. Not on one single day was it invested in the task of genuinely acting to serve the religion. Genuine service would have lent it moral authority over Islamic peoples residing in or beyond the empire, along with a religiously based capacity to act effectively. The government would then have had to respect, fear, and support it, and likewise the caliph, the caliph who had relinquished to it the role of supervising religious and Islamic affairs.

THE STATE'S WEAKNESS IN EVERYTHING BUT THE MILITARY

The truth that I must declare is that the Ottoman Empire was so beset by social problems and the effects of foreign teachings and conspiracies that all of its powers, material and spiritual, were weakened. As a result, the only power that remained effectively intact was military power, which benefited from having had a degree of organization and modern weaponry. Hence, nobody could overthrow it except by using the power of the army—the Ittihadists were aware

The Caliphate

of that, and thus they used it as they did. They committed misdeeds until they had terminated this sultanate (the empire), and our statement about them at the time when the Coalition Party took power from them proved true: "when they come back, it will be decisive."[280]

OUR ADVICE TO THE TURKS ON THE ISSUE OF THE CALIPHATE

But God Almighty granted victory to this destructive military power, whose politics were unrestrained and unjust. He did so by saving most of the Turkish lands from the claws of the European powers after they had attacked them and the entire world was at the point of losing all hope. The Turks then formed a republican Turkish government, and it acted as it did on the matter of the Islamic caliphate. After lengthy deliberation and reflection on the issue from two angles, the Islamic and the social, what we have discerned is:

- that what they initially determined must be a temporary expedient, not permanently established;
- that following peace the military authority should hand control of government over to a council elected by the people through a process that is genuinely free, not directed by the government or the army;
- that the matter of the caliphate should be left to all of the Islamic peoples and their wholly or partially independent governments;
- that a committee or a free and diverse society headquartered in Constantinople should be formed and tasked with examining everything that those with knowledge and sound opinions have written and recommended on the issue, preparing the way for the convening of an Islamic congress a year or more after peace.

We also find that the supreme Turkish government should form another committee tasked with determining the form that its relationship with the Arab community and other Islamic peoples should take, and, in view of its military, civil, and religious standing, how it might assist and be assisted by them. The two committees' members, or at least some of them, should be influential members of a congress on the caliphate, those who set down its agenda and determine how it would be configured, having carefully examined all pertinent opinions and information that they have gathered.

The newspapers have reported that the government in Angora (Ankara) will consult with the Islamic world on the matter of the caliphate. But genuine consultation, consultation that actually has effect, cannot occur unless the process is properly organized and the individuals and peoples involved are judiciously selected. For this reason, it is hoped that intelligent people be selected for each committee, and that through its actions each committee successfully sets down the right course of action. The desired result is that those among the Turks who loose and bind be persuaded to use their influence to establish the true imamate. Thereby, what the Muslims' ignorance and Europeans' materialism have corrupted on earth would be restored to its proper state. Destiny has turned. Mankind's need for the Qur'an's reform has intensified. The opposition of inflexible and traditionalist Muslims has weakened. The harms resulting from the partisan actions of the Umayyads, 'Abbasids, and Ottomans have become apparent, as has the error of the Europeans and the Europeanized Muslims. So blessed be the renewers, the reformers, and woe unto the conceited traditionalists. And the future belongs to the pious.

"This is the certain truth" [Qur'an 56:95].

"You will know the truth of it after a while" [Qur'an 38:88].

GLOSSARY

'adalah: justice, integrity.

'adl: justice, integrity, and piety of character required to hold office, denoting a sovereign's just character in dispensing fairly and equally.

A.H.: after the *Hijrah*, the migration of the Prophet from Mecca to Medina in 622, the base-year for the Islamic calendar.

'ahd: designation by testament; contract; used in the Qur'an to refer to agreements temporarily drawn up by Muhammad with the unbelievers.

ahkam: see *hukm*.

ahl al-'ahd: non-Muslims temporarily living in Muslim territories who have been given a pledge of security by their Muslim rulers, or who are in a treaty relationship with them.

ahl al-baghy: rebels.

ahl al-bayt: "people of the house," Muhammad's family and descendants, particularly his cousin and son-in-law 'Ali (d. 661); his daughter and 'Ali's wife Fatimah; their sons Hasan (d. 669) and Husayn (d. 680); and descendants.

ahl al-dhimmah: "people of the pact," tributaries, non-Muslims permanently resident in the Muslim state, protected and bound by certain conditions under the rules of a pact (*dhimmah*) made with Muslims. Applies particularly to Jews and Christians; also includes Zoroastrians.

ahl al-hall wa al-'aqd: those who "loose and bind"; those who may enter into a contract and dissolve it; those who represent the Muslim community and, in theory, act on their behalf in electing and deposing caliphs.

ahl al-kitab: "people of the book," namely, Jews, Christians, and Zoroastrians.

ahl al-riddah: apostates from Islam.

ahl al-shura: "people of consultation," counselors; the six Companions of the Prophet whom 'Umar appointed to elect one among themselves caliph.

ahl al-sunnah wa al-jama'ah: "people of the sunnah and the *jama'ah*" (q.v.); used by Sunni Muslims to refer to themselves, as distinct from other sects or those seen as deviationists, such as the Mu'tazilis.

Glossary

'ajam: non-Arabs, particularly Persians.

'Alids: descendants of 'Ali bin Abi Talib (d. 661), the Prophet's cousin and son-in-law.

'allamah: an especially expert or erudite scholar.

aman: pledge of security; safe conduct.

amanah: primordial covenant between God and human beings.

amir: also rendered "emir" in English, commander of a province or an army, appointed by the caliph in early Islam; a high-ranking soldier; chief; prince; governor of a city.

amir al-mu'minin: "commander of the faithful," a non-qur'anic expression and title of the caliph used from a very early date; also used by Umayyads, 'Abbasids, Fatimids, Almohads, and others; in Shi'ism this title is reserved for 'Ali.

amirate: also rendered "emirate" in English, the position or office of an amir.

al-'ammah: the common people, masses; cf. *al-khassah.*

amr bi al-ma'ruf wa al-nahy 'an al-munkar: commanding what is good and prohibiting what is rejected; this is both the ruler's duty and legitimation.

ansar (sing. *ansari*): Helpers, inhabitants of Medina who supported Muhammad; frequently used by jihadi groups today; also applied to the disciples of Jesus (in the Qur'an).

'aql: reason, mind.

'aqli: reason-based; cf. *shar'i,* shari'ah-based, and *naqli* (tradition-based).

a'rab: nomadic Arab tribespeople, as distinct from city dwellers.

'asabiyyah: partisanship or solidarity based on blood ties; partisanship for one's clan or group, or material interest; a notion emphasized by Ibn Khaldun, who argued that it was on the basis of *'asabiyyah* that groups are able to obtain and hold power. Rida rejects Ibn Khaldun's view.

baghy: dissention, rebellion.

Batinis: see *Isma'ilis.*

bay'ah: pledge of allegiance through which authority is recognized.

al-baydah: "the white," an epithet applied to Islamic territory.

bayt al-mal: the treasury.

bayyinah: evidence.

bid'ah: innovation; while a *bid'ah* may be good (*bid'ah hasanah*), the term is most often used negatively.

bid'at wilayat al-'ahd: the innovation of nominating an heir apparent; the innovation of hereditary succession.

da'i: missionary, usually of religio-political movements.

dalil: evidence; prescription, proof, source for a rule of law; also used of the four sources of law in Sunni Islam: Qur'an, hadith, *qiyas* (analogical reasoning), and *ijma'* (consensus); sign.

dar al-'ahd: non-Muslim territories in a treaty relationship with a Muslim state, also referred to as *dar al-sulh* (q.v.); the Ottoman Empire's relationship with its Christian tributary states.

dar al-aman: abode of Safety.

dar al-harb: the abode of War; regions not at peace with Islam, or not yet under Muslim control.

dar al-Islam: the abode of Islam.

Glossary

dar al-sulh: the abode of Peace; regions at peace with Islam.

darurah: necessity; synonymous with *hajah.*

da'wah: qur'anic reference for a call to invite people to Islam, call to believe in the true religion; call to Islam; call to nominal Muslims to commit fully to Islam; mission or missionary movement; cf. *da'i.*

dawlah: lit., turning; dynasty in premodern usage; state in modern usage; empire, temporal power.

dhikr: invocation, individual and communal prayer ceremony.

dhimmah: pact; pact of protection for the People of the Book (*ahl al-kitab,* q.v.).

dhimmi: tributary; see *ahl al-dhimmah.*

din: religion or way; Islam; etymologically related to the notion of humankind's relationship of indebtedness to God.

diwan: originally a list of those entitled to state salaries; government office or ministry.

dunya: this world, as distinct from the afterlife (*akhirah*).

emir: amir (q.v.).

emirate: amirate (q.v.).

faqih: expert in fiqh; jurist or jurisprudent.

fard: religious obligation, precept of the revealed law.

fasad: corruption, decay.

fasiq: sinner.

fay': property of the enemy acquired by the Muslim state without fighting on the battlefield.

fiqh: lit., understanding; commonly translated as "jurisprudence"; understanding or knowledge of the shari'ah, particularly the *furu'* (q.v.).

fitnah: discord, a period of strife for the Muslim community; civil war, sedition; temptation. The first and most crucial *fitnah* in Islam was precipitated by the murder of 'Uthman, ultimately leading to the Sunni–Shi'i split.

furu': branches, as distinct from roots (*usul,* q.v.), referring to laws or specific provisions derived from the law's roots or fundamental principles.

ghulah: extremists; those whose doctrines are so heretical as to be beyond the pale of Islam.

ghuluww: exaggeration or excess, especially in religion.

hadarah: urban life, civilization; synonymous with *madaniyyah* and *tamaddun.*

hadathah: modernity.

hadd: sing. of *hudud;* limit; a category of crime referenced in the Qur'an and hadith and assigned a fixed penalty.

hadith qudsi: "divine saying," God's thoughts expressed by the Prophet.

hakimiyyah: sovereignty; God's sovereignty.

hakimiyyah milliyyah: national sovereignty.

haqq (pl. *huquq*): what is right or rightful, claim, entitlement; truth; reality.

haqq Allah: right or claim of God.

harbi: non-Muslim; foreigner. If the person is protected by treaty, he is a *mu'ahad* (q.v.), not a *harbi,* but if that treaty lapses, he reverts to being a *harbi.*

hilah (pl. *hiyal*): legal fictions or strategies structured to evade the strict requirements of the law.

218   *Glossary*

hisbah: the duty of the ruler and of every Muslim to enjoin what is good and forbid what is evil; ensuring that the precepts of the shari'ah are followed; supervision of markets and morals.

hudud: see *hadd.*

hukm: in the Qur'an, arbitration, judgment, authority, and God's will; over time it came to refer to temporal rule and the judgment of a qadi, and the plural, *ahkam,* to specific ordinances or rules derived through *fiqh* (q.v.); wisdom.

hukumah: classically, dispensation of justice, while *wilayah, sultan,* and *imarah* referred to government. As Muslims became interested in Western governance in the nineteenth century, *hukumah* came to denote government, sometimes as distinct from the state (*dawlah,* q.v.).

'ibadat: duties toward God; acts of worship; cf. *mu'amalat.*

ifranj: "Franks," Europeans.

ihsan: righteousness or goodness.

ihya': revival.

ijma': consensus, the fourth or third source of law; in theory or ideally that of the ummah or the *jama'ah* (q.v.).

ijtihad: lit., making effort or personal intellectual effort, the process of deriving new judgments.

ikhtiyar: choice or freedom of choice; choice of caliph by election, as distinct from hereditary succession, and the Shi'i notion of Muhammad's clear designation of the imam (*nass,* q.v.).

ilhad: in the Qur'an, deviation; other meanings include heresy, apostasy, and atheism; synonymous with *zandaqah* (atheism, dualism, Manicheanism, q.v.). In Islamic texts *ilhad* is almost always used pejoratively; in the modern era it was adopted by some Arab freethinkers as a positive self-description.

'illah: the "effective cause" of a rule of law; Determining an *'illah* is a necessary step in reasoning by analogy (*qiyas,* q.v.).

'ilm: knowledge, science.

imam: one who stands "in front"; refers to various kinds of leader, most pertinently to the leader of the Muslim community and used interchangeably with *khalifah* (caliph); also refers to four founders of the four Sunni legal schools; in Shi'ism the office of the imam is restricted to members of *ahl al-bayt* (q.v.).

imamah: imamate, office of the imam; synonymous with *khilafah;* denotes a state ruled by the shari'ah or the ideal state of Islam. In Rida's explanation, *imamah,* caliphate, and *imarah* (amirate or emirate) are three words with one meaning.

imamat al-darurah: imamate of necessity.

imamat al-taghallub: imamate of tyranny; see *taghallub.* This refers to an imamate whose legitimacy derives from conquest. The extent to which it embodies tyranny depends on how it behaves once it has power.

imarah: emirate, office of the emir.

islah: reform; restoring things to their proper or rightful state.

Isma'ilis: a Shi'i sect also called "Seveners" and "Batinis" in reference to their stress upon the esoteric (*batin*) underlying the exoteric (*zahir*). The Fatimids were Isma'ilis.

Glossary

istibdad: autocratic rule, absolute monarchy; despotism.

istikhlaf: designation of one's successor. The verb *istakhlafa* is qur'anic and is common in *sirah* literature, describing the Prophet's appointment of overseers of Medina with limited authority during his absence.

istinbat: derivation, deduction; in reasoning by analogy (*qiyas*, q.v.), *istinbat* refers to methods for finding the effective cause (*'illah*, q.v.) of a rule.

istislah: the juristic principle of seeking or taking public welfare (*maslahah*, q.v.) into account; opinion based on this principle.

Ittihadists: "Unionists," members of the Committee for Union and Progress (CUP), founded in 1895. The CUP dominated Ottoman political life between 1908 and 1918. Its reforms in such areas as justice and education paved the way for further secularization and the establishment of a Turkish republic. The nationalist movement was led by former CUP members.

jama'ah: "the group," referring to the community of believers, or the main body of the Muslim community; connotes the idea of collectivity, unanimity, or a community formed through consensus; a group of people performing the prayer.

jinsiyyah: nationality, ethnic or racial identity.

jumhur: the people, the masses.

kafa'ah: competence.

khabar: report.

khalifah: caliph, successor, deputy; in Sufism, successor of a Sufi shaykh.

Khalifat Movement: Indian movement in support of the Ottoman caliph from 1919 to 1924.

kharaj: tax; later specifically land tax.

al-khassah: elites, as distinct from the common people (*al-'ammah*, q.v.).

khawarij: commonly rendered "Kharijis" or "Kharijites" in English, "those who go out on jihad," "those who go out," "seceders." A group of 'Ali's supporters who seceded in 657. They rejected the doctrine that the caliph must belong to the tribe of Quraysh (q.v.). Considered very strict—some say "puritanical"—in their views, they believed that an unrepentant sinner should be excluded from the community.

khilafah: caliphate, vicegerency; synonymous with *imamah* (q.v.).

khilafat al-nubuwwah: vicegerency of prophecy; the Madinian caliphate.

khutbah: Friday mosque sermon in which the ruler's name is mentioned, a sign of sovereignty.

madhhab: lit., direction; way of proceeding; opinion; school of law or thought.

madhhabism (ta'assub al-madhhab): being a partisan of or relying exclusively on one school of law, an orientation criticized by Rida.

Majus: Magians, Zoroastrians.

mal: property, wealth; taxes.

ma'na: concerning meaning or signification as distinct from outward form.

manaqib: virtues, meritorious deeds, miracle stories, genre of hagiographical accounts.

ma'nawi: moral; spiritual.

maqasid: goals, aims.

ma'ruf: recognized; what is right and good.

mashayikh: the collectivity of the shaykhs as an institution; elders.

220

Glossary

mashru': lawful according to the shari'ah.

mashruta: name given to denote a constitution in the early twentieth century.

mashyakhah: authority or office of the shaykh.

maslahah: public interest, public welfare, well-being; what produces benefit or has utility; matter or affair.

mawali (sing. *mawla*): non-Arab Muslims, Arabicized "clients" or "allies" of Arab tribes whose status under the caliphate was controversial. The question of Arab preeminence (or not) in Islam has never been fully settled.

millah: religion; religious community; the Muslim community, sometimes synonymous with ummah and *jama'ah* (q.v.); origin of the Turkish word *millet*, which referred to non-Muslims having a *dhimmi* status and who acquired new privileges at the end of the nineteenth century.

minhaj: path, way; program.

mu'ahad: confederate, ally.

mu'ahadah: treaty, pact.

mu'amalat: duties toward people; the realm of social interactions and relationships involving the organization of society that are subject to the shari'ah; cf. *'ibadat.*

mubaya'ah: double pledge of allegiance joining the imam and the community.

Muhajirun: Emigrants, Meccans who accompanied Muhammad to settle in Medina, an epithet frequently used by jihadi groups today, similar to *ansar* (q.v.).

muhtasib: the official in charge of the *hisbah* (q.v.).

mujaddid: renewer of the religion who according to tradition appears at the start of every century; cognate to *tajdid* (q.v.).

mujtahid: one qualified for *ijtihad* (q.v.).

mukallaf: fully competent or responsible for discharging legal duties and able to form intent; one on whom a task is imposed by God; the legal subject.

mulk: dominion, rule, power, the realm of temporal or earthly authority, state, government, royal authority or monarchy; ownership or possession.

mullah: cleric or learned man, a Persian construction derived from the Arabic *mawla* (sing. of *mawali,* q.v.), used in Turkey, Iran, Afghanistan, and the Indian subcontinent.

muqallid: one who is bound by the principle of deference (*taqlid,* q.v.).

muslih: reformer, one who engages in *islah* (q.v.); in Islamic reformist discourse, the figure of the *muslih* often counterpoints that of the *muqallid* (q.v.).

mutafarnij: "Franconizer," Europeanizer, Westernizer, one who imitates European norms; see *ifranj.*

mutaghallib: one who takes or maintains rule by force, tyrant, usurper; see *taghallub.*

mu'tamad: trusted, adopted.

Mu'tazilis: a rationalist school that was dominant in 'Abbasid circles, stressing human free will, God's unity, and the createdness of the Qur'an.

mutlaq: referring to a rule that is absolute, without restrictions or qualifications.

muwada'ah: treaty.

nabi: prophet, applied especially to Muhammad.

namudhaj: model.

Glossary

naqli: tradition-based.

nasab: lineage; notion of kinship ties with the Prophet's family.

nass: definitive text in the Qur'an, hadith, or one that results from consensus (*ijma‘*, q.v.); definitive stipulation; designation of a ruler by his predecessor; designation by divine decree. In Shi‘i doctrine, the imams are chosen by such a decree.

nizam: lit., system, order, system for organizing a society or state; plan or program of action; political order, administration.

qada': the function of the *qadi* (q.v.); adjudication or judging, administration of the law.

qadi: judge; agent of the ruler entrusted with *qada'* (civil and criminal jurisdiction).

qanun: a term of Greek origin; law; secular law; supplementary laws enacted by governments in areas not sufficiently regulated by Islamic law; applies particularly to penal and tax law. An integral part of the Ottoman legal system, *qanun* refers in particular to the sultan's legal decrees (Turk. *Kanun*). In modern usage it becomes a generic term for all regulations, similar to terms such as *nizam* (q.v.) and *dustur* (constitution).

al-qanun al-asasi: basic constitutional law.

qati‘: clear-cut or decisive; cf. *zanni*.

qawa‘id (sing. *qa‘idah*): rules, the technical principles of law, a subject of special works.

qiyas: reasoning by analogy, a source of law in Sunni Islam.

Quraysh: leading Meccan tribe in the time of Muhammad. Traditional teaching holds that the caliph must be a Qurayshi, as Rida affirms.

ra‘iyyah (pl. *ra‘aya*): subject, citizen.

rasul: messenger, used of prophets having a legislative role; when used with the definite article (*al-rasul*) refers to Muhammad.

ra'y: opinion or, more specifically, sound opinion or judgment; juristic speculation.

risalah: treatise; mission of the messenger (*rasul*, q.v.).

sabiqah: precedence, especially in conversion. The earlier a person converted, the greater his *sabiqah*.

sahifat al-madinah: constitution of Medina.

sahih: sound, correct, authentic, valid.

al-salaf: ancestors; the first Muslim generation, or the first three.

al-salaf al-salih: the pious ancestors.

salah: right or proper condition, righteousness; also a synonym of *maslahah* (q.v.).

sam‘an: known by revelation or traditional sources (Qur'an, hadith, *qiyas* [q.v.], *ijma‘* [q.v.]), as distinct from *‘aqlan* (known rationally).

saqifah: covered meeting place.

sayyid: chief of a tribe in pre-Islamic Arabia; descendant of Muhammad.

shahid: witness; martyr.

shar‘: revealed law, cognate to *shari‘ah*; when used unqualifiedly, the revealed law of Islam.

shar‘i: shari‘ah-based, occurring or applying as a matter of the shari‘ah; lawful or rightful.

shari‘ah: lit., pathway, law.

sharif (pl. *ashraf*): noble, person of prominence; descendant of the Prophet; in Umayyad times, tribal leader or chief; by the fourth/tenth century usually confined to descendants of ‘Ali; descendant of Hasan.

222 *Glossary*

shaykh: also rendered "sheikh," title for a man of authority, elder, teacher, head of a Sufi order, bestowed on those of sufficient age and experience and frequently denoting scholarly or pious renown.

shaykh al-Islam: the chief mufti and head of the Ottoman state's hierarchy of ulama.

shaytan: Satan, demon; the name given to Iblis after his expulsion from paradise.

shura: consultation; council. In the Qur'an, *shura* connotes an authority's consultation with subordinates (3:159) or consultation between peers (42:38). After 'Umar's caliphate it comes to refer to the idea of an elective assembly.

sirah: way of life.

siyasah: political system, authority or administration; governance; authority.

sultan: in the Qur'an and hadith, "power" and "authority"; by around the tenth century the word acquired the secondary sense of someone who holds power and authority; government.

sunnah: lit., well-trodden path; normative example, precedent or manner of conduct, especially that of the Prophet Muhammad. In the theory of the caliphate, or certain iterations of it, the sunnah of the rightly guided caliphs merges with that of the Prophet; the corpus of hadith.

taghallub: commonly rendered "tyranny" in English; domination, mastery, subjugation, usurpation, coercion, based on power. In regard to states, *taghallub* refers to one that comes into being and is maintained through force or military victory rather than through choice or election, and is characterized by subordination of ruled to ruler; domination in its broad political, economic, and military senses.

tajdid: renewal or reform; cognate to *mujaddid* (q.v.).

takfir: excommunicating or labeling other Muslims as heretics.

talfiq: assemblage; in the modern period, bringing together or reconciling the teaching of different law schools to form a new rule.

tanfidh: implementation or execution of rules, orders, or principles.

tanzimat: Ottoman reforms of 1836–78, derived from the Arabic *tanzim* (organizing) and *al-nizam al-jadid* (new order or organization).

taqlid: following the teachings or positions of earlier authorities; often connotes blind or unreasoned following. In Islamic reformist discourse, *taqlid* is often juxtaposed with reform (*islah*, q.v.) or *ijtihad* (q.v.).

tarjih: giving preference to a superior opinion.

tashri': to form rules of law or legislate, either in the shari'ah or in general.

tawatur: recurrence, a term used in connection to reports whose character—because they are corroborated by numerous independent sources—are known to be of certain authenticity because of the impossibility that these sources could have collaborated to concoct the report.

turath: heritage.

ulu al-amr (sing. *wali al-amr*): qur'anic expression for those who hold authority. It is not specified who they are.

ummah: the Muslim community.

ummah wasat: a middle community; also connotes justice and equity.

Glossary

'umran: from the root '-M-R, "to build"; human culture, material and spiritual; prosperity, civilization; constructing the earth; may also mean development or modernization. *'umran* is a classical term; cf. *hadarah* and *madaniyyah,* which are modern terms.

'urf: custom, common practice, law based on custom; Ottoman imperial decree.

usul: roots, as distinct from branches (*furu'*, q.v.), referring to fundamental principles of law (*usul al-fiqh*)—the Qur'an, hadith, reasoning by analogy (*qiyas,* q.v.), and consensus (*ijma'*, q.v.)—from which specific provisions or laws are derived.

vizier: see *wazir.*

wajib: what is obligatory or a duty.

wali: governor; friend of God; used of Shi'i imams; saint.

wali al-'ahd: presumptive heir, next in line; equivalent to crown prince.

wali al-amr: sing. of *ulu al-amr* (q.v.).

waqf: charitable endowment.

al-wazi' al-dini: the religious restrainer, referring to the role of the shari'ah in politics.

wazir: minister, vizier; chief administrator of a Muslim kingdom and often the second most powerful official after the king or caliph.

wilayah: guardianship, may refer to temporal governance or power as well as spiritual guidance; province; in Sufism also refers to a Sufi realm or territory.

zandaqah: word of Persian origin meaning impiety, heresy, or atheism, of which an eighth-century group (*zindiq;* pl. *zanadiqah*) were accused. These were converts from Manicheanism who secretly remained committed to that religion and who were sometimes accused of apostasy.

zanni: assumed or probable, as distinct from what is decisive (*qati'*, q.v.).

Zaydis: branch of Shi'ism deriving its name from Zayd (d. 740), the grandson of the Prophet's grandson Husayn (d. 680).

NOTES

NOTE ON THE TRANSLATION

1. Mary Snell-Hornby, *The Turns of Translation Studies: New Paradigms or Shifting Viewpoints?* (Amsterdam: John Benjamins, 2006), 145.

TRANSLATOR'S INTRODUCTION

1. Mahmoud Osman Haddad, "Arab Religious Nationalism in the Colonial Era: Rereading Rashid Rida's Ideas on the Caliphate," *Journal of the American Oriental Society* 117.2 (1997): 268.
2. For a critique of that view, see Leor Halevi's *Modern Things on Trial: Material Reformation in the Age of Rida, 1865–1935* (New York: Columbia University Press, 2019), Introduction (location 563–682) and Chapter 8 (location 6620–56). I cite the Kindle edition of Halevi's book. On Rida as a fundamentalist, or not, see Simon A. Wood, *Christian Criticisms, Islamic Proofs: Rashid Rida's Modernist Defense of Islam* (Oxford: Oneworld, 2010), 48–64.
3. Florian Zemmin, "Secularism, Secularity, and Islamic Reformism," Leipzig University—HCAS, "Multiple Secularities—Beyond the West, Beyond Modernities" (2019), 7. On 'Ali 'Abd al-Raziq, see Souad T. Ali, *A Religion, Not a State: Ali Abd al-Raziq's Islamic Justification of Political Secularism* (Salt Lake City: University of Utah Press, 2009).
4. See Elizabeth F. Thompson's *How the West Stole Democracy from the Arabs: The Syrian Arab Congress of 1920 and the Destruction of Its Historic Liberal-Islamic Alliance* (New York: Atlantic Monthly Press, 2020), 250–315. Kindle edition.
5. Malcolm H. Kerr, *Islamic Reform; The Political and Legal Theories of Muhammad 'Abduh and Rashid Rida* (Berkeley: University of California Press, 1966), 176.
6. Halevi, *Modern Things on Trial*, location 343. Kindle edition.
7. Haddad, "Arab Religious Nationalism in the Colonial Era," 253.

226   *Notes to Pages 7–15*

8. Publication of the volume was delayed for two months due to a shortage of paper. Thompson, *How the West Stole Democracy*, 608. Kindle edition.

9. Unless otherwise stated, all in-text citations in the Translator's Introduction and the translation are from the Qur'an. Translations of qur'anic verses generally follow those of Mahmoud Ayoub, M. A. S. Abdel Haleem, and Michael Sells. Mahmoud Ayoub, *The Qur'an and Its Interpreters*, Volume 1 (Albany: SUNY Press, 1984); Volume 2 (Albany: SUNY Press, 1992). M. A. S. Abdel Haleem, *The Qur'an* (Oxford: Oxford University Press, 2005). Michael Sells, *Approaching the Qur'an: The Early Revelations* (Ashland: White Cloud Press, 2007).

10. *Al-Manar* 21.1 (December 2, 1918): 2.

11. On this point, see Thompson, *How the West Stole Democracy*, 95–98. Kindle edition.

12. *Al-Manar* 21.1 (December 2, 1918): 5.

13. Sells, *Approaching the Qur'an*, 78.

14. *Al-Manar* 21.1 (December 2, 1918): 6. See also Thompson, *How the West Stole Democracy*, 95–96. Kindle edition.

15. Rashid Rida, *Al-Khilafah* (Cairo: Al-Manar, 1923), 135.

16. *Al-Manar* 21.1 (December 2, 1918): 8.

17. *Al-Manar* 21.1 (December 2, 1918): 17–33.

18. *Al-Manar* 21.1 (December 2, 1918): 28.

19. *Al-Manar* 21.1 (December 2, 1918): 29.

20. Thompson, *How the West Stole Democracy*, 86. Kindle Edition.

21. Thompson, *How the West Stole Democracy*, 86. Kindle Edition.

22. *Al-Manar* 20.1 (July 30, 1917): 48–57.

23. *Al-Manar* 21.1 (December 2, 1918): 30.

24. This language—"rising stars"—was suggested by an anonymous reviewer.

25. On these topics see also Eliezer Tauber, "Rashid Rida and Faysal's Kingdom in Syria," *Muslim World* 85:3–4 (July–October 1995): 235–45.

26. Thompson, *How the West Stole Democracy*, 410. Kindle Edition.

27. It is unclear how the comments Thompson cites from Rida's *Al-Wahy al-Muhammadi* point to an ideological shift from earlier in his career. Thompson, *How the West Stole Democracy*, 410–11. Kindle edition.

28. *Al-Manar* 23.4 (April 27, 1922): 313.

29. *Al-Manar* 23.4 (April 27, 1922): 313–14.

30. *Al-Manar* 23.4 (April 27, 1922): 314.

31. *Al-Manar* 23.4 (April 27, 1922): 314–16. Quote p. 316.

32. Rida adds the wording between brackets to the quoted text; *Al-Manar* 23.5 (May 27, 1922): 392.

33. Arabic (hereafter Ar.) *sifat al-jam'iyyah al-wataniyyah al-ta'sisiyyah.*

34. *Al-Manar* 23.5 (May 27, 1922): 392–93.

35. Thompson, *How the West Stole Democracy*, 17 and 272. Kindle edition.

36. Thompson, "Rashid Rida and the 1920 Syrian-Arab Constitution: How the French Mandate Undermined Islamic Liberalism," in *The Routledge Handbook*

Notes to Pages 15–23

of the Middle East Mandates, ed. Cyrus Schayegh and Andrew Arsan (New York: Routledge, 2015), 244.

37. See Haddad, "Arab Religious Nationalism in the Colonial Era," 269. Haddad reproduces the substance of Rida's proposal.
38. Thompson, *How the West Stole Democracy*, 263. Kindle edition.
39. Rida, *Al-Khilafah*, 4.
40. Rida, *Al-Khilafah*, 114.
41. While, as noted, Thompson's research is valuable, the narrative arc as it relates to Rida is at times difficult to follow. Later in her discussion she notes that the 1950 Syrian Constitution specifies that "Islam shall be the main source of legislation," typifying the regrettable defeat of a "liberal Islam" that had briefly governed in 1920. Yet she shows Rida calling for just that—Islam as the source of legislation—in the 1920 diary entry quoted above. Thompson, *How the West Stole Democracy*, 422–23. Kindle edition.
42. *Al-Manar* 23.5 (May 27, 1922): 394–95.
43. Rida, *Al-Khilafah*, 107–8.
44. *Al-Manar* 22.6 (June 6, 1921): 478.
45. On Rida's articles and his Geneva trip and its aftermath, see also Thompson, *How the West Stole Democracy*, 425–51. Kindle edition.
46. *Al-Manar* 23.9 (November 19, 1922): 699.
47. *Al-Manar* 23.9 (November 19, 1922): 696–702.
48. *Al-Manar* 12.4 (May 19, 1909): 288. Simon A. Wood, "Reforming Muslim Politics: Rashid Rida's Visions of Caliphate and Muslim Independence," *Journal of Religion and Society*, Supplement 18 (2019): 66.
49. On Rida's long engagement with the issue of the Caliphate in the period leading up to the publication of *The Caliphate*, see Wood, "Reforming Muslim Politics" and Haddad, "Arab Religious Nationalism in the Colonial Era," 253–77.
50. *Al-Manar* 23.4 (April 27, 1922): 282. See John Willis, "Debating the Caliphate: Islam and Nation in the Work of Rashid Rida and Abul Kalam Azad," *International History Review* 32:4 (2010): 711–32.
51. *Al-Manar* 23.6 (June 25, 1922): 431–35. Quote p. 432. For an English translation see Mahmoud Osman Haddad, "Muhammad Rashid Rida," in *Islamic Legal Thought: A Compendium of Muslim Jurists*, ed. David Powers, Susan Spectorsky, and Oussama Arabi (Leiden: Brill, 2013), 480–81. See also Haddad, "Arab Religious Nationalism in the Colonial Era," 272.
52. *Al-Manar* 23.6 (June 25, 1922): 431–32.
53. While Rida noted that he had two homelands, his identification as Syrian took precedence; Rida, *Al-Khilafah*, 108.
54. Haddad, "Arab Religious Nationalism in the Colonial Era," 269.
55. *Al-Manar* 23.9 (November 19, 1922): 713–20.
56. *Al-Manar* 23.10 (December 18, 1922): 785.
57. See for instance Ahmed Ibrahim Abushouk's "Muhammad Rashid Rida's Reformist Project to Establish a True Caliphate: Prospects and Challenges," in *Ways of Knowing*

228   *Notes to Pages 24–37*

Muslim Cultures and Societies: Studies in Honour of Gudrun Krämer (Leiden: Brill, 2018), 55–80. Referring to the passage quoted above, he writes, "The passage reveals that Rida anticipated that the Kemalists were capable of leading the revival of the Islamic caliphate" (p. 70).

58. Henri Laoust, *Le califat dans la doctrine de Rašīd Ridā* (Paris: Librairie d'Amérique et d'Orient, 1986). Laoust's translation does not include Rida's Introduction. Laoust's notes contain a great deal of valuable details.

59. See Abushouk, "Muhammad Rashid Rida's Reformist Project," 55–57 for an overview of some of the key works, along with Abushouk's reading of their relative merits. In addition to the works cited above, see also Mahmoud Osman Haddad, "Rashid Rida and the Theory of the Caliphate: Medieval Themes and Modern Concerns" (Ph.D. diss., Columbia University, 1989); Hamid Enayat, *Modern Political Thought in Islam* (London: I. B. Tauris, 2005), 69–83; Malcolm H. Kerr, *Islamic Reform; The Political and Legal Theories of Muhammad 'Abduh and Rashid Rida* (Berkeley: University of California Press, 1966).

60. Rida, *Al-Khilafah*, 105.

61. Rida, *Al-Sunnah wa al-Shi'ah aw al-Wahhabiyyah wa al-Rafidah* (Cairo: Al-Manar, 1929), 29. On this point and on Rida and Wahhabism more generally, see Henri Lauziere's *The Making of Salafism: Islamic Reform in the Twentieth Century* (New York: Columbia University Press, 2016).

62. Rida, *Al-Khilafah*, 9.

63. *Al-Manar* 25.4 (May 4, 1924): 289.

64. Rida, *Al-Khilafah*, 6.

65. Rida, *Al-Khilafah*, 8.

66. Rida, *Al-Khilafah*, 11.

67. Rida, *Al-Khilafah*, 20.

68. Rida, *Al-Khilafah*, 38.

69. Rida, *Al-Khilafah*, 46.

70. Rida, *Al-Khilafah*, 44–45.

71. Rida, *Al-Khilafah*, 44.

72. Rida, *Al-Khilafah*, 46.

73. Rida, *Al-Khilafah*, 47.

74. Rida, *Al-Khilafah*, 52.

75. See also *Al-Manar* 25.10 (July 2, 1924): 390–400, where Rida critiques Sharif Husayn's attempt to usurp the caliphate.

76. Rida, *Al-Khilafah*, 56.

77. Rida, *Al-Khilafah*, 61.

78. Rida, *Al-Khilafah*, 61.

79. Rida, *Al-Khilafah*, 70.

80. Rida, *Al-Khilafah*, 71.

81. Rida, *Al-Khilafah*, 76–77.

82. Rida, *Al-Khilafah*, 77–78.

83. Rida, *Al-Khilafah*, 78.

84. Rida, *Al-Khilafah*, 78.

Notes to Pages 37–50

85. See for instance Enayat, *Modern Political Thought in Islam*, 69–83.
86. Rida, *Al-Khilafah*, 92.
87. Rida, *Al-Khilafah*, 107–8.
88. See for instance Haddad, "Arab Religious Nationalism in the Colonial Era," 276.
89. Rida, *Al-Khilafah*, 103.
90. Rida, *Al-Khilafah*, 80.
91. Rida, *Al-Khilafah*, 85.
92. Rida, *Al-Khilafah*, 96.
93. Rida, *Al-Khilafah*, 97–98.
94. Rida, *Al-Khilafah*, 101.
95. Rida, *Al-Khilafah*, 103.
96. Rida, *Al-Khilafah*, 110.
97. Rida, *Al-Khilafah*, 112.
98. Rida, *Al-Khilafah*, 106–12.
99. Rida, *Al-Khilafah*, 114.
100. Rida, *Al-Khilafah*, 117.
101. Rida, *Al-Khilafah*, 142.
102. *Al-Manar* 25.4 (May 4, 1924).
103. *Al-Manar* 25.4 (May 4, 1924): 285.
104. *Al-Manar* 25.4 (May 4, 1924): 286.
105. *Al-Manar* 26.6 (October 18, 1925): 421–24; 26.7 (January 14, 1926): 496–98. See Haddad's translation: Haddad, "Muhammad Rashid Rida," 484–89.
106. *Al-Manar* 25.4 (May 4, 1924): 288.
107. On Kemalism, see *Al-Manar* 24.9 (September 11, 1923): 692–706. On Sharif Husayn, see *Al-Manar* 25.4 (May 4, 1924): 260–68; 25.5 (July 2, 1924): 390–400. On 'Ali 'Abd al-Raziq, see *Al-Manar* 26.2 (June 21, 1925): 100–104; 26.3 (July 21, 1925): 230–32; 26.5 (September 18, 1925): 363–82; 27.9 (December 5, 1926): 715–17. See also Ali, *A Religion, Not a State*, 15; 59–64. See also *Al-Manar* 26.10 (March 14, 1926): 789–91; 25.7 (October 24, 1924): 525–34; 27.2 (May 13, 1926): 138–43; 27.3 (June 11, 1926): 208–32; 27.4 (July 10, 1926): 280–94; 27.5 (August 18, 1926): 370–77; 27.6 (September 7, 1926): 449–58; 32.2 (February 1932): 113–32; 32.3 (March 1932): 193–208; 32.4 (April 1932): 284–92.
108. *Al-Manar* 26.10 (March 14, 1926): 790.
109. *Al-Manar* 27.2 (May 13, 1926): 138–43.
110. *Al-Manar* 28.1 (March 3, 1927): 1–8.

THE CALIPHATE

1. Ayoub, *The Qur'an and Its Interpreters*, Volume 1, 150.
2. Ar. *hum al-fasiqun*; alternatively, "they are wrongdoers."
3. See Qur'an 21:105, "My righteous servants will inherit the earth."
4. A stock phrase in Islamic discourse.
5. Rida's note: In his book *Ordinances of the Qur'an* [*Ahkam al-Qur'an*], Abu Bakr al-Jassas, a fourth-century [A.H.] Hanafi imam, states in regard to the Almighty's statement to Abraham — "My covenant shall not include the wrongdoers" (2:124) — that it

230   *Notes to Pages 51–52*

was given in answer to his question about God making imams from among his progeny, and as a clarification: the wrongdoers among them would not be imams. He then states that it is impermissible for a wrongdoer to be a prophet, prophet's successor (caliph), judge, or anyone whose opinion regarding matters of religion the people are obligated to accept, such as a mufti, witness, or narrator of a report from the Prophet, God's prayer and peace be upon him. Thus, the verse conveys that the prerequisite for all who are in the position of following his example is that they embody justice, purity, etc.

Qadi al-Baydawi states: "The statement conveys the answer Abraham received to his question, and that the wrongdoers among his progeny are excluded from the imamate because it is a trust from God and a covenant, and that the wrongdoer is not fit for the imamate" (abridged). The meaning is that an imamate lacking justice is not genuine. Thus, there is no legal imam, because the imamate has not come into being. Jassas and others reported from Ibn 'Abbas (may God be pleased with him) that he said: "In the case of a wrongdoer, there is no obligation to fulfill a pledge. Thus, if one enters into a contract with you in sin, break it."

6. Ar. *muqallidun*, imitators, referring to those who practice *taqlid*, imitation or following of their madhhabs' teachings, rather than ijtihad, or independent reasoning. In Rida's understanding, the mentality of the reformer (*muslih*) and that of the imitator stand opposed, a theme he elaborates upon in such works as *Muhawarat al-Muslih wa al-Muqallid* (*Debates of the Reformer and the Traditionalist*, 1906), regarded as recrafted or fictional. See Jakob Skovgard-Petersen, "Portrait of the Intellectual as a Young Man: Rashid Rida's *Muhawarat al-muslih wa al-muqallid*," in *Islam and Muslim—Christian Relations* 12 (2001): 93–104. The *muqallid* emerges as a figure who lives in an intellectual world unfitted to the realities of his day, and who is unequipped to provide leadership to the common Muslims. In some respects, Rida's muqallid resembles the Zionist image of the effete diaspora rabbi who remains preoccupied with traditionalist learning and who likewise fails to provide effective leadership or modern solutions to modern problems. On the terms *taqlid* and *muqallid*, see for instance Wael B. Hallaq, *A History of Islamic Legal Theories: An Introduction to Sunni Usul Al-Fiqh* (Cambridge: Cambridge University Press, 2004), 121–22.

7. Ar. *al-mawasim wa al-ahzab wa al-awrad*, celebrations, incantations, or prayers formed of qur'anic sections and phrases and the names of God, and litanies of strung-together *adhkar*, or remembrance formulae. See Beirut J. Spencer Trimingham, *The Sufi Orders in Islam* (Oxford: Oxford University Press, 1998), 214–15, 301, 307.

8. See Qur'an 42:38: "who conduct their affairs by mutual consultation."

9. Gustave Le Bon (1841–1931), *Lois psychologiques de l'évolution des peuples* (Paris: F. Alcan, 1894).

10. Ar. *jil al-muqallid, jil al-mukhadram, jil al-mustaqill. Mukhadram*: referring to living across more than one generation or epoch; the generation bridging the pre-Islamic and Islamic periods.

11. Ar. *ata 'ala al-nas hin min al-dahr*, a qur'anic expression. See Qur'an 76:1.

12. Ar. *al-matami' al-ash'abiyyah*, a literary allusion to greed.

Notes to Pages 52–56

13. Herbert Spencer (1820–1903): known as the founder of sociocultural evolution and an influence on Charles Darwin; an agnostic rather than an atheist with evolutionary and progressive views on religion. His interpretation is consistent with the Enlightenment project of replacing religion not with atheism but with a scientific version of religion that would be free of beliefs that people depended upon in earlier eras of history. See for instance Michael Taylor, *The Philosophy of Herbert Spencer* (London: Continuum, 2007), 141.

14. Abdul Hamid II (1842–1918; r. 1876–1909): Ottoman sultan known for autocratic and oppressive rule and modernizing reforms in the areas of justice, education, and transportation that contributed to the infrastructural basis of modern Turkey. By the time of his rule the Ottoman Empire was in decline, and he appealed to his role as caliph in an effort to inspire the support of Muslims both within and without the empire. "Caliph" had been among the titles of the Ottoman sultans. Abdul Hamid's manner of asserting the role was novel. He dissolved Parliament during the Russo-Ottoman War of 1877–78. Increasing repression under his rule led to the development of the Young Turks opposition, from which the Committee for Union and Progress (CUP; Ittihadists) forced him to restore Parliament in 1908 by establishing a network of support in the army. He was deposed following the Revolt of March 31, 1909. See Selcuk Aksin Somel, *The A to Z of the Ottoman Empire* (Lanham: Scarecrow Press, 2010), 3–5, 244–45.

15. Ar. *yajrimannaka*; cf. the qur'anic *yajriimannakum* (Qur'an 5:8, 11.89).

16. Ayoub, *The Qur'an and Its Interpreters*, Volume 2, 392.

17. Ayoub, *The Qur'an and Its Interpreters*, Volume 1, 94.

18. Ar. *fasl al-khitab*. Cf. Qur'an 38:20.

19. Rida's note: Sa'd al-Din died in the year 791. His *Commentary on Goals* was published in Constantinople in 1305. Among Arab, Turkish, and other scholars of theology he is chief.

20. Ar. *sam'iyyah*, known on the basis of revelation, authority, or traditional sources (Qur'an, hadith, *qiyas, ijma'*), as distinct from what is known on the basis of reason (*'aqli*).

21. *Maqasid al-Talibin fi 'ilm usul al-Din* (*Goals of Students Regarding the Fundamental Principles of the Religion*, 1383) by Sa'd al-Din al-Taftazani (1322–1390), a Shafi'i scholar also associated with the Hanafi school who wrote on grammar, rhetoric, theology, law, and exegesis; referred to by Rida as "Al-Sa'd" and "Al-Taftazani." Not a great deal is known of his life and environment. A native of Taftazan in Khurasan, he is said to have been a student of 'Adud al-Din al-Iji; his work was approvingly cited by Ibn Khaldun. His works are widely studied in Islamic madrasahs. For some general background on Taftazani and his place in the kalam tradition, see Muammar Iskenderoglu's entry in *The Biographical Encyclopedia of Islamic Philosophy*, ed. Oliver Leaman (New York: Theommes Continuum, 2006), 298–300, and Earl Edgar Elder, trans., *A Commentary on the Creed of Islam: Sa'd al-Din al-Taftazani on the Creed of Najm al-Din al-Nasafi* (New York: Columbia University Press, 1950), xx–xxxi. Taftazani's commentary became a standard text in Islamic theology. Rida's lengthy

232   Notes to Pages 56–57

citations suggest that he regards him as an authoritative voice. Taftazani separated the rightly guided period from that of the dynasties but regarded both as caliphates. See Elder, 141–51, and Haddad, "Rashid Rida and the Theory of the Caliphate," 67–68.

22. Rida's note: He died in the year 450 [A.H.]. His book is unique in its subject matter. It was published in Egypt in 1228, and has been translated into a number of languages.

23. Asadullah Yate, trans., *Al-Ahkam As-Sultaniyyah: The Laws of Islamic Governance* (London: Ta-Ha Publishers, 1996), 10. Wafaa H. Wahba, trans., *The Ordinances of Government: A Translation of Al-Ahkam al-Sultaniyya w'l-Wilayat al-Diniyya* (London: Garnet, 1996), 3. Abu al-Hasan al-Mawardi (974–1058): the son of a rose-water merchant who lived in Basra, Iraq; a specialist in the Shafi'i legal school who also studied the other schools of law, and a practicing judge (*qadi*) who earned the so-briquet "the most judicious of judges." His *The Ordinances of Government (Al-Ahkam al-Sultaniyyah)* was published around the beginning of the eleventh century and is a seminal work on the relationship between Islam and politics. Its pertinence to modern Islamic politics is reflected, for instance, in two English translations published in 1996. He wrote the work during a time of political turmoil between the 'Abbasid caliphs and Shi'i Buyids, a Persian dynasty that ruled large areas of the 'Abbasid domain from 945 to 1055. Mawardi's book is believed to have been commissioned by one of the caliphs. It attempts to demonstrate that in spite of their apparent weakness, they were legitimate in Islamic terms: the legitimacy of the caliphate must be preserved at all costs. Ingrid Mattson suggests that his evidences and examples are unconvincing, or constrained by his historical situation and transparent need to justify the status quo. Thus, his discussion is not to be taken as an ideal model to be followed by later generations. Mawardi's other concern is to describe the features of public law and the functions of the judiciary. His discussion is brief in comparison with that in his much longer work, *Al-Hawi*, a commentary on Shafi'i law. *The Ordinances of Government* is more of a sketch than a comprehensive analysis. See Ingrid Mattson, "Al-Ahkam Al-Sultaniyyah: The Laws of Islamic Governance," *Journal of Law and Religion* 15.1–2 (2000–2001): 399–403.

24. On Razi and Taftazani, see Laoust, *Le califat dans la doctrine de Rašīd Ridā*, 245n3.

25. See Taftazani, *Sharh al-Maqasid* (Qom: Al-Manshurat al-Sharif al-Radi, 1412 A.H.), 235.

26. Ar. *sahih*, sound or genuine, referring to hadiths fulfilling all conditions for acceptance.

27. Taftazani references this declaration in his commentary on the Creed of Nasafi, finding that a caliph-imam must be appointed on the basis of authority, rather than on the basis of reason, as held by certain Mu'tazilis, or on the basis of both, as held by some authorities. Elder, trans., *A Commentary on the Creed of Islam*, 145n17.

28. Ar. *marfu'*, elevated or exalted, a hadith attributed to the Prophet and narrated by a Companion. See *Musnad*, IV, 96.

29. Mu'tazilis or Mu'tazilah: a political and religious movement that emerged in the same climate as the Kharijis and Murji'ites ("postponers") and characterized by its rationalist approach to doctrine; known particularly for the doctrine of the created Qur'an. Kharijis, "seceders" or "those who go out," also rendered "Kharijites" in English: a sectarian group taking its name from "those who went out" on jihad, or

Notes to Pages 58–61

233

"those who went out" from 'Ali's army during his dispute with Mu'awiyah following the murder of 'Uthman in 656. They divided into several branches. Today they survive as the Ibadis.

30. Rida's note: In regard to their statement that they are people of distinction Shibramilsi states: This is a case of linking the general to the specific, because the people of distinction are the greatest among them in terms of power, or knowledge, or other things. P. 120. Part 7.

31. Nawawi, *Minhaj al-Tallibin* (Beirut: Dar al-Minhaj, 2005), 500. See also Laoust, *Le califat dans la doctrine de Rašīd Ridā*, 245–46n4.

32. Ramli, *Nihayat al-Muhtaj ila Sharh al-Minhaj* (Beirut: Dar Al-Kotob al-Ilmiyah, 2003), 410.

33. Ar. *faltah,* here referring to something occurring on an ad hoc basis that, while not invalid, should not be taken as normative or setting a precedent. On the pertinence of this term to the form of Islamic governance, see Asma Afsaruddin, *The First Muslims: History and Memory* (Oxford: Oneworld, 2007), 184. For Afsaruddin this is one of several instances where the record undermines the claim that Islamic history or teaching establishes that an Islamic state has a divinely mandated form.

34. This refers to the covered meeting place in Medina where the Prophet's companions gathered to choose his successor, a process not recognized as valid in Shi'ism. For a survey of classical accounts of the Saqifah debate and its significance, see Mahmoud Ayoub, *The Crisis of Muslim History: Religion and Politics in Early Islam* (Oxford: Oneworld, 2005), 8–25, and Khalid Blankinship, "Imarah, Khilafah, and Imamah: The Origins of the Succession to the Prophet Muhammad," in *Shi'ite Heritage: Essays on Classical and Modern Traditions,* ed. Lynda Clarke (Binghamton: Global Publications, 2001), 32–38. Also see Wilferd Madelung, *The Succession to Muhammad: A Study of the Early Caliphate* (Cambridge: Cambridge University Press), 3, 35–45, and A. Guillaume, *The Life of Muhammad: A Translation of Ibn Ishaq's Sirat Rasul Allah* (Oxford: Oxford University Press, 2004), 683–88.

35. On this matter see also Rida's critique of a Palestinian delegation's pledge to Sharif Husayn: "Intihal al-Sayyid Husayn Amir Makkah li al-Khilafah: Muqaddimat Mubaya'at Wafd Filistin wa Nass al-Mubaya'ah," *Al-Manar* 25.5 (July 2, 1924): 397n1.

36. Mu'awiyah (c. 605–680): the first Umayyad caliph, who contested 'Ali's election to the caliphate. After 'Ali's death in 661 Mu'awiyah's status was no longer under challenge. Mu'awiyah didn't technically proclaim himself caliph. Reports mention that he was either given allegiance or recognized as caliph by others.

37. Mawardi notes the opinion that five pledges bring the imamate into being because five people pledged allegiance to Abu Bakr, and because 'Umar set up a council of six so that one of them should take up the imamate with the acceptance of the other five. Wahba, trans., *The Ordinances of Government,* 12–13. Only five of the six electors whom Umar had designated were present to deliberate.

38. Rida's note: Ramli, *Sharh al-Minhaj.* P. 120. Part 7.

39. Rida's note: That is, the necks of the animals bearing those traveling to him.

40. See Madelung, 28–30.

41. See Muslim, *Sahih Muslim,* Book 20, Hadith 4555.

234   Notes to Pages 61–66

42. Ar. *mashhur*, widely accepted, referring to a hadith accepted by a large number of scholars; a hadith narrated or vouched for by one or only a few Companions, with many transmitters then taking it from this one or few. There are differing legal views on how such hadiths should be categorized. See Yasin Dutton, *The Origins of Islamic Law: The Qur'an, the Muwatta' and Madinan 'Amal* (New York: Routledge, 2002), 196n62.

43. Rida uses a version of the hadith narrated by Nasr bin 'Asim, who personally asked Khalid al-Yashkuri about Hudhayfah bin al-Yaman's hadith.

44. Ar. *wa fi riwayat ziyadah*, which Laoust renders: "Dans la version de Ziyadah on lit." Laoust, *Le califat dans la doctrine de Rašīd Ridā*, 22.

45. See Ibn Hajar, *Fath al-Bari* (Damascus: Dar al-Risalah al-'Alamiyyah, 2013), Volume 23, 73. Ibn Hajar al-Asqalani (1372–1449): historian and eminent hadith scholar, whom Rida refers to both by name and by his epithet "Al-Hafiz" — "the memorizer" — acquired through his reputation for memorizing hadiths. His *Fath al-Bari fi Sharh Sahih al-Bukhari* (1428), a multivolume commentary on Bukhari's *Sound Collection (Sahih al-Bukhari)*, is regarded as the most important work in the genre of Sunni hadith commentary. See Norman Calder, Jawid Mojaddedi, and Andrew Rippin, eds., *Classical Islam: A Sourcebook of Religious Literature* (New York: Routledge, 2003), 42.

46. 'Adud al-Din al-Iji (d. 1355), *Book of Stations (Kitab al-Mawaqif)*, a multivolume work on the discipline of theology (*kalam*). See shiaonlinelibrary.com: Al-Iji, *Al-Mawaqif*, Part 3. P. 595.

47. 'Ali ibn Muhammad ibn 'Ali al-Husayn al-Jurjani, al-Sayyid al-Sharif (1340–1413), *Commentary on Stations of the Discipline of Kalam (Sharh al-Mawaqif fi 'ilm al-Kalam)*. On Jurjani, see Alnoor Dhanani, "Jurjani," in *The Biographical Encyclopedia of Astronomers*, ed. Thomas Hockney et al. (New York: Springer, 2007), 603–4.

48. *The Study Quran*, ed. Seyyed Hossein Nasr (New York: HarperCollins, 2015), 189. Kindle Edition.

49. Rida's note: See the explanation of the verse "obey God and obey the messenger and obey those in authority over you" (Qur'an 4:59) at the end of the commentary in *Al-Manar*, Volume 13, and the beginning of Volume 14; or in Part 5 of the *Qur'an Commentary* [*Tafsir al-Manar*], pp. 180–222.

50. There is an omission in Rida's quotation of Mawardi: the *la* in *la sha'(an)* is omitted. Mawardi, *Al-Ahkam al-Sultaniyyah wa al-Wilayat al-Diniyyah* (Cairo: Mustafa al-Babi al-Halabi, 1966), 6.

51. Mawardi, *Al-Ahkam al-Sultaniyyah*, 5–6; Wahba, trans., *The Ordinances of Government*, 4; Yate, trans., *Al-Ahkam As-Sultaniyyah*, 11–12.

52. See Ibn Hajar, *Fath al-Bari*, Volume 13 (Al-Maktabah al-Salafiyyah), 198.

53. See Nawawi, *Rawdat al-Talibin* (Beirut: Dar Ibn Hazm, 2002), 1715–18. The work is a summary of Rafi'i's *Al-Sharh al-Kabir*, which is a commentary on Ghazali's *Wajiz*. Rida's text literally reads, "He says in *Al-Rawdah*: its *asl* is that one of them must be qualified for ijtihad," where *asl* refers to Rafi'i's *Al-Sharh al-Kabir*.

54. See Ibn Hajar, *Fath al-Bari*, Volume 13 (Al-Maktabah al-Salafiyyah), 198–99.

55. Rida's note: *Sharh al-Maqasid*, 272, part 2.

56. Ar. *mukallaf*, legally capable and responsible, of sound mind.

Notes to Pages 66–74

57. Rida's note: P. 271, part 2 also.

58. Kamal bin al-Humam (d. 1457): a Hanafi theologian. Abul-Fadl Qasim Ibn Qutlubugha (1399–1474): author of a dictionary of Hanafi writers and jurists entitled *Crown of Biographies (Taj al-Tardjim)*, a significant source on historic names. See Clement Huart, *A History of Arabic Literature* (New York: D. Appleton and Company, 1903), 366.

59. Rida's note: *Ordinances of Governance [Al-Ahkam al-Sultaniyyah]*, 4–5.

60. Ar. *al-baydah*, the territory of Islam (*baydat al-Islam*). See Rida's note 89 below.

61. Dirar ibn 'Amr (c. 730–c. 800). On Dirar and his views on the caliphate, see Hayrettin Yucesoy, "Political Anarchism, Dissent, and Marginal Groups in the Early Ninth Century: The Sufis of the Mu'tazila Revisited," in *The Lineaments of Islam: Studies in Honor of Fred McGraw Donner*, ed. Paul Cobb (Leiden: Brill, 2012), 76–78.

62. Ar. *al-siddiq*, the truthful or the veracious, an epithet often applied to Abu Bakr.

63. Wahba, trans., *The Ordinances of Government*, 4–5; Yate, trans., *Al-Ahkam As-Sultaniyyah*, 12.

64. Ar. *manaqib*, glorious deeds or virtues, referring to works written in praise of a famous shaykh or saint.

65. 'Adud al-Din al-Iji, *Kitab al-Mawaqif (Book of Stations)*.

66. See Ibn Hajar, *Fath al-Bari*, Volume 7 (Al-Maktabah al-Salafiyyah), 32.

67. See Marcia K. Hermansen, trans., *The Conclusive Argument from God: Shah Wali Allah's Hujjat Allah al-Balighah* (Leiden: Brill, 1996), an important work conveying the thought of the influential South Asian Muslim intellectual Wali Allah (1703–1762). See also Laoust, *Le califat dans la doctrine de Rašīd Ridā*, 248–49n11.

68. Rida's note: Born 1101 A.H., died 1176 A.H. A reformer [*mujaddid*] of the religious sciences in India in the twelfth century. This book of his, on the rationale of legislation, has been published in India and Egypt a number of times.

69. Rida's note: This wording is found in *Surat Yusuf* (Qur'an 12), *Surat Zumar* (Qur'an 39), *Surat Fussilat* (Qur'an 41), *Surat Shura* (Qur'an 42), and *Surat Ahqaf* (Qur'an 46).

70. Rida's note: *Surat al-Ra'd* (Qur'an 13), verse 37.

71. Ar. *Mawali*, non-Arab Muslims, Arabicized "clients" or "allies" of Arab tribes whose status under the caliphate was controversial. The question of Arab preeminence (or not) in Islam has never been fully settled. See Patricia Crone, *God's Rule: Government and Islam* (New York: Columbia University Press, 2004), 332–33.

72. I.e., the Ka'bah.

73. On Abu Mu'ayt bin Abi 'Amr bin Umayyah and Banu Abi Mu'ayt, see Madelung, 73. See also G. Rex Smith, *The History of al-Tabari*, Volume 14: *The Conquest of Iran* (Albany: SUNY Press, 1994), 91.

74. See Ibn Hajar, *Fath al-Bari*, Volume 13 (Al-Maktabah al-Salafiyyah), 111.

75. Ar. *hasan*, good or satisfactory, referring to a chain of transmission that is not completely flawless for such reasons as the integrity of the transmitters being concealed or unknown, or shortcomings in their memories and expertise as compared with those of others.

76. Ar. *ahl al-bayt*, people of the house: Muhammad's family and descendants, particularly his cousin and son-in-law 'Ali; his daughter and 'Ali's wife Fatimah; their sons Hasan (d. 669) and Husayn; and descendants.

236

Notes to Pages 74–77

77. Ar. *Shu'ubiyyah*: a social, cultural, and literary movement originating in the eighth century that rejected the notion of Arab preeminence in Islam. Shu'ubi authors ridiculed Arab claims to nobility and virtue. Scholarship on the Shu'ubis relies mostly on works written by their opponents, including Ibn Qutaybah, who wrote a book-length refutation of their arguments. Ibn Qutaybah, himself of Persian descent, critiqued the Shu'ubi view that Arabs were inferior to Persians. See Sarah Bowen Savant, "Shu'ubis," in *The Princeton Encyclopedia of Islamic Political Thought* (Princeton: Princeton University Press, 2013), 513; Israel Gershoni and James P. Jankowski, *Egypt, Islam, and the Arabs: The Search for Egyptian Nationhood, 1900–1930* (Oxford: Oxford University Press, 1987), 102–4; Roy P. Mottahedeh, "The Shu'ubiyah Controversy and the Social History of Early Islamic Iran," *International Journal of Middle Eastern Studies* 7 (1976): 161–82. 'Abd Allah ibn Muslim Abu Muhammad Ibn Qutaybah (d. 889): Qur'an and hadith scholar from Kufa and Baghdad and a seminal figure in Islamic theology and literature. See Calder et al., *Classical Islam*, 202.

78. 'Abd al-Malik (d. 705; r. 685–705), the fifth Umayyad caliph. 'Abd Allah bin al-Zubayr (d. 692) and 'Abd Allah bin 'Umar (d. 693) were the sons of Zubayr and 'Umar. Given their experience, pedigree, and notoriety, they would have been likely candidates for the caliphate.

79. That is, he refused to take sides. A reference to the second civil war or *fitnah* in Islam, also known as the *"fitnah* of Ibn Zubayr," a struggle between Ibn Zubayr and the Umayyads that had its beginnings during the caliphate of Yazid bin Mu'awiyah (r. 680–83) and ended with Ibn Zubayr's death, probably in 692. Some leading Muslims had refused to acknowledge Yazid, Mu'awiyah's son and successor, as caliph. These included Husayn, the third Shi'i imam, killed during an unsuccessful rebellion against the caliphate in Karbala', and Ibn Zubayr, who upon Yazid's succession fled to Mecca. Following Yazid's death, he put himself forward as caliph. See G. R. Hawting, *The First Dynasty of Islam: The Umayyad Caliphate, AD 661–750* (London: Routledge, 2000), 46–57.

80. The verse reads in full: "Prophet, when believing women come and pledge to you that they will not ascribe any partner to God, nor steal, nor commit adultery, nor kill their children, nor lie about who has fathered their children, nor disobey you in what is right, then you should accept their pledge of allegiance and pray to God to forgive them: God is most forgiving and merciful."

81. See Bukhari, *Sahih al-Bukhari*, Book 9, Volume 88, Hadith 178.

82. See Bukhari, *Sahih al-Bukhari*, Book 9, Volume 89, Hadith 307.

83. By jihad Rida doesn't mean "fighting" alone, since both men and women are expected to participate. Rida explains this below.

84. Rida's note: *Intadalu* and *tanadalu*: competing in shooting arrows, and likewise bullets. *Al-jishr*: moving animals to a place where they can sleep and rest, which is now called *tarbi'*.

85. Alternatively, "each one weakening the preceding one." Rida's note: *Yuraqqiqu al-fitanu ba'duha ba'd(an)*: makes weak (*raqiq(an)*), namely weak (*da'if(an)*).

86. Haleem, trans., *The Qur'an*, 53.

87. See Muslim, *Sahih Muslim*, Book 20, Hadith 4546.

Notes to Pages 78–83

88. See Bukhari, *Sahih al-Bukhari*, Judgments, 252 (Book 9, Volume 89, Hadith 252): Narrated 'Abdullah bin 'Umar:

> Allah's Apostle said, "Surely! Every one of you is a guardian and is responsible for his charges: The imam of the people is a guardian and is responsible for his subjects; a man is the guardian of his family [household] and is responsible for his subjects; a woman is the guardian of her husband's home and of his children and is responsible for them; and the slave of a man is a guardian of his master's property and is responsible for it. Surely, every one of you is a guardian and responsible for his charges."

89. Rida's note: *Baydah* means bird's egg, iron helmet [*baydat al-hadid*], or the entire territory, which is what is being referred to here, namely, the imam protects the community's territory. Today, this is referred to as protecting "public security."

90. Ar. *iqamat al-hudud*; in Yate's translation, "establish the hadd-punishments." What Mawardi means is not the idea of legislation, but that the imam must execute the hudud laws that God and the Prophet have already established. Yate, trans., *Al-Ahkam As-Sultaniyyah*, 28.

91. Ar. *mu'ahad*. Rida's note: *Mu'ahad* here includes "The People of the Pact [*dhimmah*]" and foreigners [*al-ajanib*] with whom we have treaties [*mu'ahadat*].

92. Wahba, trans., *The Ordinances of Government*, 16–17; Yate, trans., *Al-Ahkam As-Sultaniyyah*, 27–29.

93. The doctrine that the Qur'an was created in time was a Mu'tazili position that came to be rejected by the majority.

94. *Mu'adhad*, ally, confederate, or contractee; *dhimmi*, one of the "People of the Pact," Christians and Jews who are bound by a pact to pay a tribute (*jizyah*) to their Muslim rulers, and accept secondary status to Muslims in return for freedom of worship and certain other rights.

95. These verses are commonly cited in reformist discourse to establish the necessity of consultation, along with *bay'ah* (allegiance, ratification) and *ijma'* (consensus), for legitimate governance. On the views of Rida and other reformists, see Afsaruddin, *The First Muslims*, 169–73. See also Ayoub, *The Qur'an and Its Interpreters*, Volume 2, 341.

96. Ibn 'Adi (d. 976).

97. Battle fought in March 624 in which the Muslims were victorious over their Meccan enemies. Tradition holds that victory resulted from divine intervention, per the qur'anic verse: "God helped you at Badr when you were very weak" (Qur'an 3:123).

98. In the account Rida refers to, Hubab ibn al-Mundhir suggests that the Muslim fighters deprive the enemy of water, while securing plenty for themselves by building a cistern. On this incident, see F. E. Peters, *A Reader on Classical Islam* (Princeton: Princeton University Press, 1994), 77; Guillaume, *The Life of Muhammad*, 296–97.

99. See for instance Muslim, *Sahih Muslim*, Book 19, Jihad and Expeditions, Hadith 4360.

100. Ayoub, *The Qur'an and Its Interpreters*, Volume 2, 341.

101. "The House of Imran": Qur'an 3.

102. "Women": Qur'an 4.

238   *Notes to Pages 84–92*

103. See *Sunan Darimi*, 161.

104. *The Study Quran*, 189. Kindle Edition.

105. See Tabarani (873–970), *Al-Mu'jam al-Awsat al-Juz' al-Thani* (Cairo: Dar al-Haramain, 1995), 172. Hadith 1618.

106. See Bukhari, *Sahih al-Bukhari*, Book 6, Volume 60, Hadith 166; Book 7, Volume 71, Hadith 625; Book 9, Volume 92, Hadith 389. Muslim, *Sahih Muslim*, Book 26, Hadith 5504.

107. Rida's note: *Ordinances of Governance [Al-Ahkam al-Sultaniyyah]*, bottom of p. 9. [See Wahba, trans., *The Ordinances of Government*, 9–10].

108. Rida's note: Mawardi, *Ordinances of Governance [Al-Ahkam al-Sultaniyyah]*, end of p. 11. [See Yate, trans., *Al-Ahkam As-Sultaniyyah*, 22. See also Wahba, trans., *The Ordinances of Government*, 12. The complete sentence in Mawardi's text reads: "This council, in which people fit for the imamate participated, and the consensus it reached, formed the basis for the imamate coming into being by an agreement, and for the pledge of allegiance being made by a number of persons from among whom one was designated for the imamate through being selected by the people who loose and bind."]

109. Ar. *Kutub al-Manaqib*, a genre of hagiography and biography praising the works of famous shaykhs or saints.

110. Rida's note: We will cite some of the narrations on his designation of him as his successor that are cited by hadith scholars when we discuss Yazid bin Mu'awiyah.

111. Ibn Hajar al-Haytami (1504–1567), a famous Egyptian Shafi'i. See C. van Arendonk and J. Schacht, "Ibn Hadjar al-Haytami," in *The Encyclopedia of Islam* (Leiden: Brill, 2001), hereafter *EI*; and Laoust, *Le califat dans la doctrine de Rašīd Ridā*, 250n14.

112. Wahba, trans., *The Ordinances of Government*, 11; Yate, trans., *Al-Ahkam As-Sultaniyyah*, 20.

113. See Ibn Hajar, *Fath al-Bari* (Damascus: Dar al-Risalah al-'Alamiyyah), Volume 23, 15.

114. The eighth Umayyad caliph (r. 717–20). Known for having a pious persona, his popularity among his subjects, and for enacting significant military and taxation reforms, 'Umar has a distinctive reputation among the Umayyad caliphs. 'Abbasid historians regarded him as a unique exception to the Umayyad tendency toward depravity, and elevated him to the rank of the rightly guided caliphs, as Rida's language reflects. See Steven C. Judd, "'Umar ibn 'Abd al-'Aziz," in *Medieval Islamic Civilization: An Encyclopedia*, ed. Josef W. Meri (New York: Routledge, 2006), 843.

115. See Ibn Hajar, *Fath al-Bari* (Damascus: Dar al-Risalah al-'Alamiyyah), Volume 7, 307.

116. Rida's note: Pp. 278–79.

117. See Kamal bin al-Humam, *Al-Musayarah fi 'Ilm al-Kalam wa al-'Aqa'id al-Tawhidiyyah al-Munjiyyah fi al-Akhirah* (Cairo: Al-Maktabah al-Mahmudiyyah al-Tijariyyah, 1929), 170.

118. Rida's note: P. 275. Part 2.

119. See Kamal bin al-Humam, *Al-Musayarah*, 171–72.

120. Rida's note: P. 277.

121. Ar. *shubhah*; in Yate's translation, "dubious opinions"; in Wahba's translation, "suspicious acts." Yate, trans., *Al-Ahkam As-Sultaniyyah*, 29–30; Wahba, trans., *The Ordinances of Government*, 17. Here, it might also mean "heretical idea."

Notes to Pages 92–102   239

122. Yate, trans., *Al-Ahkam As-Sultaniyyah*, 29–30; Wahba, trans., *The Ordinances of Government*, 17. Rida omits several lines from the passage he quotes here. At issue is the question of whether this is sufficient grounds for disqualification, in contrast to unbelief, in which case disqualification is beyond question and not in dispute.

123. Yate, trans., *Al-Ahkam As-Sultaniyyah*, 34; Wahba, trans., *The Ordinances of Government*, 20–21.

124. Wahba, trans., *The Ordinances of Government*, 21; Yate, trans., *Al-Ahkam As-Sultaniyyah*, 35.

125. Rida's note: P. 272. Part 2.

126. See Bukhari, *Sahih al-Bukhari*, Book 9, Volume 88, Hadith 178.

127. See *Kitab al-Mu'jam al-Awsat*, Hadith 2978.

128. See Ibn Hajar, *Fath al-Bari* (Damascus: Dar al-Risalah al-'Alamiyyah), Volume 23, 12–15.

129. Midhat Pasha (1822–1884): Ottoman statesman and reformer who was twice grand vizier, architect of the first constitutional period (1876–78). The constitution of 1876 underscored the sultan's absolute power and rendered the Parliament an advisory assembly. Somel, *The A to Z of the Ottoman Empire*, 61, 188–89.

130. See Muslim, *Sahih Muslim*, Book 20, Hadiths 4555, 4556, and 4557.

131. Rida's point is that the problem lies not with the shari'ah as such, but with the manner in which it has been interpreted and applied in support of unjust rule. He reiterates the point below.

132. See Bukhari, *Sahih al-Bukhari*, Book 6, Volume 60, Hadith 352.

133. Abu Muhammad Ibn Abi Hatim al-Razi (854–938).

134. Ar. *Kisra* (Per. *Khusraw*; Gr. *Chosroes*): the name of several Sasanian kings in the pre-Islamic period and often referring to any Sasanian king, as qaysar (caesar) refers to any Roman or Byzantine emperor.

135. See Ibn Hajar, *Fath al-Bari* (Damascus: Dar al-Risalah al-'Alamiyyah), Volume 23, 40.

136. On Hasan al-Basri, see Laoust, *Le califat dans la doctrine de Rašīd Ridā*, 251n17.

137. On the term *huffaz*, see Recep Şentürk, *Narrative Social Structure: Anatomy of the Hadith Transmission Network*, 610–1505 (Stanford: Stanford University Press, 2005).

138. Ar. *nawasib*, Nasibis, referring to those hostile toward 'Ali, his descendants, and the Shi'ah generally. The term is said to derive from the appointment of Abu Bakr. In Twelver Shi'i fiqh, *nawasib* are considered non-Muslims. The term counterpoints *rafidah* ("rejectors")—that is, rejectors of Abu Bakr and 'Umar—a polemical term referring to Shi'is, as in Rida's book *The Sunnah and the Shi'ah or the Wahhabis and the Rejectors (Al-Sunnah wa al-Shi'ah aw al-Wahhabiyyah wa al-Rafidah)* (Cairo: Maba'at al-Manar, 1929). On these terms, see Werner Ende, "Shi'i Islam," in *Islam in the World Today: A Handbook of Politics, Religion, Culture, and Society*, ed. Werner Ende and Udo Steinbach (Ithaca: Cornell University Press, 2010), 51–52.

139. Ar. *al-sihah*, works including only hadiths deemed sound by the compiler, such as *Sahih al-Bukhari*. Ar. *al-masanid* (sing. *musnad*), works organized according to hadiths' narrators rather than their subject matter, such as *Musnad Ahmad*.

140. Died 685.

141. See Bukhari, *Sahih al-Bukhari*, Book 4, Volume 56, Hadith 802.

240   *Notes to Pages 102–10*

142. See Ibn Hajar, *Fath al-Bari* (Damascus: Dar al-Risalah al-'Amaliyyah), Volume 23, 20.

143. See Ibn Hajar, *Fath al-Bari* (Damascus: Dar al-Risalah al-'Amaliyyah), Volume 23, 20.

144. Rida's note: P. 280. As mentioned previously, the author of *Al-Musayarah* is Kamal bin al-Humam, a Hanafi. As for the commentary upon it, named *Al-Musamarah*, its author is Kamal ibn Abi Sharif, a Shafi'i.

145. See Muslim, *Sahih Muslim*, Book 20, Hadith 4568.

146. See Kamal bin al-Humam, *Al-Musayarah*, 171. Rida inserts "Hujjat al-Islam al-Ghazali," identifying Ghazali. On Ghazali, see also Wood, *Christian Criticisms, Islamic Proofs*, 153–80; Laoust, *Le califat dans la doctrine de Rašīd Ridā*, 250n15.

147. Wahba, trans., *The Ordinances of Government*, 7–8; Yate, trans., *Al-Ahkam As-Sultaniyyah*, 16.

148. Rida's description of Fanari is puzzling. Laoust left it out of his French translation, perhaps for that reason.

149. Sayyid Siddiq Hasan Khan (1832–1890): Indian writer, statesman, and poet. See Zafarul-Islam Khan, "Nawwab Sayyid Siddik Hasan Khan," *EI*. See also Richard Gauvain, *Salafi Ritual Purity: In the Presence of God* (New York: Routledge, 2013), 252n19.

150. Rida's note: Here, and in what follows, the plural should be omitted.

151. Rida's note: P. 413 of the edition published by Al-Matba'ah al-Amiriyyah in Egypt, 1296.

152. Haleem, trans., *The Qur'an*, 115.

153. It is a well-known rule of Islamic law that inheritance does not take place between individuals in different religions. For that reason some people took this verse to refer to that doctrine, not to the more universal question of political jurisdiction which Rida believes is its proper referent.

154. Turko-Afghan Treaty, concluded in Moscow March 1, 1921; ratified by Afghanistan October 4, 1922. This recognizes the independence of the Turkish and Afghan nations and the rights of all Eastern nations to independence. It further stipulates that the Turkish nation holds the caliphate, and that the two nations will be allied in the effort to resist British imperialism, with Article 4 referring to the two nations supporting each other in resisting acts by "a foreign state in pursuance of a policy of invasion and exploitation in the East." The treaty made Afghanistan the second state after the Soviet Union to recognize Turkish independence. The treaty was strengthened in 1928. See J. C. Hurewitz, ed., *The Middle East and North Africa in World Politics: A Documentary Record* (New Haven: Yale University Press, 1979), 248–50; Bill Park, *Modern Turkey: People, State and Foreign Policy in a Globalised World* (London: Routledge, 2012), 140.

155. Turanian: referring to various peoples speaking Ural-Altaic languages.

156. See Ibn Hajar, *Fath al-Bari* (Damascus: Dar al-Risalah al-'Amaliyyah), Volume 10, 255, 354.

157. Sayyid Muhammad 'Ali al-Idrisi (d. 1922): leader of the Sayyid clan of 'Asir. Rida refers to him as "an 'Alid Sayyid," although "Sayyid" does not necessarily mean a descendant of the Prophet in this case. Following the collapse of Ottoman authority in Arabia, he established an approximation of an organized independent state in 'Asir

Notes to Page 110

during the first quarter of the twentieth century. Following its collapse after his death in 1922, its territories were occupied by Imam Yahya and the Saudis. See Robert D. Burrowes, *Historical Dictionary of Yemen* (Lanham: Scarecrow Press, 2010), 172–73; and Eliezer Tauber, *The Emergence of the Arab Movements* (New York: Routledge, 1993), 114–15.

158. Sharif Husayn bin 'Ali of Mecca of the 'Awn branch of the Hashimi family in the Hijaz, born 1853 or 1856 in Istanbul, died 1931 in 'Amman. Emir and grand sharif of Mecca and the Hijaz (1908–16); king of the Hijaz (1916–24). Father of 'Abd Allah bin Husayn, who was appointed emir of Transjordan by the British, and Faysal bin Husayn. Husayn was bilingual in Turkish and Arabic, and was appointed to the Ottoman Council of State. In 1908, with the backing of Grand Vizier Kamil Pasha, he was named emir of Mecca—an office whose history dated back to the 'Abbasid period, in which role he initially appeared to be loyal. Yet he also had ambitions of being a leader of Arab lands, to which end he was in contact with secret organizations in Syria and with the British in Egypt. World War I provided further impetus to that endeavor. Husayn equivocated over raising troops to support the Turkish cause, and did not support the proclamation for jihad in support of the caliph. His contacts with the British in Cairo resulted in the so-called McMahon letters, which were suggestive of Arab-Anglo cooperation. The impulse to rise up against the Turks was reinforced by British assurances of support for a revolt. Husayn proclaimed the Arab Revolt in 1916, and the Turks were expelled from most of the Hijaz, with the exception of Medina. In autumn of that year Husayn proclaimed himself "King of the Arab Lands," but Britain and the other European powers substituted the title "King of the Hijaz." British and French occupation of Arab lands, the Sykes-Picot Agreement of 1916, and the mandates did not preclude independent Arab rule in the Arabian Peninsula during the war and in the postwar era. The Hijaz remained independent, despite its association with Britain. Husayn's role did not extend beyond the Hijaz from 1918 onwards. In 1924, two days after the Turkish Parliament abolished the caliphate, Husayn proclaimed himself caliph during a visit to 'Amman, a move that Stephen H. Longrigg characterizes as "a crowning mistake," one that aroused significant opposition and criticism, including that of Rida. Ibn Sa'ud rejected this move and began a campaign against him, leading to his defeat and then exile in Cyprus and 'Amman. See S. H. Longrigg, "Husayn," *EI*.

159. Yahya bin Muhammad Hamid al-Din (c. 1869–1948): Zaydi imam and first ruler of the Mutawakkili kingdom of Yemen, whose rule (1904–48) represents the zenith of the Hamid al-Din dynasty, the family that provided the last of the Zaydi imams. Upon the death of his father in 1904, Yahya received the pledge of allegiance from most of Yemen's tribes and clans, assuming the title "Al-Mutawakkil 'ala Allah" (He Who Relies on God), rejecting Ottoman authority, and rebelling. With Muhammad bin 'Ali al-Idrisi he raised another revolt in 1911, resulting in a treaty agreement between Yahya and the Ottomans: in return for recognizing Ottoman authority his authority over the Zaydi parts of Yemen was recognized, leading to the birth of the modern state of Yemen. He remained loyal to the Turks until the end of World War I, but then took control of the whole country. In 1920 he changed the Zaydi imamate into the Mutawakkili kingdom. Alain Rouaud characterizes Yahya's rule as isolationist,

242 *Notes to Pages 110–12*

tyrannical, and obscurantist, which undermined his expansionist ambitions. Yayha later came into conflict with the British and the Saudis. See A. Rouaud, "Yahya bin Muhammad," *EI*; and Burrowes, *Historical Dictionary of Yemen*, 154–55. Imam Yahya was not a sayyid in the genealogical sense of the term. He and the other members of the Hamid al-Din family were descendants of Hasan. Therefore, they were sharifs, not sayyids.

160. 'Abd Allah bin al-Husayn (1882–1951): emir of Transjordan and later king of the Hashimite kingdom of Jordan, second son of Husayn bin 'Ali, king of Hijaz. After the Revolution of 1908 'Abd Allah represented the Hijaz in the Ottoman Parliament. Before World War I he joined the Arab League (Al-Jami 'ah al-'Arabiyyah), founded in Cairo by Rida. He met with Lord Kitchener and Ronald Storrs, the oriental secretary of the British Consulate in Cairo, in April 1914, and took part in the discussions leading to the Arab Revolt proclaimed by his father, but played only a minor role in the conflict. In March 1920 an Iraqi congress meeting in Damascus proclaimed him king of Iraq, but he never took the throne, which the British awarded to his brother, Faysal, in June 1921. In March 1921 Winston Churchill, at that time the British colonial secretary, offered 'Abd Allah the role of heading an Arab government in Transjordan, separate from Palestine, and he became emir of Transjordan. He became king of Jordan in 1946, which role he held until his assassination in Al-Aqsa Mosque in Jerusalem on July 20, 1951. See for instance M. Colombe, "'Abd Allah bin al-Husayn," *EI*.

161. Sharif Husayn's newspaper, published in Mecca from August 1916 to 1924, the mouthpiece of the Arab Revolt. See A. A. Duri, *The Historical Formation of the Arab Nation: A Study in Identity and Consciousness*, trans. Lawrence I. Conrad (New York: Routledge, 2012), 303–13; and William L. Cleveland, "The Role of Islam as Political Ideology in the First World War," in *National and International Politics in the Middle East: Essays in Honor of Elie Khedouri*, ed. Edward Ingram (New York: Routledge, 2013).

162. See also Rida's discussion in "Intihal al-sayyid husayn amir makkah li-al-khilafah," 394.

163. 'Adnan is the eponymous grandfather of the northern Arabians, and is thus a stand-in for the Arabs generally.

164. Sultan Muhammad VI Wahid al-Din (Mehmed VI Vahideddin, 1861–1926; r. 1918–22): the last Ottoman sultan. Born in Constantinople, he came to the throne on July 3, 1918, after the death of his brother, Mehmed V, and led the empire during its final decline. He was hostile to the nationalist movement, acquiescing to moves made by the Allies against it after the Ottoman Empire's surrender on October 30, 1918, and the flight of the Young Turks' leadership on a German ship on November 1, 1918. On December 8, 1918, Wahid al-Din accepted an Allied military administration in Istanbul, and on December 21 he dissolved Parliament in an effort to maintain control. In 1919, Mustafa Kemal's nationalist movement forced him to agree to elections, and following its subsequent victory he again dissolved Parliament on April 11, 1920. The nationalists set up a provisional government in Angora (Ankara), and, having under Kemal's leadership prevailed over the Greeks in the Greco-Turkish War (1921–22), were in effective control of Turkey. After the Grand National Assembly abolished the sultanate on November 1, 1922, Wahid al-Din fled to Malta on a British battleship on November 17. The next day his cousin, 'Abd al-Majid II (Abdülmecid II), was

Notes to Pages 112–18 243

proclaimed caliph. After the abolition of the caliphate in 1924, Wahid al-Din unsuccessfully attempted to reestablish himself in the Hijaz. He died in San Remo, Italy, in 1926.

165. 'Abd al-Majid II (Abdülmecid II, 1868–1944): the last Ottoman caliph and crown prince. Born in Constantinople, he was proclaimed caliph by the Grand National Assembly on November 18, 1922, the day after the flight of his deposed cousin, Wahid al-Din (Mehmed VI). In response to Muslims rallying for 'Abd al-Majid II in India and elsewhere, the Grand National Assembly abolished the caliphate on March 3, 1924. He was exiled the following day. Upon his deposition Sharif Husayn declared himself caliph, but he received little support beyond his domain in Hijaz and that of his sons in Iraq and Transjordan. He abdicated in favor of his elder son, 'Ali, in the fall of 1924. 'Abd al-Majid II died in Paris in 1944.

166. Angora was renamed Ankara in 1930.

167. Mahdi, "the well-guided one," a kind of messiah in Islam. The term has been given to a number of figures in Islamic history, including the twelfth imam of the Imami Shi'ites, who went into occultation in 874.

168. This sense is reinforced in an October 4, 1922, letter from Fakhri Pasha to Gen. Mohammad Wali Khan, Afghan foreign minister, which recognizes that Afghanistan views Turkey as "the seat of the Great Islamic Caliphate," not as a "government to be followed." Hurewitz, *The Middle East and North Africa in World Politics*, 250.

169. Ar. *rabibuhu*, which Laoust renders "son fils spirituel." Laoust, *Le califat dans la doctrine de Rašīd Ridā*, 101. Here Rida probably means no more than to identify Sa'd Pasha Zaghlul as 'Abduh's disciple or student. Qasim Amin is also referred to as 'Abduh's "rabib." Sa'd Pasha Zaghlul (1859–1927): Egyptian statesman and nationalist, leader of the 1919 revolution against the British, and founder of the Wafd Party. In 1924 he was briefly prime minister. In 1873 he entered Al-Azhar, where he became a disciple of Jamal al-Din al-Afghani and 'Abduh. In 1880 'Abduh hired him as an editor for the Egyptian government's official gazette. On his legal and political career, see for instance "Zaghlul, Sa'd," in Arthur Goldschmidt, *Biographical Dictionary of Modern Egypt* (Boulder: Lynne Reinner, 2000), 234–35. See also Emad Eldin Shahin, "Renewal, Renewing and Renewers," in Charles Kurzman, ed., *Modernist Islam, 1840–1949: A Sourcebook* (New York: Oxford University Press), 77–85, a translation of Rida's *Al-tajdid wa al-tajaddud wa al-mujadiddun*.

170. In 1919 Sa'd Zaghlul was arrested and deported to Malta. He was later exiled to Aden, the Seychelles, and Gibraltar, and did not return to Egypt until the 1923 constitution had been written. Goldschmidt, *Biographical Dictionary of Modern Egypt*, 234.

171. For a comparison of Rida's and Abul Kalam's views on the caliphate, see John Willis, "Debating the Caliphate: Islam and Nation in the Work of Rashid Rida and Abul Kalam Azad," *International History Review* 32.4 (2010): 711–32.

172. Muhammad 'Ali (1878–1931) and Shawkat 'Ali (1873–1938), the 'Ali Biradaran, "'Ali Brothers." They received a modern education at the insistence of their illiterate mother, Abadi Begum, known as "Respected Mother." Shawkat 'Ali was a supporter of his younger brother's activities. In 1913, he founded the "Association of the Servants of the Ka'bah" to facilitate pilgrimage from India. He also managed the Urdu and

244   *Notes to Page 118*

English newspapers published by Muhammad, *Hamdard* and *Comrade*. Muhammad was a supporter of the Turkish cause during the First World War, and was involved in the "Silk Letter Conspiracy" to overthrow the British government in India with Turkish and Afghan assistance. The brothers were imprisoned from May 1915 to December 1919 on charges of agitating Muslims against the British. In September 1917, while in detention, Muhammad was elected leader of the Muslim League. In subsequent years the brothers played an important role in Indian Muslim life through their involvements with the freedom movement, the Indian National Congress, the Non-Cooperation Movement, and the Khalifat Movement, which arose in India to protest the treatment of Turkey in the wake of the First World War (see note 173 below). Muhammad led a Khalifat delegation to Europe in 1920. The brothers were arrested again in 1921 for having called upon Muslim soldiers in the Indian British army to desert at the All-India Khalifat Conference, July 9, 1921. With the rise of Hindu nationalism, most Muslim leaders moved away from the congress and toward seeking a separate state for Muslims.

Muhammad, having earlier been a proponent of Hindu–Muslim brotherhood, came to believe that Indian Muslims needed to protect themselves from Hindu assertiveness, a claim that later developed into the argument for the state of Pakistan. When the Khalifat Movement died in 1924, he tried in vain to revive it through Ibn Sa'ud. Shawkat resigned from the congress and worked for Muslim causes through the Urdu publications *Khalifat* and *Khalifal-e 'Uthmaniyya*. See Zafarul-Islam Khan, "Muhammad 'Ali" and "Shawkat 'Ali," *EI*.

173. Rida had ties with the leaders of the Khalifat Movement, and published many articles by and about its leaders, such as Abul Kalam Azad's *Kitab al-Khilafah al-Islamiyyah* (*The Islamic Caliphate*), translated by 'Abd al-Razzaq al-Mulihabadi in *Al-Manar* 22 (1922): 45–56, 102–6, 193–201, 282–89, 361–72, 466–71, 509–12, 691–702, and 753–57. Azad did not subscribe to the stipulation that the caliph be a Qurayshi. The Khalifat Movement (1919–24) was a movement of Indian Muslims working in alliance with Indian nationalists following the First World War. It sought to pressure the British government to preserve the authority of the Ottoman sultan as caliph, and to restore the 1914 boundaries of the Ottoman Empire. The movement crystalized anti-British sentiments among Indian Muslims that had increased since the British declared war against the Ottomans in 1914. Most of its leaders, including the 'Ali brothers, were imprisoned during the war because of their pro-Turkish sympathies. The movement's legacy lies less in its influence on pan-Islamism than on Indian nationalism. See Gail Minault, "Khalifat Movement," in *1914–1918 Online: International Encyclopedia of the First World War*, ed. Oliver Janz, published by the Freie Universität Berlin. See also Gail Minault, *The Khilafat Movement: Religious Symbolism and Political Mobilization in India* (New York: Columbia University Press, 1982) and M. Naeem Qureshi *Ottoman Turkey, Ataturk, and Muslim South Asia* (Oxford: Oxford University Press, 2014).

174. Najaf is a shrine city in southern Iraq where 'Ali is buried, and a center of Shi'i religious scholarship.

175. Sayyid Jamal al-Din al-Afghani (1838/9–1897): along with 'Abduh and Rida, one of the trio known as the key figures in the Salafiyyah, which in English has often been

Notes to Pages 118–23 245

referred to as "the Islamic modernist movement." Some authorities find that "Islamic modernist" is inaccurate, a misnomer, or an Orientalist construct. As indicated above, "modernist" does not correlate very well to Rida's self-understanding, or to that of those who inspired him. Although named "the Afghan" (Al-Afghani) by himself and others, Afghani was a Shi'ah from western Iran. Rida emphasized the influence that Afghani's prescriptions for Islamic revival had had on him when he was a young man. On Afghani's journal *Al-'Urwah al-Wuthqa* (*The Indissoluble Bond*), he commented: "Every issue was like an electric current . . . no other Arabic discourse . . . has done what it did in touching the seat of emotion in the heart and persuasion in the mind." Rida, *Ta'rikh al-Ustadh al-Imam al-Shaykh Muhammad 'Abduh* (Cairo: Dar al-Manar, 1931), 303; quoted in Albert Hourani, *Arabic Thought in the Liberal Age: 1798–1939* (Cambridge: Cambridge University Press, 1983), 226. See also for instance Mangol Bayat, "al-Afghani," in *The Princeton Encyclopedia of Islamic Political Thought*, 17–19; Nikki R. Keddie, *An Islamic Response to Imperialism: Political and Religious Writings of Sayyid Jamal al-Din al-Afghani* (Berkeley: University of California Press, 1968); Elie Kedourie, *Afghani and Abduh: An Essay on Religious Unbelief and Political Activism in Modern Islam* (London: Frank Cass, 1966).

176. The Tobacco Revolt of 1891–92 was an important moment in the politicization of Shi'ism. In 1891, Mirza Hasan al-Shirazi (d. 1896), at that time the leading jurist in Najaf, wrote two letters to the Qajar shah, Naser al-Din, stating his opposition to the tobacco concession. He then wrote to an Iranian cleric, Mirza Hasan Ashtiyani (d. 1901), requesting that he lead the protest on his behalf. Hamid Dabashi, a scholar of Iranian studies, observes that this communication is the last factual evidence of Shirazi's involvement, and that there is no evidence that he issued the fatwa against tobacco use that appeared in Tehran in December 1891 and was signed with his name. Hamid Dabashi, *Islamic Liberation Theology: Resisting the Empire* (London: Routledge, 2008), 77–79. In a 1977 speech in Najaf, Ruhollah Khomeini spoke of the Tobacco Revolt as an instance of the political efforts of earlier generations of scholars such as a Mirza Hasan al-Shirazi, which he contrasted with the political quiescence of the scholars of his own day. Devin J. Stewart, "The Portrayal of an Academic Rivalry: Najaf and Qum in the Writings and Speeches of Khomeini, 1964–78," in *The Most Learned of the Shi'a: The Institution of the Marja ' Taqlid*, ed. Linda S. Walbridge (Oxford: Oxford University Press, 2001), 224.

177. On this theme, Haddad finds Rida following his mentor 'Abduh. Haddad, "Arab Religious Nationalism in the Colonial Era," 275–76.

178. Ar. *madaniyyat al-qawanin*, the secularity of laws. See *Al-Manar* 23.8 (October 20, 1922): 625–33. See also *Al-Manar* 23.7 (July 26, 1922): 539–48 and *Al-Manar* 23.6 (June 25, 1922): 435–45.

179. Grand vizier (*mustashar al-sadarah*): the sultan's deputy in civil and military affairs. Following the constitutional reforms of 1909, the grand vizier became prime minister in the modern sense, choosing his own ministers. Somel, *The A to Z of the Ottoman Empire*, 101. Ibrahim Haqqi Pasha (1862–1918): Ottoman statesman, diplomat, and grand vizier (1910–11), described by the *Encyclopedia of Islam* as a moderate influence in the conflict between the Committee for Union and Progress (CUP) and the opposition.

246   *Notes to Pages 123–34*

180. Mehmed Talat Pasha (1874–1921): grand vizier (1917–18) and head of the CUP. He played a major role in the Revolution of 1908. While minister of the interior (1913–17) he organized the deportation of the Armenian population from eastern Anatolia to Syria (1915) and is considered one of those responsible for the Armenian genocide. Somel, *The A to Z of the Ottoman Empire*, 288–89.

181. Musa Kazim (1858–1920): a member of the ulama branch of the CUP, an Ottoman senator, and the Ottoman Empire's Shaykh al-Islam, head of the ulama and the empire's highest religious official. He was appointed Shaykh al-Islam in 1910 and after a series of resignations and removals was reappointed in 1911, 1916, and 1917. See M. Sukru Hanioglu's Introduction to Kurzman, *Modernist Islam, 1840–1940*, 175.

182. A qur'anic expression.

183. Muhammad Rashad (Mehmed V, 1844–1918; r. 1909–18): son of 'Abd al-Majid (Abdülmecid), successor of his brother, Abdul Hamid II. He acceded to the throne in 1909, when Abdul Hamid II was deposed by the CUP after the revolt of March 31, 1909. As sultan he acted within the limits of a constitutional monarch. During his reign the Ottoman Empire lost Libya, its last directly governed North African province, after it was attacked by Italy in 1911, and during the Balkan Wars of 1912–13 it lost nearly all of its Balkan provinces. The CUP organized a coup d'état (January 1913), and under their dictatorship Mehmed V acted as a symbolic head of state. During World War I, at the CUP's urging, he issued a fatwa calling upon Muslims to join a jihad against the Allies (1914). Somel, *The A to Z of the Ottoman Empire*, 182. Nurallah Ardic notes that the issuing of the fatwa was the last occasion on which the CUP made use of the ideological power of the caliphate. Nurallah Ardic, *Islam and the Politics of Secularism: The Caliphate and Middle Eastern Modernization in the Early Twentieth Century* (London: Routledge, 2012), 191–94.

184. A formula occurring nine times in the Qur'an referencing the Muslim community's obligation to act righteously and reject immorality, and applied in the ethical, legal, economic, and political spheres. Connected to the office of the *hisbah*, whose functionary, the *muhtasib*, was responsible for overseeing public morality and the activities of artisans and merchants.

185. Muhammad 'Ali Pasha (Mehmed Ali) (1769–1849): Albanian soldier and commander born in Kavala, Macedonia; Ottoman governor of Egypt (1805–48), dubbed the founder of modern Egypt. He introduced long-lasting reforms and fought both for and against the Ottomans. His expansionist policies threatened the Ottoman Empire. In 1839 the Ottomans unsuccessfully attempted to expel his forces from Syria, leading to intervention by Britain and other European states.

186. The Sunni Muslims of Yemen, followers of the Shafi'i school, were politically allied with the Ottomans.

187. Ar. *imtiyazat*, privileges or concessions granted to European states.

188. Ar. *jaza'ir al-muhit al-janubi*, "the islands of the southern ocean," by which Rida seems to be referring to the Dutch Indies, present-day Indonesia.

189. Ar. *al-islah al-dunwayi*, reform in everyday affairs, secular reform.

190. Ibn Qayyim al-Jawziyyah (1292–1350): a Hanbali jurist, best known as a disciple of Ibn Taymiyyah, who wrote on most branches of the Islamic sciences. On Rida's views on

Notes to Pages 138–55

Ibn Taymiyyah and Ibn Qayyim, see for instance Martin Riexinger, "Ibn Taymiyyah's Worldview and the Challenge of Modernity: A Conflict among the Ahl-i Hadith in British India," in *Islamic Theology, Philosophy and Law: Debating Ibn Taymiyya and Ibn Qayyim*, ed. Birgit Krawietz and Georges Tamer (Berlin: De Gruyter, 2013), 515; W. Ende, "Rashid Rida," *EI*; and Laoust, *Le califat dans la doctrine de Rašīd Ridā*, 260n32.

191. Ar. *mawsil*, a juncture or place where things come together. See also Laoust, *Le califat dans la doctrine de Rašīd Ridā*, 260–61n33.

192. See Muslim, *Sahih Muslim*, Book 1, Hadith 271.

193. See Bukhari, *Sahih al-Bukhari*, Book 4, Volume 56, Hadith 835.

194. Compare Qur'an 55:24: "His are the moving ships that float high as mountains on the sea."

195. Rida is here referring to Jamal al-Din al-Afghani.

196. Rida's note: See pp. 220–35 and 270–76 of Volume 20.

197. Ibrahim Pasha (1789–1848): presumed eldest son of Muhammad 'Ali, Egyptian general and governor of Syria (1831–41). Octave Joseph Anthelme Seve, "Sulayman Pasha" (1787–1860): French army officer in Egyptian service who married into Muhammad 'Ali's family, converted to Islam, and took the name Sulayman.

198. Rida's note: See Volume 9, pp. 35–51 and 141–47.

199. Ar. *al-mahkamah al-ahliyyah*, referring to native national courts with jurisdiction over Egyptian nationals set up by the British after their occupation of Egypt. Nathan J. Brown, *The Rule of Law in the Arab World: Courts in Egypt and the Gulf* (Cambridge: Cambridge University Press, 1987), xvi; Samira Haj, *Reconfiguring Islamic Tradition: Reform, Rationality, and Modernity* (Stanford: Stanford University Press, 2009), 138.

200. Ar. *'ulama' al-din wa 'ulama' al-dunya*, literally, ulama of religion and ulama of the world.

201. Le Bon, *Lois psychologiques de l'évolution des peuples*.

202. Mehmed V hosted Kaiser Wilhelm I (1859–1941), his World War I ally, in Constantinople on October 15, 1917. The kaiser also toured the Gallipoli battlefields. Previously the kaiser had visited the Ottoman Empire in 1898.

203. Al-Khalil ibn Ahmad al-Farahidi (718–786 or 791): distinguished lexicographer, phonologist, grammarian, educator, and musicologist. See Karin C. Ryding, ed., *Early Medieval Arabic: Studies on Al-Khalil ibn Ahmad* (Washington, DC: Georgetown University Press, 1998). Ishaq bin Rahwayh (d. 853): described in premodern biographical works as a renowned scholar of hadith and jurist. See Susan A. Spectorsky, "Sunnah in the Responses of Ishaq b. Rahwayh," in *Studies in Islamic Legal Theory*, ed. Bernard G. Weiss (Leiden: Brill, 2001), 51–74.

204. Ar. *'irq*, conveying the sense of root. It may also be rendered "race," yet the sense of Rida's meaning here is perhaps not best captured by an openly racial vocabulary.

205. As noted in the Translator's Introduction above, Rida does not explicitly suggest that legislation could be independent of religion. He often distinguishes between religion and worldly or mundane matters, *din wa dunya*, but does not claim or suggest that mundane (*dunyawi*) legislation is "secular" in the sense that it operates outside the framework of Islam. For Rida, the principles enabling independent lawmaking—necessity

248   *Notes to Pages 155–68*

and public interest or *maslahah*—have a canonical or Islamic legal basis. On this issue see also Enayat, *Modern Political Thought in Islam*, 79–80.

206. Ar. *al-ahkam al-qada'iyyah aw al-'amaliyyah*, the latter (*al-akham al-'amaliyyah*) referring to practical rules or rulings of shari'ah pertaining to the conduct of individuals.

207. Rida suggests that Islamic lawmaking is based on deliberation and not simply majoritarian. In that respect it differs from and is preferable to European lawmaking.

208. Rida, *Tafsir al-Manar* (Beirut: Dar Ehia al-Tourath al-Arabi, 2002), Volume 5, 171–89.

209. Rida's note: A *mursal* tradition related by Ahmad [ibn Hanbal], Abu Dawud, and Tirmidhi, and supported by what Bukhari traced to a hadith of 'Amr bin al-'As, and which Abu Hurayrah and Abu Salamah concurred with, may God be pleased with them: "He who makes a ruling on the basis of his ijtihad and rules correctly will have two rewards; and if he makes a ruling and makes an error, he will have one reward."

210. Mu'adh ibn Jabal (d. 639): a Companion sent by the Prophet to Yemen to serve as a judge. The report of the Prophet giving Mu'adh permission to use ijtihad has served as one of the primary justifications for the practice of ijtihad. Al-Qadi al-Nu'man, *Disagreements of the Jurists*, trans. Devin J. Stewart (New York: NYU Press, 2017), 385.

211. Ar. *manhaj al-'ilm al-istiqlali*, the path of independent reasoning. Here, Rida has ijtihad in mind.

212. Rida's note: This is the text of the recently published edition of the book. One of the meanings of *al-zamanah* is love [*mahabbah*]. He appointed Abu al-Akhwas as qadi out of love, and as a reward for a favor, as the book discusses.

213. Rida's note: Died 384. [See R. Paret, "al-Tanukhi," *EI*; Laoust, *Le califat dans la doctrine de Rašīd Ridā*, 265n39.]

214. Muqtadir: 'Abbasid caliph (r. 908–32); Mutawakkil bin al-Mu'tasim: 'Abbasid caliph (r. 847–61); Mu'tasim: 'Abbasid caliph (r. 833–42).

215. Ayoub, *The Qur'an and Its Interpreters*, Volume 1, 225.

216. On Rida's attitudes toward the status of women under Islam, see also Rida, *The Muhammadan Revelation*, trans. Yusuf Talal DeLorenzo (Alexandria, VA: Al-Saadawi Publications, 1996), 140–42; and Rida, *Nida' Ila al-Jins al-Latif* (Cairo: Al-Manar, 1932).

217. Verse 82 of Ibrahim bin Ibrahim al-Laqani's *al-Jawharah* or *Jawharat al-Tawhid*, a creed in verse that produced many commentaries. Laqani (d. 1631 or 1632) was a Maliki Al-Azhar professor. See W. Montgomery Watt, *Islamic Philosophy and Theology* (Edinburgh: Edinburgh University Press, 1985), 140, and http://marifah.net/articles/JawharatalTawhid.pdf. On the French translation of the creed, see Laoust, *Le califat dans la doctrine de Rašīd Ridā*, 266–67n43.

218. Ar. *a'immat al-'itrah*, referring to Shi'i authorities.

219. Ar. *sadd al-dhari'ah*, blocking the means. On this principle, see for instance Justin Stearns, "Enduring the Plague," in *Muslim Medical Ethics: From Theory to Practice*, ed. Johnathon E. Brockopp and Thomas Eich (Columbia: University of South Carolina Press, 2008), 51n22.

220. Ar. *al-ma'sum*, referring to the Prophet.

221. That is, one that is based on interpretation (*ta'wil*), a word originally used synonymously with *tafsir*, exegesis, but coming to denote the effort to uncover the Qur'an's most fundamental or hidden meanings, and particularly associated with Shi'ism and

Notes to Pages 168–79

Sufism. The term occurs seventeen times in the Qur'an, notably Qur'an 3:7: "As for those in whose hearts is deviation from the truth, they will follow what in it [the Qur'an] is unspecific, seeking discord and seeking an interpretation suitable to them [lit., "seeking its ta'wil (ta'wilihi)]" (trans. Hussein Abdul-Raof). In this instance, Rida's reference to ta'wil—to people issuing fatwas on the basis of ta'wil—implies a criticism, as Laoust's French translation also suggests. Laoust, *Le califat dans la doctrine de Rašīd Ridā*, 172. The literature on ta'wil and tafsir is extensive; see for instance Hussein Abdul-Raof, *Schools of Qur'anic Exegesis: Genesis and Development* (London: Routledge, 2013), 84–110.

222. Laoust finds Rida here following Ghazali. Laoust, *Le califat dans la doctrine de Rašīd Ridā*, 267–68n46.

223. Ar. *al-umur al-khassah*, which Laoust renders "leurs affaires personnelles." Laoust, *Le califat dans la doctrine de Rašīd Ridā*, 173.

224. *Al-Manar* 23.8 (October 20, 1922): 584–92; See also Laoust, *Le califat dans la doctrine de Rašīd Ridā*, 268n47.

225. Rida critiques the practice. *Al-Manar* 24.3 (March 18, 1923): 179; See also Laoust, *Le califat dans la doctrine de Rašīd Ridā*, 268n48.

226. On this stipulation as a Shafiʿi prescription, and Rida's position, see Laoust, *Le califat dans la doctrine de Rašīd Ridā*, 268n47.

227. A common Arabic expression.

228. Cf. Qur'an 103:3: "urge one another to the truth, and urge one another to steadfastness."

229. Ayoub, *The Qur'an and Its Interpreters*, Volume 2, 290.

230. Ar. *hisbah*, calculation, verification, reckoning; an institution for implementing norms—what is proper—and preventing what is improper, serving to supervise commercial and other this-worldly activities. Muhammad Akram Khan, *Islamic Economics and Finance: A Glossary* (New York: Routledge, 2003), 76.

231. See also Eyal Zisser, "Rashid Rida: On the Way to Syrian Nationalism in the Shade of Islam and Arabism," in *The Origins of Syrian Nationhood: Histories, Pioneers and Identity*, ed. Adel Beshara (New York: Routledge, 2011), 123–40. Zisser notes the political aspect of Rida's career, as compared with Rida's intellectual legacy, highlighted by Albert Hourani and others.

232. Rumelia/Roumeli, literally, "the land of the Rum or Romans" (Turk. *Rumeli*), the name the Ottomans gave to territory formed by their conquests in the Balkan Peninsula. See Ipek K. Yosmaoglu, *Blood Ties: Religion, Violence and the Politics of Nationhood in Ottoman Macedonia, 1878–1908* (Ithaca: Cornell University Press, 2013), 79.

233. Haleem, trans., *The Qur'an*, 63.

234. Ar. *sighat al-mubalaghah*, "exaggerating" the action described.

235. See Laoust, *Le califat dans la doctrine de Rasid Rida*, 269n51.

236. Haleem, trans., *The Qur'an*, 78.

237. Qur'an 65:1–7 outlines rules for divorce.

238. Ayoub, *The Qur'an and Its Interpreters*, Volume 2, 215.

239. Shams al-Din Muhammad ibn al-Qayyim al-Jawziyyah (d. 1350), *Iʿlam al-Muwaqqaʿin ʿan Rabb al-ʿAlamin*, a multivolume fiqh work. See Mustafa Abdul Rahman, *On Taqlid: Ibn Al Qayyim's Critique of Authority in Islamic Law* (New York: Oxford University Press, 2013).

250   *Notes to Pages 181–93*

240. Rida frequently wrote about European policies in the Middle East. On this point see for instance Wood, *Christian Criticisms, Islamic Proofs*, 30n11, and Laoust, *Le califat dans la doctrine de Rašīd Ridā*, 271n53. On Rida and Britain see also Haddad's "Arab Religious Nationalism in the Colonial Era" and Umar Ryad, "Anti-Imperialism and the Pan-Islamic Movement," in *Islam and the European Empires*, ed. David Motadel (Oxford: Oxford University Press, 2016), 131–49.

241. On Rida's memorandum to Lloyd George, see A. L. Tibawi, "From Rashid Rida to Lloyd George," *Islamic Quarterly* 20–22 (1978): 24–29, and Haddad, "Arab Religious Nationalism in the Colonial Era," 270–71.

242. On Rida and pan-Islamism, see for instance Muhammad Qasim Zaman, *Modern Islamic Thought in a Radical Age: Religious Authority and Internal Criticism* (New York: Cambridge University Press, 2012), 10–11.

243. For a comparison of Rida's rendering with Cromer's original English, see Cromer, *Memorandum by Lord Cromer on the Present Situation in Egypt. Printed for the Use of the Foreign Office*, September 1906, 2–3.

244. Rida, "al-jami'ah al-islamiyyah wa al-siyasiyyah," *Al-Manar* 17.1 (December 28, 1913): 75–79.

245. Rida, "al-jami'ah al-islamiyyah wa al-siyasiyyah," *Al-Manar* 17.1 (December 28, 1913): 76–77.

246. Critiques of Cromer were not limited to those of *Al-Manar*. Cromer's views on Islam and proposals for its reform were outlined in his annual reports; his farewell address (May 4, 1907); *Modern Egypt* (New York: Macmillan, 1908), a book that prompted many rebuttals from Muslim intellectuals; and *Abbas I* (London: MacMillan, 1915). In 1905, Cromer proposed to critical Egyptian reception the creation of a Ministry of Waqfs, whose minister would be part of the Council of Ministers and subject to British influence. Cromer's ideas were taken up by Lord Kitchener in 1913. See also Laoust, *Le califat dans la doctrine de Rašīd Ridā*, 272–73n59.

247. Rida's note: We published this in *Al-Manar*, Volume 17, p. 77.

248. The notion of transcendence (*tanzih*) exempts God from any resemblance to anything created, on which basis anthropomorphism (*tashbih*) is prohibited in Islam.

249. Sells, *Approaching the Qur'an*, 76.

250. "Those whose hearts are to be reconciled to Islam" (*mu'allafah qulubuhum*) refers to those the Prophet is reported to have given proceeds from the zakat to draw them to Islam, or because their faith was weak, or to deter them from harm. Cf. Qur'an 9:60: "Alms are meant only for the poor, the needy, those who administer them, those whose hearts need winning over, to free slaves and help those in debt, for God's cause, and for travelers in need. This is ordained by God."

251. Batinis (*Batiniyyah*), "those who follow the hidden meaning," a name given to the Isma'ili Shi'ah, who emphasized the notion that the Qur'an has an external meaning (*zahir*) accessible to all, as well as a hidden meaning (*batin*), a notion also emphasized in Sufism.

252. See Mahmoud Ayoub, *A Muslim View of Christianity*, ed. Irfan A. Omar (New Delhi: Logos Press, 2009), 213–16. See also Laoust, *Le califat dans la doctrine de Rašīd Ridā*, 273n61.

Notes to Pages 193–200

253. Sells, *Approaching the Qur'an*, 76.

254. Rida's note: A reference to what Matthew related from the Messiah in his gospel: "Truly I tell you, whatever you bind on earth will be bound in heaven, and whatever you loose on earth will be loosed in heaven" (Mt 18:18).

255. Sells, *Approaching the Qur'an*, 116.

256. Ayoub, *The Qur'an and Its Interpreters*, Volume 2, 272.

257. Rida's note: That is, [without] the mediation of any individual for himself. As for them being able to mediate through their teachings and guidance, this was affirmed at the beginning and at the end. [Rida's point is that while there is no individual mediation in Islam, there is a broader, collective kind of mediation. He may have added the note because he felt he needed to rationalize 'Abduh's statement, or that it might potentially mislead.]

258. Rida's note: Among the testimonies to this is the ulama's elevation in rank above the caliphs, who are beneath them in understanding and knowledge. Have you not heard of the story of Imam Malik and Caliph Harun al-Rashid, God have mercy upon them both, how when giving a lesson the imam directed the caliph to come down from the pulpit and sit among the common people, as he had the rank of a student?

259. Rida's note: Testimonies to this include the statement of the first caliph, may God be satisfied with him, in his sermon: "If I deviate from the right way, correct me." See p. 734 of *Al-Manar*, Volume 4.

260. Rida's note: A hadith related by Bukhari, Muslim, and others. See p. 32 of *Al-Manar*, Volume 4.

261. Rida's note: An example of that would be when he has partisan support stronger than the community, so that it be feared that he would destroy the community with it. And: "Preventing corruption comes before procuring benefit."

262. Rida's note: An Egyptian magazine that the Master has rebutted on this issue.

263. On *Al-Jami'ah* see also Wood, *Christian Criticisms, Islamic Proofs*, 20, 25, 30, 63, 153n145, 153–208.

264. Rida's note: This article was the first of those that we wrote on the issue of the caliphate. It then appeared to us that we should foreground it with an explanation of its ordinances. That was followed by an investigation into the means of its establishment, and the obstacles to that. The discussion of this matter grew lengthy, to the point that we forgot about this article. We then revisited it. We saw that we might make it a conclusion, so as to stimulate interest in it, although some of its investigations are repeated in the sections that precede it.

265. Rida's Conclusion, as he indicates, predates the book that precedes it. See also Laoust, *Le califat dans la doctrine de Rašīd Ridā*, 273n63, who finds it serving the function of a conclusion rather poorly.

266. See Qur'an 2:143: "We have made you a community of the middle path." See also Ayoub, *The Qur'an and Its Interpreters*, Volume 1, 170–72; and Qur'an 42:38.

267. Chosroism (*al-kisrawiyyah*) refers to the pre-Islamic Persian form of rule.

268. Qaramitah, a political-religious movement derived from Isma'ili Shi'ism founded by Hamdan Qarmat (disappeared c. 899) in the Kufa area, recognizing Muhammad bin Isma'il as imam, and ending in the eleventh century with the rise of the Fatimids.

Notes to Pages 200–13

269. Abu Shuja' Fanna Khusraw (936–983), usually known by the honorific 'Adud al-Dawlah ("Aid of the Dynasty") granted by Caliph Muti' in 962: a Buyid emir who ruled Baghdad from 977 until his death. He acted as if an independent king, but for legitimation maintained the fiction of subservience to the caliph. John P. Turner, "'Adud al-Dawla," in *Medieval Islamic Civilization*, Volume 1, ed. Josef W. Meri and Jere L. Bacharach (New York: Routledge, 2006), 16. On 'Adud al-Dawlah and Ta'i', see also Patricia Crone and Martin Hinds, *God's Caliph: Religious Authority in the First Centuries of Islam* (Cambridge: Cambridge University Press, 2003), 14–15n35. Ta'i': 'Abbasid caliph (r. 974–91) whose authority was overshadowed by the Buyids, including 'Adud al-Dawlah, his father-in-law, de facto ruler of much of Iraq and Iran.

270. Jalal al-Din 'Abd al-Rahman bin Abi Bakr al-Suyuti, *Tarikh al-Khulafa'* (Qatar: Wizarat al-Awqaf wa al-Shu'un al-Islamiyyah, 2013), 629; On this incident, see Gavin R. G. Hanbly, "The Emperor's Clothes: Robing and 'Robes of Honour' in Mughal India," in *Robes of Honour: Khil'at in Pre-Colonial and Colonial India*, ed. Steward Gordon (Oxford: Oxford University Press, 2003), 33–34.

271. See Bukhari, *Sahih al-Bukhari*, Book 9, Volume 89, Hadith 251.

272. Ar. *tasnif*, writing things down, which Laoust renders "de codifier leurs lois." Laoust, *Le califat dans la doctrine de Rašīd Ridā*, 225. In *An Introduction to Islamic Law* (Cambridge: Cambridge University Press, 2011), Wael B. Hallaq notes that the codification of Islamic law did not begin until the eighteenth century under colonial pressure. Mawardi in his *Ordinances of Islamic Governance* provides opinions rather than codes.

273. "The Truthful," a qur'anic epithet applied by Muhammad to Abu Bakr. A. Rippen, "al-Siddik," *EI*.

274. Rida's note: See Sections 8 and 14.

275. See Bukhari, *Sahih al-Bukhari*, Book 9, Volume 88, Hadith 228.

276. Ibn Khaldun, *The Muqaddimah*, trans. Franz Rosenthal (Princeton: Princeton University Press, 2005), 267–68. See also Ali Abdel Razeq, *Islam and the Foundations of Political Power*, trans. Maryam Loutfi (Edinburgh: Edinburgh University Press, 2012), 29–30.

277. The Italo-Turkish or Italo-Ottoman War, September 1911–October 1912, considered a precursor of the First World War and notable for involving the first use of bombing from an airplane in war. The war revealed Ottoman weakness. Italy easily prevailed, taking the territories that would form Italian Libya.

278. Shakib Arslan (1869–1946).

279. Bâb-ı Meşîhat is the Shaykh al-Islam's office. With the abolition of the Janissary Corps in 1826, the meşihat makam (Office of Şeyhulislam) was moved to Ağakapısi (the residence of the Janissary chief) together with all shari'ah institutions, and it was called the Bâb-ı Meşîhat. There were around 150 officials in the department.

280. Ar. *Hizb al-i'tilaf*, The Freedom and Coalition Party (Hürriyet ve Itilaf Firkast, HIF).

INDEX

Abadi, Begum, 243–44n172
'Abbas ibn 'Abd al-Muttalib, 70
'Abbasid caliphate/dynasty, 20–21, 23, 27, 31, 33, 34, 68, 69, 71, 72, 73, 86–87, 89, 101, 102–3, 112, 160, 192, 196, 200, 201, 207, 208, 214, 232n23
'Abd al-Hamid (Abdul Hamid II), 4, 18, 19, 53, 68, 127, 169, 172, 209; 231n14, 246n183
'Abd Allah ibn al-Husayn, 34, 110, 111, 241n158, 242n160
'Abd Allah ibn al-Sa'ib, 68
'Abd Allah ibn al-Zubayr, 75, 206, 236n78
'Abd Allah ibn 'Amr ibn al-'As, 77
'Abd Allah ibn Saba', 73, 199
'Abd Allah ibn 'Umar, 75, 78, 236n78
'Abd al-Majid (Abdülmecid), 246n183
'Abd al-Majid II (Abdülmecid II), 21, 42, 43, 112, 242–43n164, 243n165
'Abd al-Malik ibn Marwan, 75, 207, 236n78; sons of, 207
'Abd al-Rahman ibn 'Abd Rabb al-Ka'bah. *See* 'Abd al-Rahman ibn Abi Bakr
'Abd al-Rahman ibn Abi Bakr, 77, 99
'Abd al-Rahman ibn 'Awf, 59, 60, 65, 73, 75, 85
'Abd al-Raziq, 'Ali, 4, 44
'Abd al-Shams, 72

'Abduh, Muhammad, 4, 35, 63, 117, 120, 193, 243n169, 244–45n175
Abdul Hamid II. *See* 'Abd al-Hamid (Abdul Hamid II)
Abdülmecid II ('Abd al-Majid II), 21, 42, 43, 112, 242–43n164, 243n165
Abraham, Prophet, 50, 204, 229–30n5
Abu al-'Abbas al-Asfahani/Isfahani al-Katib, 160
Abu al-Darda', 65
Abu al-Husayn ibn 'Abbas, 160
Abu al-Sa'ud al-'Imadi, 177
Abu Bakr, 29, 58, 60, 62, 64, 65, 67, 68, 69, 72, 83, 84, 98, 99, 160, 203, 205; designation of successor, 86; pledge of allegiance to, 233n37; on qualifications of caliph, 229–30n5; rejectors of, 239n138; sons of, 99
Abu Bakr ibn Abi Shaybah, 95
Abu Bakr ibn Khaythamah, 100
Abu Barzah, 206
Abu Dawud, 248n209
Abu Hanifah, 168
Abu Hurayrah, 68, 97, 101, 102, 248n209
Abu Sa'id, 85
Abu Sa'id al-Khudri, 104, 192
Abu Salamah, 248n209
Abu Sufyan, 72

Index

Abu 'Ubadah, 94, 95
Abu 'Ubaydah, 85
Abu Umayyah al-Ahwas al-Fulani al-Basri, 160
Aden, 180
Adib, Khalidah, 121
'Adnan, 110, 163n242
'Adud al-Dawlah, 200–201, 252n269
adultery, 212
Afghani, Sayyid Jamal al-Din al-, 118, 243n169, 244–45n175, 247n195
Afghanistan, 34–35, 53, 113; emir of, 113; government of, 109; Muslim renaissance in, 142; Muslims in, 169; Persian language in, 122; treaty with Turkey, 109, 240n154
Africa, Muslims in, 126, 198
Ahmad Mukhtar Pasha, 117, 181
'A'ishah, 82, 191
Al-Azhar, 109, 118
Albanians, 152
alcohol consumption, 149
Aleppo, 11
Algeria: Muslims in, 114; opposition to government of the Hijaz, 135
'Ali, 59, 65, 68, 73, 85, 129, 199, 203, 235n76; army of, 232–33n29; burial location, 244n173; as Commander of the Faithful, 75, 99, 110, 199, 201, 205
'Ali, Muhammad (brother of Shawkat), 35, 118, 243–44n172, 244n173
'Ali, Shawkat (brother of Muhammad), 35, 118, 243–44n172, 244n173
'Alids, 31, 72, 73–74, 88, 110
Allenby, Edmund, 14
All-India Khalifat Conference, 243–44n172
altruism, 40, 173
Amin, Qasim, 243n169
'Amman, 110
'Amr ibn al-'As, 65, 100, 248n209
anarchism, 104, 128, 137
Anas ibn Malik, 73, 82

Anatolia: Christians in, 175; Kemal in, 143; lands contested by, 138; Muslims in, 179; nationalist movement, 121; Turks in, 183, 185
Andalusia, 177, 196
Angora (Ankara), 112, 113, 117, 172
Ankara. See Angora (Ankara)
annulment, 166
anti-imperialism, 1
apocalypticism, qur'anic, 7
apostasy, 33, 95, 123
apostates: fighting, 64; Muslim, 36, 173. See also heretics
appointment and deposition, 29–30
Arab Caliphate, 40, 181. See also caliphate
Arab community, 53, 180; relationship with England, 183; relationship with Turkey, 213
Arab emirs, 125, 136
Arab Federation, 15, 35
Arab government, 5–6, 12
"Arab Government of Damascus, The" (Rida), 11
Arab independence, 21
Arab lands: colonization of, 134; reform in, 120; Turks expelled from, 7
Arab League, 242n160
Arab Revolt, 241n158, 242n160
Arab unity, 131, 200
Arabian Peninsula: and the Arab Federation, 15; and the British, 131–32; Europeanization on, 125; government on, 129–30; Islamic governments in, 180; Muslims on, 130, 132; as proposed seat of caliphate, 133
Arabic language, 39, 70, 74, 125, 129, 136, 142, 149–53, 181, 183, 189–90, 194, 209; in Afghanistan, 142; duty to learn, 194; and Islam, 151–52; obligatory learning of, 209; and the Qur'an, 150, 152; and the revealed law, 149–53; translations into, 8, 20; in Turkey, 136
Arabism, 4

Index

Arabs: conquests by, 178; cooperation with Turks, 36–37, 152–53; criticism of, 74; factionalism among, 130; Hadrami, 131; as inferior to Persians, 236n77; Muslim, 125, 130, 132, 136, 183, 199; opposition to caliphate in the Turks' lands, 136; recognizing a caliph in Turkey, 138; relationship with the caliphate, 129–33; relationship with Turks, 1, 20, 129; rights of, 2; as the root of Islam, 119–20; solidarity among, 207; subjugation of, 183; territories where they predominate, 138; Turkish treatment of, 4; and the Umayyads, 206

Armenian genocide, 246n180

Armenians, 7, 40, 175, 179

Arslan, Shakib, 44, 211

Ash'ari, 30

Ashtiyani, Mirza Hasan, 245n176

'Asir, 34; Sayyid clan, 240–41n157

Association of the Servants of the Ka'bah, 243–44n172

Atassi, Hashim al-, 12, 13

authority: absolute, 208, 209; autocratic, 96; of the caliph, 203, 211–12; of the caliphate, 21, 23, 55, 88, 91, 121, 126, 136, 138, 145, 158, 186, 192, 199, 211; of caliphs and emirs, 192; civil, 195–96; of the Congress, 14; delegating, 79, 127; divine, 195; of emirs, 192; European, 173; executive, 38, 42, 127; foreign, 135; to give good counsel, 196; of God, 191; of imams, 90, 109, 156, 168–69; in Islam, 157, 173, 194–96; Islamic, 173; Ittihadist, 210; legislative, 127, 154, 162, 165; military, 213; monarchal, 202, 207; moral, 212; of the Muslim community, 38, 42, 51, 61–63, 76, 78, 112, 127, 156–57, 195, 198, 203; obedience to, 78, 83, 157, 158, 234n49; Ottoman, 33, 152, 158, 240–41n157, 241–42n159, 244n173; personal, 42, 96, 172, 208; political, 169, 193; of the Quraysh, 69, 73, 89; religious, 193–94, 195, 196; of religious leaders, 52, 121, 197; of the Shaykh al-Islam, 211–12; of the sultanate, 21, 33, 42, 53, 55, 68; supreme, 115; temporal, 42, 192, 196; of those who loose and bind, 29, 35, 62–63, 84, 98, 116, 119, 127, 157, 159, 203; of unlawful rulers, 116–17

autocracy, 4, 5, 13, 14, 19, 96, 118, 134, 136, 200

Azad, Abul Kalam, 20, 35, 118, 244n173

Azerbaijan, 109

Azhar ibn 'Abd Allah, 95

Azharis, 110

Bâb-ı Meşîhat, 252n279

Badr, battle of, 82, 191, 237n97

Balkan Wars, 175, 246n183

Banna, Hasan al-, 4

Banu 'Abd al-Shams, 72

Banu Abu Mu'ayt, 73

Banu 'Adi, 72–73

Banu Hashim, 72, 73

Banu Taym, 72

Banu Umayyah, 72, 73

Basrah, governor of, 59

Batini Shi'ah, 22, 192, 200

Baydawi, 229–30n5

Bayhaqi, 68, 82, 84

Bazzar, 68

Bedouinism, 111, 143

Bedouins, 118

Berbers, 72

Bolshevism, 19, 54, 128, 137

Book of Stations (Iji), 62, 68, 105

Britain: and the Arab Community, 183; and the Arabian Peninsula, 131–32; and the caliphate, 180, 181–84; conspiracies of, 126; and Egypt, 131, 132, 169, 241n158; and Greater Syria, 6, 12; in the Hijaz, 131; and Iraq, 17, 21, 118; Middle Eastern view of, 18; and the Ottoman Empire, 181, 185; recognizing Arab independence, 13, 40–41; and Russia, 181; in Syria, 13

256   *Index*

Bukhara, 109

Bukhari, 59, 60, 68, 75, 78, 85, 99, 102, 151, 192, 248n209; *Sound Collection*, 87, 94, 110, 206

Bulgaria, 123

Buyids, 232n23

Caesar, 33, 99, 239n134

Cairo, 13, 19, 20, 35, 36; statues in, 145. *See also* Egypt

Cairo Caliphate Congress, 6, 25, 44

caliphate: abolition of, 28, 42–44, 241n158; of Abu Bakr, 72; administrative and financial offices and councils, 140–41; advice concerning, 213–14; in Anatolia, 185; in Angora, 112; Arab, 40, 181; characteristics and benefits of, 36; and claims about pan-Islamism, 183–88; and the colonial states, 180–83; in corruption of, 103, 158–59, 192, 202, 208; defined, 56; elimination of, 104; establishment in an intermediate zone, 138–39; establishment of, 185–86; establishment of tyranny under, 98–104; genuine, 133; history and theory, 28–29; independent governments tied to, 130; Islamic, 96, 122, 128, 153, 171, 185; legitimacy of, 232n23; location of, 37; models of programs required for, 139–41; of necessity and tyranny, 32, 88–92, 125; no appointment of one who seeks to rule, 87–96, 135; non-Arab, 31; non-Muslims resistance to the government of, 172–80; non-Qurayshi, 31; and the Ottoman Turks, 208–10; and the papacy, 190–96; people's intentions regarding, 125–28; and prophethood, 204; prophetic, 171, 182, 199; proposed seat of, 133; and the public welfare, 140; qualifications for, 139, 169; qur'anic, 27; rebellion against, 31, 32, 34; recognition of, 36; relationship to Arabs and Turks, 129–33; religious, 109; respect for, 212; restoration/revival of, 39, 53–55, 133, 135, 136; Rida's

discussion of, 1, 3, 20–21, 44; rights of, 187; shari'ah-based, 24, 25, 55, 103, 125, 130, 133, 153–62, 172, 180; as source of legislation, 158–59; spiritual, 22, 26, 53, 112, 127, 193, 209; in Turkey, 34, 41, 68, 110, 112, 113, 121, 136–38, 143, 161, 180, 181, 186, 192, 240n154, 243n168; Turks' resistance to, 40; of tyranny, 122, 127; of 'Umar, 72–73; universal, 24, 34, 111. *See also* 'Abbasid caliphate/dynasty; imamate; Ottoman caliphate/sultanate; Umayyad caliphate

Caliphate or Supreme Imamate, The: overview, 24–26; proposal for reviving the caliphate, 34–42; rhetorical and pedagogical dimension, 3; Rida's introduction to, 26–28; Rida's reasons for writing, 2–3, 25; Rida's review of theory, 28–34; secondary literature, 24; translations of, 24; writing of, 1

caliph(s): 'Abbasid, 207; accountability to people who loose and bind, 70, 140, 157; allegiance of people who loose and bind to, 29, 57, 74, 76, 84, 89, 114, 140; allegiance to, 30, 31; appointment of, 56–61, 85–87, 232n27; Arab, 132; and the Arabic language, 150; authority of, 21, 23, 55, 88, 91, 121, 126, 136, 138, 145, 158, 186, 192, 199, 203, 211–12; called to account, 140; in Constantinople, 110, 169; constrained by Qur'an and sunnah, 32; disqualification from imamate, 92–96; election of, 21, 138; errors of, 159–60; as head of state, 209; ignorant, 171; limited power of, 192; in Mecca, 16; mujtahid, 39; obedience to, 207, 209; obligation to consult, 31–32; Ottoman influence over, 36; power taken from, 123; qualifications of, 30–31, 37, 66–74, 183; Qurayshi lineage required for, 20, 30, 31, 37, 66–72, 88–91, 112, 129, 133, 206, 244n73; relationship with sultans, 201; righteous, 198, 201–2, 203; role of, 51–52, 194;

selection of by people who loose and bind, 32, 57, 86, 87, 91, 98, 101, 105, 138, 168, 238n108; shari'ah rights of, 36; single vs. multiple, 104–8; spiritual, 55, 150, 169; as supreme leader, 127; as temporal ruler, 41; in Turkey, 143, 183, 192; tyrannical, 127, 160; unjust/disbelieving, 31, 86. *See also* imams; mujtahids

capitalism, 137, 164

Carmathians (Qaramitah), 200

Caucasus region, 109

Central Powers, 23

charitable endowments, 188

children of Ishmael, 50

children of Israel, 50

China, 106

Chosroes, 99, 239n134

Chosroism, 200, 251n267

Christianity: in Bulgaria, 123; conversion to, 186; dismissal of, 4; genuine, 40; legal recognition of, 21; in the Middle Ages, 195; missionaries, 123, 186; patriarchs, 169; social-political form of, 173; virtues of, 53. *See also* papacy

Christians: Europeanized, 173; living in Muslim lands, 40, 174, 175–78; resistance to the government of the caliphate, 172–73; in Rumelia and Anatolia, 175; in Syria, 12, 17; tribute paid by, 237n94

Churchill, Winston, 242n160

Circassians (Jarkas), 132, 152

civil government, 128, 153–54, 176

civil society, politics of, 17, 51–52

civil transactions, 122, 155, 162, 166, 195

civilization, 153–54; development of, 52; European, 52; Islamic, 28, 53, 135, 137

Coalition Party, 213

colonial aggression, 18

colonial rule, 34, 53, 99

colonial states, 40–41; and the caliphate, 180–83

colonization, 185–86

Commander of the Faithful. *See* 'Ali

Commentary on Goals (Taftazani), 58, 68, 89, 90–91, 94, 182

Committee for Union and Progress (CUP), 172, 187, 231n14, 246n181, 246n183

Companions, 23, 51, 57–60, 62, 64, 68, 71, 75, 83, 89, 166, 191, 199, 200, 205, 206, 233n34, 234n42

Conclusive Argument from God, The (Ahmad Wali Allah al-Dihlawi), 69

congregational prayer, 170

consensus, 30, 56–57, 59, 60, 62, 65, 66, 67, 69, 71, 74, 81, 86, 104, 135, 150, 154, 156–57, 159, 168, 237n95, 238n108

Constantinople, 35, 68, 71, 88, 110, 112, 117, 118, 121, 126, 150, 208, 213; as seat of caliphate, 130, 133, 136, 169

constitutional government/law, 117, 203

consultation, 21, 23, 27, 29–32, 51, 58–59, 60, 74, 100, 133, 140, 156, 158, 161, 189, 191, 198, 203, 206, 213–14, 237n95; in Islam, 81–85

contracts, 166. *See also* civil transactions

corruption, 7, 39, 42, 73, 88, 91, 96, 162; of Arab Islamic rule, 199–201; avoiding, 50; of the caliphate, 103, 158, 161; causes of, 33, 163, 165, 171; elimination of, 208; financial/political, 52; moral, 211; preventing, 82, 124, 144, 153, 161, 189

Council of Deputies, 123

Cromer (Lord): critiques of, 250n246; Rida's letter to, 189; Rida's rebuttal to, 184–85; statement on pan-Islamism, 184; statement on shari'ah, 189–90

crusades, 21

Curzon (Lord), 183

Dabashi, Hamid, 245n176

Damascus, 5, 110, 174; France in, 13; Rida in, 19, 20, 27, 34; Syrian government in, 10–17

Dar al-Da'wah wa al-Irshad (The Institute for Outreach and Guidance), 185

Dar al-Fatwa, 124
Darimi, 84
Dawidi, 95
democracy: under Faysal, 10–11; liberal, 15
Deoband Madrasah (India), 118
Development of Nations, The (Le Bon), 52
Dhahabi, 160
dhimmis, 162–63, 177–78
Dihlawi, Shah Ahmad Wali Allah al-, 69–70, 235n67, 235n68
Dirar, 67
divorce, 166, 170, 178
Dutch Indies, 246n188

Egypt: Arab caliphate in, 131; Britain and, 132, 169, 185; Europeanization in, 121, 130, 147; foreign rule in, 33, 117; governor of, 59; leaders of, 181–82; Muslim renaissance in, 142; Muslims in, 35, 91, 99, 101, 114, 117, 130–31, 147, 164, 169; obedience to the caliph, 209; opposition to government of the Hijaz, 135; Ottoman governor of, 246n185; pan-Islamism in, 184; qadi of, 109; recognition of caliphate by, 36; Rida in, 13; socialism in, 164; statues erected in, 143, 145; support for new caliphate in, 126; ulama in, 124; Wafd, 118. *See also* Cairo
Egyptian government, 166, 182–83
Egyptian revolution, 116, 117
Emigrants, 59, 60, 62, 85, 199, 205
emirs, Arab, 125, 136
England. *See* Britain
English Leather Company, 118
equality, 4, 6, 8, 12, 15, 121, 154, 164, 173, 178
ethnicity: and community unification, 153; foreign, 132; preferential treatment for, 54; Turanian, 122; Turkish, 122
Europeanization, 21, 24, 28, 36, 39, 41, 42, 118, 123, 128; on the Arabian Peninsula, 125; of Christians, 173; in Egypt, 121, 130, 147; of Muslims, 130, 143, 162, 173,

186, 210–11, 214; of the Ottoman Turks, 208–10; party of the Europeanized, 120–22; in Turkey, 42, 136, 142, 147, 175

Fakhri Pasha, 243n168
Fanari, 105, 40n148
fanaticism, 120
Fath al-Bari. See Ibn Hajar al-'Asqalani
Fatih Mosque (Constantinople), 118
Fatimah, 129, 235n76
fatwas: on alcohol, 149; in *Al-Manar*, 145; collections of, 144; council responsible for, 140; deviating from sound teaching, 168; explanation of, 170; issuing, 165; for jihad against Allies, 246n183; of Kemal, 143, 144, 145, 146; permission to issue, 166; of Rida, 3; of Sulayman, 177; against tobacco use, 118, 245n176
Faysal ibn Husayn, 5, 10, 11, 12, 13, 14, 17, 18, 44, 110, 118, 241n158; failure of, 12, 13; in Iraq, 110, 242n160; Rida's advice to, 13, 14; Rida's critique of, 34; in Syria, 11–12
fiqh, 27, 53, 76, 113, 120, 122, 149, 155, 166, 189, 239n138. *See also* Hanafi madhhab
France: and Greater Syria, 6, 12; in the Middle East, 13; Middle Eastern view of, 18; recognizing Syrian independence, 13; relationship with Tunisia and Algeria, 114; in Syria, 13, 17, 21
freedom, 6, 12, 18, 19, 190; and the caliphate, 67; lack of, 34, 43, 175; for non-Muslims, 175; personal, 173, 174; political, 22; of religion, 14, 80, 123, 132, 187, 237n94; of speech and association, 12, 114; in Turkey, 200

gambling, 164
Gandhi, Mohandas, 1, 35, 117
"General Syrian Congress, The" (Rida), 11
Geneva, 10, 11, 17, 19, 20
Germany, 7, 8, 19
Ghazali, 90, 104, 187, 234n53, 240n146, 249n222

Gouraud, Henri, 12, 13
government: civil, 128, 153–54, 176;
    Egyptian, 116, 117; Ibadi, 112; religious,
    173; representative, 21, 26, 117. *See also*
    Ottoman government; Syrian Congress;
    Turkish government
grand vizier, 123, 149, 211, 239n129, 241n158,
    245n179, 246n180
Great Powers, 9, 11, 13, 17, 18, 123; as ene-
    mies of Islam, 4; Muslim subjects in,
    210; politics of, 170; respect for the cal-
    iphate, 212
Great War (World War I), 52–53, 175, 181,
    185
Greater Syria, 6. *See also* Syria
Greco-Turkish War, 242–43n164
Greek Orthodox church, 8
Greeks, 40, 41, 175, 179, 183; in
    Anatolia, 121

Haddad, Mahmoud, 5
hadith: and the Arabic language, 129, 150;
    designations of, 239n139; as example
    and source of knowledge, 194, 203; guid-
    ance of, 198; requirement for caliph to
    be learned in, 29; shari'ah derived from,
    154; use for resolving disputes, 157
hadith topics: actions in accordance with,
    74; avoiding epidemics, 85; caliphate/
    emirate, 68, 71; challenging power, 95;
    consultation, 156; day of resurrection,
    100; imams from Quraysh tribe, 68–69;
    imitating non-Arabs, 201; infliction of
    injury or repayment for injury, 17; the
    Muslim community, 61, 62; obligations
    of the faithful, 62; pledge of the ma-
    jority, 104–5; responsibility for the flock,
    202; revelation, 82; rulings, 248n209;
    testimony and integrity, 178–79; women
    pledging allegiance, 75
Hadrami Arabs, 131
hajj, 59, 60, 99, 125, 150, 182; council re-
    sponsible for, 141

Hakam ibn Abi al-'As, 103
Hakim al-Naysaburi, al-, 62, 73, 94
Halevi, Leor, 3, 5
Hamid al-Din dynasty, 241–42n159
Hanafi madhhab, 109, 122
Hanafis, 66–67, 89, 90, 122, 140, 144,
    240n144
Hanbalis, 111, 166, 246–47n190
Haqqi Pasha, 123
Haramayn, council responsible for, 141
Harun al-Rashid, 207
Hasan (grandson of the Prophet), 74,
    235n76
Hasan al-Basri al-, 81, 100
Hashim, 72; clan of, 58
Hashimi 'Alid lineage, 111
Hashimi Qurayshis, 204. *See also*
    Qurayshis
Helpers, 59, 60, 67, 69, 85, 199, 205
Heraclius, 33, 99
heresiography, 139
heretics, 174, 200; on the Arabian
    Peninsula, 125; Europeanized, 121, 137;
    Muslims as, 40, 143; Muslims favoring
    nonreligious government described as,
    17. *See also* apostates
hijab, 146, 211
Hijaz, 34, 36, 37, 71, 99, 109, 111, 130, 131,
    180, 198; government of, 110, 135; in-
    dependence of, 40–41, 182, 241n158;
    king of, 111, 112, 158n241; obstacles to
    caliphate in, 134–35; as proposed seat of
    caliphate, 133–36; subjugation of, 102;
    Turks expelled from, 241n158
hijrah, 180, 204–5
History of the Caliphs (*Tarikh al-Khulafa'*),
    100, 200–201
Ho Chi Minh, 1
Hubab ibn al-Mundhir, 82–83, 191,
    237n98
Hudhayfah ibn al-Yaman, 61
hudud laws, 57, 70, 79, 90, 109, 111, 174,
    187, 194, 237n90

Index

Husayn (grandson of the Prophet), 235n76, 236n79

Husayn ibn 'Ali, 4, 18, 21, 34, 40, 41, 42, 44, 102, 110, 126, 241n158; as king of the Hijaz, 111, 112, 241n158

Husni Effendi, 185

hypocrites, 173, 181, 192, 200

Ibadi government, 112

Ibadi school of law, 112, 171, 232–33n29

Ibn 'Abbas, 61, 82, 83, 85

Ibn Abi Hatim, 99

Ibn 'Adi, 68, 82

Ibn al-Furat, 160

Ibn al-Humam, Kamal, 66, 235n58, 240n144; *Al-Musayarah*, 66, 88–89, 90, 104

Ibn al-Tin, 95

Ibn Battal, 102

Ibn Hajar al-'Asqalani, 30, 33, 62, 65, 68–69, 73, 75–76, 78, 87, 88, 94–95, 100, 102, 103, 109–110, 234n45

Ibn Hajar al-Haytami, 32, 86–87, 238n111

Ibn Hanbal, 65, 82, 88, 94, 111, 151, 168, 247n203, 248n209

Ibn Khaldun, 41, 204–8

Ibn Majah, 65

Ibn Mardawayh (Ibn Mardawyhi), 83

Ibn Mas'ud, 65

Ibn Qayyim al-Jawziyyah, 134, 179, 246–47n190

Ibn Qutaybah, 74, 236n77

Ibn Qutlubugha, Abu-Fadl Qasim, 66, 235n58

Ibn Sa'd, 83

Ibn Sa'ud, 4, 5, 25, 44, 45, 241n158, 243–44n172

Ibn Taymiyyah, 134

Ibrahim Pasha, 145, 247n197

identity: ethnic, 119, 121–22, 129; Islamic, 122; Muslim, 21; national, 54, 122, 210; Turanian, 210

Idrisi, Sayyid Muhammad 'Ali al-, 44, 110, 240–41n157, 241–42n159

Idrisids, 74

ignorance, 127, 135, 137, 159, 167, 171–72, 180, 181, 196, 200, 205, 206, 214; of the caliph, 160; Era of, 57, 61, 72, 89, 205, 206; pre-Islamic, 97, 115

Iji, 'Adud al-Din al-, 62, 105

ijtihad: of the caliph, 140; call for, 39–40; capacity to exercise, 159; defined, 27; errors in, 162; of imams, 69, 79, 80, 81, 91, 96, 105, 156, 158, 168, 248n210; madrasah for, 167; on multiple imams, 106; in the Muslim community, 51, 167, 168; Muslim dependence on, 141–44; and positive human legislation, 154, 155, 158; prohibition of, 165–66, 167; and public welfare, 65; qualifications for, 30, 64, 66, 67, 89, 140, 157, 234n53; in the revealed law, 139, 149–53, 170; Rida's call for, 39; rules for, 130; science of, 38, 40, 139, 167, 171; Turks' need for, 144–49; unrestricted, 122, 129, 165–66. *See also* Islamic legislation

I'lam al-Muwaqqa'in (Ibn Qayyim al-Jawziyyah), 179

images, permissibility of, 144–45

Imam Muhammad the Madhi, 113

imamate: as contract, 74; corruption of, 192; disqualification from, 92–96; elimination of, 87; establishment of, 214; genuine, 170; of Husayn, 110–11; influence on Islamic reform, 168–72; Islamic, 141; lacking justice, 229–30n5; of necessity or tyranny, 88–92; restricted to 'Alids, 31; shari'ah-based, 180; unity of, 108–15; universal, 49–50, 115, 119. *See also* caliphate

Imami Shi'ites, 113, 243n167

imams: appointment of, 115, 119, 124; authority of, 90, 109, 156, 168–69; coercion of, 93–94; defense of, 97; deposition of, 94; dismissal for cause, 62–63; duties of, 92, 127; ijtihad of, 69, 79, 80, 81, 91, 96, 105, 156, 158, 168, 248n210; of the jurists, 40; multiple, 104; of necessity or tyranny, 76; obedience to, 76; obligation to the religion and the community, 78–81; qualifications of, 86, 87, 182; rebellion against, 75, 96; righteous, 27; taken captive by hostile force, 93–94; unjust/disbelieving, 75, 86, 98; in Yemen, 130, 131, 180, 182; Zaydi, 37, 74, 241–42n159. *See also* caliph(s); mujtahids

India: Europeanization in, 121; foreign occupation of, 117; Khalifat Movement, 118; leaders in, 117–18; leaders of, 181; Muslim community in, 35, 91, 117, 120; Muslims in, 36, 114, 122, 126–27, 198, 243–44n172, 244n173; obedience to the caliph, 209; opposition to government of the Hijaz, 135; people of, 106; pilgrimage from, 243–44n172; reform in, 120

Indian National Congress, 243–44n172

Indonesia, 246n188

inheritance: in Islamic law, 240n153; of the land, 50

injustice, 18, 31, 33, 91, 95, 103, 123, 137, 138, 141, 155, 166, 176, 180, 197–98, 200; abode of, 96–98. *See also* justice

Institute for Outreach and Guidance (Dar al-Da'wah wa al-Irshad), 36, 123, 185, 187

integrity: of caliphs, 30, 88–89, 161; in human communities, 179; of imams, 67, 89, 90, 130, 171; impairment of, 92; lack of, 89, 90, 143, 179; loss of, 143; of madrasah graduates, 139; of Qurayshis, 206; of rulers, 195, 198; of those who loose and bind, 30, 63, 64, 116; of Umayyads, 206

intermediate zone, 138–39

international dispute resolution, 8

international law, 139

Iran, 34, 53, 113; division of, 181; Muslims in, 118; Persian language in, 122; tobacco trade in, 118

Iraq, 17, 33; Europeanization in, 121; King Faysal in, 110; king of, 242n160; lands contested by, 138; Muslims in, 99, 131;

occupation of, 18–19; as part of an Arab federation, 15; treaty with Britain, 118

Ishaq ibn Rahwayh, 151

Ishmael (Isma'il), 71; children of, 50

Islam: abode of, 96, 107; Arabic, 18, 71; and the Arabic language, 151–52; authority of, 157, 173, 194–96; and the Berbers, 72; call to, 71, 132, 139, 141, 187; consultation in, 81–85; conversion to, 107, 132, 170, 175, 177; defense of, 139; disestablishment of, 11, 14–15; egalitarianism of, 72; enemies of, 42, 137, 141, 170; fifth principle of, 193–94; forbidden practices, 38, 51, 90–91, 92, 95, 143, 145, 146, 149, 155, 157, 162–63, 166, 167, 173–74; forced conversion to, 177; fundamental principles of, 203; Hanafi, 66–67, 109, 122, 140, 144, 240n144; historic accounts of, 100–101; Imami Shi'i, 113; imam's obligations to, 78–81; Khariji, 101; Nasibi, 101; as national and cultural bond, 173; in need of revival, 37–38; and non-Muslim rights, 4; ordinances added to, 51; and the Ottoman Empire, 182; partisanship as contrary to, 204–8; pillars of, 125; as politics of civil society, 51; principles of, 28; purification of, 138; reform of, 137, 184; reformist, 7; as religion of freedom and independence, 190; restrictions based on, 16; revival of, 143; Salafi, 3, 5, 111; Shafi'i, 66, 68, 168, 170, 240n144; Shi'ah, 72, 101, 171, 192; Shi'i, 31, 44, 118, 232n23, 233n34, 239n138, 243n167, 244n174, 245n176, 248–49n221; as spiritual guidance, 51; spiritual-political character of, 26, 27; spread of, 198–99, 207; as state religion, 14–15; Sufi, 27, 51, 110; Sunni, 26, 27, 44, 66, 69, 101, 104, 109, 113, 118, 129, 166, 172; true nature of, 123, 124; Turkish, 20; Turkish leadership as enemy of, 1; as unifying force, 153; Wahhabi, 4, 25, 45; weakening of, 202, 210–12; Western culture as inimical to, 5. *See also* Muslims

Islam and Christianity between Science and Civilization ('Abduh), 193

Islam and the Bases of Rule ('Abd al-Raziq), 4, 44

"Islamic Caliphate, The" (Azad), 20

Islamic civilization, 28, 53, 135, 137

Islamic governance, 20, 21, 26, 83, 106, 233n33

Islamic government, 16–17, 21, 27–28, 51, 122, 128, 133–34, 144, 154, 161, 162, 169, 173; in the Arabian Peninsula, 180; as divinely mandated, 233n33; establishment of, 187; Muslims' disarray over, 201–4; in Najd, 111; non-Arab corruptions of, 199–201; treatment of non-Muslims, 177–78; as weak regarding religion, 162

Islamic law, 15, 20, 35, 120, 134, 144; and the Arabic language, 149–53; codification of, 252n272; Cromer's statement on, 189–90; and human legislation, 177; on inheritance, 240n153; jurisdiction of, 11; knowledge of, 135; positive, 139; principles of, 205; revealed, 209. *See also* shari'ah

Islamic legislation, 37, 153–62

Islamic modernism, 5

Islamic renaissance, 187

Islamic revival, 244–45n175

Islamic university, 186

Isma'il ibn 'Abd Allah, 94

Israel, children of, 50

Italo-Turkish (Italo-Ottoman) War, 252n277

Italy, 252n277

Ittihadists (Unionists), 7, 14, 42, 43, 123, 149, 186, 210, 211, 212

jama'ah, 29, 30, 96, 97, 106, 111, 120, 123, 169, 171, 198; authority of, 127–28; dispersal of, 102; meaning of term, 62; qualifications of, 63–66. *See also* people who loose and bind

Jami' (Tirmidhi), 62

Al-Jami'ah, 196, 251n263

Janissaries, 200, 252n279

Jarkas (Circassians), 132, 152

Java, 135, 170

Jawharat al-Tawhid (Ibrahim al-Laqani), 166

Jesus, 204

Jews, 199; tribute paid by, 237n94; in Yemen, 180; Zionist, 12, 230n6. *See also* Judaism

jihad, 79, 80–81, 97, 121, 132, 181, 241n158, 246n183

Jisr, Husayn al-, 101

Jordan, 242n160

Judaism, 4, 21. *See also* Jews

jurists, 144; Hanafi, 144; in India, 149; Muslim, 31, 36, 38, 40, 58, 59, 63, 64, 65, 69, 85, 87, 91, 155, 163, 165–67, 179, 189; Sunni, 56, 67; traditionalist, 35, 122–25

Jurjani, Sayyid al-, 62

justice: abode of, 76, 94, 96–98, 106, 107, 111; divine, 22; and equity, 128; establishment of, 78, 96, 153, 207; God's command to uphold, 176; and the government of the caliphate, 173; and imams, 105; in Islam, 38, 66, 93, 99, 176, 188, 198, 207, 208; lack of, 229–30n5; path of, 127; Rida's reflections on, 11–12, 18; and shari'ah, 154, 175, 180, 190, 209; and truth, 9, 18, 19, 98; in Turkey, 180; universal, 2, 6, 8, 40, 77; Wilson's definition of, 9–10. *See also* injustice

Juwayni, Imam al-Haramayn al-, 63, 66

Juwayriyyah bint Asma', 100

Kamal ibn Abi Sharif, 144n240

Al-Kamil (Ibn 'Adi), 68

Kamil Pasha, 241n158

Karmi, Sa'id al-, 110

Kazim, Musa, 123–24, 246n181

Kemal, Mustafa, 4, 18, 20, 21, 23, 24, 39, 143–44, 172, 242–43n164; fatwas of, 145, 146; Rida's critique of, 1, 22–23, 25, 28, 43–44

Kemalists, 22, 227–28n57; as enemies of Islam, 42–43; as opportunistic, 43; rejection of personal authority by, 96
Khalid ibn al-Walid, 192
Khalifat Movement, 118, 243–44n172, 244n173
Khalil ibn Ahmad al-Farahidi al-, 151, 247n203
Khan, Siddiq Hasan, 105–6
Khan Musaylun, battle of, 13
Kharijis, 57, 69, 101, 112, 171–72, 206–7, 232–33n29
Khiva (Uzbekistan), 109
Khosrau (Chosroes), 99, 239n134
Kinana tribe, 66
King-Crane Commission, 13, 16
Kitchener (Lord), 242n160; statement on shari'ah, 190; statement to Al-Zahrawi, 190
Kufah, governor of, 59
Kurdistan, 109
Kurds, 7, 132, 138, 152

language: Persian, 122; Urdu, 122. See also Arabic language
Laqani, Ibranim ibn Ibrahim al-, 248n217
laxity, 161
Le Bon, Gustave, 52, 148
leadership: misinterpretations of, 30; spiritual, 190–96
League of Nations, 4, 17, 18; League Council, 17, 18
Lebanon, 12
legislation, 165–66; and the caliphate, 158–59; different types of, 158; entrusted to the Muslim community, 156; Islamic, 37, 153–62; and the Muslim community's condition, 162–68; Qur'an-based, 167; restrictions on, 162; secular, 247–48n205; shari'ah-based, 158
Lenin, Vladimir, 42, 43
liberalism, 2, 5, 6, 13, 15, 18
libertinism, 147
Libya, 246n183, 252n277

Lloyd George, David, 16, 22, 40, 182
loosing and binding. See people who loose and bind

madhhabism, 124
madhhabs, 101, 111, 114, 118, 129, 143, 149, 168, 177; Ash'ari, 59; Hanafi, 109, 122
madrasahs, 37, 139, 140, 146, 164; Dar al-Da'wah wa al-Irshad, 185; for ijtihad, 140–41, 167
Magians, 73, 199, 203
Mahdi, 113, 243n167
Malik ibn Anas, 168
Al-Manar: addressing the abolition of the caliphate, 42; under al-Banna, 4; article on civil character of laws, 120; article on foreign Muslims, 170; on Britain and the Ottoman Empire, 181; on the caliphate, 3, 6, 24, 55, 251n264; censorship of, 181; defense of Islam, 72; "The European Trip," 17; on Europeanized Muslims, 123; on evidence and testimony, 179; on fatwas, 145, 170; on the king of the Hijaz, 134; on pan-Islamism, 184, 186–87; report on the Cairo Caliphate Congress, 6, 25; suggestions regarding reform, 171; Volume 21, 7; Volume 23, 24; Volume 24, 24
mandates, 4, 17, 18, 24, 241n158
Al-Ma'rifah (Bayhaqi), 68
marriage, 166, 170, 173
Marwan, 89, 99, 102–3, 206, 207
maslahah 'ammah, 5
materialism, 52, 173
Mawali, 235n71
Mawardi, 24, 29, 30, 31, 56, 63–64, 67, 68, 78–80, 86, 87, 92–94, 105, 232n23
Maymun ibn Mahran, 84
Mazdaism, 200
McMahon letters, 241n158
Mecca, 7, 15, 72, 99, 100, 110, 126, 207; caliph in, 15; Emir of, 182; sharif of, 4, 34, 181, 183, 241n158
Medina, 99, 100, 233n34

Index

Mehmed V (Muhammad Rashad), 59, 60, 102, 186, 211, 242–43n164, 247n202

Mehmed VI. *See* Muhammad VI Wahid al-Din (Mehmed VI Vahideddin)

Midhat Pasha, 33, 96, 209, 239n129

militarism, 52

Al-Minhaj (Nawawi), 58

missionaries, Christian, 123, 186

Mohammad Wali Khan, 243n168

monarchy, 43, 202, 208; absolute, 45; limited, 209

Morocco, 74, 106; Muslims in, 169

Moses, 50, 204

mosques, 77, 102, 106, 138, 141, 182; Al-Aqsa, 242n160; in 'Amman, 110; in Constantinople, 118; in Tunis, 118

Mosul, 138

Mu'adh ibn Jabal, 158, 248n210

mu'ahad, 177–78

Mu'awiyah, 30, 31, 33, 65, 77, 86, 98, 99, 100, 199, 203, 204, 205, 206, 207; 'Ali's dispute with, 232–33n29; as caliph, 233n36; son as successor, 236n79

Mughirah ibn Shu'bah, 65, 100

Muhallab, 88

Muhammad. *See* Prophet (Muhammad)

Muhammad 'Ali Pasha, 130, 145, 246n185, 247n197

Muhammad ibn Sa'id ibn Zamanah, 99

Muhammad Rashad (Mehmed V), 211, 242–43n164, 246n183, 247n202

Muhammad VI Wahid al-Din (Mehmed VI Vahideddin), 22, 29, 42, 112, 126, 242–43n164, 243n165

Muhammadan Revelation, The (Rida), 11

Al-Mu'jam Al-Awsat (Tabarani), 85

Al-Mu'jam al-Kabir (Tabarani), 62, 68

mujtahids, 38, 39, 64, 66, 90, 111, 118, 138, 140, 149, 150, 156, 159, 166, 168, 194, 205

muqallidun, 167, 230n6

Al-Muqattam, 8, 9

Murji'ites, 232–33n29

Al-Musayarah (Kamal ibn al-Humam), 66, 88–89, 90, 104

Muscat, 112

music, prohibition of, 143, 146

Muslim (shaykh), 77, 78, 82, 97, 191, 192; *Sound Collection*, 87–88, 94

Muslim Brotherhood, 4

Muslim community (ummah): adherence to, 169; authority of, 38, 42, 51, 61–63, 76, 78, 112, 127, 156–57, 195, 198; characteristics of, 136; consensus of, 168; consultation with, 155–56; core values of, 136, 147–48, 153, 165; disparity and conformity in, 162–68; early generations, 56; in Egypt, 117; God's promises to, 50; ijtihad in, 51, 167, 168; imam's obligations to, 78–81; in India, 117; legislation entrusted to, 156; and the people who loose and bind, 115–19; protection of, 79; and public welfare, 172; reform of, 139; and the right of universal leadership, 63; right to dismiss imams, 62–63; ruin of, 208; subjugation of, 192; unification of, 108–15, 129

Muslim ibn 'Uqbah, 33, 99–100

Muslim independence, 3, 5, 20, 33, 40, 92

Muslim League, 243–44n172

Muslims: afflicted with weakness, 51, 52; in Afghanistan, 169; in Africa, 126, 198; 'Alids, 31, 72, 73–74, 88, 110; in Anatolia, 179; as apostates, 173; on the Arabian Peninsula, 125, 130, 132, 136, 183, 199; conversion to Christianity, 186; core values of, 39; disarray over their governments, 201–4; duties of, 76; in Egypt, 130–31, 147, 164, 169; Egyptian, 101; Europeanized, 124, 128, 143, 162, 173, 186, 210–11, 214; in foreign lands, 114, 170–71; in the Great Powers, 210; heretical, 40, 174; in India, 36, 120, 122, 126–27, 198, 243–44n172, 244n173; in Iran, 118; in Iraq, 131; in Java, 170; in Morocco, 169; in Najd, 169; non-Arab, 70, 235n71; Persian, 183; reformist, 36; renaissance of, 141–44; rights of, 2; Shafi'i, 246n186; Shi'ah, 131; in

Index

265

Siam, 170; subjugation of, 134; Sunni, 56, 68, 131, 246n186; in Syria, 131, 171, 199; in Turkey, 34–35, 121, 125, 130–31, 147, 164, 183; unification of, 137; women, 146–49, 162, 164–65, 173, 178, 211, 212; in Yemen, 130, 169, 246n186

Musnad (Bazzar), 68

Musnad Ahmad (Ibn Hanbal), 62, 68, 88, 232n28, 239n139

Mustadrak (Hakim), 62

Mu'tasim, 200

Mutawakkil ibn al-Mu'tasim, 160

Mutawakkili kingdom, 241–42n159

Mu'tazilis, 30, 56, 57, 59, 232–33n29, 237n93

Muttaqi, 160

Najaf, 118, 244n174, 245n176

Najd, 34, 36; government of, 109; Muslims in, 169; people of, 111, 130

Napoleon (Bonaparte), 43

Nasa'i, 97, 99

Naser al-Din Shah Qajar, 245n176

Nasibis, 101, 239n138

National Assembly (Turkish), 1, 21, 24, 36, 117, 144, 161, 172, 186, 209, 242–43n164, 243n165; Mustafa Kemal's speech to, 22

nationalism: in Anatolia, 121; Hindu, 243–44n172; Indian, 244n173; liberal, 5; Syrian, 4; Turkish, 20, 21, 242–43n164; warning about, 184

Nawawi, 58, 95

Nazim (Doctor), 124

Nimr, Faris, 8, 9

Nisaburi, 63

Non-Cooperation Movement, 243–44n172

non-Muslims: and the caliphate, 193; cooperation with, 10; defeat of Turkey by, 5; equality of, 15; lending money, 162–63; living in Muslim lands, 12, 162–63, 172–80, 187; as minorities, 21; resistance to the government of the caliphate, 172–80; rights of, 4, 175; shari'ah protections for, 40; subjugation of, 177;

testimony of, 179; treaties with Muslims, 177; treatment of Muslims by, 103; under tyrants, 33; 'Umar's actions regarding, 30; welfare of, 177

obedience: to authority, 78, 83, 157, 158, 234n49; to caliphs/imams, 80, 89–91, 106, 195, 207; to God, 77, 138–39, 198; to Islamic law, 177; to the Messenger, 77, 191; to tyrants/unjust rulers, 98, 113

Oman, 34, 112

oppression, 18, 19, 91, 95, 96, 97, 103, 105, 180; preventing, 198, 209; struggle against, 95

Ordinances of Government (Mawardi), 30, 31, 56, 63–64, 67, 68, 78–80, 86, 87, 92–94, 105, 232n23

Ottoman caliphate/sultanate, 5, 20–21, 23, 27, 34, 42, 53, 69, 137, 176, 181, 192; abolition of, 1, 21, 175, 213; and Britain, 181. *See also* caliphate; sultanate

Ottoman Constitution, 15, 175, 209

Ottoman dynasty/Empire, 11, 22, 36, 96, 123, 132, 152, 161, 180–81, 200, 214; aftermath of, 1; authority of, 33, 240–41n157, 241–42n159, 244n173; and Britain, 185; and the caliphate, 208–10; decline of, 231n14; and Egypt, 246n185; Europeanization in, 208–10; Kitchener's thoughts on, 190; loss of Libya, 246n183; loyalty to, 182; military capabilities of, 212–13; restoration of, 244n173; surrender of, 242–43n164; weakening of, 212–13

Ottoman government, 166

Pakistan, 243–44n172

Palestine, 12, 233n35, 242n160

pan-Islamism, 4, 41, 121, 122, 244n173; claims made about, 183–88

pan-Ottomanism, 122

papacy, 37, 103, 123, 169; and the caliphate, 190–96

Paris Peace Conference, 4

partisanship, 204–8, 214

266   Index

party of inflexible traditionalist jurists, 122–25

party of moderation and Islamic reform, 119–22, 140, 147–48, 150–51, 168–72; obligations of, 125–28

peace, 8, 36, 43, 64, 122, 156, 213

people who loose and bind, 30–31; allegiance to caliph of, 29, 57, 74, 76, 84, 89, 114, 140; authority of, 29, 35, 62–63, 84, 98, 116, 119, 127, 157, 159, 203; caliph's accountability to, 70, 140, 157; characteristics of, 119–20, 124; consulting function of, 29, 58, 60, 86, 98, 127, 158, 160; election/selection of caliph by, 32, 57, 86, 87, 91, 98, 101, 105, 138, 168, 238n108; endorsement of, 87; as leaders, 56, 58, 59, 84, 199, 202; legal duty of, 30; obligations of, 116–19; and the popular will, 29; and the public welfare, 31, 116; qualifications of, 30, 63, 64, 65, 99, 117, 124; representative bodies, 35; resisting injustice, 33, 66, 76, 95; responsibility of, 205–6; righteousness of, 116; role of, 20, 22, 65, 115–19; selection of, 35, 62, 63; selection of caliph by, 32, 57, 86, 87, 91, 98, 101, 105, 138, 168, 238n108; in Turkey, 35, 214

People's Development (Le Bon), 52, 148

Persia, 109

Persian Empire, 99

Persian language, 122

Persians, 33, 73, 183, 199, 200, 236n77

Peter the Great, 43

pledge of allegiance, 59, 60, 62, 65, 84, 93; to Abu Bakr, 233n37; form of, 74–76; to imam in Yemen, 130; to imams, 106; to king of the Hijaz, 110; of the majority, 104; and the Muslim community, 76–78; to new caliph, 126; by the people who loose and bind, 140; in the Qur'an, 198; to someone unfit, 60; to Turkish caliph, 114, 136; to 'Uthman, 75;

by women, 75; to Yahya, 241–42n159; to Yazid, 99

pope. *See* papacy

positive law, 134, 139, 209

power: and partisanship, 87; unjust use of, 96; of the West and the global North, 7

prayers: congregational, 170; validity of, 106

preaching, responsibility for, 141

Prophet (Muhammad): on the appointment of governors or emirs, 87–88; caliph of, 169, 210; Companions consulting with, 81, 83, 84, 191–92, 198; descendants of, 240–41n157; on the duties of imams, 78–79; era of, 30, 163, 194; family of, 109, 166, 200, 235n76; glorifying the House of, 101; hadiths, 61, 73, 82, 85, 139, 156, 232n28; on holding fast to *jama'ah*, 29, 57, 61; on imams from Quraysh, 67, 69, 70, 72, 74; imams of, 90, 104, 166; on independence, 145–46; on Islam in the Hijaz, 71; and the law, 155, 237n90; lifestyle of, 199; in Mecca, 72; and Mu'adh, 158; on obedience, 31, 138–39, 198; opposition to, 33, 204–5; on partisanship, 151; pledging allegiance to, 75, 94; receiving revelation, 82–83; on responsibility, 80, 202; role of, 155–56; sanctifying Medina, 100; successor of, 200, 233n34; and the universal imamate, 50; way of, 109

prophethood, 72, 198, 204, 206

prophets, 8, 51, 197, 198, 229–30n5; Wilson as, 9–10

prostitution, 211

public morality, 174

Qajars, 245n176

Qaramitah (Carmathians), 200, 251n268

qaysar. *See* Caesar

Qur'an, 7, 22, 25, 27; actions in accordance with, 74; and the Arabic language, 129, 150, 152; and the caliph/caliphate,

29, 30, 32; created, 232–33n29, 237n93; as example and source of knowledge, 194, 203; exegesis of, 95, 248–49n221; guidance by, 27, 52, 198; on human history, 49–50; and the Qurayshis, 74; recitations of, 150; requirement for caliph to be learned in, 29, 195; revelation of, 70; Rida quoting, 26–27; shari'ah derived from, 154; use for resolving disputes, 157; Wilson's echoing, 10

Qur'an Commentary (Rida), 61, 63, 83, 234n49. See also *Tafsir al-Manar* (Rida)

Qur'an topics: angelic forces, 8; authority, 30, 209; burden on those with knowledge, 3; burdens imposed by God, 41; caliphate, 26–29; change, 148; commandment to defend sovereignty, 108; conduct of caliphs, 71; consultation, 81–82, 83, 156; contracts, 166; covenants and promises of God, 55; Day of Resurrection, 142; description of Muslims, 174; forbidden foods, 157; God's care for his servants, 188; God's requirements, 186; gratitude, 55; healing of the Muslim community, 51; holders of authority, 63; messengers, 190–91; military preparations, 80–81; the Muslim community, 62; Muslims ills and errors, 39–40; obedience, 30, 77–78, 84–85, 198; obedience to God, 157; obligations of imams, 79; obligations of the faithful, 62, 246n184; omniscience of God, 162; pledge of allegiance, 75, 198; preparing power, 31, 141; promises/covenants of God, 49, 50, 128; protection of believers, 107; religious authority, 193; resources, 163–64; restraint and submission, 204; setbacks and defeat, 21; signs from God, 7; succession, 26–27; suffering abuse, 204–5; testimony and integrity, 178–79; those who are favored and/or grateful, 197; those who resist

Islam, 7–8; truth and justice, 9, 25, 55, 176, 214; victory of spiritual over material power, 7; wisdom, 180; women, 75, 164–65

Qurayshis: authority of, 69, 73, 89; and the caliphate, 20, 30, 31, 37, 66–72, 88–91, 112, 129, 133, 206, 244n173; consultation with, 85; criticism of, 74; Hashimi, 204; and Islam, 70; opinions of, 85

Rafi' ibn Khudayj, 82, 191

Al-Rawdah (Nawawi), 64, 234n53

Al-Rawdah al-Nadiyyah (Siddiq Hasan Khan), 105–6

Razi, 56, 63

realism, 2, 5

religion: as obstacle to progress, 136–37; reform of, 135; scientific approach to, 231n13; state, 43. *See also* Christianity; Islam; Judaism

Republic of Turkey, 1, 21. *See also* Turkey

revelation, 82–83, 129, 155, 163, 194

Rida, (Muhammad) Rashid, 1; admiration for Wilson, 2, 5, 8–10, 11; as advocate of Gandhi, 35; calls for reform, 7, 12–13; characterization of, 3–4; as community advocate, 5; critique of Faisal, 34; critique of Kemal, 1, 22–23, 25, 28, 43–44; Cromer's letter to, 189–90; Islamic-American postwar vision, 7–10; memorandum to Lloyd George, 16; multiple identities of, 21; as Muslim writer, 2, 3–4; non-Islamic ideas and agendas, 2; political agenda of, 3, 7; as pragmatist, 20, 22; as president of Congress, 14, 16, 25; proposed institution for Islamic outreach and guidance, 36; publishing Wilson's speeches, 6, 8; as realist, 2, 5; reasons for writing *The Caliphate*, 2–3, 25; as reformer, 5; in Syria, 11–12; Thompson's portrayal of, 8, 10–11, 227n41; trip to Geneva, 17–20

Index

Rida, (Muhammad) Rashid, works of:
Al-Wahy al-Muhammadi, 226n27; "The
Arab Government of Damascus" (Rida),
11; "The Arab Question," 17; "A Call
from the East to the Liberals of the
West," 17, 22; "The European Trip,"
17; "The General Syrian Congress"
(Rida), 11; later works, 44–45; letter to
Lord Cromer, 189; memorandum to
Lloyd George, 182–83; *Muhammadan
Revelation* (Rida), 11; *Muhawarat
al-Muslih wa al-Muqallid*, 230n6;
Qur'an Commentary, 61, 63, 83; *Tafsir
al-Manar*, 179; "The Turks' Victory
over the Greeks; Their Toppling of the
Ottoman Throne; and Their Turning
the Islamic Caliphate into a Spiritual,
Moral Institution," 22. See also
*Caliphate or Supreme Imamate, The;
Al-Manar*
righteousness, 27, 49, 50, 97, 116, 134, 159,
171, 176, 202, 203–4, 246n184
Rikabi, 'Ali Rida Pasha al-, 12, 13
ritual devotions, 155
Roman Empire, 99
Romans, 33
Rumelia, 175, 208, 249n232
Russia, 9, 10, 43; and Britain, 181; Empire
of, 181; tsarist, 109
Russo-Ottoman War, 231n14

Sabaeans, 199, 203
Sa'd ibn Abi Waqqas, 59
Sa'd ibn 'Ubadah, 67, 68, 75
Salafism, 3, 5, 111
Salafiyyah, 244–45n175
Salim I, 112
Saqifah Assembly, 58, 67, 68, 69,
233n34
Sasanians, 239n134
Saudis, 240–41n157, 241–42n159
Saudi-Wahhabi kingdom, 4, 7
secularism, liberal, 10, 11

self-determination, 6, 19, 26
Seve, Octave Joseph Anthelme
("Sulayman Pasha"), 145, 247n197
Shafi'i, 170
Shafi'i school, 66, 68, 168, 170, 246n186
shari'ah: abandonment of, 102, 154; acting
in accordance with, 148, 165; acts contrary to, 111; in Anatolia, 185; on the
Arabian Peninsula, 129; on the caliphate, 91, 112, 172; caliphate based on,
24, 25, 55, 103, 125, 130, 133, 153–62, 172,
180; caliph's rights, 36; canceling the
need for socialism, 164; cases not covered by, 17; and the Christian community, 175–76, 177–78; compatibility with
civilization, 139; councils responsible
for, 140–41; derivation from the Qur'an,
154; duty of the community under,
115; forbidden practices, 163; on forced
conversions, 177; fundamental principles of, 179; illegal governments under,
116; institution of imamate under, 109,
130; interpretation of, 239n131; on the
Islamic caliphate, 55; in Islamic states,
10, 16, 92, 144, 158, 168, 178, 209; and
lawful tyranny, 98; Lord Cromer's statement on, 189–90; Lord Kitchener's
statement on, 190; and Muslim government, 166; obligatory fighting under, 97;
ordinances and norms of succession, 27,
49; and the people who loose and bind,
116; protections for minorities, 40; and
selection of the caliph, 133; submission
to, 204; in Syria, 15, 16; in Turkey, 161,
180; in the Turkish-Turanian nation,
210. See also Islamic law
Shaykh al-Islam, 123, 124, 177, 185, 196,
246n181, 252n279; authority of, 211–12
Shi'ah and Shi'ite Islam, 14, 31, 72, 101,
118, 171, 192, 232n23; 233n34; 243n167,
244n174, 245n176, 248–49n221; Batini,
22, 192, 200; Imami, 113, 243n167;
Twelver, 239n138

Shirazi, Mirza Hasan al-, 118, 245n176
Shirt of Fire, A (Adib), 121
Shu'ubis, 74, 236n77
Siam, 170
Sibawayh, 151
Silk Letter Conspiracy, 243–44n172
social order, 208
social relations, 155, 157
socialism, 9, 164
Society for Science and Guidance, 123
sociology, 52
Sound Collection (Bukhari), 59, 68, 75, 85, 87, 94, 110, 206
Sound Collection (Muslim), 77, 82, 87–88, 94
sovereignty: communal, 2; of the community, 51; establishment of, 204; Muslim, 4, 21, 25, 26, 36, 41, 92, 108, 182; national, 209; popular, 5, 18, 26; Syrian, 6; Turkish, 113; of Turkish-Turanian nation, 210
Spanish Empire, 177
Spencer, Herbert, 52, 231n13
statues: erected in Egypt, 143, 145; permissibility of, 39, 88, 143, 145–46
Storrs, Ronald, 242n160
succession, 26, 99, 160; designation by imam in office, 85–86; of people and dynasties, 49–50
Sudan, 181
Sufi Islam, 27, 51, 110
Sulayman I, 177
Sulayman Pasha, 145, 247n197
Suleymaniye Mosque (Constantinople), 118
sultanate: abolition of, 42, 242–43n164; in Angora/Ankara, 117; authority of, 21, 33, 42, 53, 55, 68. *See also* caliphate; Ottoman caliphate/sultanate
sultan-caliphs, 22, 212
sunnah, 198; and the caliph, 32; of Heraclius and Caesar, 33. *See also* hadith topics; Qur'an topics

Sunni Islam, 26, 27, 44, 66, 69, 101, 104, 109, 113, 118, 129, 166, 172; Hanafis, 66–67, 89, 90, 109, 122, 140, 144, 240n144; Hanbali, 111, 166, 246–47n190
Suyuti, 200–201, 252n270
Sykes, Mark, 4
Sykes-Picot Agreement, 241n158
Syria: Armenians deported to, 246n180; Declaration of Independence, 12, 13; Egyptian troops in, 246n185; Europeanization in, 121; Faysal in, 110; foreign rule in, 33; governor of, 59; as independent state, 6, 11–12, 16, 20, 21; Islamic law in, 35; and the king of Hijaz, 110; Muslims in, 99, 131, 171, 199; occupation of, 18–19; as part of an Arab federation, 15; Rida in, 20; Rida's commentaries on, 21; territories claimed by, 12, 138; ulama in, 124
Syrian Congress, 4–5, 11, 13–14, 16, 21, 26, 29, 174
Syrian Constitution, 5, 14–15, 16, 37, 174; Article 1, 15; Article 5, 15; Article 6, 15; Article 14, 15; Article 147, 15
Syrians: Christian, 175; rights of, 2; sovereignty of, 6; unification of, 20

Tabarani, 62, 68, 85, 94, 99
Tabari, 27, 30, 64
Tafsir al-Manar (Rida), 169, 179, 234n49. *See also* Qur'an Commentary (Rida)
Taftazani, 29, 56–57, 58, 63, 66, 89, 91, 231–32n21; on the appointment of caliph-imams, 232n27; *Commentary on Goals*, 89, 90–91, 94
Ta'i', 200–201
Talat Pasha (Talat Bey), Mehmed, 36, 123, 124, 149, 211, 246n180
Talhah, 59
Tanukhi, 160, 248n213
Tatars, 132, 200
Thompson, Elizabeth F., 8, 9, 10–11, 14–15
Tihamah, 36, 130

270 Index

Tirmidhi, 62, 65, 248n209
Tobacco Revolt, 118, 245n176
traditionalism, 42, 120, 122–25, 214; inflexibility of, 124; in Turkey, 136
Transjordan, 111; Emir of, 110, 111, 241n158, 242n160
Transoxiana, 106
Treasure of the Laborers (Al-Hindi), 86
Treaty of San Remo, 18
Treaty of Sevres, 18
Treaty of Versailles, 18
Trotsky, Leon, 42, 43
Al-Tuhfah (Ibn Hajar al-Haytami), 86
Tunisia, 114, 135, 209
Turanian ethnicity, 121–22, 132, 210
Turanian union, 109
Turkey: anti-Islamic actions of, 42; and the Arab community, 213; caliphate in, 34, 41, 68, 110, 112, 113, 121, 136–38, 143, 180, 181, 186, 192, 240n154, 243n168; defeat by non-Muslims, 5; Eastern view of, 18; elimination of Ottoman dynasty, 96; Europeanization in, 121, 136, 142, 147; government of, 109; and government of the Hijaz, 135; Islam in, 20, 53; as Islamic nation, 161–62; Ittihadists in, 14; military capabilities of, 137; Muslim community in, 91; Muslim renaissance in, 142; Muslims in, 121, 125, 130–31, 147, 164; nationalism in, 20, 21, 242–43n164; and the Ottoman sultanate, 53; postwar, 35; as proposed seat of caliphate, 133, 136–38; reform in, 120; Revolt (1909), 231n14; Rida's commentaries on, 21; Rida's recommendations for, 28; socialism in, 164; supervision of caliph's election in, 37; traditionalism in, 136; War of Independence, 6; women in, 143
Turkish government, 25, 113, 114, 126, 167, 172, 213–14; and Islamic reform, 137; Rida's support for, 55. *See also* Angora (Ankara)
Turkish language, 121–22, 152

Turkish republic, 23
Turkish War of Independence, 20, 117
Turkish-Turanian nation, 210
Turko-Afghan Treaty, 109, 240n154
Turks: and the ʿAbbasids, 68, 73, 200–201; advice to, 213–14; in Anatolia, 183, 185; cooperation with Arabs, 36–37, 152–53; Europeanized, 130, 175, 208–10; exhorted to renew the caliphate, 53–55; expansionist, 132; Greek and Armenian revolt against, 179; as Islam's sharp sword, 119–20, 152; Kemalist, 22; misconduct of, 160; Muslim, 7, 183; need for ijtihad, 144–49; Ottoman, 74; relationship with the caliphate, 129–33, 138; resistance to the caliphate by, 40; territories where they predominate, 138; ulamas of, 105; uniting with the Arabs, 129
Twelver Shiʿism, 239n138
tyranny, 32–33, 66, 76, 91, 103, 207; abode of, 96–98; annihilation of, 52, 202; of the caliphate, 122, 127; establishment of, 98–104, 161; in Islam, 99; of leaders, 123; obedience to, 113; rule of, 199–201

ʿUbadah ibn al-Samit, 75, 87, 94
ʿUbaydis (Fatimids), 74
Uhud, battle of, 22, 191
ʿUmar, 23, 29, 30, 58, 59, 60, 62, 64, 65, 72–73, 83, 84, 85, 98, 99, 160, 192, 199, 202, 203; as Abu Bakr's successor, 86; as caliph, 84; and the council of six, 233n37; rejectors of, 239n138; son of, 236n78
ʿUmar ibn ʿAbd al-ʿAziz, 88, 101, 153, 206, 238n114
ʿUmar ibn Yahya ibn Saʿid ibn ʿAmr ibn Saʿid ibn al-ʿAs, 102
Umayyad caliphate, 20–21, 23, 27, 31, 33, 69, 71, 72, 78, 87, 89, 101, 102–3, 196, 201, 205, 208, 233n36, 238n114. *See also* caliphate

Index

271

Umayyad dynasty/Empire, 73, 98–99, 199–200, 203, 206, 207, 214; struggle with Ibn Zubayr, 236n79

ummah. *See* Muslim community (ummah)

United States: and the King-Crane Commission, 13, 16; postwar interventions, 8; Rida's admiration of, 8

Universal History (Tanukhi), 160

Urdu language, 122

usury, 162–64

'Uthman, 29, 30, 59, 60, 62, 65, 73, 84, 199, 200, 206; allegiance to, 75; murder of, 232–33n29

Uzbekistan (Khiva), 109

viziers, 160. *See also* grand vizier

Wafd Party, 118, 243n169

Wahhabis, 4, 25, 45

Wahid al-Din. *See* Muhammad VI Wahid al-Din (Mehmed VI Vahideddin)

war, 7, 8; apocalyptic, 18; destruction of Europe through, 19

War of Tripoli, 210

Washington, George, 9

Western culture, as inimical to Islam, 5; Rida's critique of, 3

Wilhelm I (Kaiser), 149, 211, 247n202

Wilson, Woodrow: definition of justice, 9–10; postwar vision of, 5, 9, 10; Rida's admiration of, 2, 6, 7, 8–10, 11; speeches published by Rida, 6, 8; viewed as prophet, 9–10

women: independence of, 164–65; Muslim, 146–47, 148–49, 173, 178, 211; Muslims, 162, 212; in Turkey, 143

World War I (Great War), 52–53, 175, 181, 185

Yahya ibn Muhammad Hamid al-Din, 34, 37, 44, 110, 111, 240–41n157, 241–42n159

Ya'rub ibn Qahtan, 151

Yazid ibn Mu'awiyah, 32, 33, 86, 98, 99–100, 101, 103, 205; as caliph, 236n79

Yemen, 34, 40, 44, 106, 130, 132, 180; imams in, 74, 131, 182, 241–42n159; independence of, 131; Jews in, 180; Lower, 109; Muslims in, 169, 246n186; Upper, 109

Young Turks, 5, 18, 231n14, 242–43n164

Zaghlul, Sa'd Pasha, 35, 117, 126, 243n169, 243n170

Zahrawi, Sayyid 'Abd al-Hamid al-, 190

zakat, 76, 141, 162, 174, 250n250

Zaydi imams, 37, 74, 241–42n159

Zaydi school (madhhab), 109, 129, 171, 172

Zaydism, 34, 37

Zaytunah Mosque (Tunis), 118

Zionism, 12, 230n6

zone of neutrality, 138–39

Zoroastrians, 73, 199

Zubayr, 59, 99, 236n78